SQL

P O W E R !

The Comprehensive Guide

By Kenneth Hess

THOMSON

™

COURSE TECHNOLOGY

Professional ■ Technical ■ Reference

ISBN-10: 1-59863-212-4
ISBN-13: 978-1-59863-212-5

Library of Congress Catalog Card Number: 2006920354

Printed in the United States of America

07 08 09 10 11 TW 10 9 8 7 6 5 4 3 2 1

THOMSON

COURSE TECHNOLOGY

Professional ■ Technical ■ Reference

Thomson Course Technology PTR, a division of Thomson Learning Inc.
25 Thomson Place
Boston, MA 02210
http://www.courseptr.com

Publisher and General Manager, Thomson Course Technology PTR:
Stacy L. Hiquet

Associate Director of Marketing:
Sarah O'Donnell

Manager of Editorial Services:
Heather Talbot

Marketing Manager:
Mark Hughes

Senior Acquisitions Editor:
Todd Jensen

Marketing Coordinator:
Meg Dunkerly

Project Editor:
Tonya Cupp

Technical Reviewer:
Les Bate

PTR Editorial Services Coordinator:
Elizabeth Furbish

Interior Layout Tech:
Digital Publishing Solutions

Cover Designers:
Mike Tanamachi and Nancy Goulet

Indexer:
Sharon Hilgenberg

Proofreader:
Kezia Endsley

I dedicate this book to my mother, who encouraged me; to my wife, who gave me space and support; and to my children, who are proud of me.

I also dedicate this book to the good people at MySQL AB for MySQL, all of those brilliant minds that laid the groundwork for our digital existence, and to those of you who are compelled to learn.

} Acknowledgments

I wish to thank my family for putting up with me during these past few months while I worked on this book. Thanks to my college freshman composition instructor, Terry Dalrymple, Ph.D., who singlehandedly inspired me to write creatively. And to my agent, Dr. Neil Salkind of Studio B, who keeps me focused on authorship.

I also wish to acknowledge and extend thanks to Tonya Cupp, the project editor, and to Les Bate, the technical editor.

About the Author

Kenneth Hess is an avid database enthusiast and administrator. He has worked with many different types of database software over the past 20 years. Ken currently focuses his database interests and research on MySQL and SQLite. He has worked with every version of Windows since 3.0, most versions of Linux, most MacOS versions since 7.x, and almost every flavor of commercial UNIX, although Linux remains as his passion and favorite amongst all the others.

Ken maintains his technical edge through his day job; his research with Linux, PHP, MySQL, SQLite; and other open-source applications. He maintains his sanity through involvement with his family, fiction writing, art, and watching a few select TV shows.

Ken is a Studio B (www.studiob.com) author who owes his continued success to his agent, Dr. Neil Salkind, and the supportive staff at Studio B. Ken may be reached through his web site at www.kenhess.com.

TABLE OF } Contents

viii
❄ ❄ ❄

} Introduction

SQL (pronounced ess-queue-ell) is the language of relational databases. It was the conception of relational databases that provided the impetus for the creation of the language. Originally developed by IBM in the 1970s, the language, then known as SEQUEL (Structured English Query Language), has gone through several iterations and updates to give us the very powerful and ubiquitous language in use today. Now known as SQL (Structured Query Language), it is the standard language we use to interface with databases. SQL has no looping or flow control components and therefore is not a procedural language such as C or Perl. It cannot stand alone like a shell script nor can it be executed at a command line, but it does qualify as a language because it has syntax and semantics. It has been classified as a sublanguage that is used in association with another language, such as PHP, to access a database. SQL is composed of several language subtypes such as Data Manipulation Language (DML), Data Definition Language (DDL), Data Control Language (DCL), and programmatic statements.

SQL was born out of a need to access data in advanced ways and for ad hoc data retrieval. It is primarily used as an interactive query language, as its name suggests. It is interactive in that users carry on dialogs with the database to extract data in a desired fashion. Data is usually retrieved via query statements from a database using SQL, but data can also be inserted, deleted, changed, moved, indexed, and exported.

I hope that you are going through this book chronologically because the concepts will be easier to understand and digest if you do. Please keep all of the databases and tables that you create, so you may use them for future chapters. Some of the examples build on work done in previous chapters. I have a tendency, when reading a book, to skip around and never really read it in order. My assumption is that some of you are using this as a text and will probably follow it in an orderly fashion. Additionally, errors might occur on some machines; fixes will be posted at www.courseptr.com/downloads if possible.

My personal experience with SQL has been very positive and I feel honored to bring this version of it to you. SQL has been a part of my career for the past 15 years or so and since discovering it, have never looked back. My contributions, up until now, have been in showing others how to use SQL and databases in unique and creative ways, rather than actually contributing to the language itself. This book represents many years of experience and hundreds of hours sitting in front of a keyboard tapping out SQL statements, doing database research, and performing database administrative tasks. It also represents many and varied experiences, frustrations, and joys of working with such a language. I hope you find *SQL Power!* useful in your career and as a welcomed addition to your technical library.

What You'll Find in This Book

You will find practical examples of every aspect of SQL in this book. I have attempted to create a readable, accessible reference book that you can use while creating, maintaining, and fixing your own databases. If you are ready to take your SQL knowledge to the next level, then you will find this book useful. Listed here are some of the main features you find inside:

- ✽ Many examples using a live database that you create.
- ✽ Information on different brands of RDBMSs.
- ✽ Embedded SQL instructions and examples.
- ✽ An introduction to stored procedures.
- ✽ An introduction to data warehousing.
- ✽ A step-by-step example of database normalization.

* An appendix showing almost every available function, with examples.
* Questions and exercises that challenge you and teach concepts.

Who This Book Is For

This book is for you if you have read one of the many introductory SQL books or have been working with databases and want to increase your knowledge without plunging headlong into a 1,000-plus–page tome. *SQL Power!* puts you into real-life situations with database design, implementation, and administration. This book is also for those who want to go beyond the basics of SQL in a relatively short amount of time. While the chapters build on each other somewhat, you may use them independently for reference on a particular subject.

It could be part of your career roadmap to some database certification or promoting yourself into a DBA (database administrator) position, where knowing SQL is a significant part of the job. This book is also good for those who manage a technical team that includes DBAs. *SQL Power!* is designed as an intermediate text focusing on some of the higher-level aspects of SQL while still covering the basics. I provide the basics for each section as baseline knowledge just in case you need a refresher before heading into unknown territory.

How This Book Is Organized

This book is organized in 14 chapters and 7 appendices. Each chapter orders concepts so that they build upon each other. The chapters build somewhat upon each other but also may be used independently for reference. The examples and some of the SQL syntax are specific to MySQL but can be generalized to other DBMSs.

* Chapter 1, "SQL: The Language." The book begins with an introduction to SQL and the concept of relational databases. The chapter continues by looking at SQL standards from the early days on up to the present.
* Chapter 2, "Relational Databases." This chapter looks at the relational model and its components. Covered topics include tables, primary keys, relationships, and foreign keys.

❊ Chapter 3, "Database Software." An overview of ACID and the major players in the commercial and open-source DBMS world are given. Each DBMS is looked at from a feature standpoint without playing favorites among vendors.

❊ Chapter 4, "Data Definition Language." The major aspects of the Data Definition Language are covered. You learn CREATE, ALTER, and DROP with many examples to guide you through the usage. Syntax is given for each keyword.

❊ Chapter 5, "MySQL." Take a fairly in-depth look at MySQL, the DBMS used for the examples in this book. The various table types (also known as engines) are covered, as well as some of MySQL's quirks, advantages, and special applications.

❊ Chapter 6, "Data Manipulation Language." SELECT, INSERT, UPDATE, and DELETE are covered in this chapter to illustrate the Data Manipulation Language. Syntax for each keyword is given. Examples and exercises are used to engage you in the material.

❊ Chapter 7, "Data Control Language." Access Control Language and Transaction Control Language are covered here. Security aspects are discussed in the Access Control Language section, including user accounts and how to grant and revoke privileges. The Transaction Control Language discussion covers how to use transactions manually and what happens behind the scenes during a transaction.

❊ Chapter 8, "Advanced Queries." Chapter 8 covers advanced query keywords and concepts such as JOINs, unions, subqueries, and summary queries. Many examples and comparisons accompany the text.

❊ Chapter 9, "Views." Also known as virtual tables, this chapter provides examples of the different types and when to use them. There is a discussion of the advantages of using views for cloaking the structure of your database from users. Updatable views are also covered.

❊ Chapter 10, "SQL Optimization." Here is where you learn how to get the best performance out of your DBMS; you examine all the variables affecting that performance.

❋ Chapter 11, "Normalization." This chapter takes you through the different normal forms, what they mean, and how to achieve each one. A normalization tutorial guides you through the process of normalizing a database.

❋ Chapter 12, "Embedded SQL." Embedding SQL in host languages that are optimized for database applications are covered. One example is taken through each language for a comparison of the syntax of each.

❋ Chapter 13, "Stored Procedures." Stored procedures are a fascinating new addition to MySQL. This is a basic introduction to the syntax and use. The MySQL implementation of stored procedures was taken directly from the SQL2003 standard.

❋ Chapter 14, "Data Warehousing." Data warehousing is one of the hottest areas of database technology today. This mild introduction to the vast subject includes my own experiences in creating a data warehouse.

1 } SQL: The Language

I have heard it said that SQL no longer stands for Structured Query Language, but for our purposes, it does. SQL has a structure, as do most languages, and rules of usage. It is generally used for asking questions and extracting data from a database. These questions and extractions are called *queries*. From a user standpoint, SQL is only a query language because most users of any database will only have read-only access to data. This chapter focuses on bringing you a brief look at the history and standards of SQL beginning with SQL92. You should become familiar with the major aspects of each standard and what they bring to the language. While it is possible to go through a career in database management without ever looking at the history or standards, it will certainly round out your database education and allow you to contribute to the ongoing effort and evolution of the language.

A Bit of History

In 1970, Edgar F. Codd wrote the now-famous paper on relational data modeling: "A Relational Model of Data for Large Shared Data Banks." The original relational database language, developed by IBM, was called *SEQUEL (Structured English Query Language)* to support its prototype *RDBMS (Relational Database Management System)* called System/R. The name SEQUEL was later changed to SQL (Structured Query Language) but the pronunciation *sequel* persists. SQL has become the de facto standard language for processing relational database systems and it was accepted by ANSI, FIPS, and ISO organizations.

 IN THE BEGINNING, CODD...
Edgar F. Codd (1923–2003) was a mathematician at IBM in 1970 when he came up with the Relational Data Model. He is the father of the relational database model but did so much more. He also worked in the fields of self-reproducing *automata* (theoretical computers) and multiprogramming. He was said to

❅ ❅ ❅

have complained that SQL did not meet his mathematical model but it was his model that produced what is the RDBMS standard language some 35 years later and for the foreseeable future.

SQL is not owned by any particular entity, but IBM was at the forefront of the research that was instrumental in developing the language. After E.F. Codd wrote his paper on Relational Data Modeling, IBM spent a great deal of money, time, and energy developing and researching the implementation of Codd's model. In 1979, a new product called Oracle was released by a company then known as Relational Software. The Oracle database was the first commercially available relational database software that utilized SQL. Once SQL gained commercial appeal, standards discussion began taking place within standards organizations and universities. The first standards for SQL were published in 1986 and 1987 as SQL86 and SQL87, respectively. An enhanced version of SQL86 was published in 1989 (SQL89).

The 1992 standard, known as SQL92, was a huge improvement over earlier versions and has come to be the most widely accepted and implemented standard by DBMS vendors to date. SQL92 has three levels of conformance: Entry, Intermediate, and Full. One of the significant things to note here is that no product currently available is fully SQL92 conformant due to serious flaws in the conformance standard's language. Vendors whose database software is SQL92 conformant are generally so at the Entry level. Most database software is SQL92 conformant with exceptions. These exceptions are typically published in the software documentation.

SQL99 was published to address many of the newer features of modern relational database systems. Included in the SQL99 standard are such improvements as call-level interfaces, object-relational database models, and integrity management. SQL99 has two levels of conformance known as Core SQL99 and Enhanced SQL99. Entry level SQL92 conformance maps favorably to Core SQL99 to making SQL99 conformance an easy transition for database vendors.

SQL Defined

I need to cover some basic SQL definitions before plunging into SQL standards and the rest of the book. The following definitions are part of the SQL standards and bear learning due to their value as a basis for the rest of the book. If you don't understand these terms upon first reading, don't be discouraged; they will become clear as you cover the book.

SQL-environments

An SQL-environment comprises the following:

* One SQL-agent.
* One SQL-implementation.
* Zero or more SQL-client modules, containing externally invoked procedures available to the SQL agent.

* Zero or more authorization identifiers.
* Zero or more catalogs, each of which contains one or more SQL-schemas.

The sites, principally base tables, that contain SQL-data, as described by the contents of the schemas. This data may be thought of as "the database."

SQL-agents

An *SQL-agent* causes the execution of SQL-statements. In the case of the direct invocation of SQL, it is implementation defined. Alternatively, it may consist of one or more compilation units that, when executed, invoke externally-invoked procedures in an SQL-client module.

SQL-implementations

An *SQL-implementation* is a processor that executes SQL-statements, as required by the SQL-agent. An SQL-implementation, as perceived by the SQL-agent, includes one SQL-client, to which that SQL-agent is bound, and one or more SQL-servers. Because an SQL-implementation can be specified only in terms of how it executes SQL-statements, the concept denotes an installed instance of some software (database management system).

SQL-clients

An *SQL-client* is a processor, perceived by the SQL-agent as part of the SQL-implementation, that establishes SQL-connections between itself and SQL-servers and maintains a diagnostics area and other state data relating to interactions between itself, the SQL-agent, and the SQL-servers.

SQL-servers

Each SQL-server is a processor, perceived by the SQL-agent as part of the SQL-implementation, that manages SQL-data. Each SQL-server

* Manages the SQL-session taking place over the SQL-connection between itself and the SQL-client.
* Executes SQL-statements received from the SQL-client, receiving and sending data as required.
* Maintains the state of the SQL-session, including the authorization identifier and certain session defaults.

SQL-client modules

An *SQL-client module* is a module that is explicitly created and dropped by implementation-defined mechanisms. An SQL-client module does not necessarily have a name; if it does, the permitted names are implementation defined. An SQL-client module contains zero or more externally invoked procedures. Exactly one SQL-client module is associated with an SQL-agent at any time. However, in the case of either direct binding style or SQL/CLI (command-line interface), this may be a default SQL-client module whose existence is not apparent to the user.

User Identifiers

A *user identifier* represents a user.

Catalogs

A *catalog* is a named collection of SQL-schemas in an SQL-environment. The mechanisms for creating and destroying catalogs are implementation-defined.

SQL-schemas

An *SQL-schema,* often referred to simply as a *schema,* is a persistent, named collection of descriptors that describe SQL-data. Any object whose descriptor is in some SQL-schema is known as an *SQL-schema object.* A schema, the schema objects in it, and the SQL-data described by them are said to be owned by the authorization identifier associated with the schema. SQL-schemas are created and destroyed by execution of SQL-schema statements (or by implementation-defined mechanisms).

Information Schema

Every catalog contains an SQL-schema with the name INFORMATION_SCHEMA that includes the descriptors of a number of schema objects (mostly view definitions) that, together, allow every descriptor in that catalog to be accessed, but not changed, as though it were SQL-data. The data available through the views in an information schema includes the descriptors of the information schema itself: It does not include the schema objects or base tables of the definition schema. Each information schema view is so specified that a given user can access only those rows of the view that represent descriptors on which he has privileges.

Definition Schema

The *definition schema* is a fictitious schema with the name DEFINITION_SCHEMA; if it existed, the SQL-data in its base tables would describe all the SQL-data available to an SQL-server. The structure of the definition schema is a representation of the SQL data model.

SQL-data

SQL-data is data described by SQL-schemas—data under the control of an SQL-implementation in an SQL-environment.

Tables

A *table* has an ordered collection of one or more columns and an unordered collection of zero or more rows. Each column has a name and a data type. Each row has, for each column, exactly one value in the data type of that column. The rows of a table have a type, called the *row type;* every row of a table has the same row type, which is also the table's row type. See Table 1.1.

Table 1.1   Table Types

Table Name	Description
Base table	SQL-data consists entirely of these table variables. A base table is either a schema object or a module object. No two columns of a base table or a viewed table can have the same name.
Created base table	A base table whose descriptor is in a schema, and may be either persistent or temporary (though its descriptor is persistent in either case).
Persistent base table	Contains zero or more rows of persistent SQL-data.
Declared temp table	A base table declared in a module may only be temporary.
Derived table	An operation that references zero or more base tables and returns a table is called a *query,* and its result is a *derived table.* Derived tables, other than viewed tables, may contain more than one column with the same name.
Typed table	A declared table based on some structured type; its columns correspond in name and declared type to the attributes of the structured type. Typed tables have one additional column, called the *self-referencing column,* whose type is a reference type associated with the table's structured type.
Viewed table	A *view* is a named query, which you can invoke by name. The result of such an invocation is called a *viewed table.* Some queries, and hence some views, are updatable, meaning they can appear as targets of statements that change SQL-data. The results of changes expressed this way are defined in terms of corresponding changes to base tables. No two columns of a base table or a viewed table can have the same name.
Temporary table	An SQL-session object that cannot be accessed from any other SQL-session. A *global* temporary table can be accessed from any associated SQL-client module. A *local* temporary table can be accessed only from the module to which it is local. A temporary table is empty when an SQL-session is initiated and all its rows are deleted either when an SQL-transaction is terminated or when an SQL-session is terminated, depending on its descriptor.

SQL as a Language

SQL unquestionably is a language. It is a language of *action*. Each time you interact with a database using SQL, you are acting on data. You either ask a question by formulating a query to extract a results set or you submit a statement that has some action, like creating a table or column. SQL is simple in form and only uses 30 or so basic keywords to get the job done. The words themselves are simple and familiar. An example is SELECT Names FROM Customers WHERE Names LIKE 'H%'. which simply means, "I want to select data from the Names column in the Customers table where the data in the Names column begins with the letter H." The % is a wildcard, like the familiar *.

I capitalize SQL keywords for clarity. It isn't necessary to do so but it helps separate SQL keywords from column names and other non-SQL words in a query or statement and using all caps for SQL keywords is somewhat of a tradition among database nerds. SQL keywords are not case sensitive, but table names and columns are. However, you get the same results set if you enter 'h%' instead of 'H%' in the query. There are ways to make the results set case sensitive; I detail that in Chapter 6.

SQL, like other languages, has clauses, statements, queries, predicates, commands and so on. In fact, the SELECT query just given has an example of a WHERE clause. It also has an example of a predicate with the inclusion of LIKE. Don't worry, you will not be required to go back to middle school. These terms are included only in the context of database management and later chapters further explain them. The main point to gather from this section is that SQL is a language with all of the potential, pitfalls, and promise of any language.

SQL Standards

SQL standards have brought database administrators to a place where, for the most part, a SQL query you create for one particular database will work on any other database with little or no change. These universal standards make SQL a *portable* language, which means that queries are database independent. For instance, I switched a web application from Microsoft SQL Server to MySQL with no changes to the SQL. After importing the data to the MySQL database, adjusting my username and password, and changing mssql calls to mysql, I was done. The application, written in PHP, worked as originally written and the application users never knew the difference. As long as all of your queries stay within the ANSI standards, they will be portable from database to database. A good programmer will document any non-standard, or database-specific, SQL calls.

This section gives you an overview of the different iterations of SQL standardization. I am beginning the section on SQL standards with SQL92 because it was the first major expansion of SQL into standards that included levels of conformance. Each standard is covered in enough detail to give you an adequate survey of the conformance levels and major enhancements over previous versions.

SQL92

There are three levels of conformance with the SQL92 standard: Entry, Intermediate, and Full. The standard was constructed in this manner to allow vendors to comply in stages. SQL92 was designed to be a standard for RDBMSs and is based on SQL89 and SQL86. SQL92 does not address objects but does set the stage for *JDBC (Java Database Connectivity)* and *SQLJ (Java optimized SQL)*. At over 600 pages, SQL92 is a major expansion over earlier versions. Significant improvements in existing features include a better definition of direct invocation of SQL language and improved diagnostic capabilities, especially a new status parameter (SQLSTATE), a diagnostics area, and supporting statements.

Many significant new features follow:

- ❋ Support for additional data types (DATE, TIME, TIMESTAMP, INTERVAL, BIT string, variable-length character and bit strings, and NATIONAL CHARACTER strings)
- ❋ Support for character sets beyond that required to express SQL language itself and support for additional collations
- ❋ Support for additional scalar operations, such as string operations for concatenate and substring, date and time operations, and a form for conditional expressions
- ❋ Increased generality in the use of scalar-valued and table-valued query expressions
- ❋ Additional set operators (for example, union join, natural join, set difference, and set intersection)
- ❋ Capability for domain definitions in the schema
- ❋ Support for Schema Manipulation capabilities (especially DROP and ALTER statements)
- ❋ Support for bindings (modules and embedded syntax) in the Ada, C, and MUMPS languages
- ❋ Additional privilege capabilities
- ❋ Additional referential integrity facilities, including referential actions, subqueries in CHECK constraints, separate assertions, and user-controlled deferral of constraints
- ❋ Definition of an information schema
- ❋ Support for dynamic execution of SQL language
- ❋ Support for certain facilities required for remote database access (especially connection management statements and qualified schema names)
- ❋ Support for temporary tables
- ❋ Support for transaction consistency levels
- ❋ Support for data type conversions (CAST expressions among data types)
- ❋ Support for scrolled cursors
- ❋ A requirement for a flagging capability to aid in portability of application programs

SQL92 was such a major update that it still remains as the most widely adopted standard for RDBMSs. You will notice, when evaluating database software, that usually some notation of standards conformance is there. You will most likely either see some level of SQL92 or SQL2 conformance in the software literature. Most database implementations do not conform 100 percent to the ANSI standard. Generally, database software is written as a *superset of a subset* of ANSI-SQL. This means that most software vendors have made conformance decisions and trade-offs based on performance benchmarks. For example, MySQL AB states the following on the issue of standards conformance: "One of our main goals with the product is to continue to work toward conformance with the SQL standard, but without sacrificing speed or reliability. We are not afraid to add extensions to SQL or support for non-SQL features if this greatly increases the usability of MySQL Server for a large segment of our user base."

SQL99

SQL99 greatly expands and extends the capabilities of SQL as laid out in SQL92. Like SQL92, SQL99 has different levels of conformance to the standard. The level I discuss in this book is called Core SQL99. Since many database software vendors seem to have gotten stuck at the Entry level of conformance with SQL92, SQL99 has made it easy to make the transition to SQL99 conformance. Core SQL99 is actually a superset of Entry SQL92, and Core SQL99 is a prerequisite of all other levels of conformance to that standard. At over 1,000 pages, SQL99 is a standard to be reckoned with. Many of the standards' parts were composed independently of each other and incorporated into the standard separately. Table 1.2 is a brief overview of the standard and its individual parts.

Table 1.2   Overview of SQL99

Standard	Definition
SQL Framework	Provides underlying material for the other parts of the standard. Core conformance is based on material in this section.
SQL Foundation	Builds on the material in SQL Framework and describes the more fundamental parts of the standard rather than just the conceptual framework.
SQL/CLI (Call-Level Interface)	Specifies a standard *API (Application Programming Interface)* through which SQL operations are called. SQL/CLI and ODBC are very similar, so if you know ODBC, you should be able to write to a SQL/CLI interface with only minor modifications.
SQL/PSM (Persistent Stored Modules)	SQL/PSM can be used to support *triggers,* which are modules of code automatically executed in response to specified changes in the data.
SQL/Bindings	Specifies how SQL is to be bound to various programming languages (excluding Java which has its own area). This section is

Standard	Definition
	relevant to embedded and dynamic SQL and although neither is a new feature, various new features, such as multimedia and user-defined data types, require extensions to the interface between SQL and other languages.
SQL/MM (Multimedia)	This extends SQL to deal intelligently with large, complex, and even streaming bits of data, such as audio, video, and spatial.
SQL/OLB (Object Language Bindings)	*Part 0* (as they call it) of the SQLJ specification for embedding SQL in Java. Strictly speaking, this is a distinct standard based on Entry-level SQL92 and developed parallel to SQL99.

The different parts of SQL99 in Table 1.2 do not correspond, in general, with the levels of conformance to the SQL99 standard. The various levels of conformance and keywords/phrases for each are shown in Table 1.3:

Table 1.3 SQL99 Conformance Levels

Level	Description
Core	Standard SQL features.
Enhanced Datetime Facilities	Most DATETIME functions were applied in SQL92.
Enhanced Integrity Management	Referential Integrity.
Active Database	Triggers.
OLAP (Online Analytical Processing)	Joins.
PSM	Stored procedures.
CLI	SQL/CLI.
Basic Object Support	User-defined data types.
Enhanced Object Support	Constructors and multiple inheritance.

Core SQL99 consists mostly of Entry SQL92 but with a few new additions. The following list gives you a generic view of new additions to the SQL99 Standard that DBMSs must support to be conformant.

- ❋ SQL-flagger: Syntax flagging
- ❋ Multiple module support
- ❋ Flexible identifiers: Lowercase names support

- ❊ Flexible syntax: compatibility related syntax flexibility
- ❊ INFORMATION_SCHEMA: System catalog tables
- ❊ CREATE SCHEMA statement
- ❊ Additions to views: GROUP BY, FROM, and UNION
- ❊ New data types: LOBs, UDTs, VARCHAR, and additional DATETIME
- ❊ Changes to cursors and some DDL additions
- ❊ Many SQL keyword additions
- ❊ Multi-row INSERT
- ❊ Additional transactional statements

SQL2003

SQL2003 is the current SQL standard as of this writing. When I refer to the SQL standard, it means SQL2003. Probably the most significant change to the SQL standard for SQL2003 is the support for XML (Extensible Markup Language). XML is used as a data *bridge* between dissimilar platforms. It also is a universal standard and the universal World Wide Web markup language. It may, in time, replace HTML as the de facto Internet markup language. With XML, you can define richly formatted documents but a document does not have to be just words. It can define graphics, mathematical equations, object metadata, and a vast number of other data types.

XML DEFINED
Extensible Markup Language, or XML, is a markup language for documents containing structured information. The XML specification defines a standard way to add markup to documents.

SQL2003 introduces a new data type: XML. This new data type allows SQL operations on XML data. Inversely, SQL data can be operated on via XML. Table 1.4 lists other new and interesting features of the new standard.

Table 1.4   Notable SQL2003 Features

Feature	Description
Elementary OLAP functions	Adds an *Online Analytical Processing (OLAP)* amendment, including a number of windowing functions to support widely used calculations such as moving averages and cumulative sums. Windowing functions are aggregates computed over a window of data: ROW_NUMBER, RANK, DENSE_RANK, PERCENT_RANK, and CUME_DIST. OLAP functions are fully described in

Feature	Description
	T611 of the standard. Some database platforms are starting to support the OLAP functions.
Sampling	Adds the TABLESAMPLE clause to the FROM clause. This is useful for statistical queries on large databases, such as a data warehouse.
Enhanced numeric functions	In this case, the standard was mostly catching up with the trend in the industry, since the new functions are already supported by one or more of the database platforms.
SQL/XML	Adds the new XML data type. Also adds four new XML operators, several new functions, and the new IS DOCUMENT predicate. It also includes rules for mapping SQL-related elements (like identifiers, schemas, and objects) to XML-related elements.

The SQL2003 Foundation section includes all of the foundation and bindings standards from SQL99, but a new section called Schemata was created. Core SQL99 requirements did not change for SQL2003 so that any RDBMS that conforms to Core SQL99 automatically conforms to Core SQL2003. Core SQL2003 is a superset of Core SQL99. SQL2003 has a few additional reserved keywords and some deletions were made, such as the bit and bit varying data types, the UNION JOIN clause, and the UPDATE...SET ROW statement.

Speculating on the Future of SQL

Now is the time that I get to take out my crystal ball and play the role of futurist. I think that if someone had asked me 10 years ago what I think databases and database technology will be like today, I would have predicted that we would be further along than we currently are. I won't tell you what my predictions would have been, because hindsight is always perfect; I will just continue with my current predictions.

Database Technology

Embedded databases, data warehouses, data malls, data marts, desktop databases, workgroup databases, enterprise databases, global databases, and so on, already exist. What does not exist, at least to my knowledge, is an underlying protocol for the databases to speak to each other in an automated fashion. I am not talking about ODBC, attaching remote databases for queries, clustering, replication, or even a data-exchange language, per se. I am speaking of real communications between databases to connect to other resources, provide security, monitor processes and alerts, and so on.

I think that eventually someone will develop a database operating system that has an embedded database server as part of the kernel, or at least part of the core operating system, that manages user accounts, tracks files and directories, manages memory, controls CPU allocation, manages processes and other daemons, and the like. It wouldn't surprise me to find that someone is developing along those lines. An integrated database with an operating system would be more than just searching for files, in my opinion. In my wildest dreams, I see this operating system's integrated database actually connecting to its mother-ship database to collect updates, update user information, grant access to resources, and communicate globally. About three years ago, I had a complete design for this system on paper. In this plan, I had integrated access to resources right into the operating system shell, so that once a user logged on to her computer, the desktop and applications would become available along with email, voicemail, videomail, and so on. The user would be unaware of the actual location of any of the applications and resources. This would all be done through the magic of databases of all sizes, including embedded, all the way up to global data warehouse.

In my database-centric future, all databases will be able to speak to each other by a common database API. All databases will find out about each other through a database cloud kind of like DNS. I propose that this new service be called DIS for Data Interchange Service. Routers will use embedded databases to locate other routers. Instead of routing tables, there will be routing databases. These services will be useful in the future because I want to be able to open my tablet in any location, even riding in my car, and be able to access all my information and resources without having to know anything about my location. It will be easier than using a cellular phone: open up your tablet and there you are, connected, working, productive—anywhere and at any time. Now I realize that wireless communications will have to improve to the broadband level to do this, but if you can pinpoint your location in the middle of nowhere with a GPS device, then why couldn't I find my home desktop or my work desktop on my tablet the same way? Did you get that: work desktop and home desktop. Sounds almost like a roaming profile, only better. Depending on my login name, password, or context, I could have an entirely different experience on the same device because my local database would connect to the mother-ship database granting my desktop experience.

In the future, databases and the data they acquire, exchange, and manage will be integrated into our lives so deeply that most of us will cease to notice. We will just take this technology for granted, like turning on the television and switching channels.

The SQL Language

SQL is a fluid and evolving entity. From its meager beginnings, it has grown into a ubiquitous amalgam of commands, statements, queries, and management utilities. The future of SQL is certain: It will remain as the primary interface language for some time to come. I do foresee a time, however, when SQL is pulled out of the DBMS almost completely with just a stub language remaining for low-level maintenance or for database-to-database communications. Where will SQL go, you ask? I think it will become external to the DBMS, eventually evolving into a complete procedural language. Think about how much smaller this would make the DBMS. I think that this is a logical progression, especially for embedded databases that need to fit into smaller and smaller spaces and provide greater and greater functionality and features.

SQL will, of course, become object oriented and perhaps evolve into the next Java. Someday everyone will want to be certified in what I am going to call SPOIL for Structured Procedural Object Interactive Language. Instead of statements, queries, and commands, we will retrieve data by means of procedural statements, much like stored procedures—but the procedures themselves will be able to stand alone, like a shell script or compiled program. It will also remain interactive because interactivity is the basis for all human languages. We feel comfort in carrying on a dialog, even if it is with a computer.

SQL Standards

My crystal ball view of standards reveals they will continue to proliferate and bloat until no single person will have ever read an entire SQL standard. People will become "SQL Module Experts" and be certified professionals in areas such as high-definition queries or the like. Though I may be making light of some of these things, it should be seriously considered that there are many professionals and paraprofessionals who currently work with and enforce the laws of the land. What is so far fetched about having professionals and paraprofessionals who study SQL and database technology standards and audit DBMS software and data for compliance—especially for government or large-corporation work?

I feel that as SQL develops into future incarnations that standards will have to keep up with its new features. Standards are what keep us honest and not only measure us against the competition, but maintain an ideal for all to strive toward. It isn't difficult to predict that the standards will grow exponentially with each new revision. I think the SQL standard probably should be almost like our Constitution, where a relatively small document lays out the general standards and any updates to those standards are actually added as amendments. Trying to keep up with every new standard that comes out is like trying to keep up with each new revision of a software product that hits the market.

Database Vendors

I predict that there will be a great consolidation movement amongst database vendors. There will be buyouts and mergers taking place over the next few years. Some of them will be positive but most will not. Look at the major database vendors now, and in 10 years if half of them are still standing alone. I see some of the big companies buying up the smaller ones (in terms of capital) to collect their user base. My guess is that when a large company acquires a smaller one, that the large company's user base will more than double. I see database vendors making a big play for the individual user instead of just large corporations. Some of these companies will offer desktop or small-server versions of their prized database software to try and win over the public at large. Some of this has already begun, with some vendors releasing *lite* versions of their DBMSs for little or no cost to try and seduce the home user and small business owner into using their products.

Vendors may actually pull back the reins a bit when it comes to software evolution and pare their offerings down to just one or two products. The two products probably will be a single, all-purpose DBMS that scales from the desktop to the data warehouse and beyond, and an embedded DBMS for devices of all scales.

Open Source

Open-source DBMS software (and open-source software in general) is my favorite soap box. I love to sing its praises and shout out its advantages for all to hear. Unfortunately, I see greed knocking at the open-source door. I foresee many open-source companies being acquired by large corporations who promise to continue development and maintain the open-source ideals. If you wave enough money in someone's face, they will probably take it. There is nothing wrong with making money. Don't get me wrong. I am a great fan of money. I also believe that some of the best things in life are free and should remain so. On the other hand, for every open-source "sellout," there will be at least 10 more freedom fighters who create great software and release the code to the public for free.

Open-source software will become an even bigger contender in the global software market in the next few years as corporations adopt it and companies form to support it. It makes good sense for large companies because their in-house programmers and contractors can edit the code to make needed enhancements. Large corporations also benefit from open source products like MySQL, PostgreSQL, PHP, Perl, and hundreds of others. It also makes sense for small companies with limited budgets that cannot afford expensive software. If you would like to see the cost savings in print, visit their respective web sites and see for yourself how large corporations are lowering their cost of ownership by using open-source software.

Summary

This chapter briefly summarizes SQL history and its modern standards. SQL is a living entity that is ever changing and growing to meet the needs of a world that is undeniably dependent on its data. But to be perfectly honest, you don't have to know anything about database standards to use, develop, create, maintain, or administer databases. It is helpful to become familiar with each standard's major features, if you are truly interested in database development, because you can contribute to the evolution of your database of choice. Even in the case of closed-source commercial databases, you can submit bug reports and suggestions via the vendor web site. Open-source database software can be enhanced by anyone who wishes to contribute. If you are a programmer, then you may contribute directly to the database code. Most of us have to settle for submitting bug reports and using online suggestion boxes.

Chapter Review

Multiple Choice

1. Which of the following SQL standards is the most widely implemented?

    a) SQL89

    b) SQL92

    c) SQL2003

    d) ANSI SQL

2. Of the many SQL standards and implementations, which one is considered pure?

    a) SQL89

    b) SQL92

    c) SQL2003

    d) ANSI SQL

3. SQL is what kind of language?

    a) Procedural

    b) Low level

    c) Non-procedural

    d) Basic

4. What company did the preliminary research into relational databases and SQL?

    a) Oracle

    b) Alpha

    c) Relational Software

    d) IBM

5. Online Analytical Processing (OLAP) was added into which SQL standard?

    a) SQL89

    b) SQL92

    c) SQL2003

    d) ANSI SQL

6. The company that owns Structured Query Language is

    a) IBM

    b) Oracle

    c) Microsoft

    d) None of the above

7. Which of the standards introduced the XML data type?

    a) SQL89

    b) SQL92

    c) SQL2003

    d) ANSI SQL

8. Who is considered the father of the Relational Database Model?

    a) E. F. Codd

    b) Larry Ellison

    c) Bill Gates

    d) Kenneth Hess

9. What practice has assisted database vendors in conforming to newer standards?

    a) Allowing vendors to pick and choose conformance levels

    b) Carrying SQL92 Entry-level conformance up to SQL99 and SQL2003

    c) Lowering the conformance expectations so that vendors can catch up

    d) Allowing open-source database vendors to participate in standards drafting

10. Why was there a push to create SQL standards?

    a) To prevent SQL forking.

    b) Database theoreticians demanded it.

    c) Commercial acceptance.

    d) ANSI and ISO lobbied for standardization.

Concepts

1. Explain what is meant by "contemporary SQL is a superset of a subset of ANSI SQL."

2. Is SQL portability a good thing? Why or why not?

3. Why does SQL qualify as a language?

2 } Relational Databases

A *database* is defined as a structured and persistent set of data. A *relational database* is composed of multiple relational tables. *Relational,* in simple terms, refers to the ability of data in one table to be related to data in other tables. Formally, by theoretical definition, a table is not necessarily a *relation,* although the terms are used interchangeably. A *relation* is a two-dimensional table that satisfies all of the following requirements:

* Each cell in the table must contain a single value, if any. Cells are not allowed to contain arrays or repeated groups.
* Each column must have a unique name.
* The order of the columns is irrelevant.
* The order of the rows is irrelevant.
* A column must contain the same type of data throughout.
* No two rows may be identical.

Databases may have tables that are not relations and that is perfectly fine, but to be a relation they must meet all of the listed requirements. Theoretical definitions, while precise, are rarely descriptive enough on their own to be illustrative. For example, if you maintain a database of people who order books from you, you would probably have a table named Customers that contains Name, Address, City, State, Zip Code, Phone Number, and a Customer Number. To keep track of the orders, you could have a table called Orders that contains the Order Number, the Item Number, the Number of Items Ordered, Shipping Method, the Total of Items Ordered and the associated Customer Number. That Customer Number associated with a Customer is the relationship between Customers and Orders. If needed, you can now query the database and find out, for example, how much money each Customer has spent or how often he purchases from you by matching the two tables by Customer Number. Figure 2.1 shows what your tables look like.

Figure 2.1

Customers table and Orders table for the Books database.

Customers	
PK	**Customer ID**
	Name
	Address
	City
	State
	Zip
	Phone

Orders	
PK	**Order ID**
	Customer_ID
	Item_Number
	Item_Count
	Shipping_Method
	Total

THE SAMPLE DATABASE

I use the sample database, Books, throughout this book for examples of an actual database. You will be creating it from scratch in Chapter 4, so don't worry about the column names or structure right now.

You may now be asking yourself why you would not just keep all of that information in one single table. If you have ever created a spreadsheet with many columns in it, you know how difficult it is to maintain the columns that are way out to the right. You have to continually scroll back and forth to maintain the data. Database software has the same issue with many columns. It is more efficient to create a table for each type of data than to put everything into a single table. The database, like you, has an easier time scrolling up and down through rows of data than across columns. An additional issue is data size. If, as in the preceding example, you only have one table, that table would increase by one complete row of data each time one item is ordered (because you would have to duplicate the entire row). By using two tables, the Customers table remains the same size for each new order made by an existing customer and only increases by one small row in the Orders table for each order. We have already increased our database efficiency by having two tables.

In this chapter, you learn the theoretical aspects and the components of the Relational Data Model. Examples are given, where feasible, for each area.

The Relational Data Model

In his 1970 "A Relational Model of Data for Large Shared Data Banks," E.F. Codd proposed the following 12 basic rules to be satisfied by a Relational DBMS:

Table 2.1 E.F. Codd's Basic Relational DBMS Rules

Codd's Rule	Plain-English Interpretation
All information is represented in relational tables.	This is basically the informal definition of a relational database.

Codd's Rule	Plain-English Interpretation
All data is accessible using the table name, primary key value, and column name.	Stresses the importance of primary keys for locating data in the database. The table name locates the correct table, the column name finds the correct column, and the primary key value finds the row containing an individual item of interest.
Systematic support for missing information (null values, independent of data type) must be provided.	Requires support for missing data through NULL values.
The relational schema itself is represented in tables and is accessible in the same way as the database.	Requires that a relational database be self describing. In other words, the database must contain certain *system tables* whose columns describe the structure of the database itself.
A relational query language must be provided that supports data definition, view definition, data manipulation, integrity constraints, authorization, and transaction boundaries (begin, commit, and rollback).	Mandates using a relational database language, such as SQL, although SQL is not specifically required. The language must be able to support all the central functions of a DBMS: creating a database, retrieving and entering data, implementing database security, and so on.
Basic support for view updatability is provided.	This rule deals with views, which are *virtual tables* that give various users different views of its structure. It is one of the most challenging rules to implement in practice, and no commercial product fully satisfies it today. Views are covered in Chapter 9.
Table-at-a-time retrieval and update operations are provided.	Stresses the set-oriented nature of a relational database. It requires that rows be treated as sets in insert, delete, and update operations. The rule is designed to prohibit implementations that support only row-at-a-time, navigational modification of the database.
Application programs are logically unaffected by changes to internal storage or access methods.	This rule states specific access or storage techniques used by the DBMS should not affect the user's ability to work with the data.

Codd's Rule	Plain-English Interpretation
Application programs are logically unaffected by information-preserving changes to the base tables.	Like the preceding rule, states that low-level changes to physical storage and retrieval should not adversely affect the user.
Integrity constraints must be definable in the query language and storable in the system tables.	The database language should support integrity constraints that restrict the data that can be entered into the database and the database modifications that can be made. This rule is not supported in most commercial DBMS products.
The DBMS has distribution independence.	The database language must be able to manipulate distributed data located on other computer systems.
If record-at-a-time processing is supported, this cannot be used to bypass the constraints declared in the set-oriented query language.	Prevents other paths into the database that might subvert its relational structure and integrity.

❄ Ahead of His Time

Codd came from a world in which databases were flat files or network databases. He was truly a visionary and the major force in relational database development that we enjoy today. And some 36 years after that landmark paper, some of his rules are still not implemented in contemporary database software. Some say that Codd could have combined Rules 8 and 9 into a single rule, but 11 rules leave the feeling of an unfinished work. Codd later refined and expanded his 12 (1970) basic rules to a whopping 333 (1990). I must confess that I have never read them all. I doubt that many database vendors will ever conform to all 333, since the initial 12 have proven somewhat ambitious, but it is interesting to note that he evolved his own relational theories to that point. Codd did not propose the specific mechanism by which a relational database is interacted with, as you can see in Rule 5. He knew nothing of SQL in 1970. It was developed later as part of the research into RDBMS.

Tables

Tables are the database entities that hold your data. They contain all of the rows and columns of data and are the primary database structural elements. You can think of individual tables of data as being like a spreadsheet. In fact, a lot of people take spreadsheets and create database tables from them. Tables, like databases, have names. The columns in a table are also named. Rows are not named but are typically numbered. Rows are your actual data entries or records. Each column defines the data type for each entry in that column.

Naming

Tables and other database entities (such as columns) should be named descriptively but without using spaces. If you feel that you need to separate words in a descriptive name, use a dash (-) or an underscore (_). For example, if you have a database for allowing customers to order different items, you may want to put the items into separate tables with descriptive names. For books, you can use Book_Orders and for pens you can use Pen_Orders. You can be as descriptive as you like in your naming of entities, but keeping the names short is a big advantage later on. There aren't any hard and fast rules about names, except to be descriptive enough so as not to be confusing. Naming tables A, B, and C won't tell you very much about the data within.

The convention used among database administrators is to use the *fully qualified name* for a table. You are likely to have a database with more than one table or multiple databases and would need to be able to distinguish between them. A fully qualified table name is defined as the Database_Name.Table_Name. Our Customers table from the Books database would be Books.Customers. This may seem useless at this point, with only one database, but if you have several databases, you can be attached to one and select data from others simultaneously. Similarly, you can use Table_Name.Column_Name to specify a particular column within a table. This comes in very handy when selecting data from different tables where column names are the same. For instance, even in our simple Books database, you need to distinguish between Customer_ID in the Customers table and Customer_ID in the Orders table. In practice, this would look like: Customers.Customer_ID and Orders.Customer_ID.

> ❋ **WHAT'S IN A NAME?**
> When you begin naming the parts of your database, such as tables, you should pick a naming convention and stick with it. Being consistent with your naming will help you later on when performing routine maintenance or webifying your database. Some examples for naming: Books, Customers, Orders or Books, CUSTOMERS, ORDERS. Using more descriptive names: Book_Orders, Customer_Info, Zip_Codes or book_orders, customer_info, zip_codes.

Data Types in Columns

Unlike naming a table, there are some rules about designing one. Designing a table requires some thought and, most likely, some revision. Very few people who design databases create all of their tables at once and never have to go back and add, change, or delete parts or even entire tables.

Before plunging right into table design and design theory, take a look at column types. When you create a table, you have to specify what type of data that column will hold. There are some basic things you need to know about column types before proceeding. The following tables show you the various column types and the different choices for each. The tables give you a general survey and quick column reference. Each data type is covered in more detail later in this section.

The following lists things to consider before choosing a particular column type for your data:

* The kind of values that the column can store.
* the amount of space the values take. Some column types take up a static amount of space, and *variable-length* types take up an amount of space that is equivalent to the size of the data in the column.
* Whether NULL values are allowed.
* Whether the data can be indexed.
* How the data are compared and sorted.

Each column in a table must have a declared data type. The data type is part of the column definition. Column definition examples are given in Chapter 4. In the meantime, know that when creating a table, you must declare the column name, the column data type, and the data type size. The data type you choose is actually a *constraint* because you are stating in the declaration that this is the only type of data that this column will contain. Some DBMSs enforce this more than others by throwing errors if an attempt at inserting the incorrect data type occurs.

DATATYPE OR DATA TYPE

You will see, or may have seen, the word datatype in articles or other books about databases. Both are understood and refer to the same concept of the type of data that is defined in a column. I prefer the two word spelling, data type, and use it this way throughout the book.

All data types fit into seven official data type categories given in Table 2.2.

Table 2.2   Official Data-Type Categories

Data Type	Description
Character String	Text. Character-set independent.
National Character	Text. National character set.
Bit String	Binary data. 0s and 1s.
Exact Numeric	Precise numeric data.
Approximate Numeric	Numeric data that represent approximations. Exponential data.
Datetime	Date and/or time-related data.
Interval	Describes amounts of time between dates or times.

ANSI SQL provides the following list of data types. Can you determine to which category each one belongs?

BINARY LARGE OBJECT (BLOB)	BOOLEAN
CHARACTER VARYING	DOUBLE PRECISION
INTERVAL	NATIONAL CHARACTER VARYING
SMALLINT	TIMESTAMP WITH TIME ZONE
BIT	CHARACTER
DATE	FLOAT
NATIONAL CHARACTER	NUMERIC
TIME	TIME WITH TIME ZONE
BIT VARYING	CHARACTER LARGE OBJECT (CLOB)
DECIMAL	INTEGER
NATIONAL CHARACTER LARGE OBJECT	REAL
TIMESTAMP	

Vendors use other, non-ANSI data types. You see those in Chapter 3, when you survey features of popular RDBMS software.

Primary Keys

A *primary key* is a column in a table that contains only unique values (usually sequentially numbered integers). These unique values are known as a primary key *constraint*. You are constraining the values in that column to be UNIQUE and NOT NULL. There is no need to specify a primary key as NOT NULL in DBMSs that are at least SQL92 conformant. NOT NULL means that the value in that column must contain a valid entry for the column type. It cannot, by definition, be blank or *null*. UNIQUE means that no two values may be the same. There can be only one primary key in a table. Primary key values should be considered *immutable*, meaning that its value is not subject to change under ordinary circumstances. A primary key is not required in a table. Remember that your tables do not have to be relations in the pure sense of the word. You must have a primary key, however, if you want to create any sort of relationships between tables. By definition, a table that is a true relation must have a key. The rule of no two identical rows dictates this.

❄ **BEST PRACTICE**
It is so important to have a primary key in a table that some DBMSs will prompt you to create one. A warning pops up after saving your new table if you didn't create a primary key while creating your table. By default, it creates a column named ID as an automatically numbered integer type.

Let's look again at your simple Books database in Figure 2.2. Can you identify the primary key in each?

Figure 2.2

Customers table and Orders table for the Books database.

Customers	
PK	**Customer_ID**
	Name
	Address
	City
	State
	Zip
	Phone

Orders	
PK	**Order_ID**
	Customer_ID
	Item_Number
	Item_Count
	Shipping_Method
	Total

Though you can't readily tell from just looking at the columns in this manner, it is safe to say that Customer_ID in the Customers table and Order_ID in the Orders table are the primary keys. The type of primary key we have defined is a *single-field primary key*. If you cannot guarantee that your IDs will be unique such that a single-field primary key will work , you can define a multiple-field primary key. The next section discusses multiple-field primary keys. In this figure, primary keys are separated from the other columns and labeled PK. Foreign keys are in bold.

You will note that there is a Customer_ID in the Orders table too. Its existence creates a relationship between the two tables. In the next section, we look at relationships that can be formed between tables. It is this ability to form table-to-table relationships and to enforce those relationships with constraints that makes databases relational.

It is my practice, habit, or neurotic tendency to always begin every table with a primary key field, usually with the name of the table with an underscore and ID (Customer_ID), or simply ID. I probably developed the habit from years of working with Microsoft Access. I am glad for the practice regardless of its origin for several reasons: First, it keeps me organized because I know it is always there, ready to be used for referential integrity; second, it fulfills the unique column requirement for a relation; and finally, it helps me retrieve the last record ID entered into the database for web programming. (You find out about this in Chapter 12 on embedded programming.)

Indexes

An *index* is a database feature that allows quick access to the rows in a table. The index, created using one or more columns, is a separate file or part of a tablespace, smaller than the original table (due to having fewer columns) and is optimized for quick searching, usually via a balanced tree *(b-tree)*. If you have two million name and address records, you don't want to scan the entire table every time someone wants to search for the name John Smith. Indexes speed access to records by creating sorted pointers to the data. This makes searches faster, because the index is searched instead of the table itself. Once the records of choice are found, the pointers access the table data.

> ❋ **CAUTION**
>
> Indexes can speed data access, but they can also slow data updates. The index has to be updated each time a record is added, updated, or deleted; that can take some time. You can work around this time delay giving the user the feeling that the update is instantaneous. I personally believe that the benefits of indexing far outweigh the negatives. You must be careful to only index those columns that will be involved in a lot of searches and the data in the indexed columns should be as unique as possible.

You already have a little experience with indexes. Think of the index at the back of this book. If you had to go through the entire book to find the term *index*, you would be searching for some time. Instead, the work has been done for you: Someone created an index that is considerably smaller than the book and points to key words. This is exactly how a database index works. It makes you wonder where they got the idea for it.

From the earlier discussion of primary keys, you have even more experience with indexes. A primary key is an index. It happens to be a unique index that is also set to NOT NULL. You don't have to tell the database that this type of index is unique or NOT NULL, because that is the definition of a primary key. Indexes can have NULL values and they don't have to be unique. Indexes don't have to be limited to referencing textual data any more since the addition of spatial indexes for *geometric (GIS)* data. The following sections look at the different index types.

Normal (Non-Unique) Indexes

A *non-unique index* allows duplicate values in the indexed column. Values can be NULL. Such an index speeds data access, but efficiency is lost because of the allowed duplicate values.

Unique Indexes

A *unique index* does not allow duplicate values in the indexed column. Values can be NULL. Unique indexes are more efficient than non-unique because the unique characteristic enforces no redundancy of values.

Full-Text Indexes

A *full-text index* allows duplicates and NULL values and has the added feature of allowing scans of all of the text contained in the indexed column. Full-text indexes are only supported in MyISAM tables and only on certain column types (char, varchar and TEXT).

Spatial Indexes

Spatial indexes are new in MySQL and represent a new object-relational model and a new indexing scheme. This type of index is for what is called Geometric data referring to GPS (Global Positioning System) or other geographic and multi-dimensional data.

Relationships

A *relationship* between tables is usually accomplished by matching data in key fields—usually with the same name in both tables as in our Books database. Look back at Figure 2.2 and you will see that in each of the tables there is a column named Customer_ID.

Foreign Keys

A *foreign key* is a column or group of columns in a table that correspond to or reference a primary key in another table in the database. You have already been introduced to the idea of a foreign key in Chapter 1 when we first created our new Books database with the two tables: Customers and Orders. Refer to Figure 2.2 to locate the foreign key in the Orders table. A foreign key is also an indexed column that is unique and NOT NULL.

One-to-Many Relationship

A *one-to-many relationship* is the most common type of relationship. In a one-to-many relationship, a record in the Customers table can have many matching records in the Orders table, but a record in Orders has only one matching record in Customers.

Many-to-Many Relationship

You can see a many-to-many relationship in Figure 2.3. I have added two new tables for this illustration named Order_Details and Products.

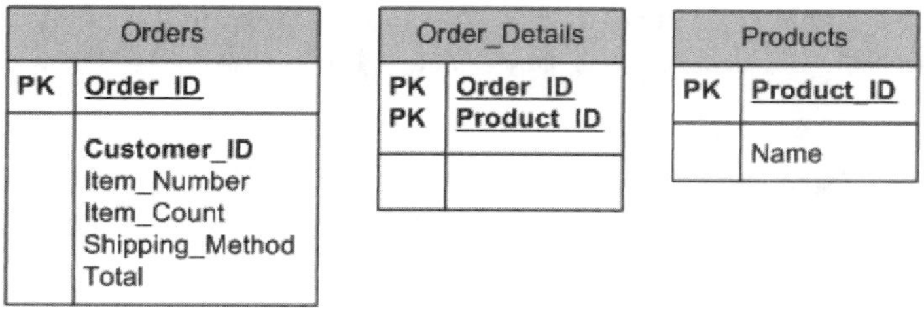

Figure 2.3

Many-to-many relationship with Orders, Order_Details, and Products tables.

Orders	
PK	Order_ID
	Customer_ID Item_Number Item_Count Shipping_Method Total

Order_Details	
PK PK	Order_ID Product_ID

Products	
PK	Product_ID
	Name

In a *many-to-many relationship*, a record in Table A can have many matching records in Table B, and a record in Table B can have many matching records in Table A. This type of relationship is only possible by defining a third table (called a *junction table*) whose primary key consists of two fields—the foreign keys from both Tables A and B. A many-to-many relationship is really two one-to-many relationships with a third table. For example, the Orders table and the Products table have a many-to-many relationship that's defined by creating two one-to-many relationships to the

Order_Details table. One order can have many products, and each product can appear on many orders.

One-to-One Relationship

In a *one-to-one relationship*, each record in Table A can have only one matching record in Table B, and each record in Table B can have only one matching record in Table A. This type of relationship is not common, because most information related in this way would be in one table. You might use a one-to-one relationship to divide a table with many fields, to isolate part of a table for security reasons, or to store information that applies only to a subset of the main table. For example, if you have an Employees table in your company database, you may also create a Managers table to isolate data associated with managers. Each manager will have an entry in the Managers table and a corresponding one in the Employees table.

Referential Integrity

Referential integrity is a system of rules that ensures that relationships between records in related tables are valid and that you don't accidentally delete or change related data. You can set referential integrity when all of the following conditions are met:

✻ The matching field from the primary table is a primary key or has a unique index. A unique index does not allow duplicate entries in the indexed field. Setting a field as the primary key automatically defines the field as unique.

✻ The related fields have the same data type.

✻ Both tables belong to the same database.

The following rules apply when you use referential integrity:

✻ No value may be entered into the foreign key field of the related table that doesn't exist in the primary key of the primary table. However, a NULL value may be entered into the foreign key, specifying that the records are unrelated. For example, you can't have an order that is assigned to a customer if that customer doesn't exist, but you can have an order that is assigned to no one by entering a NULL value in the Customer_ID field.

✻ Records from a primary table cannot be deleted if matching records exist in a related table. For example, you can't delete a Customer record from the Customers table if there are orders assigned to the Customer in the Orders table.

✻ A primary key value cannot be changed in the primary table if that record has related records. For example, a Customer ID in the Customers table cannot be changed if there are orders assigned to that Customer in the Orders table.

For relationships in which referential integrity is enforced, you can specify whether you want the database to automatically cascade update and cascade delete related records. If you set these options, delete and update operations that would normally be prevented by referential integrity rules are allowed. When you delete records or change primary key values in a primary table, the database makes necessary changes to related tables to preserve referential integrity.

> ❄ **CASCADING UPDATES AND DELETES DEFINED**
>
> Cascading update: For relationships that enforce referential integrity between tables, the updating of all related records in the related table(s) when a record in the primary table is changed.
>
> Cascading delete: For relationships that enforce referential integrity between tables, the deletion of all related records in the related table(s) when a record in the primary table is deleted.

Referential integrity has its advantages, but there are disadvantages as well. I discuss some of them at length in Chapters 4 and 11, but for now, these notes on cascading updates and cascading deletes are very important to consider.

If you use cascade update when defining a relationship, any time you change the primary key of a record in the primary table, the database automatically updates the primary key to the new value in all related records. For example, if you change a customer's ID in the Customers table, the Customer_ID field in the Orders table is automatically updated for every one of that customer's orders so that the relationship isn't broken. Most databases perform cascading updates without displaying any messages.

If you use cascade delete when defining a relationship, any time you delete records in the primary table, the database automatically deletes related records in the related table. For example, if you delete a customer record from the Customers table, all the customer's orders are automatically deleted from the Orders table (including records in the Order_Details table related to the Orders records). When you delete records using a delete query, most databases automatically delete the records in related tables without displaying a warning.

> ❄ **CAUTION**
>
> Cascading updates and deletes are very useful, but as the note reveals, they can be dangerous too. Many database systems are created by people who are also either avid Unix users or developers, and that leads to applications (specifically databases for us) that are not very *chatty*. Unix is a powerful operating system and is extremely useful for hosting databases but, in the same breath, if you tell a Unix server to remove an entire directory, it does so without asking if you really want to do that. I have been told that good judgment comes from experience and experience comes from poor judgment. I can testify to that. Be warned that backups won't do you any good if you accidentally remove all of the work that you did today. Before I became one, I used to make fun of Unix guys for typing in a command, staring at the screen for what seemed like an eternity, then whacking the Enter key like they were submitting a request for their last meal. They wanted to be sure that what they typed is really what they meant to do.

You should embrace this practice. The few extra seconds you take to check the query you type will save you countless hours of grief later on (and maybe your job). Be careful.

Summary

This chapter has introduced you to some database theory and a lot of database terminology. Any time you learn a new language, you just have to memorize some parts, while you learn other parts along the way. SQL has some of the same idiosyncrasies as any other language. While it is not so important to memorize Codd's 12 relational database rules, I do feel it is necessary to know about them and to realize how far we have come from those days of rickety old wooden databases to the newer, faster, and sportier models that we enjoy today.

Terminology such as primary and foreign keys, cascading updates and deletes, referential integrity, and relationships are very important to know and understand. You must not only know the definitions, but you must also comprehend their function and usage. And just as important as terminology are the concepts of how table columns can be related to one another and referential integrity.

Chapter Review

Multiple Choice

1. What is the most common type of table-to-table relationship?

   a) One to one

   b) One to many

   c) Many to many

   d) Selected

2. A table must have a name.

   a) True

   b) False

3. A key is defined by which attributes?

   a) Unique and constrained

   b) Constrained and named

   c) Unique and named

   d) Unique and NOT NULL

4. Which of the following is required for referential integrity?

   a) A named table

   b) A foreign key

   c) A one-to-one relationship

   d) Table integrity

5. How many data-type categories are there?

   a) 3

   b) 5

   c) 7

   d) 9

6. In the sample database Books, what is Orders.Customer_ID?

   a) A fully qualified table name

   b) A primary key

   c) A SQL anomaly

   d) A foreign key

7. If you use cascade delete when defining a relationship, any time you delete records in the primary table, the database automatically deletes related records in the related table.

   a) True

   b) False

8. Codd's 12 Rules are:

   a) Far too complex to be implemented, even today.

   b) The perfect number of rules to govern databases.

   c) The outline of the Relational Data Model.

   d) The outline of the Structured Query Language.

9. Referential integrity enforces what in a database?

   a) Consistency

   b) Fidelity

c) References

d) Codd's 12 Rules

10. Which of the following is true of columns?

a) They must be a static size.

b) They must be created as NOT NULL.

c) They must be referenced.

d) They must be named.

Concepts

1. Explain how all relations are tables but not all tables are relations.

2. Does a relationship between two tables imply referential integrity? Explain.

3. Explain why a unique index would be more efficient and higher performing than an index that does not enforce unique values.

3 } Database Software

Though this chapter has little to do with SQL per se, it introduces you to the major products that use it. I feel this reference is necessary to making an informed decision about a DBMS product. I cover commercial and open-source DBMSs and present their features and their limitations. This is meant to simply be an overview of my experience with each RDBMS, its features, limitations, standards compliance, pricing (where available), and other attributes. This review is in no way an advertisement for or a negative commentary on any vendor or its RDBMS. Everyone has his preferences, but I am not trying to steer you toward or away from any particular vendor or software. My purpose is to give you a look at what is available to you and provide my personal experiences with them.

By having the information contained in this chapter, you may find a DBMS that fills another need in your office or enterprise. I have found that there is no single correct answer for every problem. Products that were reviewed for this chapter are in bold in each section. I generally reviewed the standard version of each product (where applicable).

THE BIG THREE

Sybase, Oracle, and Informix are known as The Big Three in the enterprise database world. You see them referred to as such in this and other texts.

Sales

If you are not familiar with some of the database software presented here but would like to know more information, I suggest visiting the vendor web site and possibly setting up a meeting with a vendor representative to discuss your needs.

CAUTION
There are some warnings that I feel compelled to give you at this point. You should realize that sales people are going to be overly optimistic about their products and technical people always want you to wait until the next release before trying a product. You should proceed with caution in either case.

Before hosting a vendor or watching a demonstration, you should figure out your DBMS needs and, perhaps most importantly, your budget for the software, consulting, user licensing, and maintenance contracts. Your budget may put you out of certain "leagues" of software. You may want Oracle but your budget may warrant something a bit more realistic. Business decisions and technical decisions do not always mesh perfectly. While technical experts feel that Oracle or Informix may be the only options for your DBMS solution, your managerial purse strings may not be so loose. For instance, if your budget is $300,000 for hardware, software, and DBMS for a project that your projected costs estimated $500,000, you will have to make some sacrifices or adjust your vision a bit. You have to be realistic in separating your needs from your desires. If you truly need a system like Informix to process your data, then by all means you should have it, but if you are using your database to process inventory, then perhaps you should consider a lower-cost system. Lower cost does not mean lower capability. In fact, many free systems are just as capable as some of the high-cost ones. Many company executives fear free software because there is no one to blame (also called *accountability* in the corporate world) when things go wrong. Those who have stepped out of the standard corporate mindset have been very pleased. Visit the vendor web sites, check out their success stories, and read the white papers for more information on those who have taken the plunge into open-source or even free software.

One of the most important concepts regarding DBMS software is ACID compliance. This is perhaps more important than strict adherence to any SQL standard, since most DBMSs do not strictly adhere to them anyway. The ACID compliance section is here because of its importance to DBMS software, especially at the enterprise level. Any enterprise-level system should be ACID compliant. It is very important, as you read through any DBMS propaganda, to note information referring to transactions. The term *ACID* may or may not be used, so you need to learn each ACID component to make this evaluation yourself.

ACID Compliance

ACID is one of those acronyms that database people throw around quite readily to describe their RDBMS software but may have little idea what is assumed. The acronym ACID stands for atomicity, consistency, isolation, and durability. To say that a DBMS is *ACID compliant* means it is protected from certain types of corruption, especially concerning transactions. The concept of a database having ACID or being ACID compliant is quite simple. Databases are multiuser by nature and design, but this multiuser ability causes some problems as well as granting some advantages. When multiple people use a database by means of client software, like a web browser for instance, it is likely that more than one person will need to use or edit a particular record at the same time. If a database were not ACID compliant, then these types of transactions would overlap and some of the data would be corrupted or nonexistent.

A good example is our own BOOKS database. Say that you are ordering a copy of *SONAR 4 Power!* from your favorite online bookstore and, at that same time, I am also ordering a copy of the same book. There would be a contention for that transaction and it is possible, without the magic of ACID, that one or both of us would lose our copy of the book. It is also possible that our credit card could be charged but no book would be associated with the transaction or, even worse for the online vendor; the book gets ordered but the credit-card transaction did not take place. If this happened several hundred or several thousand times, the online bookstore would go bankrupt or their complaint-department phone lines would be heated up with angry customers. Either would be bad. An ACID-compliant database would save the online vendor from bankruptcy and from the wrath of unhappy customers.

The example can be explained in database lingo by saying that the online bookstore's database does not support concurrency and locking and that our transactions were *deadlocked*. *Concurrency* is how simultaneous transactions are handled. *Locking* prevents simultaneous data access; I cover this topic extensively in Chapter 7. Now turn back to ACID and take a look at what each part of it means:

❈ **Atomicity:** Database transactions that are atomic are all or nothing—either the entire transaction is completed or none of it is. It either gets committed (COMMIT) or rolled back (ROLLBACK) to a state such that the transaction has never been executed. Atomicity is maintained in the event of deadlocks, DBMS failure, application failure, disk failure, or CPU failure. Atomicity can be turned off at either the session or system level.

❈ **Consistency:** Going back to the example of ordering books—the vendor wants our credit card debited for the purchase of the book and our account with the vendor's store to be credited for the purchase and the book placed in the queue for delivery. This would be a consistent transaction. An amount of money, say $43.00 (book plus shipping, handling and tax), is debited from our Credit Card and posted to our bookstore account. Our credit card would show a −$43.00 and the bookstore would show +$43.00. This is one definition of transaction consistency.

❈ **Isolation:** Transactions should be isolated from each other as much as possible while maintaining an acceptable level of performance. If transactions can be *serialized*, then isolation is more successful. Some degree of isolation must exist for simultaneous transactions to be successful. Four degrees of isolation are offered, but lower levels lead to less consistency. The four levels of isolation are covered in Chapter 7.

❋ **Durability:** A durable DBMS guarantees proper recovery after a crash, regardless of where the transaction was in the queue, commit, store, or rollback process. The recovery is based on the most recent commits.

As you can see, ACID compliance is a significant part of decision-making when it comes to choosing a DBMS for your company or application. It can mean the difference between successful transactions with consistent data and corrupted unusable data, or worse. All of the DBMS software reviewed in this chapter, with the exception of Microsoft Access, is ACID compliant.

Database Software

This chapter is here to give you an idea of what kind of RDBMSs are available to you. I feel that I have chosen the most popular and well-known database software available today for this overview. The list is in no particular order. I have had varying experiences with each database and thus far all have been positive. You will have to choose the cost/performance/feature set that suits your needs.

You should answer the following questions before evaluating any DBMS for production use in your company. You can also answer them when creating a project budget. These questions give you focus for the project and make it easier to present your case to management. The questions are in no particular order. While they are in a yes/no answer format, you should not just answer yes or no and go on. You should use these questions as prompts for creating your plan of action.

❋ How many users will utilize the system?

❋ How will users attach to the database: browser, application, other tool?

❋ How important is database security?

❋ Do you need heavy transactional support?

❋ Do you need a full-time database administrator (DBA)?

❋ Do you require a vendor service contract?

❋ Do you need to contract a service-level agreement (SLA) from the vendor or other support entity?

❋ Do you need high-availability capability?

a. Will you need high-availability/fail-over hardware?

b. Does your database need to support high availability/fail over?

❋ What is your backup/restore/disaster-recovery plan?

❋ Do you need data warehousing capability?

❋ Do you, or will you, need historical data-retrieval capability?

- ❋ Have you accounted for growth in users, data, bandwidth, and storage needs?
- ❋ Do you have a performance and capacity-planning analysis plan?
- ❋ Will users be mostly doing queries or will they need to do updates and deletes?
- ❋ How important is update speed?
- ❋ Are you looking for low-cost or no-cost solutions?
- ❋ Have you, or would you, consider open-source solutions?
- ❋ Are you already bound to a specific vendor, like Microsoft?
- ❋ Do you need new hardware for this project?
- ❋ Have you considered alternative hosting solutions for your data?
- ❋ Have you chosen the host operating system for this project?
- ❋ Have you factored in the costs of upgrading, maintenance, and support?
- ❋ Do you, or will you, use XML data?
- ❋ Do you need stored procedures, view, triggers, or similar advanced DBMS functionality?
- ❋ Do you need Java connectivity?
- ❋ Do you need specific data types?
- ❋ Are you using/going to use a multi-tier architecture?
- ❋ How often and by what means will your data be archived?
- ❋ Does the DBMS have an auto-commit feature?
- ❋ How are transactions recovered after a crash?

These are the main questions that I encourage you to answer in developing a plan for a new system. Existing systems are a bit more complicated. For instance, are you changing architectures or vendors? Have your needs changed? You must answer a lot of questions in such a situation. I could probably write another book on just developing IT budgets and project plans for new or improving current implementations.

❋ **CAUTION**

People hear company names and buzzwords with little or no idea what they are saying or asking. If, for instance, you have decided that Oracle is your DBMS of choice and have made a case for it, someone in power may decide that Informix is the right answer without having done one bit of research. It is frustrating, but you might have to deal with it.

The rest of this chapter is dedicated to highlighting DBMS software. There are really no losers in this list. Most DBMS software these days is very complete, robust, and functional. The choice depends mostly on your corporate culture and budgetary constraints. I wish you the best of luck in making this very important decision.

> ❋ **EDITION AND HARDWARE INFORMATION**
> If multiple production products are available, the standard (or equivalent) edition is used for the overview, features, and requirements. Reviewed versions are shown in **bold** type. System requirements are given as the vendor's *recommended* (when available) requirements and not the minimum. Hardware requirements are sketchy for some implementations. Err on the high side.

Microsoft SQL Server

- ❋ **Name:** Microsoft SQL Server
- ❋ **Latest Stable Version:** 2005
- ❋ **Products Available:** Enterprise Edition, **Standard Edition**, Developer Edition, Workgroup Edition, Express Edition, Mobile Edition.
- ❋ **Vendor:** Microsoft
- ❋ **Web Site:** www.microsoft.com/sql
- ❋ **Platforms:** Windows (x86, 64bit, Itanium)
- ❋ **System Requirements:** Processor: 1GHz or higher, Windows server operating system; Memory: 1GB or more; Disk Space: 775MB (minimum), CD-ROM.

Microsoft SQL Server is Microsoft's entry into the world of enterprise database management systems. Somewhere along the way, Sybase gave Microsoft access to the source code for Sybase SQL Server and Microsoft created a Windows version of the DBMS. SQL Server and Sybase are different from each other now but both still use Transact-SQL for their stored procedure language and share many of the same attributes.

I have used Microsoft SQL Server for several years and have been very pleased with its performance and its long list of features. I especially like Enterprise Manager, which is the main tool you use if you are a SQL Server DBA. This tool is your management interface for SQL Server. It is graphical in nature, of course, and comes bundled with the server software. It is not just a single server tool but, as the name implies, a graphical tool capable of managing an entire enterprise of DBMSs. SQL Server is fast and easy to manage and has a relatively small footprint for a DBMS of its magnitude. A great deal of the taken space is in documentation. I think the documentation is very good and is quite helpful in sticky situations. Where the documentation fails, Microsoft has an online knowledge base and further documentation. SQL Server also has a very large following and many web sites that dish out gigabytes of information for free. You should have no trouble finding answers to questions should you ever run into any issues with the system.

Microsoft SQL Server has made some great improvements since the days of the 6.x versions, but SQL Server 2005 promises to be the most secure version yet with a lot of other enhancements, some of which are shown here:

- ❋ High availability: Failover clustering and database mirroring
- ❋ A new suite of management tools
- ❋ Security enhancements
- ❋ Scalability advancements: Table partitioning, replication enhancements, and 64-bit support
- ❋ *Common language runtime (CLR)* integration
- ❋ New XML data type
- ❋ Transact-SQL enhancements
- ❋ SQL service broker: Distributed asynchronous application framework for new levels of scalability
- ❋ Analysis services
- ❋ A complete redesign of *data transformation services (DTS)*
- ❋ A new report server and tool set for reporting
- ❋ Enhanced data mining

Microsoft SQL Server is a very high-quality database at a reasonable price. If you are a fan of Windows and Windows software, then this just may be a good fit for you. Microsoft SQL Server is worth a serious look for any company that needs continual updating and improvement.

Microsoft Access

- ❋ **Name:** Microsoft Access
- ❋ **Latest Stable Version:** 2003
- ❋ **Products Available:** Access (part of the Microsoft Office Suite)
- ❋ **Vendor:** Microsoft
- ❋ **Web Site:** www.microsoft.com/access
- ❋ **Platform:** Windows (x86, 64bit, Itanium)
- ❋ **System Requirements:** Processor: Pentium III or higher, Windows operating system; memory: 256MB or more; disk space: 360MB (minimum), CD-ROM

Microsoft Access is probably the most popular desktop database in the world today. I personally have used it since version 1.0 and have to say that it was love at first sight. Access is so easy to use that even the most timid of database dabblers will be able to create and use a database within a very short time. The ease of use is in no way an indication that it might be a lightweight product. Access is very complete and has many desirable features. It isn't just for single users either. I know many people (myself included) who have created multiuser databases that operate on *local area networks (LANs)*. Some of those databases have been in use since 1995 and are still being used, on a daily basis, by 50 or more users. Access will never be a Microsoft SQL Server contender but it has made significant inroads into even the largest of companies.

Once back in 1994, while using Access version 1.0 or 1.1, I had the feeling that Microsoft wasn't all that committed to Access, but far more invested in FoxPro and SQL Server. Fortunately for me, and a lot of other people, I was wrong. I happily upgraded to Access 2.0, then Access 97, Access 2000, and now to Access 2003.

Users who are new to Microsoft Access will find that Microsoft has done a superb job of writing online help for the application. The Access web site is also an excellent resource for information, updates, and downloads. There is also a huge amount of Microsoft Access information on the Internet for users of all levels of expertise. Before I had multiple computers at home, I used Access to design all of my databases before going to production with them, regardless of the actual DBMS in the end product. I have used Access as a development template for databases that ended up as MySQL, SQL Server, and even Oracle databases.

Though Microsoft Access is not ACID compliant, it is still a very good individual and workgroup DBMS. A well-designed database and interface should suffice for most non-enterprise, non-transactional database implementations. Access is file based, serverless, very robust, and definitely worth a second look if you are looking to get into a multiuser database inexpensively and easily. It has the standard intuitive interface that all Windows programs have and is forgiving to work with. The following list gives you a look at some of its features:

❈ Lots of new import/export features (data sharing)

❈ Intuitive interface

❈ Multiuser capable (limited to a theoretical maximum of 255 users)

❈ Very active user base and user community

❈ Many training materials available

❈ Can attach to other DBMSs via ODBC

❈ Very easy to use Query Builder—no SQL needed, but SQL capable

❈ Can create portable demo databases

❈ Inexpensive

❈ Built-in forms, reports, and programming language

❈ Actively developed by Microsoft

Oracle

- ❋ **Name:** Oracle
- ❋ **Latest Stable Version:** 10g Release 2
- ❋ **Products Available:** Enterprise Edition, Standard Edition, **Standard Edition One,** Personal Edition, Lite Edition
- ❋ **Vendor:** Oracle
- ❋ **Web Site:** www.oracle.com
- ❋ **Platforms:** Windows, MacOS X, Linux, Unix
- ❋ **System Requirements:** Supported operating system; memory: 512MB or more; disk space: 3GB or more; CD-ROM

What can I say about Oracle? It was the first commercial RDBMS to use SQL and is still the ultimate in enterprise DBMSs. Its reliability, stability, and support are second to none. It is pricey and does require a lot of expertise to use and maintain, but it is probably worth it if you need that kind of reliability. Your hardware will wear out long before your Oracle software will.

I once had an enterprise application that used an Oracle 7.3.4 database as a backend. The server had been up for over 1,200 days (Unix people will love that) but everyone was afraid to reboot the server. They weren't afraid to reboot it because of any Oracle fears; we just weren't sure if the hardware would fail. At almost 1,300 days, the server was accidentally rebooted, according to the system administrator who happened to be working on it at the time, and I am happy to report that both the hardware and software came through the "accidental" reboot just fine. Though it may not be the best Oracle story you will ever hear, it says something for reliability.

Oracle has made exponential advancements in the area of installation. I have installed almost every release since 7.3.3 and I can tell you for sure that those were not the good old days of installing Oracle. Oracle 10g is almost a *forehead install:* You put the CD in the drive and fall asleep on the keyboard, your forehead hitting the keyboard once to accept the license agreement. This is, of course, a slight exaggeration. It is a lot easier to install than previous versions but you need to read the documentation before starting.

> ❋ **CAUTION**
>
> Oracle is not for the database dabbler. You need a considerable amount of database experience, and certainly some Oracle training, before trying to manage an Oracle DBMS implementation. Oracle nomenclature is different than other DBMSs, and the way humans do things is also very different. Yes, you use SQL, but doing things like creating tables requires special formats that just don't exist in other DBMSs. This system is so extensive that you will never see a single "everything" book for Oracle the way you will for other DBMSs. You will most likely see a series of topical books for a particular release. I am not trying to scare you away from Oracle, by any means, because unless you are the DBA, then querying

any database and extracting data is pretty much the same as any other. Before I knew anything about Oracle databases, I *attached* (linked) to a lot of Oracle database tables from Microsoft Access and I could query them as if they were part of my own database. My point here is that if you are a database user, you aren't likely to face any particular issues that are database-vendor related. It is the administration of these systems that requires expertise and vendor-specific knowledge.

* Automated storage management (ASM)
* Grid computing
* Regular expressions
* XML
* Automated Database Diagnostic Monitor (ADDM)
* High performance
* Long history of success
* Number one of the Big Three DBMSs

Oracle is a dependable, high-end RDBMS that can serve terabytes of data with very high performance. It has been number one since day one and probably will remain so for some time to come.

Informix

* **Name:** Informix Dynamic Server
* **Latest Stable Version:** 10
* **Products Available:** IBM Red Brick Warehouse, Informix Extended Parallel Server, IDS Enterprise Edition, **IDS Workgroup Edition**, Informix Standard Engine, Informix OnLine Extended Edition
* **Vendor:** IBM
* **Web Site:** www.informix.com
* **Platforms:** Windows, Linux, Unix
* **System Requirements:** Unix and Linux—Disk space: 750MB or more; memory: 256MB; one CPU. Windows—Disk space: 600MB or more; memory: 256MB; one CPU. No recommendations beyond these are given

My experience with Informix has only been at the user level. I have never administered Informix databases but have used the data from them extensively. Historically, it has run on large Unix systems where uptime and availability are paramount. Many telecommunications businesses run Informix databases due to the high security and very fast response. The software has been around a long time and has had its ups and downs related to company management—not to the database itself. Its acquisition by IBM in 2001 was probably the best thing to happen to this very capable and much-deployed DBMS. At some point, IBM may merge this product with DB2, but so far it continues to release and enhance the Informix line of products. I see Informix continuing into the future for some time to come and IBM's service and support should help Informix remain a database of choice for big businesses. Some of Informix's features are listed here:

- ❉ High-availability backup, recovery, and replication
- ❉ Very high performance engine
- ❉ Federated data access
- ❉ Informix 4GL built-in programming language
- ❉ R-tree indexing technology
- ❉ Stored procedures
- ❉ Triggers
- ❉ IBM's service, support, and expertise

Sybase

- ❉ **Name:** Sybase Adaptive Server Enterprise
- ❉ **Latest Stable Version:** 15
- ❉ **Products Available:** Sybase IQ, Replication Server, **Adaptive Server Enterprise**, Adaptive Server Anywhere, ASE Express Edition
- ❉ **Vendor:** Sybase
- ❉ **Web Site:** www.sybase.com
- ❉ **Platforms:** Windows, MacOS X, Linux, Unix
- ❉ **System Requirements:** Supported operating system; memory: 512MB or more; disk space: 1GB or more; CD-ROM

Sybase is one of the Big Three. Reportedly Sybase only has about 3 percent of the total database market share these days; they seem to be making somewhat of a comeback in the Asian market. Focusing on small and medium-sized businesses with the Adaptive Server Anywhere product and mobile solutions seems to be boosting the company in the right direction. CEO John Chen has been the "rainmaker" for Sybase and is the leading force in its renewed vision.

My experience with Sybase has been from a web-developer standpoint. I have created PHP applications that access, update, and maintain data in databases. My limited administration of Sybase has been through creating these applications. You have to know a bit about the DBMS and some of each system's management tools to develop and create web-based management tools for DBAs. Sybase seems far easier to manage than the other two Big Three. Sybase has some great management tools, but you will probably spend most of your time in Sybase Central, the main management interface.

* On-disk encryption
* Smart partitions
* Unstructured data management
* High-performance query enhancements
* One of the Big Three DBMSs

Sybase has a long and stable history as an enterprise database solution. Name any 10 of the top 100 companies in the United States and chances are very good that most of them are using Sybase.

DB2

* **Name:** DB2
* **Latest Stable Version:** 8.2
* **Products Available:** Enterprise Edition, Express Edition, **Workgroup Server Edition**, Personal Edition, Everyplace Edition
* **Vendor:** IBM
* **Web Site:** www-306.ibm.com/software/data/db2
* **Platforms:** Windows, MacOS X, Linux, Unix, Mainframe, AS/400
* **System Requirements:** Supported operating system; memory: 512MB or more; disk space: Depends on installation options

DB2 began its life in 1983 on the Mainframe platform. Since that time, IBM has developed a suite of products, under the name DB2, that run on Windows, Linux, and most Unix implementations, as well as AS/400 and Mainframe. DB2 is a core component of IBM's e-business application framework. DB2 also has many graphical administrative tools including Control Center and Replication Center. The SMART technology (Self-Managing and Resource Tuning) has been integrated into a number of DB2 components, including installation, configuration, utilities, problem determination and resolution, and availability. IBM is continuing to improve their tools and DB2 to make DBAs more productive and to decrease management overhead. Installation has also been streamlined and improved and is graphical in nature. Installation and instance creation are done via wizards that simplify initial setup and management for those unfamiliar with DB2. The use of wizards also eases the switch from another vendor's DBMS to DB2.

I have no personal experience with DB2, but can say with some certainty that you wouldn't be disappointed with this product line. All of their editions are compatible with each other; an application developed using the Personal Edition product as your development system is compatible with any of the other versions with no code changes.

- ❋ Federated data access support
- ❋ Advisors to help you with setup and management
- ❋ XML support
- ❋ High Availability Disaster Recovery (HADR)
- ❋ Replication support
- ❋ Connection concentrator
- ❋ Scalable architecture
- ❋ Integrated business intelligence
- ❋ Partitioning
- ❋ Optimized for the web
- ❋ IBM's service and support

DB2 is vying for the number one position in the DBMS market. IBM considers Oracle and Teradata their main competitors. With IBM's vast people and monetary resources, this is one to keep an eye on unless you have already converted to DB2. Experience has taught me that IBM products are second to none and my assumption is that DB2 is no different. Remember the saying, "You never get fired for buying IBM."

MySQL

- ❋ **Name:** MySQL
- ❋ **Latest Stable Version:** 4.0.26, 4.1.16, 5.0.18
- ❋ **Products Available:** MySQL Cluster, MySQL Pro Certified Server, MaxDB, **MySQL Community Edition**
- ❋ **Vendor:** MySQL AB
- ❋ **Web Site:** www.mysql.com
- ❋ **Platforms:** Windows, MacOS X, Linux, Unix
- ❋ **System Requirements:** No specific CPU or memory, but suggests 200MB disk space for installation

Advertised as "The World's Most Popular Open Source Database," MySQL is sort of the Apache of databases. It is easy to set up and use, and that is enough to convince me to use it for all of my web database applications. It interfaces easily with Perl and PHP and requires very little from new users. Its relatively few shortcomings have all but disappeared with the latest updates. My main reason for liking MySQL, besides the cost (free for the community version), is its performance. If your web users get discouraged by long waits for your advanced features to take effect, how advanced or necessary are they, really? I like MySQL and use it for almost everything database related. Most vendors are usually willing (for a price) to help you make their system successful for you. This is the biggest argument against open-source solutions because there typically is no vendor on the other end helping you. MySQL is one exception to this open-source caveat.

NOTE
MySQL is the DBMS that I use for the examples and lessons in this book.

One of the best things about MySQL, and one that gets almost no advertisement, is the fact that a database is a directory and the tables are all files. This may seem strange but the advantage is that those files are totally cross platform. This means that if my Linux server running MySQL fails, I can restore my databases to a Windows or different Unix server and I am up and running with no changes whatsoever to my databases.

The following lists some new advanced feature offerings from MySQL 5.x:

* ACID transactions
* Stored procedures
* Triggers
* Views
* Information schema
* Distributed transactions
* Pluggable storage engine architecture
* Archive storage engine
* Federated storage engine
* Cross-platform databases and tables
* Many extended features beyond basic SQL
* Very high-performance database engine
* Modest pricing; community version is free
* Binaries available for most operating systems

MySQL has enjoyed exponential growth and acceptance over the past three years or so. I work with a group that manages one of the largest MySQL implementations in the world. It is absolutely state-of-the-art in every way and maintains a 24×7 site that is mission-critical. Just look at MySQL's web site for whitepapers and success stories and you will find some very interesting implementations and applications. Now that the 5.x versions have hit production, it is my personal opinion that MySQL will become a two-fisted competitor with some of the big names in this business. Since it has corporate support, there is no reason not to consider it along with any of the other DBMSs in this list. It has come of age and has proven that it is ready to compete in the same arena as the large commercial systems. MySQL powers some of the most influential and publicly recognized companies in the world like Google and Yahoo!.

PostgreSQL

❄ **Name:** PostgreSQL

❄ **Latest Stable Version:** 8.1

❄ **Products Available:** PostgreSQL 8.1.x, 8.0.x, 7.3.x, 7.4.x

❄ **Vendor:** Worldwide community of developers

❄ **Web Site:** www.postgresql.org

❄ **Platforms:** Windows, MacOS X, Linux, Unix

❄ **System Requirements:** Supported operating system, standard OS requirements

PostgreSQL's web site touts the software as the world's most advanced open-source database. I have no evidence to confirm or deny the claim. I do know that PostgreSQL has a very dedicated user base and an extensive online support community. I have used a few versions of it starting with PostgreS95, and found that it was a very extensive DBMS with a lot of complexity and scalability. I didn't have time to spend learning such a system and soon gave up on it. My personal experience found it large and slower than expected, but still a very viable option for those who convert from DBMSs such as Oracle, Sybase, or Informix. My experiences aside, I think that it is a very high-end DBMS that deserves a look if you are seeking to minimize your DBMS software costs and maintain enterprise-class databases.

PostgreSQL doesn't have the advantage of a single company being financially responsible for the product; neither does it have the disadvantages of such an entity. It is well maintained by a worldwide developer community. PostgreSQL boasts many features only found in very costly commercial databases. You would have to look very hard to find a commercial DBMS that can compete with its dedicated user base, price, performance, and this very extensive list of features:

❄ Fully ACID compliant

❄ ANSI SQL compliant

❄ Referential integrity

❄ Replication (non-commercial and commercial solutions) allowing the duplication of the master database to multiple slave machines

❄ Native interfaces for ODBC, JDBC, C, C++, PHP, Perl, TCL, ECPG, Python, and Ruby

❄ Rules

- ❈ Views
- ❈ Triggers
- ❈ Unicode
- ❈ Sequences
- ❈ Inheritance
- ❈ Outer joins
- ❈ Sub-selects
- ❈ Open API
- ❈ Stored procedures
- ❈ Native SSL (Secure Sockets Layer) support
- ❈ Procedural languages
- ❈ Hot stand-by (commercial solutions)
- ❈ Better than row-level locking
- ❈ Functional and partial indexes
- ❈ Native Kerberos authentication
- ❈ Support for UNION, UNION ALL, and EXCEPT queries
- ❈ Loadable extensions offering SHA1, MD5, XML, and other functionality
- ❈ Tools for generating portable SQL to share with other SQL-compliant systems
- ❈ Extensible data-type system providing for custom, user-defined data types and rapid development of new data types
- ❈ Cross-database compatibility functions for easing the transition from other, less SQL-compliant RDBMS
- ❈ Free software with the very liberal BSD license model

Zealous is the term I think of when describing PostgreSQL fans. I think that PostgreSQL is a fine DBMS and it should work well for you. There seems to be plenty of support available for it on the Internet in the form of forums and blogs but there are also companies that provide support for it. You should have no problem finding the support you need for any issues you may experience. I see PostgreSQL gaining corporate acceptance in the next few years and becoming quite competitive in the DBMS market.

SQLite

- ❋ **Name:** SQLite
- ❋ **Latest Stable Version:** 2.8.17 and 3.2.8
- ❋ **Products Available:** SQLite Version 2.x and **Version 3.x**
- ❋ **Vendor:** Hipp, Wyrick & Company, Inc.; distributed as freeware
- ❋ **Web Site:** www.sqlite.org
- ❋ **Platforms:** Windows, MacOS X, Linux, Unix
- ❋ **System Requirements:** Same as for the host operating system

SQLite is available for most platforms, no installation is required, it is free and serverless, and it conforms pretty well to SQL92. Table 3.1 shows the exceptions to its SQL92 conformance. I currently use SQLite version 3.x due to its enhanced capabilities and features. This list shows some of SQLite's highlights:

- ❋ No installation
- ❋ Serverless: no daemon or service running in memory
- ❋ Zero configuration
- ❋ Allows simultaneous access
- ❋ Database is contained in a single file
- ❋ Compact: executable is only 328K (SQLite3.x), SQLite2.x is 277K
- ❋ Manifest typing (described in the following text)
- ❋ Variable-length records, resulting in smaller database files
- ❋ Readable source code
- ❋ SQL statements compile into virtual machine code
- ❋ Software is in the public domain
- ❋ Enhanced SQL statements
- ❋ SQL92 conformant with some exceptions
- ❋ Database files are cross platform

Most SQL database engines use *static typing*. A data type is associated with each column in a table and only values of that particular data type are allowed to be stored in that column. SQLite relaxes this restriction by using *manifest typing*: The data type is a property of the value itself, not of the column in which the value is stored. Thus, you can store any value of any data type in any column regardless of that column's declared type. (There are some exceptions to this rule: An INTEGER PRIMARY KEY column may only store integers. And SQLite attempts to coerce values into the declared data type of the column when it can.)

Table 3.1   SQL92 Features That SQLite Does Not Implement

Feature	Explanation
FOREIGN KEY constraints	FOREIGN KEY constraints are parsed but are not enforced.
Complete trigger support	There is incomplete support for triggers. Missing subfeatures include FOR EACH STATEMENT triggers (currently all triggers must be FOR EACH ROW), INSTEAD OF triggers on tables (currently INSTEAD OF triggers are only allowed on views), and *recursive triggers* (triggers that trigger themselves).
Complete ALTER TABLE support	Only the RENAME TABLE and ADD COLUMN variants of the ALTER TABLE command are supported. Other kinds of ALTER TABLE operations such as DROP COLUMN, ALTER COLUMN, ADD CONSTRAINT, and so forth, are omitted.
Nested transactions	The current implementation only allows a single active transaction.
RIGHT and FULL OUTER JOIN	LEFT OUTER JOIN is implemented, but not RIGHT OUTER JOIN or FULL OUTER JOIN.
Writing to VIEWs	VIEWs in SQLite are read only. You may not execute a DELETE, INSERT, or UPDATE statement on a view. You can create a trigger that fires on an attempt to DELETE, INSERT, or UPDATE a view and do what you need in the trigger body.
GRANT and REVOKE	Since SQLite reads and writes an ordinary disk file, the only access permissions that can be applied are the underlying operating system's normal file-access permissions. The GRANT and REVOKE commands commonly found on client/server RDBMSs are not implemented because they would be meaningless for an embedded database engine.

I like SQLite and use it frequently in my niche-type applications. Especially for read-only data where your users have a web browser for information lookups, it should take care of just about any amount of data. The interesting thing is that SQLite is embedded in PHP 5.x by default so you don't have to install a SQLite binary to use it.

I would like to see SQLite's development continue for educational purposes, although I believe it has its place in commercial applications as well. To have a powerful and free piece of software that requires no installation is a real advantage to cash-strapped school systems. SQLite has a lot of potential for web-based applications.

Teradata

- ※ **Name:** Teradata RDBMS
- ※ **Latest Stable Version:** V2R6.1
- ※ **Products Available: Teradata RDBMS**, Teradata Warehouse
- ※ **Vendor:** Teradata, a Division of NCR
- ※ **Web Site:** www.teradata.com
- ※ **Platforms:** Windows, Linux, Unix
- ※ **System Requirements:** Supported operating system; memory: 2GB or more; disk space: several GB; CD-ROM

Teradata is a massively parallel processing system running a shared nothing architecture. *Massive parallelism* is a term used in computer architecture, reconfigurable computing, *application-specific integrated circuit (ASIC)*, and *field-programmable gate array (FPGA)* design. It signifies the presence of several ("many") independent arithmetic units that run in parallel. A *shared nothing architecture* is a distributed database architecture without a single point of contention. The main point with the Teradata DBMS is that it is linearly and predictably scalable in all dimensions of a database system workload (data volume, breadth, number of users, complexity of queries), which is why it is very popular for enterprise-data warehousing applications. Teradata is offered on Intel servers interconnected by the BYNET messaging fabric. Its systems are offered with either Engenio or EMC disk arrays for database storage. Wal-Mart has the world's largest data warehouse and uses Teradata to power it. Other prominent clients include AT&T, Dell, and FedEx.

The Teradata RDBMS is the product that I am reviewing for this section as it compares favorably with the other products in the list. Some of Teradata RDBMS benefits are listed here:

- ※ External stored procedures
- ※ Triggers calling stored procedures
- ※ Queue tables
- ※ IN-list processing
- ※ Recursive queries
- ※ Top *N* row operations
- ※ PPI optimization
- ※ Replication
- ※ Single sign-on
- ※ Parallel operation
- ※ Ease of manageability

* Simplified mainframe integration
* Low total cost of ownership (TCO)

Teradata is *the* name in data warehousing and is the master in supply-chain and demand-chain management. If you need Teradata, chances are very good that you already know it.

Other RDBMSs

Several other commercial, open-source, and freeware databases are viable as desktop, work-group, small business, and even enterprise-capable DBMSs, but time and space are limited here. This section surely won't do them justice (and no doubt I will miss a few), but I am including them as systems that are worth a look if you are seeking something that is special purpose or perhaps outside the mainstream. Most of those I include in this section are of the open-source, shareware, and freeware variety.

For this section I supply the DBMS name, web site, and summary information. My personal comments, if any, will be included in the text. This list is in alphabetical order:

* **AlphaFive:** www.alphasoftware.com. AlphaFive version 7 is the latest incarnation of this historically easy-to-use and feature-rich DBMS. This version allows web access without a third-party programming language like PHP or Perl to program an interface. I used AlphaFour a long time ago and was very impressed at the time. This one won't do enterprise applications but if you have a database that needs a web interface, AlphaFive may be your answer. A fully functional download version is on their web site.

* **Firebird:** firebird.sourceforge.net. Firebird is an RDBMS offering many ANSI SQL features. It runs on Linux, Windows, and a variety of Unix platforms, offering excellent concurrency, high performance, and powerful language support for stored procedures and triggers.

* Firebird is perhaps the best known of the lesser-known open-source DBMSs. This relational database offers many ANSI SQL-99 features that runs on Linux, Windows, and a variety of Unix platforms. It has been used in production systems under a variety of names since 1981.

* **GT.M High end database + MUMPS compiler:** sourceforge.net/projects/sanchez-gtm. GT.M is a vetted, industrial-strength, transaction-processing application platform consisting of a database engine optimized for high TP (transaction processing) throughput and a compiler for the M (aka MUMPS) programming language. GT.M is open-source freeware on x86/Linux.

* **HSQL Database Engine:** sourceforge.net/projects/hsqldb. HSQLDB is a relational database engine written in Java, with a JDBC driver, supporting a large subset of ANSI-92 SQL. A small, fast engine with both in-memory and disk-based tables as options. This product is the continuation of HypersonicSQL.

- **Ingres:** www.ingres.com. This commercial, open-source DBMS is actually the parent database of such offspring as PostgreSQL, Sybase, Microsoft SQL Server, Non-stop SQL, and Informix. Some might argue that this should have been placed in the other lineup of products, but I made the decision based on popularity and product name recognition. Ingres has been maintained and improved over the years to contend in any size market and deserves a look if you have mission-critical data and want to support a commercial implementation of an open-source product.

- **InterBase:** www.borland.com/us/products/interbase/index.html. InterBase is an open-source DBMS now under the ownership of Borland. InterBase is distinguished from other DBMSs by its small footprint, close-to-zero administration requirements, and multigenerational architecture. InterBase runs on the Linux, Windows, and Solaris operating systems.

- **Leap RDBMS:** leap.sourceforge.net. Leap is an RDBMS implementing relational algebra, a core part of relational database theory. It is primarily used as an educational tool, but has found some novel uses and applications.

- **Metakit:** www.equi4.com/metakit.html. Metakit is an efficient database library with a small footprint. It's a cross between flat file, RDBMS, and OODBMS. Keywords: structured storage, transacted, load on demand, portable, C++, Python, Tcl, instant schema versioning.

- **One$DB:** www.daffodildb.com/one-dollar-db.html. One$DB is open-source version of Daffodil DB, a commercial Java database. This standards-based, platform-independent RDBMS can be embedded into any application with minimal administration. One$DB is available in both Embedded and Network editions.

- **tdbengine SQL Server:** tdbsql.tdbengine.org. tdbengine SQL Server (tdbSQL) is a complete implementation of an easy SQL server for the tdbengine RDBMS. It is a client/server solution that can be accessed via TCP. Its aim is to access tdbengine DBs from other programming languages than EASY (PERL, PHP, and the like) over the Internet.

Summary

This chapter hopefully has informed you of some new DBMSs and has given you enough of an overview to begin your quest of choosing a DBMS for your company or application. Take your time choosing a database server—it is an expensive undertaking. You will be in a bad position if you make a poor choice in this area. These days your data is your most valuable asset and no one can afford to lose it or have it permanently damaged by an errant or undersized system. Conversely, you don't want to spend $50,000 on a database system to manage an address book.

When evaluating any new software product, it is perfectly acceptable to ask your vendor to supply you with some current clients that you may contact for reference. It is very important to contact these clients and ask the important questions. Questions like "How do you like XYZ RDBMS?" will not help you make an informed decision. The vendor isn't going to give you a list of people who don't like their software. You need to ask pointed questions about support, response time to problems, service value, software limitations, and any second thoughts the client may have about the vendor or software. DBAs are usually willing to share their experiences, but you need to take overly negative and overly positive comments with a grain of salt.

There are no easy answers when it comes to choosing a DBMS for your company. If you do your research, call clients, check the Internet for information, and get your numbers together, then you have done your best to protect yourself and your company's data. Open-source solutions should be seen as reasonable and viable options especially where TCO is a high priority for corporate check writers.

Chapter Review

Multiple Choice

1. When considering a DBMS for a company that performs thousands of money transactions per month, which of the following is most important?

   a) The DBMS vendor

   b) 24×7 support

   c) SQL92 conformance

   d) ACID

2. One of the greatest barriers to free and open-source DBMS software is

   a) Price

   b) Performance

   c) The lack of a responsible party

   d) Shoddy source code

3. What may actually influence the decision to choose a particular DBMS more than the facts?

   a) Corporate culture

   b) Price

   c) Performance

   d) Return on investment

4. TCO stands for

   a) Total Complexity of Operations

   b) Total Cost of Operation

   c) Total Cost of Ownership

   d) Technical Costs and Operations

5. Transactions that are atomic are said to be

   a) all or nothing

   b) very small

   c) consistent

   d) compliant

6. In an ACID-compliant DBMS, a transaction that fails due to a disk crash fails due to

   a) Atomicity

   b) Consistency

   c) Isolation

   d) Durability

7. "A transaction is isolated" means that it

   a) occurs independently of other transactions.

   b) takes place in a JVM (Java Virtual Machine).

   c) occurs when the DBMS is quiescent.

   d) is processed independently of other transactions.

8. Durability refers to which attribute?

   a) Recovery

   b) Speed

   c) Strength

   d) Overhead

9. Microsoft Access is ACID compliant.

 a) True

 b) False

10. In the DBMS world, Oracle, Sybase and Informix are

 a) Expensive

 b) Awesome

 c) The Big Three

 d) Open source

Concepts

1. A database fails at your company due to a hardware problem. After the server is repaired and comes back up, you find that your database is just fine. Explain how the database is okay despite the fact that there were probably several transactions in progress when the crash occurred.

2. Describe the features that you want in your perfect DBMS.

3. Now discuss the trade-offs you are likely to make in your perfect DBMS.

Data Definition Language

The first three chapters cover a lot of material to prepare you for the actual purpose of this book, which is to learn SQL. The title of this chapter is "Data Definition Language," which implies that you are learning something other than SQL. This is not the case at all. *Data Definition Language (DDL)* is that part of SQL that is involved in the creation, deletion, and changing of databases, database structure, and data itself. DDL is not a separate language within SQL. It is a logical separation based on the function of the commands.

> ❄ **A CAPITAL IDEA**
> The convention is to use ALL CAPS when using any SQL keywords and I will adhere to that convention in this book. This convention makes it easier to recognize SQL keywords from all other words like names of tables, columns, indexes, and so on.

Before I began writing this book, I decided to use a database called SQLite (reviewed in Chapter 3) for the SQL examples and SQL lessons. There are places where SQLite breaks from the SQL92 standard to which it adheres so closely. Since SQLite lacks many of the advanced features of contemporary DBMSs, I use MySQL 5.x for the examples in this book. I chose MySQL for the same reasons that I chose SQLite with a few exceptions. MySQL has to be installed, is much larger than SQLite, and requires that you run a service in memory. But there is much to like about MySQL and it gets my highest praise. While this is not a book on MySQL, the program is free, easy to install, and is comfortable to use. You may use MySQL or the database of your choice for the examples.

You learn about these DDL statements in this chapter:

* CREATE DATABASE
* CREATE TABLE
* CREATE INDEX
* DROP DATABASE
* DROP TABLE
* DROP INDEX
* ALTER DATABASE
* ALTER TABLE
* RENAME TABLE

This chapter takes you through the uses of the DDL commands CREATE, ALTER, DROP, and RENAME. You use each command repeatedly to gain practice and understanding of its uses and hazards.

Preparing

Download a copy of the latest version of MySQL from http://dev.mysql.com/downloads/mysql. I suggest getting the latest stable version of the product, but feel free to get any one you want to work with. I am using MySQL on Windows, but feel free to install it on Linux, Unix, MacOS, or other operating system. It works the same regardless of platform. Full installation instructions are given for Windows and Unix/Linux in Appendix C.

> ❊ **YOU KNOW WHAT I'M SAYING?**
> In teaching the various SQL keywords, I will discuss what you are about to do, then give the generic version of the command with options and the SQL command that you actually execute. An example follows:
>
> ```
> Create a database (Books) using CREATE.
>     CREATE DATABASE Database_Name
>     CREATE DATABASE Books
> ```

It is a good idea to have a system all to yourself for working through the examples, because you need sufficient privileges to create, delete, change, update, and modify databases, tables, and data. In other words, you need administrative rights to a database server. At this point, you need a DBMS that you can log in to and use. First, start your DBMS server, confirm that it is running, and log in to the server. You either need a command-line interface or a familiar graphical tool that has a query builder.

For MySQL, change directory (cd) to the mysql\bin directory and issue the following command:

```
mysql -uroot <ENTER>
```

If you have some experience with MySQL and have changed the root password, then issue the following:

```
mysql -uroot -ppassword <ENTER>
```

Replace *password* with your password.

CREATE

Using CREATE to begin talking about SQL keywords is a great way to start since it is the first step in creating a new database. You will, for the most part, be using SQL at the command line. With the CREATE keyword, one can create many types of database objects. Table 4.1 shows the DDL uses of CREATE in alphabetical order. There are many others but I feel these are the most common.

Table 4.1 The Many Uses of CREATE

Statement	Description
CREATE DATABASE	Creates a new database
CREATE INDEX	Constructs a secondary index
CREATE TABLE	Creates a new table
CREATE TABLE AS	Creates a new table from the results of a SELECT

CREATE DATABASE

Jump right in with the CREATE statement to create a database.

Objective
Create a database named Books.

```
CREATE DATABASE Database_Name;

CREATE DATABASE Books;
```

You may have noticed the semicolon at the end of the CREATE command. If you are using a DBMS with a command-line interface, you probably need the semicolon. You definitely need it with MySQL, SQLite, and Oracle if you are using SQLPlus. Most graphical tools don't require them.

You now have a database named Books. If you are on Windows, then the case does not matter. I am used to using Unix/Linux where case is used, so out of habit I create databases with the first letter capitalized. To use the database you have just created, type the following:

```
USE Books; <ENTER>
```

❄ ENTER NOT

To alleviate confusion and on-page clutter, <ENTER> is assumed at the end of a command or SQL statement. Operating system commands, such as logging in to the DBMS, are offset with a new line. SQL statements always end with a semicolon (;). Look at these examples:

Operating system command: `mysql -uroot -ppassword`

SQL statement: `CREATE DATABASE Test;`

Creating a database is relatively simple, as you can see. The most difficult part is coming up with a descriptive name. I don't know that there are any real rules about naming databases, but I suggest that you keep them short and descriptive. Don't use spaces, even if the DBMS allows it. Spaces in names make it more difficult for other people to use your data. If I feel the need for a separator, I use an underscore for the name.

So just what are you making when you create a database in MySQL? The answer may surprise you. Look in the data directory (folder) where you installed MySQL and you see a folder named Books. That's it. You created a folder named Books. MySQL uses a file-based system and all databases are just folders where, in most cases, your tables will reside. The question now is whether you can create a new database by simply creating a new folder under the data directory. The answer is yes. Try it for yourself. Later in this chapter you learn some other commands to view the databases and tables you have created.

❄ TRADING SPACES

Spaces in names of database objects, should someone use them, can still be used by enclosing the name in square brackets. Use the following for a table named Bad Table Name:

```
[Bad Table Name]
```

CREATE TABLE

Creating a table is more complex because of the number of options involved. The list given here shows those options. When looking at syntax lists like these, don't get bogged down in the length or perceived complexity. Simply read through it; once you gain some experience with syntax, you will appreciate this level of detail. The syntax for CREATE TABLE is given in this list. It isn't as bad as it looks—really. Once you create some tables, you will see how the options fit together.

```
CREATE [TEMPORARY] TABLE [IF NOT EXISTS] tbl_name
    [(] LIKE old_tbl_name [)];
create_definition:
    column_definition
  | [CONSTRAINT [symbol]] PRIMARY KEY [index_type] (index_col_name,...)
  | KEY [index_name] [index_type] (index_col_name,...)
  | INDEX [index_name] [index_type] (index_col_name,...)
  | [CONSTRAINT [symbol]] UNIQUE [INDEX]
        [index_name] [index_type] (index_col_name,...)
  | [FULLTEXT|SPATIAL] [INDEX] [index_name] (index_col_name,...)
  | [CONSTRAINT [symbol]] FOREIGN KEY
        [index_name] (index_col_name,...) [reference_definition]
  | CHECK (expr)


column_definition:
    col_name type [NOT NULL | NULL] [DEFAULT default_value]
        [AUTO_INCREMENT] [UNIQUE [KEY] | [PRIMARY] KEY]
        [COMMENT 'string'] [reference_definition]


type:
    TINYINT[(length)] [UNSIGNED] [ZEROFILL]
  | SMALLINT[(length)] [UNSIGNED] [ZEROFILL]
  | MEDIUMINT[(length)] [UNSIGNED] [ZEROFILL]
  | INT[(length)] [UNSIGNED] [ZEROFILL]
  | INTEGER[(length)] [UNSIGNED] [ZEROFILL]
  | BIGINT[(length)] [UNSIGNED] [ZEROFILL]
  | REAL[(length,decimals)] [UNSIGNED] [ZEROFILL]
  | DOUBLE[(length,decimals)] [UNSIGNED] [ZEROFILL]
  | FLOAT[(length,decimals)] [UNSIGNED] [ZEROFILL]
  | DECIMAL(length,decimals) [UNSIGNED] [ZEROFILL]
  | NUMERIC(length,decimals) [UNSIGNED] [ZEROFILL]
```

```
    | DATE
    | TIME
    | TIMESTAMP
    | DATETIME
    | CHAR(length) [BINARY | ASCII | UNICODE]
    | VARCHAR(length) [BINARY]
    | TINYBLOB
    | BLOB
    | MEDIUMBLOB
    | LONGBLOB
    | TINYTEXT [BINARY]
    | TEXT [BINARY]
    | MEDIUMTEXT [BINARY]
    | LONGTEXT [BINARY]
    | ENUM(value1,value2,value3,...)
    | SET(value1,value2,value3,...)
    | spatial_type

index_col_name:
    col_name [(length)] [ASC | DESC]

reference_definition:
    REFERENCES tbl_name [(index_col_name,...)]
                [MATCH FULL | MATCH PARTIAL | MATCH SIMPLE]
                [ON DELETE reference_option]
                [ON UPDATE reference_option]

reference_option:
    RESTRICT | CASCADE | SET NULL | NO ACTION

table_options: table_option [table_option] ...

table_option:
    {ENGINE|TYPE} = engine_name
  | AUTO_INCREMENT = value
  | AVG_ROW_LENGTH = value
  | [DEFAULT] CHARACTER SET charset_name [COLLATE collation_name]
```

```
| CHECKSUM = {0 | 1}
| COMMENT = 'string'
| CONNECTION = 'connect_string'
| MAX_ROWS = value
| MIN_ROWS = value
| PACK_KEYS = {0 | 1 | DEFAULT}
| PASSWORD = 'string'
| DELAY_KEY_WRITE = {0 | 1}
| ROW_FORMAT = {DEFAULT|DYNAMIC|FIXED|COMPRESSED|REDUNDANT|COMPACT}
| UNION = (tbl_name[,tbl_name]...)
| INSERT_METHOD = { NO | FIRST | LAST }
| DATA DIRECTORY = 'absolute path to directory'
| INDEX DIRECTORY = 'absolute path to directory'
```

```
select_statement:
    [IGNORE | REPLACE] [AS] SELECT ...    (Some legal select statement)
```

Create your first table now, and I can distill it to what you need to know for now. The following is not official **CREATE TABLE** syntax, but it is enough to give you the requirements for creating a table:

```
CREATE TABLE Table_Name (Column_Name1 Data Type(Size), Column_Name2 Data Type
(Size)...);
```

In creating a table, you must have **CREATE TABLE**, a table name, and at least one named column with a defined data type and a column size (for each column). Pay close attention to the use of parentheses. You will see these requirements demonstrated in creating your first table.

Objective
Create a table named Customers.

```
CREATE TABLE Table_Name;
```

```
CREATE TABLE Customers;
```

You should have received an error similar to "A table must have at least one column." When you create a table, you must create at least one column and the column must have a name and a data type. Try that again—this time with the correct syntax.

Objective
Create a table named Customers with an integer column named ID.

```
CREATE TABLE Customers (Column_Name Data Type);

CREATE TABLE Customers (ID integer);
```

This time the Customers table is created successfully. Now you can create a table that is a bit more complex with multiple columns, data types, and column sizes. Column sizes are important because they set a limit on the amount of information allowed in the column. For instance, if you define a varchar column with size 50, only 50 characters will fit into that column. Do a bit of thinking ahead before creating columns. For now don't worry about these constraints; you are just getting the basics of creating tables down.

Objective
Create a table named Publishers with multiple columns.

```
CREATE TABLE Table_Name (Column_Name1 Data Type(Size), Column_Name2 Data Type
(Size));

CREATE TABLE Publishers (ID integer(4), Name varchar(50), Address varchar(50),
City varchar(25), Zip varchar(10), Phone varchar(12));
```

I use varchar as my catch-all column type, as it will hold text, numbers, dashes, underscores, and just about any other character you can produce. I also prefer the varchar over char because varchar takes less space for an equivalent amount of data. To be more specific, if I put my name, Kenneth Hess, into a char(50) column, my name takes up 50 bytes of space. If I put my name into a varchar(50) column, it takes up 12 bytes of space. If your data will vary in size (as in a name, address, city, and the like), then varchar is a good choice. If your data will all be a static size, then char is a better choice.

Adding a primary key to a table is very easy. It is part of the description of a column or columns. For now, stick with a single column primary key. Remember that a true relation is defined as having at least one unique column. If you just enhance the CREATE TABLE statement from earlier, your table can easily be transformed into a true relation by adding a primary key.

Objective
Create a table named Vendors with a primary key.

```
CREATE TABLE Table_Name (Column_Name Data Type(Size) PRIMARY KEY),
Column_Name2 Data Type(Size));

CREATE TABLE Vendors (ID integer(4) PRIMARY KEY, Name varchar(50));
```

It is great that you now have a primary key for your table, but how do you make sure the values that go into it are always unique and that a value actually goes into the column? If you are a programmer, you can get the last inserted value in that field (column) and add 1 to it; or perhaps your order numbers are generated by some other program and will be inserted into that field. Either of those ways is fine, but you can also have the DBMS do this for you with an automatically incrementing number. This assures that each time a row of data is inserted into the table, a unique number (ID in this case) is created. You set this attribute as part of the column description when the column is created.

Objective
Create a table named Orders with a primary key that is auto-incremented.

```
CREATE TABLE Table_Name (Column_Name1 Data Type(Size) PRIMARY KEY
AUTO_INCREMENT), Column_Name2 Data Type(Size));
```

```
CREATE TABLE Orders (ID integer(4) PRIMARY KEY AUTO_INCREMENT, Name varchar
(50));
```

Creating the ID column in this way assures that anytime a new row of data is inserted into the table Orders, a unique number is inserted and automatically incremented by 1 more than the last inserted number in that column. Numbering starts with 1, not 0, and the column type has to be one of the integer types.

To create a temporary table, you use the same syntax as when creating a permanent table except you add the keyword TEMPORARY to the statement.

Objective
Create a temporary table named Lists.

```
CREATE TEMPORARY TABLE Table_Name (Column_Name Data Type(Size) PRIMARY KEY
AUTO_INCREMENT), Column_Name2 Data Type(Size));
```

```
CREATE TEMPORARY TABLE Lists (ID integer(4) PRIMARY KEY AUTO_INCREMENT, Name
varchar(50));
```

Temporary tables are handy if they are increasing an application's performance; then a user can write to a temporary table during a database session, then update the permanent tables after final information submission. Temporary tables can speed up a system's perceived performance for the user, but the data only lasts for that database session. A temporary table can have all of the same attributes as a permanent table.

CREATE TABLE AS
CREATE TABLE AS is a very useful SQL command because you can create a new table based upon a query that gives you a permanent set of data, as a table, that would ordinarily only be available by query. It is also a good way to create a quick copy of another table. Creating a table in this way does not copy any keys, indexes, or other constraints. It only copies the structure and data. I show you how to use CREATE TABLE AS in Chapter 5.

CREATE INDEX

Normally, you would create an index when you create a table's definition, but CREATE INDEX allows you to add an index after the table has been created. The following list shows the syntax:

```
CREATE [UNIQUE|FULLTEXT|SPATIAL] INDEX index_name
       [USING index_type]
       ON tbl_name (index_col_name,...)


index_col_name:
       col_name [(length)] [ASC | DESC]
```

Indexes are used to quickly find rows with specific column values. Without an index, the DBMS must begin with the first record and then read through the entire table to find the relevant rows; therefore, the larger the table, the greater the cost. If the table has an index for the columns in question, the DBMS can quickly determine the position to seek in the middle of the data file without having to look at all the data. If a table has 1,000 rows, then this is at least 100 times faster than reading sequentially. Note that if you need to access most of the rows, it is faster to read sequentially, because this minimizes disk seeks. Table 4.2 shows the different index types and valid properties for each.

Table 4.2   Index Types and Their Attributes

Index Type	Attribute
Primary Key	Unique values and NOT NULL.
Regular	Allows non-unique values and NULL values.
UNIQUE	Values are unique but may be NULL.
FULLTEXT	char, varchar, and text data types only. Non-unique and may be NULL.
SPATIAL	Used for geometric and geographic data.

Indexes are important to databases because generally they speed up data lookups. But they can also adversely affect database performance. How can something like an index adversely affect performance? If you create an index (other than a primary key) on a table that has only a few rows, the index does not speed up the search. You should stick with just a primary key. Performance can also take a hit when you update data because each time a record is updated, the index is updated. Use indexes only on columns that are searched often.

Objective

Create an index for the Name column on the Vendors table.

```
CREATE INDEX Index_Name ON Table_Name(Column_Name);

CREATE INDEX Vendor_Idx ON Vendors(Name);
```

You just created a regular non-unique index, which means that values may be repeated and they also may be NULL. If you know beforehand that you want the column to always have a value, then specify NOT NULL for that column when creating the table. If you also want the values to be unique, then you have to specify UNIQUE either when creating the index or when creating the column in the table definition.

Objective

Create an index for the Name column on the Publishers table.

```
CREATE UNIQUE INDEX Index_Name ON Table_Name(Column_Name);

CREATE UNIQUE INDEX Pub_Phone ON Publishers(Phone);
```

A FULLTEXT search is good on a City field for the Publishers table because the fields don't need to be unique. That is true because there may be multiple Publishers in a city like New York or Los Angeles.

Objective

Create a FULLTEXT search for the City column on the Publishers table.

```
CREATE FULLTEXT INDEX Index_Name ON Table_Name(Column_Name);

CREATE FULLTEXT INDEX Pub_City ON Publishers(City);
```

Creating a spatial index works the same way as the other specific indexes but can only be placed on spatial data-type columns: GEOMETRY, POINT, LINESTRING, POLYGON, MULTIPOINT, MULTILINESTRING, MULTIPOLYGON, and GEOMETRYCOLLECTION. The GEOMETRY type can store geometry values of any type. The other single-value types—POINT, LINESTRING, and POLYGON—restrict their values to a particular geometry type. The other data types hold collections of values.

Use the USING clause, when creating an index, when there are index type options. DBMSs use BTREE, RTREE, or HASH. R-TREE type indexes are typically used for spatial data.

You now have the introductory CREATE statements for creating databases, tables, and indexes. You also know how to create a primary key on a column. The rest of the CREATE commands are presented in their respective chapters so that the material is presented in a more logical format.

DROP

DROP is the next most logical command to learn since it is the opposite of CREATE. In SQL, you don't delete database objects; you drop them. Yes, there is a DELETE keyword, but that deletes data from a table. If you DROP a database, table, index, or the like, it is removed from the DBMS and cannot be retrieved. DROP should be used with caution. You can destroy an entire day's work with a DROP providing you have backups sufficient to get you where you were last night. Careless use of DROP has caused many a DBA to be sent to the Classifieds section of the newspaper. Table 4.3 shows the various DROP statements.

Table 4.3   SQL DROP Statements

Statement	Description
DROP DATABASE	Removes an existing database
DROP INDEX	Removes existing indexes from a database
DROP TABLE	Removes existing tables from a database

DROP DATABASE

This is perhaps the most dangerous of all the DROP commands because it removes the named database and all tables, data, and so on contained within the database. To demonstrate DROP DATABASE, you will create a database, add a table, and then drop the database.

Objective

Create a new database named Temp. In it create a table named Table1 with a column named ID. Drop the database.

```
CREATE DATABASE Temp;

USE Temp;

CREATE TABLE Table1 (ID integer(4));

SHOW DATABASES;
```

> ❋ **SHOW BUSINESS**
>
> MySQL has a few SHOW commands that are very useful to a DBA. These are relevant to you at this point:
>
> ```
> SHOW DATABASES;
> SHOW TABLES;
> SHOW COLUMNS FROM Table_Name;
> ```

```
SHOW CREATE TABLE Table_Name;
The SHOW commands are unique to MySQL.
```

When you issue the SHOW DATABASES command, you should see (at a minimum) four databases: mysql, test, Temp, and Books. SHOW DATABASES is a MySQL command that reveals all the databases you have permission to view. I like this feature and wish other vendors would implement it as well, although each vendor has its own way of doing the same thing. A full list of SHOW and other useful administrative commands is included in Appendix A.

```
DROP DATABASE Temp;

SHOW DATABASES;
```

You will now see that Temp is missing from the list. This is how easy it is to remove a database, whether it is 20KB or 20GB.

DROP TABLE

DROP TABLE does exactly what it says: It drops (deletes, removes) a table and all the data in it. You may also drop temporary tables and multiple tables with this command.

```
DROP [TEMPORARY] TABLE [IF EXISTS]
        tbl_name [, tbl_name] ...
        [RESTRICT | CASCADE]
```

Objective
Drop the Vendors table from the Books database.

```
USE Books;
```

Always select your database before doing any manipulation to a table since you may have multiple databases with table names that are the same.

```
SHOW TABLES;
```

SHOW TABLES is a MySQL command that reveals the tables in the current database. Like SHOW DATABASES, SHOW TABLES is a very handy tool.

```
DROP TABLE Table_Name;

DROP TABLE Vendors;
```

The Vendors table has now been deleted. You can do another SHOW TABLES to be sure it is gone. You won't receive any real confirmation working with the command-line interface, but you receive an error if a table doesn't exist. Try the DROP command again to see the error.

Objective

Drop a table that doesn't exist.

```
DROP TABLE Table_Name;

DROP TABLE Vendors;
```

You get an error similar to "Unknown table 'Vendors'." Some DBAs use the IF EXIST clause, but I don't see much point in it. If it exists, it will be deleted and if it doesn't, it won't be. You can try it if you want to see the difference.

Objective

Drop a non-existent table with the IF EXISTS clause.

```
DROP TABLE IF EXISTS Table_Name

DROP TABLE IF EXISTS Vendors;
```

You will receive a standard message or warning instead of an error about the non-existence of the table. You may do it either way. If you are constructing a web-based application, you may want to use IF EXISTS to keep the database from throwing an error, unless you have some way in your programming to suppress those errors.

Multiple tables can be dropped in a single SQL statement by naming the tables in a comma-separated list.

Objective

Drop the Customers and Orders tables from the Books database.

```
DROP TABLE Table_Name1, Table_Name2;

DROP TABLE Customers, Orders;

SHOW TABLES;
```

The Customers and the Orders tables are now dropped from the Books database. The RESTRICT and CASCADE portions of DROP TABLE protect a database's integrity. Issuing the RESTRICT keyword ensures that only a table with no dependent views or integrity constraints can be destroyed. Using CASCADE means that any referencing views or integrity constraints are also dropped from the database.

DROP INDEX

DROP INDEX drops the index named Index_Name from the table Table_Name. This statement is actually mapped to an ALTER TABLE statement to drop the index.

```
DROP INDEX Index_Name ON Table_Name
```

You created two indexes on the Publishers table. First, you created a unique index on Phone, then a full-text index on City. To see the indexes that were created on this or any other table, you may issue the following command:

```
SHOW CREATE TABLE Table_Name;
```

Objective
Remove the full-text index from the Publishers table.

```
DROP INDEX Index_Name ON Table_Name;
```

You may not remember the index names on the Publishers table, or even how many there were. To see this, use this:

```
SHOW CREATE TABLE Publishers;
```

The response you get should look like the following:

```
| publishers | CREATE TABLE 'publishers' (
    'ID' int(4) default NULL,
    'Name' varchar(50) default NULL,
    'Address' varchar(50) default NULL,
    'City' varchar(25) default NULL,
    'Zip' varchar(10) default NULL,
    'Phone' varchar(12) default NULL,
    UNIQUE KEY 'Pub_Phone' ('Phone'),
    FULLTEXT KEY 'Pub_City' ('City')
) ENGINE=MyISAM DEFAULT CHARSET=latin1 |
```

Though we added the indexes after creating the table, it looks as if they were created at the same time the Publishers table was created. As you can see from the code listing, the UNIQUE index (KEY) is named Pub_Phone and the FULLTEXT index is named Pub_City. Our objective is to drop the full-text index. You don't need to know the index *type* to drop, but you do need to know the index *name*. You now have the information you need to complete the objective.

```
DROP INDEX Pub_City ON Publishers;

SHOW CREATE TABLE Publishers;
```

You will see that the full-text index has been dropped from the Publishers table and the CREATE TABLE code is changed accordingly.

ALTER

The ALTER keyword is perhaps my favorite SQL keyword of all. It is the great fixer of mistakes made when creating. With ALTER, you can change the column name or column type, add columns to a table, add foreign keys, change a user's password, change or reset auto-increment values, and so on. Sometimes I think I rely on ALTER too much, but it is available to use and a very powerful tool to boot. I will say, though, that until a database has been field tested, chances are pretty good that you will have to make a few ALTER statements to get things just right. Table 4.4 shows common uses of the ALTER keyword.

Table 4.4   SQL ALTER Syntax

Statement	Description
ALTER DATABASE	Changes the characteristics of a database.
ALTER TABLE	Changes the structure of an existing table.

ALTER DATABASE

ALTER DATABASE allows you to change the overall characteristics of a database. MySQL currently only supports a few attributes. Each vendor has its own ALTER DATABASE syntax, if it is supported at all, and you need to read up on your specific DBMSs implementation.

```
ALTER {DATABASE | SCHEMA} [db_name]
        alter_specification [, alter_specification] ...


alter_specification:
        [DEFAULT] CHARACTER SET charset_name
    | [DEFAULT] COLLATE collation_name
```

You may change the default character set with the ALTER DATABASE command but be careful as you can make your data unreadable depending on the character set you choose. Collation refers to the sort order of objects in the database.

Objective
Change the default character set to latin1.

```
ALTER DATABASE Database_Name CHARACTER SET Charset_Name
ALTER DATABASE Books CHARACTER SET latin1;
```

ALTER TABLE

ALTER TABLE allows you to change the structure of an existing table. You can add or delete columns, create or destroy indexes, change the type of existing columns, or rename columns or the table itself. You can also change the comment for the table and table type. MySQL has a very full-featured ALTER TABLE capability, as you can see from its syntax:

```
ALTER [IGNORE] TABLE tbl_name
        alter_specification [, alter_specification] ...

alter_specification:
        ADD [COLUMN] column_definition [FIRST | AFTER col_name ]
    | ADD [COLUMN] (column_definition,...)
    | ADD INDEX [index_name] [index_type] (index_col_name,...)
    | ADD [CONSTRAINT [symbol]]
            PRIMARY KEY [index_type] (index_col_name,...)
    | ADD [CONSTRAINT [symbol]]
            UNIQUE [index_name] [index_type] (index_col_name,...)
    | ADD [FULLTEXT|SPATIAL] [index_name] (index_col_name,...)
    | ADD [CONSTRAINT [symbol]]
            FOREIGN KEY [index_name] (index_col_name,...)
            [reference_definition]
    | ALTER [COLUMN] col_name {SET DEFAULT literal | DROP DEFAULT}
    | CHANGE [COLUMN] old_col_name column_definition
            [FIRST|AFTER col_name]
    | MODIFY [COLUMN] column_definition [FIRST | AFTER col_name]
    | DROP [COLUMN] col_name
    | DROP PRIMARY KEY
    | DROP INDEX index_name
    | DROP FOREIGN KEY fk_symbol
    | DISABLE KEYS
    | ENABLE KEYS
    | RENAME [TO] new_tbl_name
    | ORDER BY col_name
    | CONVERT TO CHARACTER SET charset_name [COLLATE collation_name]
    | [DEFAULT] CHARACTER SET charset_name [COLLATE collation_name]
    | DISCARD TABLESPACE
    | IMPORT TABLESPACE
    | table_options
```

ALTER TABLE is the SQL command that practicing DBAs probably spend most of their time with. It handles most of the post-build aspects of tables. Once a table is built, ALTER TABLE allows you to add and drop columns, add and drop keys, and so on. Graphical tools can take the sting out of some of the complexities of ALTER TABLE. For instance, if you add a column via a graphical tool, you don't need to know the SQL ALTER TABLE syntax. You would simply use the graphical tool to drop in a new column where you want it.

Since graphical tools are not covered in this book, you have to go through the pain of learning the actual SQL to perform these functions. The *command-line interface (CLI)* can be very good to know, if for some reason you don't have your graphical tools available. This can happen quite often if you are connecting to Unix/Linux servers remotely where only ssh (text-based) sessions are allowed.

Objective
Add a new column to the Publishers table named Contact after the Name column.

```
ALTER TABLE Table_Name ADD COLUMN Column_Name Data Type(Size) AFTER
Column_Name;

ALTER TABLE Publishers ADD COLUMN Contact varchar(100) AFTER ID;

SHOW CREATE TABLE Publishers;
```

You will now see that Contact has been added after the ID column as a varchar type with size of 100 bytes. Note that it looks as if the Publishers table was originally created with the Contact column. The next couple of examples show how to add constraints such as indexes and foreign keys.

Objective
Add an index to the Publishers table on the Contact column.

```
ALTER TABLE Table_Name ADD INDEX Index_Name (Column_Name);

ALTER TABLE Publishers ADD INDEX Pub_Contact (Contact);

SHOW CREATE TABLE Publishers;
```

You see that the index has been added to the table on the Contact column. It should have been made a full-text index but have already created the index. No problem. ALTER TABLE allows you to drop an index as well.

Objective
Remove the regular index from the Contact column of the Publishers table and replace it with a full-text index.

```
ALTER TABLE Table_Name DROP INDEX Index_Name;

ALTER TABLE Publishers DROP INDEX Pub_Contact;
```

The index has been removed. You may check with the SHOW CREATE TABLE Publishers command, if you wish.

To add your full-text index, use a slightly different syntax. The keyword INDEX is actually not used for a specific INDEX type. Instead, you use just the index type keyword FULLTEXT.

Objective
Add a full-text index to the Publishers table on the Contact column.

```
ALTER TABLE Table_Name ADD FULLTEXT Index_Name (Column_Name);

ALTER TABLE Publishers ADD FULLTEXT Pub_Contact (Contact);
```

You can check to see that the ALTER TABLE worked like you think it should have with a SHOW CREATE TABLE statement.

The final example of ALTER TABLE is to show you how to create a foreign key constraint. This is a multi-step process, so follow along carefully.

Objective
Create a foreign key constraint in the Publishers table that references Table1.

First, you have to create a new table: Table1. Then create a new column in the Publishers table that is of the same type as the column you reference in Table1. Since a foreign key references a primary key in another table, you must create an integer column with a size of 4 bytes.

```
CREATE TABLE Table1 (ID integer(4) PRIMARY KEY, Name varchar(50));

SHOW CREATE TABLE Table1;
```

Into the Publishers table, add the new column that will become the foreign key:

```
ALTER TABLE Table_Name ADD COLUMN Column_Name Data Type(Size);

ALTER TABLE Publishers ADD COLUMN Table1_ID integer(4);
```

Now create a unique index on Table1_ID:

```
ALTER TABLE Table_Name ADD UNIQUE Index_Name (Column_Name);

ALTER TABLE Publishers ADD UNIQUE FK_Table1 (Table1_ID);
```

You can now set the foreign key constraint:

```
ALTER TABLE Table_Name ADD FOREIGN KEY Index_Name (Column_Name) REFERENCES
Foreign_Table_Name (Column_Name);

ALTER TABLE Publishers ADD FOREIGN KEY FK_Table1 (Table1_ID) REFERENCES Table1
(ID);
```

You now have a foreign key (Publishers.Table1_ID) that references (Table1.ID). Take a look at the foreign key by issuing the following:

```
SHOW CREATE TABLE Publishers;
```

You may notice from the table design that you do not see any references to your foreign key. The SHOW CREATE TABLE looks like this:

```
| publishers | CREATE TABLE 'publishers' (
    'ID' int(4) default NULL,
    'Contact' varchar(100) default NULL,
    'Name' varchar(50) default NULL,
    'Address' varchar(50) default NULL,
    'City' varchar(25) default NULL,
    'Zip' varchar(10) default NULL,
    'Phone' varchar(12) default NULL,
    'Table1_ID' int(4) default NULL,
    UNIQUE KEY 'Pub_Phone' ('Phone'),
    UNIQUE KEY 'tab' ('Table1_ID'),
    FULLTEXT KEY 'pub_contact' ('Contact')
) ENGINE=MyISAM DEFAULT CHARSET=latin1 |
```

The foreign key you set up looks just like any other unique index. What could have gone wrong? Nothing. The problem is the last line you see in the CREATE TABLE statement:

```
) ENGINE=MyISAM DEFAULT CHARSET=latin1 |
```

The part that says ENGINE=MyISAM is the glitch for your foreign key and reference to the other table. MyISAM is the default table type or storage engine in MySQL, and it does not support foreign key constraints nor does it enforce any referential integrity between tables. Why didn't you receive an error to that effect when you typed in the SQL statement for the foreign key and table reference? MySQL allows the statement to be processed, but as you can see, it is not stored nor will it be enforced.

This is the way the table Publishers should look from a SHOW CREATE TABLE Publishers statement:

```
| Publishers | CREATE TABLE 'Publishers' (
    'ID' int(4) default NULL,
    'Contact' varchar(100) default NULL,
    'Name' varchar(50) default NULL,
    'Address' varchar(50) default NULL,
    'City' varchar(25) default NULL,
```

```
'Zip' varchar(10) default NULL,
'Phone' varchar(12) default NULL,
'Table1_ID' int(4) default NULL,
UNIQUE KEY 'Pub_Phone' ('Phone'),
UNIQUE KEY 'FK_Table1' ('Table1_ID'),
KEY 'Pub_Contact' ('Contact'),
CONSTRAINT 'Publishers_ibfk_1' FOREIGN KEY ('Table1_ID') REFERENCES 'Table1'
('ID')
) ENGINE=InnoDB DEFAULT CHARSET=latin1 |
```

Notice that the last line has changed to ENGINE=InnoDB. InnoDB is a transaction-safe (ACID-compliant) table type. Also notice that in the preceding lines, you can clearly see that the foreign key constraint and the reference to Table1 are there. You may also see that the Pub_Contact index is no longer FULLTEXT. This is because InnoDB tables do not support full-text indexes. I explain all of these details in Chapters 5 and 7, when you get to transactions.

RENAME TABLE

A few DBMSs support RENAME TABLE, so I include it in here since it is part of DDL. Those DBMSs that do not support RENAME TABLE use ALTER TABLE with a RENAME clause.

```
RENAME TABLE tbl_name TO new_tbl_name

        [, tbl_name2 TO new_tbl_name2] ...
```

Objective
Rename table Table1 as Table2.

```
RENAME TABLE Table1 TO Table2;

SHOW TABLES;
```

You should now see Table2 in the list instead of Table1.

Summary

Congratulations on completing your first real lesson in SQL! Now you know what I meant earlier about SQL being *interactive* in nature. It is a lot to take in all at once. You may want to read this chapter again before going on to the Chapter Review questions. I also suggest working through the examples again so you feel more comfortable writing SQL statements; this material is the basis for all of the rest of the book.

You will be using CREATE, DROP, and ALTER in just about every chapter from this point on, and the discussions will assume knowledge of their usage and syntax. You have learned quite a bit in this chapter using the data definition language: commands to create, drop, and alter database entities such as databases, tables, and indexes; some non-DDL commands such as USE and SHOW CREATE TABLE; some MySQL-specific commands such as SHOW DATABASES and SHOW TABLES. From the syntax boxes and the examples, you should now be able to formulate some of your own SQL statements. Try some on your own.

Chapter Review

Multiple Choice

1. The CREATE Orders; SQL statement

   a) does nothing.

   b) gives an error.

   c) creates a table named Orders.

   d) creates a database named Orders.

2. The DROP TABLE Products; SQL statement

   a) detaches you from the table Products.

   b) deletes the table Products.

   c) stops querying the table Products.

   d) copies the structure and data of Products to an external file.

3. If you want to see how a table was created, which command would you issue?

   a) SHOW TABLES;

   b) USE TABLE Table_Name;

   c) SHOW CREATE DATABASE Table_Name

   d) SHOW CREATE TABLE Table_Name

4. To interactively switch from one database to another, which command would you use?

   a) CREATE DATABASE Database_Name;

   b) USE DATABASE Database_Name;

   c) USE Database_Name;

   d) SHOW TABLES;

5. The SHOW TABLES command

   a) gives a list of databases.

   b) gives a list of tables.

   c) returns the error: No such command.

   d) does nothing.

6. Identify the correct CREATE TABLE syntax.

   a) CREATE TABLE Fruit (ID integer(4), Name varchar(25));

   b) CREATE TABLE Fruit (ID (integer(4)), (Name (varchar(25));

   c) CREATE Fruit (ID integer(4), Name varchar(25));

   d) CREATE TABLE Fruit (ID, Name) VALUES (4, 25);

7. Which phrase creates an index on a column?

   a) CREATE INDEX

   b) ALTER INDEX

   c) DROP INDEX

   d) INDEX CREATE

8. In MySQL, a database is simply a

   a) database.

   b) table.

   c) column.

   d) folder.

9. One correct way to remove an index is

   a) ALTER TABLE Table_Name DROP INDEX;

   b) ALTER TABLE Table_Name DELETE INDEX Index_Name;

   c) ALTER TABLE Table_Name DROP INDEX Index_Name;

   d) ALTER DATABASE Table_Name DROP INDEX Index_Name;

10. Another way to remove an index is

   a) DROP INDEX Index_Name ON Table_Name;

   b) DELETE INDEX Index_Name ON Table_Name;

   c) DROP INDEX ON Table_Name;

   d) DROP INDEX Index_Name ON Column_Name;

5 } MySQL

Since I am using MySQL for the DBMS in this book, this chapter highlights it and its features for you. My purpose in presenting this material now is that I have to use language in this chapter that you are familiar with from Chapter 4. It makes more chronological sense to put this information here since you now have the knowledge to grasp it successfully.

I have personally worked with MySQL since version 3.23 and fell in love with it as soon as I logged in the first time. Most of my MySQL experience has been in writing web-based applications that use it as a back-end DBMS. Now that it has reached version 5.x, it now supports views, triggers, stored procedures, and many other enterprise-level features. I can say honestly that I never really missed any of those advanced features because I programmed workarounds in Perl or PHP (my programming languages of choice). Now that the features are available, my programming has been streamlined somewhat—but I still prefer embedded SQL to other options. My preferences and prejudices do not necessarily reflect the opinions of the masses. I know I am in the minority, but my applications work, they are easy to use and maintain, and they are very, very fast. Enough about me; let me enlighten you about the MySQL DBMS, its features, and even some of its shortcomings.

MySQL AB

MySQL AB is the company that owns and maintains MySQL, the DBMS. MySQL AB, a Swedish company that was started by founders David Axmark, Allan Larsson, and Michael "Monty" Widenius, is truly a global company. It has employees on six continents and users on all seven. For those of you who don't know, AB is the Swedish version of Inc.

MySQL AB has two sets of core values: one for how it interacts with its software and the other for how it interacts with its employees and users.

These are the core values relating to how MySQL AB works with MySQL Server software:

* To be the best and the most widely used database in the world
* To be available and affordable by all
* To be easy to use
* To be continuously improved while remaining fast and safe
* To be fun to use and improve
* To be free from bugs

The first one is debatable, but it is a matter of opinion and choice. The rest of the list is, in my experience, a fair assessment. The software certainly is affordable, available, fast, safe, and easy and fun to use; I have never personally discovered any bugs. Generally, I have had only good experiences with all of the DBMSs that I have used but MySQL is the right database software for me.

These are the company's core values, as given on its web site at dev.mysql.com/doc/refman/4.1/en/what-is-mysql-ab.html:

* We subscribe to the Open Source philosophy and support the Open Source community
* We aim to be good citizens
* We prefer partners that share our values and mindset
* We answer email and provide support
* We are a virtual company, networking with others
* We work against software patents

I can verify that they definitely do answer their email and provide support. During the early stages of writing this book, I submitted an email query from their web site about something that I thought was pretty far down on the list of priorities, but to my surprise I received a phone call from a MySQL representative about it. I was very impressed with the response (a few days) and the willingness to assist me in my quest. I was trying to find an interesting little application, called Crash-me, on their site that I had used in the past. Crash-me is a detailed comparison of several DBMSs, and it is a very fair comparison. You can see how MySQL compares to other systems in a very short amount of time. My point is that, even for such a trivial question, someone contacted me directly with a phone call and not just an email.

I have also taken MySQL AB-supplied training. The instructor was very knowledgeable and able to answer all of our questions with ease and confidence. He spent time with me figuring out some issues with my implementations; that probably could have been handled in online forums, but he took his own time to assist.

The MySQL Database Management System

MySQL was originally associated with mSQL and used *Indexed Sequential Access Method (ISAM)* tables. As the developers continued their work, they found that this setup was not sufficient in either speed or flexibility. The code was then developed independently of mSQL and diverged into a new interface. Somewhere lost in the annals of history is the exact origin of the name MySQL. One of the developers has a daughter named My, but even the folks at MySQL aren't sure exactly why or when they started using MySQL. I assumed, since these guys were all developers that it had something to do with localization, referring to its inherent security like one does with variables. I have never posed this theory to any of the developers or other MySQL employees.

SOUNDS LIKE...

The official way to pronounce *MySQL* is "My Ess Que Ell" (not "my sequel"), but the people at MySQL AB don't mind if you pronounce it some other localized way.

MySQL was written with speed, portability, and flexibility in mind. This list shows why MySQL is so fast:

❋ Written in C and C++.

❋ Fully multi-threaded using kernel threads.

❋ Uses very fast b-tree disk tables (MyISAM) with index compression.

❋ Very fast thread-based memory allocation system.

❋ Very fast joins using an optimized one-sweep multi-join.

❋ In-memory hash tables, which are used as temporary tables.

❋ SQL functions implemented using a highly optimized class library and should be as fast as possible. Usually there is no memory allocation at all after query initialization.

❋ File system-based structure. Databases are directories and tables are files.

I really like MySQL's file system-based structure. This feature alone is worth a pound of gold because I can easily port databases and tables to other platforms with a simple file transfer. To be able to pick up an entire database from a Windows system and drop it, unchanged, onto a Linux system and have it immediately available on the Linux system without even a restart of the MySQL server is extremely valuable. In the next section, I cover the different DBMS table types in detail and explain the features and limitations of each.

MySQL AB maintains several editions of MySQL that all have their specific uses and applications in the business world:

* Community Edition: Free.
* MySQL Pro Certified Server: I believe this is the same as the Community Edition except with stable code and commercial support.
* MaxDB: A rebranded version of SapDB.
* MySQL Cluster: A high-availability system that delivers 99.999 percent uptime for mission-critical applications.

Tables

Most, if not all, DBMSs support table variants such as permanent tables, virtual tables, or views and temporary tables. All of the DBMSs in Chapter 3 support virtual tables and *view* is the commonly used term for that database entity. Temporary tables are a universally supported table type. Typically, they are used for *scratch* (temporary) data that is discarded or transferred to a permanent table at or near the end of a database session.

TABLE IT
You will see the terms *storage engine* and *table type,* as well as others. They are the same thing. Storage engine is the newer, more accepted, term for table type. I use the terms interchangeably, as do most database administrators.

Most DBAs would not consider these as table *types* per se because they do not represent unique storage engines. Many DBMSs only have a single default storage engine that is a permanent-transaction safe storage engine. I separate these descriptions as special tables because of their functionality and role within the DBMS. They differ in the way that they are created, where they reside, their lifespan and, very often, their uses. You can create them with any of several storage engine types. In other words, a temporary table can be an InnoDB, MyISAM, or even a memory table.

Permanent Tables

Permanent tables are what come to mind when one thinks of tables. They are the basic entity in a database where data is stored. This named entity resides on disk and is composed of named columns and rows of data. For many DBMSs, this is a default table and there is no other to choose from. You will see several permanent table types from MySQL in this chapter. The two main are InnoDB and MyISAM. MyISAM is typically the default table type or storage engine, although you can change this, so it is always good practice to define the engine type when creating a new table. The following example shows how to create an InnoDB table:

```
CREATE TABLE Example (ID integer(4), Name varchar(50), Phone varchar(12))
ENGINE=INNODB;
```

And now the same example with MyISAM as the storage engine:

```
CREATE TABLE Example (ID integer(4), Name varchar(50), Phone varchar(12))
ENGINE=MYISAM;
```

These statements produce the permanent tables types shown by specifying ENGINE=*TYPE* after the column definitions. The various storage engine types are shown in Table 5.1. The permanent table types are InnoDB, MyISAM, BDB, CSV, Archive, Merge, and Federated.

Virtual Tables (Views)

This addition came with the release of the 5.x versions. Views are nothing more than *virtual* tables. You don't create a view with standard CREATE TABLE syntax, though. They are created from a query of existing table data. They can be created from multiple table sources via a SELECT statement. A view is often a set of data that wouldn't exist in any other form but possibly represents a popular or often-requested data set. Views don't actually contain any data but give the appearance of a table and can be updateable. Views show up in a SHOW TABLES statement but look very different when a SHOW CREATE TABLE View_Name is issued. The SHOW CREATE TABLE statement reveals that the table is actually a view. I cover this topic in detail in Chapter 9, but I thought they were worth mentioning here in the discussion of database tables.

Temporary Tables

Temporary tables are an interesting entity in the DBMS realm and are considered to be an advanced feature. In MySQL, at least, they can be created easily enough with the CREATE TEMPORARY TABLE command and they exist for what used to be known as scratch data, but they don't show up when you do a SHOW TABLES command. My assumption is that they exist to assist developers in creating a semi-persistent or intermediate data set to refer to without having to repeat an SQL query. I can think of many instances where I would create a temporary table for a web user to hold session data while the user shops or makes a series of choices before a final submit is issued.

Temporary tables only exist for the user who creates them and once that user is no longer active, the tables are removed. Once the user session that created the temporary tables is closed, the files associated with the temporary tables are also removed from the file system and are not retrievable. When a temporary table is created, its corresponding disk files are also created. These files are created in /tmp on my Linux system and in C:\WINDOWS\TEMP on my Windows system. The created files are not named with the table names as you might expect, but with random, incremented, temporary names. A single file is created for InnoDB temporary tables, and the usual three files are created for MyISAM tables. On my Windows system, the InnoDB temporary table I created is represented by the file sql1dc_1c_0.frm, which holds the table definition. The MyISAM temporary table is represented by three files: sql1dc_1c_3.frm (table definition), sql1dc_1c_3.MYI (index), and sql1dc_1c_3.MYD (data). The comparable files on my Linux system are sql40f6_56_0.frm (InnoDB table definition), sql40f6_56_1.frm (MyISAM table definition), sql40f6_56_1.MYI (index), and sql40f6_56_1.MYD (data). The reason for the discrepancy in the number of files between InnoDB and MyISAM tables is a mystery that will have to wait until later in this chapter to be revealed.

You may have noticed that the filenames for temporary tables are random and do not correspond in any way with the actual table names. This means that any number of users may connect to the DBMS to create a temporary table named Temp1 and none of them will receive an error that a table with that name already exists. A single user, however, may not create multiple tables with the same name because there would be no logical way to refer to them and their contents.

Temporary tables can be created as any of the following types: HEAP, ISAM, MyISAM, MERGE, or InnoDB.

MySQL Table Types

MySQL comes equipped with support for several different storage engines. I don't discuss every engine in this section but I will spend some time on those I consider most important and most widely used. I highlight these storage engines in this chapter: MyISAM, InnoDB, Memory, and Federated. Some of the other storage engines have to be enabled either by compiling in support or using a slightly different DBMS engine (MySQL-Max). The default-supported storage engines and their key attributes are given in Table 5.1. This information is the response I received from the MySQL DBMS after issuing the SHOW ENGINES command.

Table 5.1   MySQL-Supported Storage Engines

Engine	Support	Comment
MyISAM	Default	Default engine with great performance as of MySQL 3.23
MEMORY	Yes	Hash based, stored in memory, useful for temporary tables
|InnoDB	Yes	Supports transactions, row-level locking, and foreign keys
|BerkeleyDB (BDB)	No	Supports transactions and page-level locking
|BLACKHOLE	No	/dev/null storage engine (anything you write to it disappears)
|EXAMPLE	No	Example storage engine
|ARCHIVE	Yes	Archive storage engine
|CSV	No	CSV storage engine
|ndbcluster	No	Clustered, fault-tolerant, memory-based tables
|FEDERATED	No	Federated MySQL storage engine
|MRG_MYISAM (MERGE)	Yes	Collection of identical MyISAM tables
|ISAM	No	Obsolete storage engine

MyISAM

MyISAM is the default table type when you create a table in MySQL. MyISAM tables, an enhanced version of ISAM tables, are proprietary to MySQL. It is a very fast access, non-transaction–safe, permanent table type. This table type should only be used when you do not need transaction-safe tables. They cannot take part in transactions at all. They also do not support foreign key constraints. The SQL commands for foreign key constraints are accepted and will give no error, but you will notice that the SHOW CREATE TABLE command shows no reference to them. Foreign key constraints are not enforced and are not saved.

When you create a new MyISAM table, three corresponding disk files are created and named the same as your table. For example, if you create a table named Orders, three disk files are created:

- ❈ Orders.MYD: The actual table data
- ❈ Orders.MYI: The Index file associated with Orders.MYD
- ❈ Orders.frm: The Orders table definition

These files are kept, by default, in a subdirectory of the data directory where you installed MySQL. The subdirectory matches the database name to which the tables belong. MyISAM tables come in three subtypes:

- ❈ Static: Contains no variable-length column types (VARCHAR, BLOB, and TEXT) and is actually the default MyISAM table type.
- ❈ Dynamic: Contains variable-length columns (VARCHAR, BLOB, or TEXT).
- ❈ Compressed: Packed with read-only versions of MyISAM tables, whether static or dynamic.

Static MyISAM Tables

Sometimes called *fixed-length MyISAM tables,* these tables contain only columns that have a fixed size regardless of the size of the data in the column. (See the discussion in Chapter 4 in the CREATE TABLE section.) This table type has many advantages over the other MyISAM types: They are the simplest in design, the least susceptible to corruption, easily recoverable in case of a crash, fastest of all the on-disk formats, and easy to cache. This format is almost always completely recoverable because the records are in fixed positions. The downside is that they require more disk space than a variable-table format. Static MyISAM tables are the MySQL default MyISAM format.

Dynamic MyISAM Tables

This MyISAM format contains at least one variable-length column type in its table definition. The biggest advantage (and possibly the only one) to this format is that it takes much less disk space than static. Using this format requires frequent table optimization and MySQL has utilities to handle these operations.

Compressed MyISAM Tables

This read-only table format saves a considerable amount of disk space over others. Tables are sometimes compressed when data is considered historical and not likely to change. The compact size and rapid data access is of particular interest when the data has been copied to CD-ROM or DVD. Either static or dynamic MyISAM tables can be compressed. MySQL comes with a utility to uncompress the tables as well.

For all of the good things I can say about MyISAM tables, there also a few negatives to inform you about. Table corruption, while not common, does happen for various reasons: hardware failure, the MySQL service being killed or abnormally stopped, unexpected power outages or performing maintenance on a live table while someone is working with the data. There are tools that fix most problems that occur, but your best defenses are good backups and some regularly scheduled preventative maintenance. MyISAM tables are not finicky by any means, but they do require some occasional TLC. I have included maintenance information in Appendix B for this reason.

MyISAM tables are fast, reliable, and easily ported from one platform to another. They are perfect for web-based applications and perform well in business-oriented applications as well. Referential integrity and transactions are better handled by InnoDB or BDB tables, but if you are a developer you can easily work around these issues in your code.

InnoDB

InnoDB tables are a proprietary table type that is transaction safe (ACID) and does enforce foreign key constraints. The InnoDB storage engine is responsible for MySQL's high availability and robust data integrity. InnoDB, the company, was purchased by Oracle in late 2005. I am hopeful that InnoDB and MySQL will continue their relationship because many companies have become dependent on the InnoDB storage engine. I also hope that the MySQL development teams are working arduously to develop their own transaction-safe storage engine just in case things don't work out favorably with Oracle. Oracle does state on its site that InnoDB will remain an open-source product and will continue to be developed.

InnoDB tables offer many advantages over MyISAM tables. The following list gives you an overview of those advantages:

* They are transactional, providing rollback and commit capabilities.
* It is the only table type in MySQL that supports foreign key constraints.
* They are fast—even faster than MyISAM tables in some applications.
* They have row-level locking: They allow higher concurrency than MyISAM tables that use table-level locking, or BDB tables, which use page-level locking. High concurrency is reflected in high multiuser performance.

❋ They provide an Oracle-style consistent read, also known as *multi-versioned concurrency control*. SELECTs do not need to set any locks and need not interfere with inserts and updates to the same table. No other MySQL table type has this property.

❋ Multi-versioning also allows you to dump tables from your database with SELECT INTO OUTFILE without setting locks on the tables: The database can keep working while a backup is made.

❋ There is a true hot backup tool available for InnoDB, which allows you to make backups of a running database in the background, without setting any locks or disturbing database operation.

❋ InnoDB has automatic crash recovery. You do not need to repair your tables if the operating system or database server crashes, when there is no disk image corruption.

❋ Tables can be any size on those operating systems where file size is restricted to <2GB.

Like MySQL, InnoDB has been designed for maximum performance, especially when processing large data volumes. Its CPU efficiency is probably not matched by any other disk-based relational database engine.

It has some limitations, but I am sure that some are going to be resolved in the near future. Some of the limitations listed here are actually features and were created by design. Some are imposed by MySQL and not really a function of InnoDB at all. The term *limitation* should not be taken to mean a shortcoming against InnoDB but rather a positive point *for* the MyISAM storage engine. There are applications in which MyISAM is the superior storage engine. Consider the following list of InnoDB limitations:

❋ The system tables in MySQL cannot be converted to InnoDB.

❋ A table may contain only 1,000 columns.

❋ The maximum row length—except for varchar, BLOB, and TEXT columns—is slightly less than half of a database page. That is, the maximum row length is about 8,000 bytes. LONGBLOB and LONGTEXT columns must be less than 4GB, and the total row length—including also BLOB and TEXT columns—must be less than 4GB. InnoDB stores the first 768 bytes of a varchar, BLOB, or TEXT column in the row, and the rest into separate pages.

❋ Although InnoDB supports row sizes larger than 65,535 internally, you cannot define a row containing varchar columns with a combined size larger than 65,535.

❋ The combined size of the InnoDB log files must be less than 4GB.

❋ The minimum tablespace size is 10MB. The maximum tablespace size is 4 billion database pages (64TB). This is also the maximum size for a table.

❋ InnoDB tables do not support FULLTEXT indexes.

* InnoDB tables do not support spatial data types before MySQL 5.0.16. I am basing this book on version MySQL 5.0.18.

* ANALYZE TABLE determines index cardinality (as displayed in the Cardinality column of SHOW INDEX output) by doing eight random dives to each of the index trees and updating index cardinality estimates accordingly. Note that because these are only estimates, re-peated runs of ANALYZE TABLE may produce different numbers. This makes ANALYZE TABLE fast on InnoDB tables but not 100-percent accurate, as it doesn't take all rows into account.

* SHOW TABLE STATUS does not give accurate statistics on InnoDB tables, except for the physical size reserved by the table. The row count is only a rough estimate used in SQL optimization.

* InnoDB does not keep an internal count of rows in a table. (In practice, this would be some-what complicated due to multi-versioning.) To process a SELECT COUNT(*) FROM t statement, InnoDB must scan an index of the table, which takes some time if the index is not entirely in the buffer pool. To get a fast count, you have to use a counter table you create yourself, and let your application update it according to the inserts and deletes it does. If your table does not change often, using the MySQL query cache is a good solution. SHOW TABLE STATUS also can be used if an approximate row count is sufficient.

* On Windows, InnoDB always stores database and table names internally in lowercase. To move databases in binary format from Unix to Windows or from Windows to Unix, you should always use explicitly lowercase names when creating databases and tables.

* For an AUTO_INCREMENT column, you must always define an index for the table, and that index must contain just the AUTO_INCREMENT column. In MyISAM tables, the AUTO_INCREMENT column may be part of a multi-column index.

* DELETE FROM *tbl_name* does not regenerate the table but instead deletes all rows, one by one.

* Under some conditions, TRUNCATE *tbl_name* for an InnoDB table is mapped to DELETE FROM *tbl_name* and doesn't reset the AUTO_INCREMENT counter.

* The LOAD TABLE FROM MASTER statement for setting up replication slave servers does not yet work for InnoDB tables. A workaround is to alter the table to MyISAM on the master, then do the load, and after that alter the master table back to InnoDB. Do not do this if the tables use InnoDB-specific features such as foreign keys.

* Currently, triggers are not activated by cascaded foreign key actions.

At first glance, it may look as if InnoDB has too many limitations, but improvements are constantly being made.

InnoDB introduces the concept of *tablespace* to MySQL. All of the InnoDB tables are collected into a single disk file named ibdata1 in the MySQL data directory. This architecture is very scalable because the single file sort of creates its own very efficient, tiny universe. To copy a single table from one place to another requires a *dump* of the structure and data to an external file. This is fine for probably everyone but me since I like the way MyISAM tables are laid out where I can see, copy, repair, compact, and so on, at will. The tablespace scenario is a little too "black boxish" for my primitive tastes. Most of the competing enterprise-quality DBMSs use tablespaces and I will eventually get used to the idea that things work very well inside the black box.

Federated

Federated tables types became available in version 5.x of MySQL. The federated storage engine accesses tables in remote databases rather than local ones but allows you to access remote tables as if they were local by creating a local table definition. Only the Max version of MySQL has support for the Federated storage engine in a binary version. If you want it, you have to compile in federated support from a source-tree download (should you choose not to use the Max binary). The structure of the local table must be exactly the same as the remote table as far as column names and descriptions. They need not be named the same and the engine for the local table is FEDERATED. A connection string to the remote table is also part of the table definition.

The FEDERATED storage engine supports SELECT, INSERT, UPDATE, DELETE, and indexes. It does not support ALTER TABLE, DROP TABLE, or any other Data Definition Language statements. Currently, you can only connect to another MySQL table, although other APIs may be added in the future. Transactions are not supported. To use a federated table setup, you must have at least SELECT permission on the remote table. If you plan to use other keywords like INSERT, UPDATE, and DELETE, you must also have those permissions on the remote table. The connect string is declared in the following format:

```
scheme://user_name[:password]@host_name[:port_num]/db_name/tbl_name
```

From a developer standpoint, this ability certainly saves a lot of extra programming if the remote database is MySQL. For more information on the federated storage engine, please visit mysql.com or the Federated Storage Engine Forum at forums.mysql.com/list.php?105.

Memory (Heap)

Heap, or *memory, tables* (as they are now known) are quite common in the DBMS world. Although memory tables, as the name would imply, are held in memory, a single disk file with the .frm extension holds the table definition. The memory storage engine uses Hash indexes by default. These tables are very fast to access, query, update, and the like, but their contents (data) are lost upon a DBMS restart. The table definition remains intact but the table data is truncated.

Characteristics of the memory storage engine in MySQL follow:

* Space for memory tables is allocated in small blocks. Tables use 100-percent dynamic hashing for inserts. No overflow area or extra key space is needed. No extra space is needed for free lists.

* Memory tables can have up to 32 indexes per table, 16 columns per index, and a maximum key length of 500 bytes.

* The memory storage engine implements both Hash and BTREE indexes. You can specify one or the other for a given index by adding a USING clause.

* You can have non-unique keys in a memory table.

* You can also use INSERT DELAYED with memory tables.

* If you have a Hash index on a memory table that has a high degree of key duplication (many index entries containing the same value), updates to the table that affect key values and all deletes are significantly slower. The degree of this slowdown is proportional to the degree of duplication (or, inversely proportional to the index cardinality). You can use a BTREE index to avoid this problem.

* Memory tables use a fixed record-length format.

* Memory doesn't support BLOB or TEXT columns.

* Memory includes support for both AUTO_INCREMENT columns and indexes on columns that contain NULL values.

* Memory tables are shared between all clients (just like any other non-temporary table).

* The server needs sufficient memory to maintain all memory tables that are in use at the same time.

* To free memory used by a memory table when you no longer require its contents, you should execute DELETE FROM or TRUNCATE TABLE, or remove the table altogether (using DROP TABLE).

* You can populate a memory table when MySQL is started.

Memory tables are never converted to disk tables, regardless of size. They will continue to grow unless you *truncate* (empty), drop, or set the max_heap_table_size system variable to limit the table size. You can also specify a MAX_ROWS table option in the CREATE TABLE statement. Memory tables are listed in a SHOW TABLES command unless the table was created as temporary. Use memory tables for a small amount of data that you need very fast access to.

Switching Storage Engines

It is possible, with the use of an ALTER TABLE command, to switch a table's storage engine. You should heed some warnings before you make such a change, though. If you convert a MyISAM table to an InnoDB table and have a full-text index in the MyISAM table, you will get an error after issuing the ALTER TABLE command and the conversion will not take place. You have to first convert the full-text index to another type before continuing with the conversion. And if you have foreign key constraints and convert from InnoDB to MyISAM, you will lose that constraint.

Locking

It would be almost impossible to discuss databases and tables without talking about locking. *Locking* is exclusive access to a resource such as a table or record and is handled by the DBMS automatically. It is one of the features built in to DBMSs to ensure data integrity. If two or more clients are trying to edit data at the same time, this could result in corrupted or outdated results. MySQL gives you a choice of what kind of locking you want by choosing your storage engine. Most DBMSs support row-level locking and do not give you a choice of any other. Locking strategies come with a price: performance. Finer-grained locking delivers less performance because of all of the system overhead of providing those locks and lock checking.

Table-Level Locking

Table-level locking has the highest performance but the least flexibility in terms of servicing multiple clients. Updates, inserts, and deletes happen so quickly that very little latency is ever experienced unless they represent large amounts of transactional data. Table-level locking is based on the assumption that the majority of table operations will be read. For table-level locking to be efficient, most client actions either need to be reads or writes because a balance of the two would result in poor performance.

MyISAM and memory tables use table-level locking. For some time, this was a big criticism of MySQL from other database vendors and administrators alike. The assumption was that MySQL wouldn't scale very well with this table-level locking strategy. The problem with the assumption is that MySQL's performance is so much higher than most other DBMSs that it really hasn't hurt MySQL's scalability. MySQL has an interesting algorithm for managing locks on table-level locking tables. If there are no locks on the table, put a write lock on it; otherwise, put the lock request in the write lock queue. If there are no write locks on the table, put a read lock on it; otherwise, put the lock request in the read lock queue. When a lock is released, the lock is made available to the threads in the write lock queue, then to the threads in the read lock queue. This means that if you have many updates for a table, SELECT statements wait until there are no more updates.

The way MySQL handles locks makes MyISAM and memory tables especially well-suited for web-based applications.

Page-Level Locking

One of the many storage engines that MySQL supports is BDB that uses page-level locking. The default page size is 8KB. A *page* is an amount of data that corresponds to a number of records that are physically located in close proximity to the record of interest that is in the same block on the disk. To clarify a bit, I said earlier that the default page size for a BDB table is 8KB. This means that when a particular record is locked that the entire 8KB block, or *page*, of data that the record is located on the disk gets locked also. Page-level locking involves a lock on a portion of a table, but not the entire table, so that only the records on the same page are affected by the lock. This locking strategy comes with a higher overhead but it seems to be offset by the increased efficiency of table reads and writes. Page-level locking strikes a balance between the high-performance, no-deadlock, all-or-nothing table-level locking and the CPU-intensive, highly transaction-oriented, row-level locking. For most operations, page-level locking will outperform row-level locking. Page-level locking, however, is not as transaction safe as row-level locking.

Row-Level Locking

InnoDB tables use row-level locking but it is not a standard row-level locking strategy. *Row-level locking* provides the highest level of concurrency at a very high performance price, although InnoDB has done an excellent job of creating a multi-version row-level locking strategy that seems to impede performance far less than standard row-level locking. This type of enhanced row-level locking is called *Multi-Version Concurrency Control (MVCC)*. What happens is that even when a row is locked for inserts, updates, and deletes, reads can still occur as non-locking reads for a particular snapshot, or *version,* of the data. Locks acquired for reading data do not conflict with locks acquired for writing data, and so reading never blocks writing and writing never blocks reading. I cover this locking strategy in greater detail in Chapter 7 when discussing transactions.

Blocks

A *block* occurs when a client requests, and is granted, a lock on a table, page, or record (row), and another client requesting the same lock gets temporarily refused. This is a standard occurrence in dealing with databases. The blocked client goes into a wait queue until the lock is released. Blocks usually resolve themselves by having clients "wait their turn" at a lock. If too many blocks are occurring, then one should closely examine the transaction, database design, and application to find out what is causing the high number of blocks and user complaints.

Deadlocks

A *deadlock* is where two or more lock requests are requesting the same lock and end up waiting on the others to release their locks. InnoDB automatically detects deadlocks and automatically resolves them by terminating one of the clients' connections. Table locking in MySQL is deadlock free for storage engines that use table-level locking (MyISAM and memory). Deadlock avoidance is managed by always requesting all needed locks at once at the beginning of a query and always locking the tables in the same order.

Summary

This chapter has been a brief overview of MySQL 5.x and some of its key features, structure, origins, and capabilities. The major table types (storage engines) were covered to give you an idea of the options you have with MySQL that you don't have with any other DBMS, commercial or open source. MySQL is extremely versatile. It is a DBMS that functions as a simple desktop database, a web-application back-end database, and an enterprise database server or data warehouse—and you never have to change products. MySQL has helped many large companies lower their TCO, much to the chagrin of certain other commercial DBMS vendors. It provides capabilities that are worth many times the cost of dedicated support from MySQL AB.

MySQL 5.x is in the realm of the biggest players in the field. The addition of such features as stored procedures, views, and triggers put MySQL in a position where it can no longer be ignored for enterprise applications. To me, MySQL is the Linux of DBMSs. It came from nowhere and has grown over time, overtaken a lot of its competitors, and squelched its critics, whose fear has replaced ridicule.

Chapter Review

Multiple Choice

1. Row-level locking is considered superior because

   a) It is faster than table-level locking.

   b) It prevents deadlocks.

   c) It has the highest concurrency.

   d) It is conservative with system resources.

2. What is one of the major features of MyISAM tables?

   a) Speed

   b) Foreign key constraints

   c) Volatility

   d) Resources

3. MyISAM tables are the default storage engine in MySQL.

   a) True

   b) False

4. Storage engine is to table as

   a) Concurrency is to blocking

   b) Latency is to drift

   c) UPDATE is to INSERT

   d) Record is to row

5. Which of the following is *not* supported by the InnoDB storage engine?

   a) Row-level locking

   b) Foreign key constraints

   c) varchar column types

   d) Full-text indexes

6. Blocking is

   a) Typical

   b) A deadlock

   c) Preventable

   d) Federated

7. What is the preferred transaction-safe storage engine in MySQL?

   a) MyISAM

   b) Memory

   c) InnoDB

   d) CSV

8. In practice, you should *never* mix storage-engine types within the same database.

   a) True

   b) False

9. MyISAM tables prevent

   a) Locks

   b) Deadlocks

   c) Lox

   d) Indexing

10. Which storage engine would you choose for an application that has money transactions?

   a) Memory

   b) MyISAM

   c) ISAM

   d) InnoDB

Concepts

1. If you were designing a database as a back end to a web-based application, which storage engine(s) would you choose? Why?

2. If you designed a database as a back end to a site that provides online banking, which storage engine(s) would you use? Why?

6 } Data Manipulation Language

Data Manipulation Language, or DML for short, is the fun part of SQL. DML allows you to query data, put data into tables, update existing data, and remove existing data. The major SQL keywords in this chapter are INSERT, SELECT, UPDATE, and DELETE. If you are a web database programmer, commands derived from these keywords will be your mainstay. DML does the bulk of the work for a web-based user interface. Web users will be manipulating data of one kind or another during a session. This chapter first takes you through the usage of INSERT to put data into a table or tables, then moves through SELECT, where you retrieve data from tables. You get an introduction to UPDATE, which replaces data how and where you specify. Finally, you take a look at the much-dreaded DELETE, which removes data from a table. At the end of the chapter I also introduce you to a few miscellaneous DML commands.

❄ **YOU KNOW WHAT I'M SAYING?**
In teaching the various SQL keywords, I discuss what you are about to do, then give the generic version of the command with options and the SQL command that you actually execute. An example follows:

Create a database (Books) using CREATE.

```
CREATE DATABASE Database_Name
CREATE DATABASE Books
```

INSERT

INSERT allows you to put data into a table or into multiple tables all at once. The data that you insert can come from just about any source, but more than likely it will come from a user community via some interface into the database. Table data entry can occur in many ways, but for now I concentrate on the SQL INSERT method.

Here's the syntax for INSERT:

```
INSERT [LOW_PRIORITY | DELAYED | HIGH_PRIORITY] [IGNORE]
    [INTO] tbl_name [(col_name,...)]
    VALUES ({expr | DEFAULT},...),(...),...
    [ ON DUPLICATE KEY UPDATE col_name=expr, ... ]

INSERT [LOW_PRIORITY | DELAYED | HIGH_PRIORITY] [IGNORE]
    [INTO] tbl_name
    SET col_name={expr | DEFAULT}, ...
    [ ON DUPLICATE KEY UPDATE col_name=expr, ... ]

INSERT [LOW_PRIORITY | HIGH_PRIORITY] [IGNORE]
    [INTO] tbl_name [(col_name,...)]
    SELECT ...
    [ ON DUPLICATE KEY UPDATE col_name=expr, ... ]
```

Before you insert any data into a table, you need to create a table. Create a table called Customers with the following columns: Name, Address, City, State, Zip, and Phone. Keeping it short will help you complete the exercises without a tremendous amount of typing.

Objective

Insert customer data into the Customers table.

```
USE BOOKS;

SHOW TABLES;
```

If you see a table here named Customers, please drop it so that you can start fresh.

```
DROP TABLE Customers;
CREATE TABLE Customers
(ID integer(4) PRIMARY KEY AUTO_INCREMENT,
Name varchar(50), Address varchar(50), City char(30),
State char(2), Zip char(10), Phone char(12));
```

Now insert some data:

```
INSERT INTO Table_Name
(Column1_Name, Column2_Name, Column3_Name, Column4_Name, Column5_Name, etc.)
VALUES ('Value1', 'Value2', 'Value3', 'Value4', 'Value5', 'etc.');
```

```
INSERT INTO Customers
(Name, Address, City, State, Zip, Phone)
VALUES ('Ken Hess', '1313 Mockingbird Lane', 'Austin', 'TX', '76470-1313', '512-555-1234');

INSERT INTO Customers
(Name, Address, City, State, Zip, Phone)
VALUES ('Fred Smith', '3520 S. Memorial Ave.', 'Austin', 'TX', '76471-3520', '512-555-9911');

INSERT INTO Customers
(Name, Address, City, State, Zip, Phone)
VALUES ('Bob Jones', '25222 E. Sheridan Rd.', 'Austin', 'TX', '76472-5222', '512-555-1225');

INSERT INTO Customers
(Name, Address, City, State, Zip, Phone)
VALUES ('Edie Anderson', '7933 N. Peoria Ave.', 'Austin', 'TX', '76475-7933', '512-555-5511');

INSERT INTO Customers
(Name, Address, City, State, Zip, Phone)
VALUES ('Melissa Humboldt', '9811 W. Wilshire Blvd.', 'Austin', 'TX', '76470-9811', '512-555-7432');
```

If the INSERTs were successfully completed, you receive a message, for each one, similar to this: Query OK, 1 row affected (0.00 sec). You don't have to use the fictitious information that I used. You may use any info you want.

> ❋ **SHORTCUT**
> A command buffer in MySQL stores your last few commands. To use this feature after you type in a command such as INSERT, use the ↑ key on your keyboard to scroll back through the commands that you have typed in. You can use the ↑ to repeat the INSERT command you just entered and the ← key to back up over the command and change parts of it. Press the Enter key when done to accept the changes.

Now use your keyboard shortcut instead of typing in each and every INSERT statement. If you received any errors when inserting the data, be sure to check that you are typing the statements exactly as shown.

Let me explain the INSERT statement syntax. The INSERT statements that you used for the Customers table always began with INSERT INTO Table_Name. Since there may be many tables in a database, you must tell INSERT into which table to insert data.

The next part of the statement declares explicitly into which columns you want to enter data. This part of the statement is optional, but I suggest that you always explicitly declare the columns that you want to add data to, as doing so alleviates some problems later. For example, if an additional column is added at a later time without changing the INSERT statement code, your statement will fail. By explicitly declaring the columns, you won't have this problem because only the columns you add data to are affected and the additional columns get a NULL value during the INSERT. If the column definition has a NOT NULL constraint, then no value is entered.

The keyword VALUES comes next in the INSERT statement followed by a list of values that are inserted into the table. The values are comma separated and usually enclosed by single quotation marks, or *ticks*. Numeric values do not have to be enclosed in tick marks unless you put in mathematical operators (-, +, *, /). A phone number is an example: 512-555-1234. If you don't use tick marks, then the mathematical operation of subtraction is carried out on this piece of data. Instead of the phone number 512-555-1234, you end up with the result of the subtraction, which is -1277.

Other INSERT options are defined in subsequent sections.

SET is another way of explicitly declaring columns except that you do it one column at a time. Some find this a more precise way to insert data into a table. Here is an example that fits our table.

Objective

Insert a new record into the Customers table using the SET keyword for David Adams (512-555-5629) at 1217 E. 21st Street, Austin, TX 76477-1217.

```
INSERT INTO Table_Name SET Column1_Name='Value1', Column2_Name='Value2', etc.;


INSERT INTO Customers
SET Name='David Adams', Address='1217 E. 21st Street', City='Austin',
State='TX', Zip='76477-1217', Phone='512-555-5629';
```

You have probably noticed the following modifiers in the INSERT syntax:

* LOW_PRIORITY: Prevents concurrent inserts and waits until no other reads are taking place from the table of interest. This should never be used in a read-heavy environment or with MyISAM tables.

* DELAYED: Puts the INSERTs into a buffer that allows the client to continue, and inserts the data into the table when it is free. Periodic read checks are done to see if read requests for the table's data are being made. If read requests are waiting, the remaining data is held in the buffer until the table is free again.

- ❋ HIGH_PRIORITY: Overrides the effect of starting the MySQL server with low-priority-updates. Also prevents concurrent INSERTs.
- ❋ IGNORE: Prevents any errors from being displayed. If errors do occur, like a duplicate in a column defined as UNIQUE, the data is not inserted but no error message is shown.

The end of this chapter explains the other INSERT features, such as SELECT and ON DUPLICATE KEY UPDATE; I wait because we have yet to discuss SELECT or UPDATE.

SELECT

SELECT allows you to retrieve data from database tables. It is probably the most often used of all the SQL keywords. It is also an often-misused keyword. With the proper SELECT command, you can retrieve records from one table, many tables, individual columns in one or more tables, and records from multiple databases. Dozens of types of SQL SELECT commands are possible. You get exposed to quite a few in this chapter but are encouraged to try as many others on your own as you want. Take a good look at the syntax for SELECT before moving on to the examples:

```
SELECT
    [ALL | DISTINCT | DISTINCTROW ]
        [HIGH_PRIORITY]
        [STRAIGHT_JOIN]
        [SQL_SMALL_RESULT] [SQL_BIG_RESULT] [SQL_BUFFER_RESULT]
        [SQL_CACHE | SQL_NO_CACHE] [SQL_CALC_FOUND_ROWS]
    select_expr, ...
    [INTO OUTFILE 'file_name' export_options
        | INTO DUMPFILE 'file_name']
    [FROM table_references
    [WHERE where_definition]
    [GROUP BY {col_name | expr | position}
        [ASC | DESC], ... [WITH ROLLUP]]
    [HAVING where_definition]
    [ORDER BY {col_name | expr | position}
        [ASC | DESC] , ...]
    [LIMIT {[offset,] row_count | row_count OFFSET offset}]
    [PROCEDURE procedure_name(argument_list)]
    [FOR UPDATE | LOCK IN SHARE MODE]]
```

The syntax for SELECT can get quite complicated in a hurry. In fact, I have seen some very lengthy and complex statements created from multiple JOINs, UNIONs, and subqueries. Most people, however, do not create these from scratch at the CLI. They use query builders that are part of a graphical database-management program. It is far easier to use these utilities when trying to design a report to get exact results, rather than attempting to use the CLI for them. I am using the CLI for teaching purposes in this book because I don't want to be partial about one graphical tool or another and because there is no standard tool to use for MySQL. Most other DBMSs come with their own proprietary tools that are actually part of the product. MySQL gives you the freedom to choose the tool that works best for you and your budget.

First take a look at the data you entered into the Customers table from the section on INSERT. You use some simple syntax at first, then add to the complexity to look at the data in new and interesting ways. You will see that changing how you select the data from a table can greatly enhance and enrich a report.

Objective

Retrieve all of the records from the Customers table.

```
SELECT Column1_Name, Column2_Name, etc. FROM Table_Name;
```

```
SELECT Name, Address, City, Zip, Phone FROM Customers;
```

Result:

Name	Address	City	Zip	Phone
Ken Hess	1313 Mockingbird Lane	Austin	76470-1313	512-555-1234
Fred Smith	3520 S. Memorial Ave.	Austin	76471-3520	512-555-9911
Bob Jones	25222 E. Sheridan Rd.	Austin	76472-5222	512-555-1225
Edie Anderson	7933 N. Peoria Ave.	Austin	76475-7933	512-555-5511
Melissa Humboldt	9811 W. Wilshire Blvd.	Austin	76470-9811	512-555-7432

You may only want a subset of the data in a table and therefore only need to select a few columns. SQL allows you to place the columns in any order when querying.

Objective

Give a report of all customers and phone numbers.

```
SELECT Column1_Name, Column2_Name FROM Table_Name;
```

```
SELECT Name, Phone FROM Customers;
```

Result:

Name	Phone
Ken Hess	512-555-1234
Fred Smith	512-555-9911
Bob Jones	512-555-1225
Edie Anderson	512-555-5511
Melissa Humboldt	512-555-7432

Objective

Give a report of all customers and phone numbers. Please give phone numbers first.

```
SELECT Column2_Name, Column1_Name FROM Table_Name;

SELECT Phone, Name FROM Customers;
```

Result:

Phone	Name
512-555-1234	Ken Hess
512-555-9911	Fred Smith
512-555-1225	Bob Jones
512-555-5511	Edie Anderson
512-555-7432	Melissa Humboldt

As you can clearly see, data can be retrieved in meaningful ways in just about any imaginable fashion. Now that you know how to pick and choose the columns that show up in reports, you may be wondering how to group or sort your data—alphabetically, numerically, or in some other way. Data is inserted into a database in somewhat of a random fashion and needs some ordering to make reports readable and interesting. Sorting your data will make it easier to use and handier to analyze. SQL gives you this ability. Using the SQL clause ORDER BY, you can sort the data alphabetically or numerically. Since I had you create the Customers table with Names instead of First_Name and Last_Name, you are somewhat limited as to the alphabetic ordering by name. You can order alphabetically, but it will be by first name only unless two first names match exactly. I provide some examples and you add more data later to fully illustrate more-advanced concepts.

Objective

Compile a report of customers, phone numbers, and zip codes ordered by zip code.

```
SELECT Column1_Name, Column2_Name FROM Table_Name ORDER BY Column1_Name;
```

```
SELECT Name, Phone, Zip FROM Customers ORDER BY Zip;
```

Result:

Name	Phone	Zip
Ken Hess	512-555-1234	76470-1313
Melissa Humboldt	512-555-7432	76470-9811
Fred Smith	512-555-9911	76471-3520
Bob Jones	512-555-1225	76472-5222
Edie Anderson	512-555-5511	76475-7933

Notice that the Zip column is, in fact, numerically ordered. You may pick any column in the table for the ORDER BY clause whether or not it is included in the query. Try the query again without the Zip column listed in the SELECT but leave it in the ORDER BY clause. You will see that the order is the same.

```
SELECT Name, Phone FROM Customers ORDER BY Zip;
```

Name	Phone
Ken Hess	512-555-1234
Melissa Humboldt	512-555-7432
Fred Smith	512-555-9911
Bob Jones	512-555-1225
Edie Anderson	512-555-5511

The default sort order is usually from the lowest number to the highest number and from a to z for alphabetic sorting. What if you want a descending sort order instead of ascending? You can request specific ordering explicitly with the ASC and DESC keywords in the ORDER BY clause.

Objective

Compile a report of customers, phone numbers, and zip codes in descending order by zip code.

```
SELECT Column1_Name, Column2_Name FROM Table_Name ORDER BY Column1_Name DESC;
```

```
SELECT Name, Phone, Zip FROM Customers ORDER BY Zip DESC;
```

Result:

Name	Phone	Zip
Edie Anderson	512-555-5511	76475-7933
Bob Jones	512-555-1225	76472-5222
Fred Smith	512-555-9911	76471-3520
Melissa Humboldt	512-555-7432	76470-9811
Ken Hess	512-555-1234	76470-1313

This query result is in reverse order from the previous two. Can you see that the zip codes are in descending sort order? Though this example may seem trivial, there are times when this type of sorting is very valuable. If you are sorting a list of choices for a pull-down list box on a web page, you may want them listed in descending numeric order. Each time I sort data for any kind of list for presentation, I always explicitly choose my sort order. To me, it is important for users to get used to a particular way that a site functions; sorting gives me, and them, that consistency.

Another type of sorting that can be useful is GROUP BY. The GROUP BY clause is normally used in conjunction with the functions COUNT, SUM, MIN, and MAX. Before demonstrating GROUP BY, you need to add more data to your Customers table. I added two more records to my table:

```
INSERT INTO Customers (Name, Address, City, State, Zip, Phone) VALUES
('Maria Klester', '985 W. Hickory', 'Manchaca', 'TX', '76499-9851',
'512-555-3456');
```

```
INSERT INTO Customers (Name, Address, City, State, Zip, Phone) VALUES ('Jon
Benner', 'Rural Route 6', 'Buda', 'TX', '76589-0006', '512-555-6789');
```

These entries will add some diversity for the next few queries. The following example is a standard type of demographic query.

Objective

Produce a report that gives the number of customers from each city.

```
SELECT Column_Name, COUNT(Column_Name) FROM Table_Name GROUP BY Column_Name;

SELECT City, COUNT(City) AS Number FROM Customers GROUP BY City;
```

Result:

City	Number
Austin	5
Buda	1
Manchaca	1

I sneaked in something. I used AS to rename a column to something more meaningful. It is true that I could have left the query as is: SELECT City, COUNT(City) FROM Customers GROUP BY City; but this may not be as legible to a non-database person so you can temporarily rename a column in a query with the keyword AS. You may also rename the other column in the query as well. In fact, you may rename every column in a query with AS to make the report more meaningful or to mask your column names from the population at large.

You now know how many customers you have from each city in the table, but how many total customers do you have? Well, for this example it is easy, but it would be more difficult and time-consuming to count hundreds or thousands of customers all by hand. Fortunately, SQL has a way to get at this information very easily. It is similar to the query where you used COUNT. This time you will use the famous COUNT(*) function. The asterisk is a *wildcard* character that means everything or all. COUNT(*) returns the number of rows retrieved even if the values are NULL. MyISAM tables return this value very quickly from a single table with no WHERE clauses or additionally queried columns. The number of rows is a stored value in MyISAM tables.

Objective

Find the total number of customers.

```
SELECT COUNT(*) FROM Table_Name;

SELECT COUNT(*) FROM Customers;
```

The answer should be 7.

Another interesting demographic query is "How diverse is your customer base?" For you, *diversity* means from how many different cities your customers come. In other words, is your customer base regional, statewide, nationwide, or worldwide? For this example, I define diversity as the number of different cities that your customers represent since all of the cities are in Texas.

Objective

Generate a report to show how many different cities are represented by your customers.

```
SELECT COUNT(DISTINCT Column_Name) FROM Table_Name;

SELECT COUNT(DISTINCT City) FROM Customers;
```

The answer is 3. Austin, Manchaca, and Buda are the three cities represented by your customer base. You obviously need to revise the marketing plan for your business.

When you have hundreds, thousands, or hundreds of thousands of records, you must narrow your results to avoid producing hundreds of pages in a report—unless that is your goal. The WHERE clause is a great tool for narrowing search results. Using WHERE generally amounts to setting a strict value for a column query. An example taken from your Customers table would be WHERE City='Austin'. This filters through the records and only returns rows that have Austin in the City column. If you are trying to send a mass mailing to everyone in Austin for a special promotion, it is easy to generate your list with this kind of filter.

Objective

Generate a list of all customers in Austin, Texas for a direct mail campaign.

```
SELECT Column1_Name, Column2_Name, etc. FROM Table_Name WHERE
Column1_Name='Value1';

SELECT Name, Address, City, State, Zip FROM Customers WHERE City = 'Austin';
```

Result:

Name	Address	City	State	Zip
Ken Hess	1313 Mockingbird Lane	Austin	TX	76470-1313
Fred Smith	3520 S. Memorial Ave.	Austin	TX	76471-3520
Bob Jones	25222 E. Sheridan Rd.	Austin	TX	76472-5222
Edie Anderson	7933 N. Peoria Ave.	Austin	TX	76475-7933
Melissa Humboldt	9811 W. Wilshire Blvd.	Austin	TX	76470-9811

Now that you have a list of all of your Austin customers, it is easy to generate your mailing labels for the marketing campaign.

At times, you may want to exclude data from a search. You can easily do this with a query like this one with one subtle difference—the ! (bang) operator, which negates the operation. An example illustrates.

Objective

Produce a report of all customers who are not in Austin.

```
SELECT Column1_Name, Column2_Name, etc. FROM Table_Name WHERE
Column1_Name='Value1';
```

```
SELECT Name, Address, City, State, Zip FROM Customers WHERE City != 'Austin';
```

Result:

Name	Address	City	State	Zip
Maria Klester	985 W. Hickory	Manchaca	TX	76499-9851
Jon Benner	Rural Route 6	Buda	TX	76589-0006

What if your marketing campaign is to cover multiple cities with a direct mailing? You can now search using zip codes and actually specify a range of zip codes to include. You may use ranges for numeric values of any kind—not just zip codes.

Objective

Produce a mailing list of all customers in or within the Austin metropolitan area.

The easiest way to do this, you surmise, is to use the zip code data in your database. You can specify a range of numbers for the zip codes knowing that zip codes are usually very similar for metro areas. The range is specified in the WHERE clause with the keyword BETWEEN, the specific low and high values, and the keyword AND. Your range is 76470 to 76500, which gives you a WHERE clause that looks like this: WHERE Zip BETWEEN '76470' AND '76500'. This takes in Austin and a surrounding area within about 10 miles. (These are not the actual zip codes for Austin, Texas or the surrounding areas. I am taking artistic license so people won't receive any errant mail inspired from reading this book.)

```
SELECT Column1_Name, Column2_Name, etc. FROM Table_Name WHERE Column2_Name
BETWEEN 'Value1' AND 'Value2';
```

```
SELECT Name, Address, City, State, Zip FROM Customers WHERE Zip BETWEEN
'76470' AND '76500';
```

Result:

Name	Address	City	State	Zip
Ken Hess	1313 Mockingbird Lane	Austin	TX	76470-1313
Fred Smith	3520 S. Memorial Ave.	Austin	TX	76471-3520
Bob Jones	25222 E. Sheridan Rd.	Austin	TX	76472-5222
Edie Anderson	7933 N. Peoria Ave.	Austin	TX	76475-7933
Melissa Humboldt	9811 W. Wilshire Blvd.	Austin	TX	76470-9811
Maria Klester	985 W. Hickory	Manchaca	TX	76499-9851

My apologies to the customers from Buda, but you are too far away for this direct mailing.

You need to add more data to your Customers table for the next few examples. I am making these entries in my table:

```
INSERT INTO Customers (Name, Address, City, State, Zip, Phone) VALUES ('Darla
Shamberg', '151 E. Pine St.', 'Albany', 'TX', '77599-0151', '915-555-9999');
```

```
INSERT INTO Customers (Name, Address, City, State, Zip, Phone) VALUES ('Lester
Baggett', '888 Peach St.', 'Abilene', 'TX', '76901-0888', '915-555-1349');
```

You need to look up a particular customer who ordered a book from you that is no longer in print, but you can't remember her name. You know that she doesn't live in Austin but the name of the city begins with an A. If you have thousands of entries, hundreds of which beginning with the letter A, you would spend a great deal of time poring over line after line to find one record. There are several ways to do a search like this; here we do it in a less-than-elegant, but effective, way.

You have the power of wildcards at your disposal. Using a wildcard in SQL is much like using a wildcard at the command line in the operating system, except you use % instead of *. Most often in SQL, wildcards are used in WHERE clauses with the keyword LIKE. A sample WHERE clause with a wildcard search looks like this: WHERE City LIKE 'b%'. This search retrieves all rows where the city name begins with the letter B. The search is not case sensitive, so any city name that begins with the letter B will be retrieved whether or not you capitalize it in the search. Similarly, if you want to search for any city with a B anywhere in the name, use WHERE City LIKE '%b%'.

Objective

Find all customers who live in a city that begins with the letter B.

```
SELECT Column1_Name, Column2_Name, etc. FROM Table_Name WHERE Column2_Name
LIKE '[character or string]%';
```

```
SELECT Name, Address, City, State, Zip FROM Customers WHERE City LIKE 'b%';
```

Result:

Name	Address	City	State	Zip
Jon Benner	Rural Route 6	Buda	TX	76589-0006

Objective

Produce a list of customers who live in cities with a B in the city name.

```
SELECT Column1_Name, Column2_Name, etc. FROM Table_Name WHERE Column2_Name
LIKE '%[character or string]%';
```

```
SELECT Name, Address, City, State, Zip FROM Customers WHERE City LIKE '%b%';
```

Result:

Name	Address	City	State	Zip
Jon Benner	Rural Route 6	Buda	TX	76589-0006
Darla Shamberg	151 E. Pine St.	Albany	TX	77599-0151
Lester Baggett	888 Peach St.	Abilene	TX	76901-0888

The query retrieved all cities with a B in the name, regardless of position within the name.

 IN CASE OF SENSITIVITY
Some DBMSs, like Oracle, are case sensitive when it comes to wildcard searches. You have to use 'B%' to get all of the cities that begin with the letter B. Read the documentation for your particular DBMS to determine whether wildcard searches are case sensitive.

In some cases, you can apply mathematical operators to character or string data. For instance, if you want all of the customers from places named alphabetically before Buda, write the WHERE clause to exclude anything above Buda by specifying the < operator. This may seem a bit esoteric, but you can apply the same logic to names or zip codes. To illustrate the concept of the <, >, and = operators and their effect on query results, the next few examples demonstrate using the operators with character and numeric data.

Objective

Produce a list of customers outside the greater Austin area (764XX-765XX).

```
SELECT Column1_Name, Column2_Name, etc. FROM Table_Name WHERE Column2_Name > '[number or string]';
```

```
SELECT Name, Address, City, State, Zip FROM Customers WHERE Zip > '76600';
```

Result:

Name	Address	City	State	Zip
Darla Shamberg	151 E. Pine St.	Albany	TX	77599-0151
Lester Baggett	888 Peach St.	Abilene	TX	76901-0888

Objective

Produce a list of customers who live in cities with names that come before Austin alphabetically.

```
SELECT Column1_Name, Column2_Name, etc. FROM Table_Name WHERE Column2_Name < '[number or string]';
```

```
SELECT Name, Address, City, State, Zip FROM Customers WHERE City < 'Austin';
```

Result:

Name	Address	City	State	Zip
Darla Shamberg	151 E. Pine St.	Albany	TX	77599-0151
Lester Baggett	888 Peach St.	Abilene	TX	76901-0888

Adding the = operator to the previous query yields different results.

Objective

Create a report that includes customers from Austin and all cities that precede it alphabetically.

```
SELECT Column1_Name, Column2_Name, etc. FROM Table_Name WHERE Column2_Name <= '[number or string]';
```

```
SELECT Name, Address, City, State, Zip FROM Customers WHERE City <= 'Austin';
```

Result:

Name	Address	City	State	Zip
Ken Hess	1313 Mockingbird Lane	Austin	TX	76470-1313
Fred Smith	3520 S. Memorial Ave.	Austin	TX	76471-3520
Bob Jones	25222 E. Sheridan Rd.	Austin	TX	76472-5222
Edie Anderson	7933 N. Peoria Ave.	Austin	TX	76475-7933
Melissa Humboldt	9811 W. Wilshire Blvd.	Austin	TX	76470-9811
Darla Shamberg	151 E. Pine St.	Albany	TX	77599-0151
Lester Baggett	888 Peach St.	Abilene	TX	76901-0888

Another way to get these same results:

```
SELECT Column1_Name, Column2_Name, etc. FROM Table_Name WHERE Column2_Name >= '[number or string]'
AND <= '[number or string];
```

```
SELECT Name, Address, City, State, Zip FROM Customers WHERE City >= 'Abilene' AND City <= 'Buda';
```

Result:

Name	Address	City	State	Zip
Ken Hess	1313 Mockingbird Lane	Austin	TX	76470-1313
Fred Smith	3520 S. Memorial Ave.	Austin	TX	76471-3520
Bob Jones	25222 E. Sheridan Rd.	Austin	TX	76472-5222
Edie Anderson	7933 N. Peoria Ave.	Austin	TX	76475-7933
Melissa Humboldt	9811 W. Wilshire Blvd.	Austin	TX	76470-9811
Jon Benner	Rural Route 6	Buda	TX	76589-0006
Darla Shamberg	151 E. Pine St.	Albany	TX	77599-0151
Lester Baggett	888 Peach St.	Abilene	TX	76901-0888

These examples give a good introduction to the depth of the SELECT keyword and its use for retrieving data. I am going to save some of the other SELECT intricacies for Chapter 8, which examines advanced queries.

UPDATE

UPDATE is the SQL keyword that allows you to replace parts (or all) of a record in a table or tables. This is useful for either correcting mistakes made when data is entered or for refreshing outdated data. UPDATE is easy to use but can be quite devastating to your data if mistakes are made in the syntax. The UPDATE syntax for single table and multiple tables is shown here:

Single-table syntax:

```
UPDATE [LOW_PRIORITY] [IGNORE] tbl_name
    SET col_name1=expr1 [, col_name2=expr2 ...]
    [WHERE where_definition]
    [ORDER BY ...]
    [LIMIT row_count]
```

Multiple-table syntax:

```
UPDATE [LOW_PRIORITY] [IGNORE] table_references
    SET col_name1=expr1 [, col_name2=expr2 ...]
    [WHERE where_definition]
```

Though the syntax shows the WHERE clause to be optional, I would have to say that it is not. I show you an example later that proves my point quite clearly. In general, the syntax for UPDATE is as follows:

```
UPDATE Table_Name SET Column1_Name = 'Value1', Column2_Name = 'Value2', etc.
WHERE ColumnX_Name = 'ValueX';
```

Objective

Someone entered the data for Fred Smith and Bob Jones incorrectly into the Customers table. Fred Smith lives in Georgetown, Texas 76552-3520 and Bob Jones lives in Round Rock, Texas 76577-5222. Please fix these errors.

First, you need to correct the info for Fred Smith, so you need to get his current information.

```
SELECT Name, Address, City, State, Zip FROM Customers WHERE Name LIKE '%Smith';
```

Result:

Name	Address	City	State	Zip
Fred Smith	3520 S. Memorial Ave.	Austin	TX	76471-3520

Now update the information with the correct values:

```
UPDATE Table_Name SET Column1_Name = 'Value1', Column2_Name = 'Value2', etc. WHERE ColumnX_Name = 'ValueX';

UPDATE Customers SET City = 'Georgetown', Zip = '76552-3520' WHERE Name = 'Fred Smith';
```

Take a look at your updated data:

```
SELECT Name, Address, City, State, Zip FROM Customers WHERE Name LIKE '%Smith';
```

Result:

Name	Address	City	State	Zip
Fred Smith	3520 S. Memorial Ave.	Georgetown	TX	76552-3520

The record has been successfully updated. Now to take care of Mr. Jones:

```
SELECT Name, Address, City, State, Zip FROM Customers WHERE Name LIKE '%Jones';
```

Result:

Name	Address	City	State	Zip
Bob Jones	25222 E. Sheridan Rd.	Austin	TX	76472-5222

```
UPDATE Table_Name SET Column1_Name = 'Value1', Column2_Name = 'Value2', etc. WHERE ColumnX_Name = 'ValueX';

UPDATE Customers SET City = 'Round Rock', Zip = '76577-5222' WHERE Name = 'Bob Jones';

SELECT Name, Address, City, State, Zip FROM Customers WHERE Name LIKE '%Jones';
```

Result:

Name	Address	City	State	Zip
Bob Jones	25222 E. Sheridan Rd.	Round Rock	TX	76577-5222

You have successfully updated the information that was erroneously entered into the Customers table.

Objective

Update information for a customer whose telephone number has changed. Darla Shamberg sent an email saying that she has a new phone number. It is 915-555-9900.

Update Ms. Shamberg's phone number with the new one:

```
SELECT Name, Address, City, Zip, Phone FROM Customers WHERE Name LIKE '%Shamberg';
```

Result:

Name	Address	City	Zip	Phone
Darla Shamberg	151 E. Pine St.	Albany	77599-0151	915-555-9999

```
UPDATE Table_Name SET Column1_Name = 'Value1', Column2_Name = 'Value2', etc.
WHERE ColumnX_Name = 'ValueX';

UPDATE Customers SET Phone ='915-555-9900';
```

Now take a look at the data to be sure everything went as planned:

```
SELECT Name, Phone FROM Customers;
```

Result:

Name	Phone
Ken Hess	915-555-9900
Fred Smith	915-555-9900
Bob Jones	915-555-9900
Edie Anderson	915-555-9900
Melissa Humboldt	915-555-9900
Maria Klester	915-555-9900
Jon Benner	915-555-9900
Darla Shamberg	915-555-9900
Lester Baggett	915-555-9900

I hope you didn't leave off the WHERE clause like I did. If you put in the WHERE clause, give yourself a pat on the back. If not, then you followed instructions but have clobbered your data in the Customers table. Imagine doing this to thousands of records. You will have to go to your backups and potentially lose all of today's work. There are ways to merge your last backup with the new data from today, but you will still lose the data that has been overwritten from today since you don't have a backup of it.

The UPDATE options of LOW_PRIORITY and IGNORE have the same effect for UPDATE as they do for SELECT. The ORDER BY clause can update rows in a specific order. The LIMIT clause updates up to the number of rows specified that also satisfy the WHERE clause.

DELETE

DELETE is one of those special SQL keywords that almost needs no explanation, since it does what it says it does: removes data from a table or from multiple tables irreversibly. DELETE is also as you suspect—even more dangerous than our persnickety friend UPDATE. By not specifying the WHERE clause, you can delete your entire table's data. If you don't trust that statement, feel free to enter the following command:

```
DELETE FROM Customers;
```

This deletes all of the data from your Customers table. If you did enter the command, you probably noticed that there was no interactive response like, "Are you sure?" The DBMS assumes that you want to perform the action.

Take a look at the DELETE syntax:

Single-table syntax:

```
DELETE [LOW_PRIORITY] [QUICK] [IGNORE] FROM tbl_name
    [WHERE where_definition]
    [ORDER BY ...]
    [LIMIT row_count]
```

Multiple-table syntax:

```
DELETE [LOW_PRIORITY] [QUICK] [IGNORE]
    tbl_name[.*] [, tbl_name[.*] ...]
    FROM table_references
    [WHERE where_definition]

DELETE [LOW_PRIORITY] [QUICK] [IGNORE]
    FROM tbl_name[.*] [, tbl_name[.*] ...]
    USING table_references
    [WHERE where_definition]
```

By now you are probably used to looking at SQL command syntax and can generalize that some options, like IGNORE, are common to many other commands and that they have the same universal effect. I want you to get some practice using DELETE, though it may seem intuitively obvious from its similarity to UPDATE.

Create a table and put some data into it for the exercises using DELETE. I will use something simple to demonstrate its use:

```
CREATE TABLE Tempdata (ID integer(4) PRIMARY KEY AUTO_INCREMENT, Name char
(50), City char(50));

INSERT INTO Tempdata (Name, City) VALUES ('Ken', 'Austin');
```

Let's speed up this data entry a bit:

```
INSERT INTO Tempdata (Name, City) VALUES ('Fred', 'Round Rock'), ('Bob',
'Georgetown'), ('Ellen', 'San Marcos'), ('Sheila', 'Wimberley');
```

This now gives us enough data to work with effectively:

```
SELECT Name, City FROM Tempdata;
```

Result:

Name	City
Ken	Austin
Fred	Round Rock
Bob	Georgetown
Ellen	San Marcos
Sheila	Wimberley

Objective

Remove Ken from the Tempdata table.

```
DELETE FROM Table_Name WHERE Column1_Name = 'Value1';

DELETE FROM Tempdata WHERE Name = 'Ken';

SELECT Name, City FROM Tempdata;
```

Result:

Name	City
Fred	Round Rock
Bob	Georgetown
Ellen	San Marcos
Sheila	Wimberley

Yes, you successfully deleted me from your table. Now I want you to use a wildcard in the WHERE clause to delete data.

Objective

Remove all users whose names have an E in them.

```
DELETE FROM Table_Name WHERE Name LIKE '%[character or string]%';

DELETE FROM Tempdata WHERE Name LIKE '%e%';

SELECT Name, City FROM Tempdata;
```

Result:

Name	City
Bob	Georgetown

There is no great mystery surrounding DELETE, but it has the downside of being easy to misuse. Caution is always recommended for intrusive commands like UPDATE and DELETE. I recommend against using the QUICK keyword for deletes, as it can leave empty space in a table. It usually isn't necessary anyway, as deleting data in MyISAM tables is very fast.

Miscellaneous Data-Manipulation Commands

These miscellaneous commands are SQL keywords that fit under DML but don't really fit in anywhere else. The first, TRUNCATE, is an immensely useful command for those who like to do things quickly, and REPLACE is the second and less utilized.

TRUNCATE

TRUNCATE is a keyword that allows you to empty a table. The difference between TRUNCATE and DELETE FROM Table_Name is that TRUNCATE resets the AUTO_INCREMENT field (if any field is set to AUTO_INCREMENT). In other words, when you empty a table with DELETE, the AUTO_INCREMENT number is not reset to 1. TRUNCATE does reset the AUTO_INCREMENT to 1. The reason this happens is that TRUNCATE drops and recreates the table which is why TRUNCATE is so fast. It takes far less time to drop and recreate a table than to delete each row.

```
TRUNCATE [TABLE] Table_Name;
```

REPLACE

REPLACE works exactly like INSERT, except that if an old record has the same value as a new record for a PRIMARY KEY or a UNIQUE index, the old record is deleted before the new record is inserted. Note that unless the table has a PRIMARY KEY or UNIQUE index, using a REPLACE statement becomes equivalent to INSERT, because there is no index to determine whether a new row duplicates another.

```
REPLACE [LOW_PRIORITY | DELAYED]
    [INTO] tbl_name [(col_name,...)]
    VALUES ({expr | DEFAULT},...),(...),...

REPLACE [LOW_PRIORITY | DELAYED]
    [INTO] tbl_name
    SET col_name={expr | DEFAULT}, ...
```

```
REPLACE [LOW_PRIORITY | DELAYED]
    [INTO] tbl_name [(col_name,...)]
    SELECT ...
```

Summary

Data manipulation is what most people think of when considering what a DBA does with SQL. Selecting, inserting, updating, and deleting data are all necessary functions of web applications as well. You have learned the highs (using DML) and lows (accidentally removing data) of DML in this chapter. You learned that WHERE clauses are universal in nature: A WHERE clause that works in a SELECT statement will also work in a DELETE or an UPDATE statement. The Data Definition Language plus the Data Manipulation Language give you a vast repertoire of SQL keywords to use when administering a database. DBAs use the same commands for every size and brand of DBMS. The syntax has some differences, but the basic functionality is universal.

Chapter Review

Multiple Choice

1. Which of the following is the correct syntax for inserting data into a table?

   a) INSERT 'Value1' INTO Table_Name ('Column_Name');

   b) INSERT INTO Table_Name (Column1_Name, Column2_Name) VALUES ('Value1', 'Value2');

   c) INSERT INTO Table_Name (Column1_Name, Column2_Name) ('Value1', 'Value2');

   d) INSERT INTO Table_Name Column1_Name, Column2_Name VALUES 'Value1', 'Value2';

2. TRUNCATE performs which function?

   a) It empties a table of all its data.

   b) It shortens a table.

   c) It deletes a table.

   d) It empties the table and then reconstructs it and its data.

3. What happens if you submit the following SQL statement?
   DELETE FROM TABLE Table_Name;

   a) All data is deleted from the table.

   b) The table is reconstructed.

   c) The table is optimized.

   d) Nothing. The syntax is incorrect.

4. What happens if you submit the following SQL statement?
   UPDATE Table_Name SET Column_Name = 'Value';

   a) All rows are updated with the new value.

   b) The column Column_Name is deleted.

   c) Only one row of data is updated.

   d) Nothing. The syntax is incorrect.

5. It is possible to insert multiple rows of data at once in a single SQL statement.

   a) True

   b) False

6. REPLACE behaves like which keyword when no PRIMARY KEY or UNIQUE index exists in a table?

   a) DELETE

   b) UPDATE

   c) INSERT

   d) SELECT

7. What will the following statement do?
   INSERT INTO Cust_Info (Name, Phone) VALUES ('Ken', '512-555-1234'), ('Bob', '512-555-6789'), ('Fred', '512-555-8899');

   a) One row of data is inserted into Cust_Info.

   b) Three rows of data are inserted into Cust_Info.

   c) An error occurs.

   d) Nothing. It is the incorrect syntax.

8. The following WHERE clause is considered to be what?
   WHERE City LIKE 'Ab%'

   a) Incorrect.

   b) Malformed.

   c) Temporary.

   d) Universal.

9. The IGNORE keyword does what?

   a) Ignores the SQL statement.

   b) Suppresses errors.

   c) Ignores any syntax problems.

   d) Suppresses the action.

10. Why does TRUNCATE reset the AUTO_INCREMENT value?

    a) The table is dropped and recreated.

    b) AUTO_INCREMENT is not reset.

    c) TRUNCATE is mapped to an ALTER TABLE statement.

    d) The table is re-sorted to reset the AUTO_INCREMENT value.

Concepts

1. Explain why most of the interaction in a database occurs via the Data Manipulation Language.

2. If you were an application developer, explain what you would do to ensure that mistakes like those demonstrated in the DELETE section (when all your data was removed by not specifying a WHERE clause) do not occur.

 # Data Control Language

Data Control Language, or *DCL,* has two main components: Access Control and Transaction Control. *Access Control* is sometimes referred to as *internal security* because it has to do with access within the database itself. In fact, sometimes the first part of this chapter is included in chapters on security and not split out as part of the language. I prefer to maintain consistency and present it as part of one of the SQL sublanguages. *Transaction Control* has to do with transactional processing within the database. It is somewhat related to security because committing (or not committing) data to a database is, and should be, related to access. Some authors split transactions into a separate chapter. I feel that the information provided here will give you enough detail into transactions that, if needed or desired, one may continue an in-depth study of them in an advanced text on the subject.

The DCL's individual components are no more or less difficult than any other aspect of SQL. The concepts are easy to grasp but the command syntax can get somewhat complicated. Even seasoned DBAs sometimes make mistakes with these commands at the CLI level. Graphical tools have taken away some of the sting (and aftermath) that is experienced by not knowing the exact syntax for the more-complex Access Control commands. I am attempting to take away some of the CLI's sting by presenting this material in a clear and concise way. There are plenty of practice exercises and the Chapter Review also helps drive home some of the subtleties of this very important aspect of SQL. As in previous chapters, the syntax reference blocks are given as your best guide to the syntax of a keyword's use.

Access Control

MySQL has an advanced but non-standard security and privilege system. Its system, in a generic way, can be described in the following way: Users are authenticated from a specific host and are able to use database resources based upon granted privileges. You may have noticed the *specific host* part of the description. MySQL considers the host and the user account when granting authorization to database resources. This is a significant security enhancement because it implies that a particular user will consistently connect from a specific host or network. It also implies that you could set up two different users with the same username but with different privileges based upon the originating host. For instance, if Bob Jones has the username bobj at work, he can also connect with the username bobj from home, but with very different privileges. This has significant implications for me because this means that I can set up users to have read-only (SELECT) privileges from hosts outside of our internal network and change privileges (SELECT, INSERT, UPDATE, DELETE) from inside our network.

GRANT

GRANT allows the DBA to bestow database privileges at several levels. The different levels and their descriptions are given in Table 7.1.

Table 7.1   Database Privilege Levels

Level	Description	MySQL Table
Global	All databases on a server	mysql.user
Database	All objects in a database	mysql.db and mysql.host
Table	All columns in a table	mysql.tables_priv
Column	Single column in a table	mysql.columns_priv
Routine	Stored routines	mysql.procs_priv

Since the sections on GRANT and REVOKE are security related, go ahead and issue some familiar commands to help secure your MySQL Server. By default, MySQL allows an anonymous user to connect from the localhost and possibly from remote hosts. It is a bit of a security flaw to allow these to remain. They are typically used for testing and have remained, though their actual use is limited. Your best bet is to remove them before allowing your database to go into production mode.

Objective

Remove anonymous users from the user table.

```
SELECT Host, User FROM mysql.user WHERE User = ' ';
```

You should see the following (or similar):

```
+-----------+------+
| Host      | User |
+-----------+------+
| localhost |      |
+-----------+------+
```

This response means that you have an anonymous user account (no user name) that can access your MySQL server from the localhost. Depending on your installation, you may see more than one entry here. You need to remove the anonymous account.

```
DELETE FROM mysql.user WHERE User = ' ';
```

The anonymous account is now deleted.

```
FLUSH PRIVILEGES;
```

The FLUSH PRIVILEGES command should always be run after making any INSERT, UPDATE, or DELETE changes to the user table so your changes take immediate effect.

```
GRANT priv_type [(column_list)] [, priv_type [(column_list)]] ...
    ON [object_type] {tbl_name | * | *.* | db_name.*}
    TO user [IDENTIFIED BY [PASSWORD] 'password']
        [, user [IDENTIFIED BY [PASSWORD] 'password']] ...
    [REQUIRE
        NONE |
        [{SSL| X509}]
        [CIPHER 'cipher' [AND]]
        [ISSUER 'issuer' [AND]]
        [SUBJECT 'subject']]
    [WITH with_option [with_option] ...]
object_type =
    TABLE
    | FUNCTION
    | PROCEDURE
with_option =
    GRANT OPTION
    | MAX_QUERIES_PER_HOUR count
    | MAX_UPDATES_PER_HOUR count
    | MAX_CONNECTIONS_PER_HOUR count
    | MAX_USER_CONNECTIONS count
```

From the syntax block, the priv_type can be any of the following shown in Table 7.2.

Table 7.2 Privilege Types (priv_type)

Privilege (GRANT/REVOKE)	Meaning
ALL [PRIVILEGES]	Sets all simple privileges except GRANT OPTION.
ALTER	Allows use of ALTER TABLE.
ALTER ROUTINE	Alters or drops stored routines.
CREATE	Allows use of CREATE TABLE.
CREATE ROUTINE	Creates stored routines.
CREATE TEMPORARY TABLES	Allows use of CREATE TEMPORARY TABLE.
CREATE USER	Allows use of CREATE USER, DROP USER, RENAME USER, and REVOKE ALL PRIVILEGES.
CREATE VIEW	Allows use of CREATE VIEW.
DELETE	Allows use of DELETE.
DROP	Allows use of DROP TABLE.
EXECUTE	Allows the user to run stored routines.
FILE	Allows use of SELECT ... INTO OUTFILE and LOAD DATA INFILE.
INDEX	Allows use of CREATE INDEX and DROP INDEX.
INSERT	Allows use of INSERT.
LOCK TABLES	Allows use of LOCK TABLES on tables for which you have the SELECT privilege.
PROCESS	Allows use of SHOW FULL PROCESSLIST.
REFERENCES	Not implemented.
RELOAD	Allows use of FLUSH.
REPLICATION CLIENT	Allows the user to ask where slave or master servers are.
REPLICATION SLAVE	Needed for replication slaves (to read binary log events from the master).
SELECT	Allows use of SELECT.
SHOW DATABASES	Shows all databases.
SHOW VIEW	Allows use of SHOW CREATE VIEW.
SHUTDOWN	Allows use of mysqladmin shutdown.
SUPER	Allows use of CHANGE MASTER, KILL, PURGE MASTER LOGS, and SET GLOBAL statements, the mysqladmin debug command; allows you to connect (once) even if max_connections is reached.
UPDATE	Allows use of UPDATE.
USAGE	Synonym for "no privileges."
GRANT OPTION	Allows privileges to be granted.

- ✳ Administrative privileges that can only be granted globally: FILE, PROCESS, RELOAD, REPLICATION CLIENT, REPLICATION SLAVE, SHOW DATABASES, SHUTDOWN, and SUPER.

- ✳ Privilege types (priv_type) that can be granted on a table: SELECT, INSERT, UPDATE, DELETE, CREATE, DROP, GRANT OPTION, INDEX, and ALTER.

- ✳ Privilege types (priv_type) that can be specified for a column: SELECT, INSERT, UPDATE, DELETE, CREATE, DROP, GRANT OPTION, INDEX, and ALTER.

GRANT is a very efficient way to create a user, set the user's password, and give privileges with a single statement. Many authors, at this point, demonstrate how to grant global privileges on all databases. I also do this, but with a word of warning first: It is highly unlikely that you will ever need to create such a user because you are already logging in as that user. To grant all privileges on all databases to any user is a bad idea. Having said this, here is how you would do it if you are so inclined:

```
GRANT ALL PRIVILEGES ON *.* TO 'username'@'localhost' IDENTIFIED BY
'password';
```

Though this is a poor example of something you should do as a DBA, the example does provide you with some valuable information about the command in general. First, you should ignore the ALL PRIVILEGES part of the statement. This should be used rarely, if ever. You should replace ALL PRIVILEGES with the privileges you wish to explicitly grant to the user. The ON part of the statement identifies the database or the table that you wish to grant privileges on. You do not have to explicitly declare the database name if you issued the command use Database_Name; prior to issuing the GRANT. Replace the first asterisk with the database name followed by the dot and then the table name. The user's identity is qualified by a username and a hostname where username is enclosed in single quotes, or ticks, followed by the @ symbol and finally the hostname where the user is allowed to connect from. IDENTIFIED BY is SQL for specifying a password. The password is enclosed in ticks. Using GRANT does two other things for you as well: It encrypts the password automatically without having to issue the Password( ) function and it alleviates the need to use FLUSH PRIVILEGES to have the server re-read the grant tables.

Objective

Create a new user account for Bob Jones for local read-only access for the Customers table.

Before jumping right into this one, you need to examine the request more closely to figure out what is being asked. As you gain experience, and see a request like this and it will become second nature, so such close scrutiny will not be necessary in the future. You need to follow some convention for creating usernames and the one that comes to mind is the standard Unix convention of first letter of the first name and the first seven letters of the last name. Bob Jones' username will be bjones. Bob needs simple read-only access to the Customers table, so he only needs the SELECT privilege; he is restricted from updating, inserting, or deleting data. You should have all of the information you need to complete the task.

```
GRANT SELECT ON Books.Customers TO 'bjones'@'localhost' IDENTIFIED BY
'password';
```

Ordinarily, you would choose a better password for Bob—one that meets your corporate standard for passwords. The following is an alternate way to complete the same task:

```
USE Books;

GRANT SELECT ON Customers TO 'bjones'@'localhost' IDENTIFIED BY 'password';
```

Note that in the first example I declared the Books database explicitly, but in the second I chose to first select the database and then issue the command only specifying the table. Unless you specify the database explicitly in the GRANT statement, the server will assume the currently selected database is the one for which you are granting privileges.

Now any good DBA will log out as the administrative user and log in as the just-created user to test the account and its privileges:

```
mysql> exit
# mysql -ubjones -ppassword Books
mysql> SHOW GRANTS;
+-------------------------------------------------------------------------+
| Grants for bjones@localhost                                             |
+-------------------------------------------------------------------------+
| GRANT USAGE ON *.* TO 'bjones'@'localhost' IDENTIFIED BY PASSWORD
'*2470C0C06D
| GRANT SELECT ON 'Books'.'Customers' TO 'bjones'@'localhost'             |
+-------------------------------------------------------------------------+
```

The SHOW GRANTS command I sneaked in shows the permissions for the user currently logged in. The command returns the username, the encrypted password, and the GRANT command used to grant privileges. You may have noticed that you did not enter the GRANT USAGE command shown first in the list. The database automatically performs this operation to allow access to the MySQL Server, but grants no privileges at the global level. USAGE, as shown in Table 7.2, is the synonym for "no privileges."

You may also notice that the IDENTIFIED BY PASSWORD clause is included in the first command but not in the second. This is a GRANT keyword design feature. Once you enter a command, you don't have to repeat certain parts of it. You would not have to repeat the password part of the command because you are entering the same username. For instance, if you log out as Bob Jones and log in again as root, you can add some privileges to Bob's account.

```
GRANT INSERT ON Books.Customers TO 'bjones'@'localhost';
```

The command should have been accepted without error. Log out as root and log in again as Bob.

```
SHOW GRANTS;
```

```
+----------------------------------------------------------------------------
| Grants for bjones@localhost
+----------------------------------------------------------------------------
| GRANT USAGE ON *.* TO 'bjones'@'localhost' IDENTIFIED BY PASSWORD
'*2470C0C06D
| GRANT SELECT, INSERT ON 'Books'.'Customers' TO 'bjones'@'localhost'
+----------------------------------------------------------------------------
```

Notice that the server has combined your two GRANT commands into a single command. This is also a good example of how to grant multiple privileges at once to a user.

Another handy demonstration of granting simple privileges is shown by the following example.

Objective
Give Bob Jones read-only access to the product table.

Log in to the server as root:

```
GRANT SELECT ON Books.product TO 'bjones'@'localhost';
```

Log out and log in as Bob. To save all of the logging in and out, you can also open a second command window, leave one of them logged in as root, and have the other as your user login.

```
SHOW GRANTS;
```

```
+----------------------------------------------------------------------------
| Grants for bjones@localhost
+----------------------------------------------------------------------------
| GRANT USAGE ON *.* TO 'bjones'@'localhost' IDENTIFIED BY PASSWORD
'*2470C0C06D
| GRANT SELECT, INSERT ON 'Books'.'Customers' TO 'bjones'@'localhost'
| GRANT SELECT ON 'BOOKS'.'product' TO 'bjones'@'localhost'
+----------------------------------------------------------------------------
```

This is a great example of how the GRANT keyword works for granting privileges to different database objects. You may grant single or multiple privileges to a database object for a user, but a separate command is needed to grant privileges to a different table or other object. In other words, you can only grant privileges to one object at a time. You can grant privileges to an entire database, including all tables, but only one table at a time. It is sort of an all-or-one situation. To get a better grasp on this, refer back to Table 7.1.

Objective

Allow Fred Smith to connect from anywhere to change data in the Customers table.

This request is a bit more complicated, as you need to decide which privileges to grant and how to allow Fred to connect from any remote host to do his job of changing data in the Customers table. Allowing access from any host only requires that you know how to use a wildcard character like you used in WHERE clauses. The privileges required to change data include INSERT, UPDATE, DELETE, and SELECT. Fred must have the SELECT privilege to be able to check the accuracy of his changes. SELECT is not absolutely needed for Fred to do his job of changing data, but it will probably be more practical if he can take a look at the data he changes so he can make further updates in case of an error.

```
GRANT SELECT, INSERT, UPDATE, DELETE ON Customers TO 'fsmith'@'%' IDENTIFIED
BY 'password';
```

Log in as Fred and check his privileges:

```
SHOW GRANTS;

+-------------------------------------------------------------------------+
| Grants for fsmith@%                                                     |
+-------------------------------------------------------------------------+
| GRANT USAGE ON *.* TO 'fsmith'@'%' IDENTIFIED BY PASSWORD
'*2470C0C06DEE42D1E19'                                                    |
| GRANT SELECT, INSERT, UPDATE, DELETE ON 'BOOKS'.'Customers' TO 'fsmith'@'%'|
+-------------------------------------------------------------------------
```

Now Fred can do his updating job and check his work afterward to make sure that it is accurate and complete. It is simpler to grant global permissions rather than restrictive ones, which is possibly why many DBAs do it despite knowing better. But sometimes you want to give a user access to all of the tables in a database so that their data entry is not impaired by a too-restrictive environment. To grant a user permissions on all the tables in a database, use the standard wildcard (*) when referring to the tables. For Books, the permissions would look like this:

```
Books.*
```

Objective

Give Justine Reed access to change data in the Books database.

Justine needs an account that will allow her to change data in any table within the Books database. Her account name is jreed and she needs SELECT, INSERT, DELETE, and UPDATE privileges on the Books database. Since her location was not specified, you must assume that it is local only since your data is sensitive and security is needed. If this is not the case, you can change it later.

```
GRANT SELECT, INSERT, DELETE, UPDATE ON Books.* TO 'jreed'@'localhost'
IDENTIFIED BY 'password';
```

You should check the permissions before contacting Justine to tell her that her database account is set up:

```
+---------------------------------------------------------------------------+
| Grants for jreed@localhost                                                |
+---------------------------------------------------------------------------+
| GRANT USAGE ON *.* TO 'jreed'@'localhost' IDENTIFIED BY PASSWORD
'*2470C0C06DEE42FD1618BB99005ADCA2EC9D1E19' |
| GRANT SELECT, INSERT, UPDATE, DELETE ON 'BOOKS'.* TO 'jreed'@'localhost'   |
+---------------------------------------------------------------------------
```

Justine now has been granted access to change data on all tables in the Books database. Refer to Table 7.2 for other privilege types to experiment with.

Limiting Resources

It often makes sense to limit the amount of data that can be *pulled* from a database in a given amount of time, or to limit the number of simultaneous user connections, especially if you are charging fees for access to data. For instance, if a user signs up for your service, you don't want her giving access to others without your getting paid for it. You may limit certain resources afforded to a user account to alleviate misuse of your resources. The following list from the GRANT keyword syntax shows the limitations that you may place on an account:

```
| MAX_QUERIES_PER_HOUR count

| MAX_UPDATES_PER_HOUR count

| MAX_CONNECTIONS_PER_HOUR count

| MAX_USER_CONNECTIONS count
```

The example that works best for purposes here is the MAX_USER_CONNECTIONS, since you can easily and directly test this.

Anne Smith of XYZ Marketing has signed up for your demographic data service and needs read-only access to your Books database. She has a single subscription to the service, so please limit her access.

Objective

Create a user account for Anne Smith for read-only access to the Books database and limit her to one simultaneous connection.

Open two command windows to complete this exercise. As the administrative user in one window, issue the following statement:

```
GRANT priv_type ON [object_type] {tbl_name | * | *.* | db_name.*} TO user
[IDENTIFIED BY 'password']WITH MAX_USER_CONNECTIONS count;
GRANT SELECT ON Books.* TO 'asmith'@'localhost' IDENTIFIED BY 'password' WITH
MAX_USER_CONNECTIONS 1;
```

Log out of MySQL and log in as asmith. In the other window, log in as asmith. You should receive the following response to your second attempt to log in as asmith:

```
ERROR 1226 (42000): User 'asmith' has exceeded the 'max_user_connections'
resource (current value: 1)
```

You see that Anne can only make one connection to the database. If you add the entry MAX_QUERIES_PER_HOUR 10 in the WITH clause, log in as Anne and issue nine SQL statements (apparently logging in takes one); you receive the following error after entering the tenth statement:

```
ERROR 1226 (42000): User 'asmith' has exceeded the 'max_questions' resource
(current value: 10)
```

The other MAX limiters work in a similar way. Feel free to explore those on your own. You only need WITH once in your statement, and the other MAX limiters are separated by a space instead of a comma.

REVOKE

REVOKE is the way privileges are taken away from a user. It also seems to be the favorite pastime activity of DBAs in large corporations. REVOKE is useful in securing your database server and restricting access if a careless GRANT has been issued. DBAs often perform database-by-database server security audits, as time allows, to better secure the data that resides within.

```
REVOKE priv_type [(column_list)] [, priv_type [(column_list)]] ...
    ON [object_type] {tbl_name | * | *.* | db_name.*}
    FROM user [, user] ...
REVOKE ALL PRIVILEGES, GRANT OPTION FROM user [, user] ...
```

In some cases, it may be necessary to quickly disable a user while network or host forensics are being performed. The best way to do this is to use the command listed in the last line of the preceding REVOKE syntax:

```
REVOKE ALL PRIVILEGES, GRANT OPTION FROM user [, user] ...
```

Fred Smith is under scrutiny from System Security. Someone from that group has contacted you and requested that you temporarily disable his account pending an investigation.

Objective

Disable Fred Smith's account on the database server.

```
REVOKE ALL PRIVILEGES, GRANT OPTION FROM user;
REVOKE ALL PRIVILEGES, GRANT OPTION FROM 'fsmith'@'%';
```

Fred's account is disabled, not deleted or dropped, and he cannot log in to the database server from any host under the username fsmith. If Fred is terminated, you may (and probably should) delete his account.

Objective

Fred Smith has been separated from our company. Please remove his database access immediately.

This objective is easily carried out, as it has nothing to do with GRANT or REVOKE. It is a simple DROP statement, which removes the user account and all associated privileges. The user account must be in the same format for DROP USER as it is for GRANT and REVOKE. More than one account may be removed at a time.

```
DROP USER user [, user] ...
```

You can remove a user account from MySQL many ways, but this is the suggested method and the only one you explore here. Per the request, Fred's account should be removed to preserve security and comply with corporate standards.

```
DROP USER 'fsmith'@'%';
```

Fred's account and all of his privileges have now been permanently removed from the database.

I must digress for a moment to give you more administrative freedom in checking user account information. You may, as the administrative user, check privileges for any user without having a second window open or logging out and logging in to check as that user. You went through those exercises to learn the importance of testing privileges as the users you create. I hear DBAs complain that they don't have time to do such things and will just filter the complaints as they come in and correct what needs to be corrected. To me, this is far less efficient than just taking a bit of time to test what you have done.

As the administrative user, issue the following statement:

```
SHOW GRANTS FOR user;
SHOW GRANTS FOR 'bjones'@'localhost';
```

```
+---------------------------------------------------------------------------
| Grants for bjones@localhost
+---------------------------------------------------------------------------
| GRANT USAGE ON *.* TO 'bjones'@'localhost' IDENTIFIED BY PASSWORD
'*2470C0C06D
| GRANT SELECT, INSERT ON 'Books'.'Customers' TO 'bjones'@'localhost'
| GRANT SELECT ON 'BOOKS'.'product' TO 'bjones'@'localhost'
+---------------------------------------------------------------------------
```

If you forget, and you most likely will, the exact username and hosts of all the users who have access to the database, there is a quick way to get that information. This information is kept in the mysql.user table in the Host and User columns.

```
SELECT User, Host FROM mysql.user;
```

Your response should look very similar to this:

```
+---------+-----------+
| User    | Host      |
+---------+-----------+
| bjones  | localhost |
| jreed   | localhost |
| root    | localhost |
+---------+-----------+
```

Instead of completely disabling a user's privileges, you may wish to limit privileges in some way. If you recall the example of Bob Jones in the GRANT section, the objective was to give Bob read-only access to the Customers table. We also gave him INSERT privilege without a request to do so. This needs to be corrected through a REVOKE statement.

Objective

A security audit has found that Bob Jones has INSERT privilege on Books.Customers. His access is supposed to be read only to that table. Please fix this.

You discover that he, in fact, does have INSERT privilege on the Customers table in the Books database and issue the following statement:

```
REVOKE INSERT ON Books.Customers FROM 'bjones'@'localhost';
SHOW GRANTS FOR 'bjones'@'localhost';
+---------------------------------------------------------------------------
| Grants for bjones@localhost
+---------------------------------------------------------------------------
```

```
| GRANT USAGE ON *.* TO 'bjones'@'localhost' IDENTIFIED BY PASSWORD
'*2470C0C06D
| GRANT SELECT ON 'Books'.'Customers' TO 'bjones'@'localhost'
| GRANT SELECT ON 'BOOKS'.'product' TO 'bjones'@'localhost'
+------------------------------------------------------------------------
```

Objective

Due to the number of errors we have recently experienced in the database, please fix Justine Reed's privileges so she can only do data entry and queries.

You should first check Justine's privileges for yourself to see what needs to be done:

```
SHOW GRANTS FOR 'jreed'@'localhost';
+---------------------------------------------------------------------------+
| Grants for jreed@localhost                                                |
+---------------------------------------------------------------------------+
| GRANT USAGE ON *.* TO 'jreed'@'localhost' IDENTIFIED BY PASSWORD
'*2470C0C06DEE4|
| GRANT SELECT, INSERT, UPDATE, DELETE ON 'Books'.* TO 'jreed'@'localhost'  |
+---------------------------------------------------------------------------
```

She will need SELECT and INSERT for queries and data entry, but you should remove UPDATE and DELETE so more mistakes are prevented. You should also schedule some training for Justine.

```
REVOKE priv_type ON [object_type] {tbl_name | * | *.* | db_name.*} FROM user;

REVOKE UPDATE, DELETE ON Books.* FROM 'jreed'@'localhost';

SHOW GRANTS FOR 'jreed'@'localhost';

+---------------------------------------------------------------------------+
| Grants for jreed@localhost                                                |
+---------------------------------------------------------------------------+
| GRANT USAGE ON *.* TO 'jreed'@'localhost' IDENTIFIED BY PASSWORD
'*2470C0C06DEE4|
| GRANT SELECT, INSERT ON 'Books'.* TO 'jreed'@'localhost' |
+---------------------------------------------------------------------------
```

Multiple privileges may be revoked in a single statement but, like GRANT, only one object at a time may be acted upon.

GRANT and REVOKE undo each other in their respective actions. These are the accepted methods, across database vendors, for creating users, granting privileges, and revoking privileges. I purposely left out the connection encryption parts of GRANT because, while useful, they are pretty far from standard. Feel free to explore them on your own.

Transaction Control

A *transaction* is a sequential set of SQL statements that encompasses or defines a block of work. The two main keywords in dealing with transactions are COMMIT and ROLLBACK. The COMMIT statement is issued to close out a successfully completed transaction. ROLLBACK is used to signal an unsuccessful transaction.

This section requires that you read through all of the keywords and their usages before any examples are presented. This is not an indication of the level of difficulty of the material. Transactions are actually quite simple to grasp. The issue is that, to look at a complete transaction, you must understand each of the steps involved.

AUTOCOMMIT

In MySQL, AUTOCOMMIT is on by default. If AUTOCOMMIT is on, each line of SQL you enter is automatically committed to the database.

```
SET AUTOCOMMIT = {0 | 1}
SET AUTOCOMMIT = 1; AUTOCOMMIT is on (Default).
SET AUTOCOMMIT = 0; AUTOCOMMIT is off.
```

Since AUTOCOMMIT is on, you still get transactions taking place but have no control as to when the SQL statements are committed to the database.

SET TRANSACTION

This statement is used to set the transaction isolation level and duration explicitly. The four transaction isolation levels are READ UNCOMMITTED, READ COMMITTED, REPEATABLE READ (default), and SERIALIZABLE. The duration can either be set to GLOBAL—which sets all transactions to the type you specify from this point forward in future transactions—or SESSION—which sets the transaction type for the current session. Since SET TRANSACTION typically takes place on the next transaction, it should go before a transaction's BEGIN statement unless the default transaction type is sufficient.

```
SET [GLOBAL | SESSION] TRANSACTION ISOLATION LEVEL

{ READ UNCOMMITTED | READ COMMITTED | REPEATABLE READ | SERIALIZABLE }
```

The details of each transaction isolation level are given here:

* READ UNCOMMITTED: Sometimes called a *dirty read* where SELECT queries are non-locking. In the case of a dirty read, one may actually be viewing data in mid-transaction (not

committed) and is inconsistent with the actual data in the database. SELECT results may not be repeatable at this level.

❋ READ COMMITTED: SELECT queries only include data from transactions that have been committed to the database. SELECT results may not be repeatable at this level.

❋ REPEATABLE READ: SELECT results are repeatable at this isolation level and are ACID compliant. SELECT queries do not take into account data committed by other transactions. InnoDB tables, which are transaction safe, use the REPEATABLE READ transaction type by default. This level of isolation is usually sufficient and is quite efficient as the InnoDB engine is optimized for REPEATABLE READ transactions.

❋ SERIALIZABLE: Like REPEATABLE READ but adds shared mode locks to the SELECT query. The SELECT query returns all records with a shared lock.

BEGIN

BEGIN is an alias for START TRANSACTION. Either signals the beginning of a transaction block.

```
BEGIN;
```

BEGIN should be the first statement in a transaction when handling transactions explicitly. It is also used after each COMMIT statement.

COMMIT

COMMIT is an explicit statement that allows the execution of all SQL statements within a transaction block. For example, an INSERT statement is not executed until the COMMIT statement has been issued if the INSERT is part of a transaction.

```
COMMIT; Commits all of the SQL statements since the last COMMIT was issued.
```

COMMIT makes all statements between the BEGIN statement and itself part of the database. Data that has been committed is no longer isolated and is available for query and update.

ROLLBACK

ROLLBACK is the SQL keyword that reverses a transaction back to the last successful COMMIT.

```
ROLLBACK; Rolls back all of the SQL statements since the last successful
commit.

ROLLBACK [WORK] [AND [NO] CHAIN] [[NO] RELEASE]

ROLLBACK [WORK] TO SAVEPOINT identifier
```

ROLLBACK is basically an *undo* statement for work that you do not want committed to the database. It has the feature/limitation of only being able to undo a single transaction.

SAVEPOINT

A SAVEPOINT is a named marker within a transaction block that designates a point to which you can ROLLBACK. It does not commit the transaction nor does it prevent you from issuing a ROLLBACK to the last successful COMMIT.

```
SAVEPOINT identifier

RELEASE SAVEPOINT identifier
```

You may have multiple SAVEPOINTs within a transaction, but they must all have unique names. If you name a SAVEPOINT with the same name within the same transaction, the older one is overwritten with the newer one.

Look at some transactions you have made through the definitions and syntax. There are no definitive objectives in this section, but there are examples.

Example 1

A transaction demonstrating a simple INSERT with the default transaction type.

First you need to create a simple transaction-safe table for the examples; see Table 7.3.

Table 7.3   A Simple Insert

Code	Description
`SET AUTOCOMMIT = 0;`	Turn off AUTOCOMMIT.
`USE Books;`	This may seem redundant but you should always put in the USE *Database* statement prior to starting a transaction.
`CREATE TABLE Demo (ID integer(4)`	
`PRIMARY KEY AUTO_INCREMENT,`	
`Name char(40)) ENGINE=INNODB;`	
`USE Books;`	
`BEGIN;`	Explicitly declare the beginning of the transaction.
`INSERT INTO Demo (Name) VALUES`	Insert some data into Demo.
`('John'), ('Paul'), ('George');`	
`SELECT Name FROM Demo;`	The data looks as if it is in the table permanently.
`+--------+`	The data is now committed to the database and viewable by others who are logged in.
`| Name   |`	
`+--------+`	You may demonstrate this to yourself by now using the ROLLBACK command.
`| John   |`	
`| Paul   |`	
`| George |`	
`+--------+`	

Code	Description
`COMMIT;`	
`ROLLBACK;`	Attempt to roll back the data.
`SELECT Name FROM Demo;`	Since the data has been committed, it cannot be rolled back.

Example 2

A transaction where data is inserted, rolled back, and then inserted again with COMMIT.

```
SET AUTOCOMMIT = 0;

USE Books;

BEGIN;

INSERT INTO Demo (Name) VALUES ('Pete');

SELECT Name FROM Demo;

+--------+
| Name   |
+--------+
| John   |
| Paul   |
| George |
| Pete   |
+--------+

ROLLBACK;

SELECT Name FROM Demo;

+--------+
| Name   |
+--------+
| John   |
| Paul   |
| George |
+--------+

INSERT INTO Demo (Name) VALUES ('Ringo');
```

143
❈ ❈ ❈

```
COMMIT;

SELECT Name FROM Demo;

+--------+
| Name   |
+--------+
| John   |
| Paul   |
| George |
| Ringo  |
+--------+
```

Your data has been successfully committed to the database.

Example 3

A transaction where data is inserted, a SAVEPOINT is used, there is a ROLLBACK to the SAVEPOINT, a new INSERT, and a final COMMIT.

```
SET AUTOCOMMIT = 0;

USE Books;

BEGIN;

INSERT INTO Demo (Name) VALUES ('Linda');

SAVEPOINT Linda;

INSERT INTO Demo (Name) VALUES ('Cynthia');

SAVEPOINT Cynthia;

SELECT Name FROM Demo;

+---------+
| Name    |
+---------+
| John    |
| Paul    |
| George  |
| Linda   |
| Cynthia |
+---------+
```

```
ROLLBACK TO SAVEPOINT Linda;
```

We have to specify SAVEPOINT Linda if we want to ROLLBACK to that SAVEPOINT. Issuing SAVEPOINT Cynthia would have no effect on the data. Issuing ROLLBACK TO SAVEPOINT Linda takes the transaction back to the point just after Linda was inserted.

```
SELECT Name FROM Demo;

+---------+
| Name    |
+---------+
| John    |
| Paul    |
| George  |
| Linda   |
+---------+

INSERT INTO Demo (Name) VALUES ('Yoko');

COMMIT;

SELECT Name FROM Demo;

+---------+
| Name    |
+---------+
| John    |
| Paul    |
| George  |
| Linda   |
| Yoko    |
+---------+
```

A COMMIT statement ends a transaction and the data is placed into the table(s) and available for query. This is a good overview of transactions for you at this level. There is really nothing magical about them: They are just multi-step SQL procedures that have their own internal syntax and top-down order.

Summary

In this chapter you learned about database security from a GRANT/REVOKE (user access) standpoint and how to manage user access to data resources. You also learned about limiting resources by connection, number of queries, and simultaneous user logins. The first rule of database security is "Only grant users the minimum privileges possible." User security is also known as internal security. MySQL provides an extra layer of security not found in many other DBMSs by adding the user's host to the username in the form of 'user'@'hostname'. This is a higher level of security because it not only requires a password but the user connect to the DBMS from a particular host.

The section on transactions introduced you to the different steps involved in an SQL transaction in which you learned how to start the procedure, execute statements within the transaction, roll back statements, and commit statements to a database. If you are interested in more information on transactions, there are entire books and sections of books written about them. I recommend that you begin with an introductory text on the subject and graduate to the more advanced ones. The Chapter Review gives you some more practice with both of these major parts of SQL.

Chapter Review

Multiple Choice

1. By issuing the "MAX_USER_CONNECTIONS 1" limitation on a user account, you are effectively doing what?

   a) Limiting a user's ability to work efficiently.

   b) Limiting a user's ability to steal your data.

   c) Limiting a user's ability to change data.

   d) Limiting a user's ability to log in more than once.

2. You have to issue a new GRANT statement for each privilege like INSERT, DELETE, and so on.

   a) True

   b) False

3. If you want to change the default transaction type, you would issue which of the following?

   a) SET TRANSACTION

   b) GRANT TRANSACTION

   c) LIMIT TRANSACTION

   d) MAX_USER_TRANSACTION

4. Consider the following transaction and choose the correct result from the SELECT statement.

USE Parts;

BEGIN;

INSERT INTO Parts (Part, Description, Vendor) VALUES ('Gear', 'Main Treddle Gear for Model X25 Series Spooler', 'ACME');

SAVEPOINT ACME;

INSERT INTO Parts (Part, Description, Vendor) VALUES ('Spring', 'Spooler Spring 20 gauge', 'EBA');

SAVEPOINT EBA;

COMMIT;

ROLLBACK TO SAVEPOINT ACME;

SELECT Part, Description, Vendor FROM Parts;

a)
```
+--------+----------------------------------------------+--------+
| Part | Description | Vendor |
+--------+----------------------------------------------+--------+
| Gear | Main Treddle Gear for Model X25 Series Spooler | ACME |
| Spring | Spooler Spring 20 gauge | EBA |
+--------+----------------------------------------------+--------+
```

b)
```
+--------+----------------------------------------------+--------+
| Part | Description | Vendor |
+--------+----------------------------------------------+--------+
| Gear | Main Treddle Gear for Model X25 Series Spooler | ACME |
+--------+----------------------------------------------+--------+
```

c)
```
+--------+----------------------------------------------+--------+
| Part | Description | Vendor |
+--------+----------------------------------------------+--------+
| Spring | Spooler Spring 20 gauge | EBA |
+--------+----------------------------------------------+--------+
```

d) Empty set (0.01 sec)

5. Which of the following is true of COMMIT?

a) It ends a transaction.

b) It submits the data to the database permanently.

c) It flushes privileges.

d) Both a and b.

147
❊ ❊ ❊

6. What effect will a ROLLBACK statement have after a COMMIT has been issued?

   a) It rolls back all of the statements in the transaction.

   b) No effect. COMMIT ends a transaction.

   c) The ROLLBACK prompts with "Are you sure?"

   d) None of the above.

7. What happens if you issue the following statements in a transaction?

   INSERT INTO Parts (Part, Description, Vendor) VALUES ('Gear', 'Main Treddle Gear for Model X25 Series Spooler', 'ACME');

   SAVEPOINT ACME;

   INSERT INTO Parts (Part, Description, Vendor) VALUES ('Spring', 'Spooler Spring 20 gauge', 'EBA');

   SAVEPOINT ACME;

   a) The server gives an error.

   b) The first SAVEPOINT is overwritten by the second.

   c) The first SAVEPOINT is saved and the second is discarded.

   d) The first INSERT is committed and the second SAVEPOINT is the new SAVEPOINT.

8. What would the following statement do?

   GRANT SELECT ON Books.* TO 'jcurtis'@'localhost' IDENTIFIED BY 'password';

   a) Nothing. The syntax is incorrect.

   b) It creates a user with full access to the Books database.

   c) It creates a user with read-only access to the Books database.

   d) Another GRANT statement would need to be issued for this to be effective.

9. Which of the following is correct for a user with access from any host?

   a) 'bjones'@'localhost'

   b) 'bjones'@'*'

   c) 'bjones'

   d) 'bjones'@'%'

10. If you are the root user, how do you check a user's privileges?

    a) SHOW GRANTS;

    b) SHOW GRANTS FOR 'user'@'localhost';

    c) SHOW GRANTS FOR Books;

    d) SHOW GRANTS FOR '%';

Concepts

1. What purpose does a SAVEPOINT serve?

2. What is meant by granting a user read-only rights to a table?

8 } Advanced Queries

This chapter will be your plunge into advanced queries. The advanced queries that it covers are multiple-table queries, subqueries, joins, unions, summary queries, batch data extraction, and batch data loading. Advanced queries are quite common in the DBMS world but are usually approached with much caution and dread by many DBAs. I don't want you to fear this chapter or the subject matter herein. I want to assure you that I make a true effort to give you a gentle introduction to each concept, then some examples for illustration. Since the material in this chapter can be a source of anxiety, I engage you with multiple examples and ways of *seeing* the concept. First, you get the gentle introduction followed by the database theory and syntax. Next, you get a graphical example followed by standard examples. The only real difference in this and the other chapters before it are the graphical examples. Some of the concepts must be visualized to be absorbed.

This chapter focuses on gathering data from multiple tables. In any well-designed database, the data of interest is in multiple tables—not just one. In gathering this data, you need to employ one or more of the aforementioned query types. The trick, if there is one, to advanced queries is to pull data from multiple tables in an organized manner and make it seem as if it has come from a single table. Very few people sit down and just knock out a complex query that works correctly the first time. I must admit that the graphical tools take away much of the frustration often imposed by more complex queries. My day goes a lot better when I can visually design a query and actually see how my data will look before spending hours finding a missing tick mark or the incorrect number of parentheses.

You will create all of the tables and enter the data for them by hand to gain more practice doing SQL from the command line. This chapter is a cumulative chapter of sorts, as it builds on everything you have learned to this point. My assumption, though possibly incorrect, is that you have gone through the material in chronological order and have arrived here after thoroughly digesting the learning objectives from previous chapters. You will be lead through the preliminary material with little explanation so that we may begin quickly with the material at hand.

I think we should start from scratch on this, so drop Books:

```
DROP Books;
```

Create a new Books database:

```
CREATE DATABASE Books;
```

You need to create five tables—Agents, Publishers, Editors, Works, and Authors:

```
USE Books;

CREATE TABLE Authors (Author_ID integer(4) PRIMARY KEY AUTO_INCREMENT,
First_Name char(30), Last_Name char(40), Phone char(12))ENGINE=INNODB;

CREATE TABLE Agents (Agent_ID integer(4) PRIMARY KEY AUTO_INCREMENT,
Author_ID integer(4) NOT NULL, First_Name char(30), Last_Name char(40), Phone
char(12), KEY Authors_idx (Author_ID), CONSTRAINT Author_FK1 FOREIGN KEY
(Author_ID) REFERENCES Authors (Author_ID))ENGINE=INNODB;

CREATE TABLE Works (ISBN integer(4) PRIMARY KEY, Title char(60), Price decimal
(4,2), Sales integer(4),Author_ID integer(4) NOT NULL, Publisher_ID integer
(4), KEY author_idx (Author_ID), CONSTRAINT Authors_FK1 FOREIGN KEY
(Author_ID) REFERENCES Authors (Author_ID), KEY publisher_idx (Publisher_ID),
CONSTRAINT Publishers_FK FOREIGN KEY (Publisher_ID) REFERENCES Publishers
(Publisher_ID))ENGINE=INNODB;

CREATE TABLE Editors (Editor_ID integer(4) PRIMARY KEY AUTO_INCREMENT,
First_Name char(30), Last_Name char(40), Phone char(12), Publisher_ID integer
(4), KEY publisher_idx (Publisher_ID), CONSTRAINT Publishers_FK1 FOREIGN KEY
(Publisher_ID) REFERENCES Publishers (Publisher_ID)) ENGINE=INNODB;

CREATE TABLE Publishers (Publisher_ID integer(4) PRIMARY KEY AUTO_INCREMENT,
Company char(60), Address char(60), City char(40), State char(2), Zip char
(10), Phone char(12), Notes text)ENGINE=INNODB;
```

Insert the data for each table.

Authors table:

```
INSERT INTO Authors VALUES ('10239', 'Lynn', 'Steele','512-555-2951');

INSERT INTO Authors VALUES ('12999', 'Robert', 'Balzer','512-555-5131');

INSERT INTO Authors VALUES ('09055', 'Anne', 'Cohen', '512-555-1555');

INSERT INTO Authors VALUES ('23469', 'Lenard', 'Dawson', '512-555-7055');

INSERT INTO Authors VALUES ('10009', 'Glen', 'Harris', '512-555-7755');
```

Publishers table:

```
INSERT INTO Publishers VALUES ('', 'No Newbies Publishing, Inc.', '1263 S.
Pittsburgh', 'Austin', 'TX', '75549', '512-555-9901', 'Agented submissions
only');

INSERT INTO Publishers VALUES ('', 'Huge Publishing House, Inc.', '339 W.
Davis Rd.', 'Sunnyvale', 'CA', '92101', '408-555-9901', 'Non-fiction
publisher');

INSERT INTO Publishers VALUES ('', 'Publish With Us, LLC.', '5689 N. Barton
Springs Rd.', 'Austin', 'TX', '75549', '512-555-9901', 'POD Publisher');

INSERT INTO Publishers VALUES ('', 'Howdy Yall Publishing, Inc', '500 S.
Guadalupe', 'Austin', 'TX', '75549', '512-555-9901', 'Country Music Lyrics');
```

Agents table:

```
INSERT INTO Agents VALUES ('', '10009', 'Paul', 'Jones', '512-555-1234');

INSERT INTO Agents VALUES ('', '23469', 'Lee', 'Smith', '512-555-2345');

INSERT INTO Agents VALUES ('', '09055', 'Ed', 'Trumbull', '512-555-3456');

INSERT INTO Agents VALUES ('', '12999', 'LeeAnn', 'Evans', '512-555-4567');

INSERT INTO Agents VALUES ('', '10239', 'Tom', 'Rosen', '512-555-5678');
```

Works table:

```
INSERT INTO Works VALUES ('1231231234', 'You Had Me At Shalom', '16.99',
'600000', '09055', '4');

INSERT INTO Works VALUES ('1002003004', 'Bruises On My Heart', '16.99',
'400000', '10239', '4');

INSERT INTO Works VALUES ('1112003111', 'Good Night, Good Chocolate',
'19.99', '14000', '10009', '2');

INSERT INTO Works VALUES ('1444561000', 'Doodling As Art', '7.99', '12000',
'23469', '1');

INSERT INTO Works VALUES ('1111223333', 'How To Write Great Queries',
'29.99', '9000', '12999', '3');

INSERT INTO Works VALUES ('1266778899', 'You Are Never Your Own Boss',
'12.95', '210000', '12999', '3');

INSERT INTO Works VALUES ('1111684321', 'Topiaries Are Tops', '9.99', '2200',
'23469', '2');
```

Editors table:

```
INSERT INTO Editors VALUES ('', 'Donna', 'Little', '512-555-0001','1');

INSERT INTO Editors VALUES ('', 'Travis', 'Dalmon', '512-555-0002','2');

INSERT INTO Editors VALUES ('', 'Terri', 'Coleman', '512-555-0002','4');
```

That is a lot of data entry, I know, but it gives you the type and amount of data you need to complete the exercises in this chapter.

Multiple-Table Queries

Very often you will need to query data from more than one table. SQL gives you a simple mechanism to perform this kind of operation. The caveat is that you need to identify the table and column instead of just the column in the query. Each column is now identified by the table name, a dot, and the column name. You have to identify the table and the column because, as you can see from your tables, if you just use Last_Name; it is very ambiguous. I like multiple-table queries because I can get richer information for a report this way. By querying multiple tables at a time, you can create very specific reports with no cut-and-paste activities. The data is already arranged for you in final form. Here is an example that specifies the Last_Name column from the Agents table and yields very different results from the column Authors.Last_Name:

```
Agents.Last_Name
```

In a multiple-table column, you must also specify each table from which you are querying. Consider the following example:

```
SELECT First_Name,Last_Name,Works.Title FROM Authors,Works WHERE
Authors.Author_ID = Works.Author_ID;
```

Result:

```
+------------+-----------+----------------------------+
| First_Name | Last_Name | Title                      |
+------------+-----------+----------------------------+
| Anne       | Cohen     | You Had Me At Shalom       |
| Glen       | Harris    | Good Night, Good Chocolate |
| Lynn       | Steele    | Bruises On My Heart        |
| Robert     | Balzer    | How To Write Great Queries |
| Robert     | Balzer    | You Are Never Your Own Boss|
| Lenard     | Dawson    | Topiaries Are Tops         |
| Lenard     | Dawson    | Doodling As Art            |
+------------+-----------+----------------------------+
```

Objective
Produce a report of authors, their works, and the publishers of each work.

Without the power of multiple-table queries, this kind of information would have to be extracted with two (or more) separate queries and the data would have to be cut and pasted into a final report. You can produce a report that is ready to be placed, as is, into a word processor, a spreadsheet, or an email for the requestor. It requires a bit of thought to do so. If you create the query incorrectly, you can tie up database resources with malformed queries and produce some nasty emails from DBAs, users, or both. The queries can be inefficient at best and, at worst, downright devastating to performance if they are malformed in some way.

The solution to this objective is relatively simple if you look at the tables' structures and the way they are related to one another. Figure 8.1 may help you visualize this better. Figure 8.2 shows the same tables with the *foreign key/primary key (FK/PK)* pairs identified.

Figure 8.1

The Books database showing table structure.

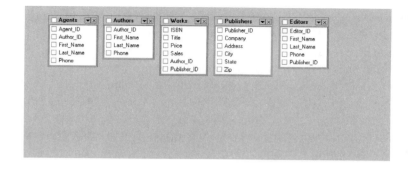

Figure 8.2

The Books database structure with FK/PK relationships.

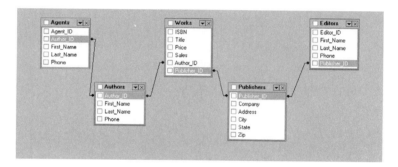

Try to construct the query that gives the following results:

```
+------------+-----------+---------------------+----------------------------+
| First_Name | Last_Name | Title               | Publisher                  |
+------------+-----------+---------------------+----------------------------+
| Lenard     | Dawson    | Doodling As Art     | No Newbies Publishing, Inc.|
| Lenard     | Dawson    | Topiaries Are Tops  | Huge Publishing House, Inc.|
| Glen       | Harris    | Good Night, Good    | Huge Publishing House, Inc.|
|            |           | Chocolate           |                            |
| Robert     | Balzer    | How To Write Great  | Publish With Us, LLC.      |
|            |           | Queries             |                            |
| Robert     | Balzer    | You Are Never Your  | Publish With Us, LLC.      |
|            |           | Boss                |                            |
| Lynn       | Steele    | Bruises On My Heart | Howdy Yall Publishing, Inc |
| Anne       | Cohen     | You Had Me At       | Howdy Yall Publishing, Inc |
|            |           | Shalom              |                            |
+------------+-----------+---------------------+----------------------------+
```

Here is the query I used to get these results:

```
SELECT First_Name,Last_Name,Works.Title,Publishers.Company  AS Publisher FROM
Authors,Works,Publishers WHERE Authors.Author_ID = Works.Author_ID AND
Works.Publisher_ID = Publishers.Publisher_ID;
```

Instead of Company, I used Publishers.Company AS Publisher to get a report that shows Publisher in the column heading because I think it sounds better—but either is correct. If you came up with a query that works for this objective, congratulations. If not, don't be discouraged; advanced queries take a lot of practice.

To construct a query that requires more than one table and potentially many columns, these steps will help you. The following is known as *Ken's Guide to Advanced Queries:*

1. Figure out exactly what you want the report to look like.

2. Isolate the tables that are needed for the query.

3. Isolate the columns that are needed for the query.

4. Look for relationships between the tables and columns.

5. Construct the query.

6. Check the results.

7. Revise, if necessary.

This is how I construct complex queries. I usually sketch out, on a sheet of paper, how I want my results to look, then isolate the tables and columns of interest. This method has a bit of trial and error to it, but when you are new to more advanced queries you need something to assist you. As you become more adept at query writing, you will find that you perform these steps without consciously sketching everything out on paper. If it is any consolation, many DBAs have to revise their queries before getting the data arranged the way they want it for a report.

You have seen queries involving two and three tables. The process is the same for many tables as well. The biggest problem with multiple-table queries, for me, is that the results get so wide (due to the number of columns involved) that it is very difficult to keep up with what is going on. Sometimes I send my query results to a file for easier viewing; I show you how to do it later in this chapter.

Subqueries

A *subquery* is a SELECT statement within another statement. This type of query is sometimes called a subselect. Subqueries are a great way of drilling down in a database. First you select some data, and then you further select data from that result set. An example is a better way of illustrating this concept.

Consider the following SELECT statement:

```
SELECT Column1_Name,Column2_Name FROM Table1_Name WHERE Column1_Name =
(SELECT Column1_Name FROM Table2_Name);
```

In this statement, the SELECT in the parentheses is the subquery, or *inner statement*. Subqueries are always enclosed in parentheses. The results returned from the subquery are used by the *outer*, or *main*, *statement* to return the desired result set. An example from your database might look like this:

```
SELECT First_Name, Last_Name FROM Authors WHERE Author_ID = (SELECT Author_ID
FROM Works WHERE Author_ID='10239');
```

Result:

```
+------------+-----------+
| First_Name | Last_Name |
+------------+-----------+
| Lynn       | Steele    |
+------------+-----------+
```

This query works because of the restriction I put on the subquery: '= 10239'. If I had chosen an Author_ID for an author with more than one work associated with his or her Author_ID, I would have received an error. Here is an example:

```
SELECT First_Name, Last_Name FROM Authors WHERE Author_ID = (SELECT Author_ID
FROM Works WHERE Author_ID='12999');
```

```
ERROR 1242 (21000): Subquery returns more than 1 row
```

This is one downside of subqueries. If you use the = and have a result set that contains more than one row, you will receive the error "Subquery returns more than 1 row". To alleviate this troublesome error, try the query again using IN in place of =.

```
SELECT First_Name, Last_Name FROM Authors WHERE Author_ID IN (SELECT
Author_ID FROM Works WHERE Author_ID='12999');
```

Result:

```
+------------+-----------+
| First_Name | Last_Name |
+------------+-----------+
| Robert     | Balzer    |
+------------+-----------+
```

The IN keyword's meaning may not be as obvious as the older form = ANY for this type of query. Instead of =, you have EQUAL TO ANY so that an error is not thrown when multiple rows are returned by the subquery. You may be wondering if you should return only a single row of data (as in the = 10239 subquery) if the IN keyword will work. The answer is yes; it does. So, why use = at all for a subquery? The answer lies in the efficiency of the search algorithm. If the values in the list are only constants, then IN is very fast; if the search criterion is a string, then IN performs a case-sensitive comparison, which can be slow.

Subqueries can also be used in the predicate of other SELECT, INSERT, UPDATE, and DELETE statements.

To duplicate my first query in the "Multiple-Table Queries" section, the following subquery is used:

```
SELECT Authors.First_Name, Authors.Last_Name, Works.Title FROM Authors, Works
WHERE Works.Title IN (SELECT Name FROM Works WHERE Authors.Author_ID =
Works.Author_ID);
```

Result:

```
+------------+-----------+------------------------------+
| First_Name | Last_Name | Title                        |
+------------+-----------+------------------------------+
| Lynn       | Steele    | Bruises On My Heart          |
| Robert     | Balzer    | How To Write Great Queries   |
| Lenard     | Dawson    | Topiaries Are Tops           |
| Glen       | Harris    | Good Night, Good Chocolate   |
| Anne       | Cohen     | You Had Me At Shalom         |
| Robert     | Balzer    | You Are Never Your Own Boss  |
| Lenard     | Dawson    | Doodling As Art              |
+------------+-----------+------------------------------+
```

The keyword SOME is a synonym for ANY. The keyword ALL is interesting, as it returns TRUE if the comparison is TRUE for all of the values in the column the subquery returns. The ALL keyword must be preceded by a comparison operator, such as <, >, = and so on. Its use can be illustrated with the following example and a comparison to the same query with the IN keyword.

```
SELECT Author_ID, First_Name, Last_Name FROM Authors WHERE Author_ID IN
(SELECT Author_ID FROM Works WHERE Author_ID < '11000');
```

Result:

```
+-----------+------------+-----------+
| Author_ID | First_Name | Last_Name |
+-----------+------------+-----------+
|      9055 | Anne       | Cohen     |
|     10009 | Glen       | Harris    |
|     10239 | Lynn       | Steele    |
+-----------+------------+-----------+
```

In this query, you want to see all of the authors with Author_IDs < 11000 and the query returns those results. In the following query, using >ALL basically reverses this query by saying that you want ALL of the matches that are greater than what is matched in the query giving you a different subset of data.

```
SELECT Author_ID, First_Name, Last_Name FROM Authors WHERE Author_ID >ALL
(SELECT Author_ID FROM Works WHERE Author_ID < '11000');
```

Result:

```
+-----------+------------+-----------+
| Author_ID | First_Name | Last_Name |
+-----------+------------+-----------+
|     12999 | Robert     | Balzer    |
|     23469 | Lenard     | Dawson    |
+-----------+------------+-----------+
```

A few queries can only be done with subqueries, but these are fairly rare. More often than not, you use a JOIN to query data from more than one table. The next section covers the different types of JOINs.

JOIN

My next sentence should illicit some angry emails, but here goes: If you can do a JOIN to get at your desired data, then you should do a JOIN. You will see a lot of debate on the Internet about subqueries versus JOINs, but there is little resolution from it all. JOINs, in some cases, can be less efficient and are admittedly less intuitive than subqueries. So why do I still prefer JOINs over subqueries after pointing out such glaring shortcomings? JOINs have fewer limitations than subqueries. For instance, they don't need any special syntax if multiple rows are returned. Maybe it is just a personal preference, but JOINs seem easier to debug than subquery statements. And most graphical tools that I have used construct a JOIN by default when you build a multiple-table query.

MySQL supports the following table references part of SELECT statements and multiple-table DELETE and UPDATE statements in JOIN syntax:

```
table_references:
    table_reference [, table_reference] …
```

```
table_reference:
    table_factor
  | join_table
```

```
table_factor:
    tbl_name [[AS] alias]
        [{USE|IGNORE|FORCE} INDEX (key_list)]
  | ( table_references )
  | { OJ table_reference LEFT OUTER JOIN table_reference
        ON conditional_expr }
```

```
join_table:
    table_reference [INNER | CROSS] JOIN table_factor [join_condition]
  | table_reference STRAIGHT_JOIN table_factor
  | table_reference STRAIGHT_JOIN table_factor ON condition
  | table_reference LEFT [OUTER] JOIN table_reference join_condition
  | table_reference NATURAL [LEFT [OUTER]] JOIN table_factor
  | table_reference RIGHT [OUTER] JOIN table_reference join_condition
  | table_reference NATURAL [RIGHT [OUTER]] JOIN table_factor
```

```
join_condition:
    ON conditional_expr
  | USING (column_list)
```

A *table reference* is also known as a *JOIN expression*.

CROSS JOIN

Cross *JOINs* are not very common and, frankly, not very useful unless you need to see all possible unique combinations of columns in a query. *JOINs* of this type are the basis for the INNER JOIN so they are worth a few words of exploration and an example.

```
SELECT Authors.First_Name, Authors.Last_Name, Works.Title FROM Authors CROSS
JOIN Works;
```

Result:

```
+------------+------------+----------------------------+
| First_Name | Last_Name  | Title                      |
+------------+------------+----------------------------+
| Anne       | Cohen      | Bruises On My Heart        |
| Glen       | Harris     | Bruises On My Heart        |
| Lynn       | Steele     | Bruises On My Heart        |
| Robert     | Balzer     | Bruises On My Heart        |
| Lenard     | Dawson     | Bruises On My Heart        |
| Anne       | Cohen      | How To Write Great Queries |
| Glen       | Harris     | How To Write Great Queries |
| Lynn       | Steele     | How To Write Great Queries |
| Robert     | Balzer     | How To Write Great Queries |
| Lenard     | Dawson     | How To Write Great Queries |
| Anne       | Cohen      | Topiaries Are Tops         |
| Glen       | Harris     | Topiaries Are Tops         |
| Lynn       | Steele     | Topiaries Are Tops         |
| Robert     | Balzer     | Topiaries Are Tops         |
| Lenard     | Dawson     | Topiaries Are Tops         |
| Anne       | Cohen      | Good Night, Good Chocolate |
| Glen       | Harris     | Good Night, Good Chocolate |
| Lynn       | Steele     | Good Night, Good Chocolate |
| Robert     | Balzer     | Good Night, Good Chocolate |
| Lenard     | Dawson     | Good Night, Good Chocolate |
| Anne       | Cohen      | You Had Me At Shalom       |
| Glen       | Harris     | You Had Me At Shalom       |
| Lynn       | Steele     | You Had Me At Shalom       |
| Robert     | Balzer     | You Had Me At Shalom       |
| Lenard     | Dawson     | You Had Me At Shalom       |
| Anne       | Cohen      | You Are Never Your Own Boss |
| Glen       | Harris     | You Are Never Your Own Boss |
| Lynn       | Steele     | You Are Never Your Own Boss |
| Robert     | Balzer     | You Are Never Your Own Boss |
| Lenard     | Dawson     | You Are Never Your Own Boss |
| Anne       | Cohen      | Doodling As Art            |
| Glen       | Harris     | Doodling As Art            |
| Lynn       | Steele     | Doodling As Art            |
| Robert     | Balzer     | Doodling As Art            |
| Lenard     | Dawson     | Doodling As Art            |
+------------+------------+----------------------------+
```

I think you get the idea by seeing all 35 rows from the query. Put scientifically: A *cross JOIN* yields the Cartesian product of the selected sets of rows between two tables. A data set's *Cartesian product* consists of unique rows that include all possibilities, or *permutations,* from the JOIN.

NATURAL JOIN

A *natural JOIN* is much like a simple multiple-table query where a foreign key and a primary key are matched in the query. This is a "natural" way to JOIN tables. We, as database designers, design our tables to have this quality and ability to be JOINed to produce useful results. To illustrate a natural JOIN, go back to my original example multiple-table query:

```
SELECT First_Name,Last_Name,Works.Title FROM Authors,Works WHERE
Authors.Author_ID = Works.Author_ID;
```

Result:

```
+------------+----------+----------------------------+
| First_Name | Last_Name | Title                     |
+------------+----------+----------------------------+
| Anne       | Cohen    | You Had Me At Shalom       |
| Glen       | Harris   | Good Night, Good Chocolate |
| Lynn       | Steele   | Bruises On My Heart        |
| Robert     | Balzer   | How To Write Great Queries |
| Robert     | Balzer   | You Are Never Your Own Boss |
| Lenard     | Dawson   | Topiaries Are Tops         |
| Lenard     | Dawson   | Doodling As Art            |
+------------+----------+----------------------------+
```

Notice the foreign key-primary key pair in the WHERE clause. Now have a look at the same query in JOIN format:

```
SELECT Authors.First_Name, Authors.Last_Name, Works.Title FROM Authors
NATURAL JOIN Works;
```

Result:

```
+------------+----------+----------------------------+
| First_Name | Last_Name | Title                     |
+------------+----------+----------------------------+
| Anne       | Cohen    | You Had Me At Shalom       |
| Glen       | Harris   | Good Night, Good Chocolate |
| Lynn       | Steele   | Bruises On My Heart        |
| Robert     | Balzer   | How To Write Great Queries |
```

```
| Robert     | Balzer    | You Are Never Your Own Boss |
| Lenard     | Dawson    | Topiaries Are Tops          |
| Lenard     | Dawson    | Doodling As Art             |
+------------+-----------+-----------------------------+
```

There really isn't much difference in the two queries, and no difference in the results. This is because, as I stated earlier, a natural JOIN is based on the foreign key-primary key pair. One type can typically be rewritten as the other. Actually, the two columns don't necessarily have to be indexed columns at all, but merely have the same name in both tables. It is just an assumption that the Agent_ID column in the Agents table and the Agent_ID column in the Listings table are associated by the PK/FK relationship.

INNER JOIN

The *inner JOIN* is the most common and the default JOIN type. In the preceding example, the JOIN is an INNER JOIN. Note the differences between the INNER JOIN and NATURAL JOIN statements. Also note the similarities between the multiple-table query and the INNER JOIN statements.

Multiple-table query:

```
SELECT First_Name,Last_Name,Works.Title FROM Authors,Works WHERE
Authors.Author_ID = Works.Author_ID;
```

NATURAL JOIN:

```
SELECT Authors.First_Name, Authors.Last_Name, Works.Title FROM Authors
NATURAL JOIN Works;
```

INNER JOIN:

```
SELECT Authors.First_Name, Authors.Last_Name, Works.Title FROM Authors INNER
JOIN Works ON (Authors.Author_ID = Works.Author_ID);
```

The parentheses around the PK/FK match are optional.

What is the big deal about a JOIN if I can easily rewrite the statement using standard syntax? You can use either one that you want.

The following section is an example for a more complex query and both syntaxes are given.

Objective
Produce a report of agents, the authors they represent, and the titles of each author's works.

This objective requires that you use three tables. The report you want should look like the following:

```
+----------+----------+----------+----------+-----------------------+
| First_Name | Last_Name | First_Name | Last_Name | Title                 |
+----------+----------+----------+----------+-----------------------+
| Ed         | Trumbull  | Anne       | Cohen     | You Had Me At Shalom  |
| Paul       | Jones     | Glen       | Harris    | Good Night, Good      |
|            |           |            |           | Chocolate             |
| Tom        | Rosen     | Lynn       | Steele    | Bruises On My Heart   |
| LeeAnn     | Evans     | Robert     | Balzer    | How To Write Great    |
|            |           |            |           | Queries               |
| LeeAnn     | Evans     | Robert     | Balzer    | You Are Never Your Own|
|            |           |            |           | Boss                  |
| Lee        | Smith     | Lenard     | Dawson    | Topiaries Are Tops    |
| Lee        | Smith     | Lenard     | Dawson    | Doodling As Art       |
+----------+----------+----------+----------+-----------------------+
```

By visualizing the data you want to see, it is easier to construct the query to match the desired result. The two queries that will produce these results are given here:

```
SELECT Agents.First_Name, Agents.Last_Name, Authors.First_Name,
Authors.Last_Name FROM Agents INNER JOIN Works ON (Agents.Author_ID =
Works.Author_ID) INNER JOIN Authors ON (Works.Author_ID = Authors.Author_ID);

SELECT Agents.First_Name, Agents.Last_Name, Authors.First_Name,
Authors.Last_Name, Works.Title FROM Authors,Agents,Works WHERE
Agents.Author_ID = Works.Author_ID AND Works.Author_ID = Authors.Author_ID;
```

OUTER JOIN

OUTER JOINs have to do with selecting data from tables based on their logical positions of left and right in a query. The "left" table is the one you select from first, and the right table is selected from second. OUTER JOINs come in three types: LEFT OUTER JOIN, RIGHT OUTER JOIN, and FULL OUTER JOIN.

LEFT OUTER JOIN

A LEFT OUTER JOIN is very different from an INNER JOIN. Instead of limiting results to those in both tables, it limits results to those in the "left" table (Authors in this case). This means that if the

ON clause matches 0 records in Works, a row in the result is returned—but with NULL values for each column from Works. In this example a NULL value is returned if an author has not yet published a title. To illustrate this point, issue the following statements:

```
INSERT INTO Authors VALUES ('10393', 'Bob', 'Fischer','512-555-1551');
```

```
SELECT Authors.First_Name, Authors.Last_Name, Works.Title FROM Authors LEFT
OUTER JOIN Works ON (Authors.Author_ID = Works.Author_ID);
```

Result:

```
+------------+----------+----------------------------+
| First_Name | Last_Name | Title                     |
+------------+----------+----------------------------+
| Anne       | Cohen     | You Had Me At Shalom       |
| Glen       | Harris    | Good Night, Good Chocolate |
| Lynn       | Steele    | Bruises On My Heart        |
| Bob        | Fischer   | NULL                       |
| Robert     | Balzer    | How To Write Great Queries |
| Robert     | Balzer    | You Are Never Your Own Boss |
| Lenard     | Dawson    | Topiaries Are Tops         |
| Lenard     | Dawson    | Doodling As Art            |
+------------+----------+----------------------------+
```

RIGHT OUTER JOIN
The RIGHT OUTER JOIN is much like the LEFT OUTER JOIN except that the tables are reversed. All of the records requested from the "right" table (Works) are returned and a NULL value for any non-corresponding record from the "left" table (Authors) is returned. You have to take my word on this one because I can't enter any data that would violate our foreign key constraints into the Authors table. It is better to adjust the query such that all OUTER JOINs were constructed as LEFT OUTER JOINS because some DBMSs do not support RIGHT OUTER JOIN syntax; that would make your code less portable to other systems.

FULL OUTER JOIN
A FULL OUTER JOIN combines the results from both tables and fills in NULLs where needed. Some DBMSs do not support FULL OUTER JOINS but LEFT OUTER JOIN and a UNION can emulate the same effect. I can't demonstrate a FULL OUTER JOIN here because MySQL does not support this syntax, but I do want you to be aware of its existence and use.

UNION

The UNION keyword is a fascinating bit of work and one of my favorite ways to construct a query. I waited for months until the 4.x version of MySQL came out so that I could use UNION queries. My fascination with UNION was short lived after MySQL implemented subqueries in version 4.1. UNIONs are very useful query types, as they are a *union* of two SELECT queries. Note that you have to use the same number of columns for each SELECT statement. It also helps if you name the columns the same in each SELECT statement. Although the data or column types don't have to match, you will find it a great advantage to name the columns the same with the AS keyword.

Basically, a UNION statement is a set of independent SELECT statements connected by the UNION keyword. Unions have a somewhat limited application, but the ability to combine SELECT statements this way is extremely valuable. Take a look at UNION's simple syntax:

```
[QUERY 1] UNION [QUERY 2] ORDER BY [sort order];
```

If you want to create a phone list of all current authors and agents, it is very easy to do with a UNION between the Authors and Agents tables:

```
SELECT Column1_Name, Column2_Name FROM Table1_Name UNION SELECT Column1_Name,
Column2_Name FROM Table2_Name;
```

```
SELECT First_Name, Last_Name, Phone FROM Authors UNION SELECT First_Name,
Last_Name, Phone FROM Agents;
```

Result:

```
+------------+-----------+
| First_Name | Last_Name |
+------------+-----------+
| Anne       | Cohen     |
| Glen       | Harris    |
| Lynn       | Steele    |
| Robert     | Balzer    |
| Lenard     | Dawson    |
| Paul       | Jones     |
| Lee        | Smith     |
| Ed         | Trumbull  |
| LeeAnn     | Evans     |
| Tom        | Rosen     |
+------------+-----------+
```

It is also possible to use more than two SELECT statements in a UNION query. It works the same way no matter how many UNIONs you *stack* together.

Objective

Construct a list of current authors, agents, and editors with phone numbers.

Fortunately, your tables are already in a convenient format for such querying. Each of the tables containing the required information has columns identically named First_Name, Last_Name, and Phone:

```
SELECT Column1_Name, Column2_Name FROM Table1_Name UNION SELECT Column1_Name,
Column2_Name FROM Table2_Name UNION SELECT Column1_Name, Column2_Name FROM
Table3_Name;
```

```
SELECT First_Name, Last_Name, Phone FROM Authors UNION SELECT First_Name,
Last_Name, Phone FROM Agents UNION SELECT First_Name, Last_Name, Phone FROM
Editors;
```

Result:

```
+------------+-----------+--------------+
| First_Name | Last_Name | Phone        |
+------------+-----------+--------------+
| Anne       | Cohen     | 512-555-1555 |
| Glen       | Harris    | 512-555-7755 |
| Lynn       | Steele    | 512-555-2951 |
| Robert     | Balzer    | 512-555-5131 |
| Lenard     | Dawson    | 512-555-7055 |
| Paul       | Jones     | 512-555-1234 |
| Lee        | Smith     | 512-555-2345 |
| Ed         | Trumbull  | 512-555-3456 |
| LeeAnn     | Evans     | 512-555-4567 |
| Tom        | Rosen     | 512-555-5678 |
| Donna      | Little    | 512-555-0001 |
| Travis     | Dalmon    | 512-555-0002 |
| Terri      | Coleman   | 512-555-0002 |
+------------+-----------+--------------+
```

Summary Queries

Summary queries are SELECTs typically limited to yielding a single or small set of numbers like counts, averages, sums, maximums, or minimums. For a database like Books, you could find out how many books a particular author has written or how many authors an agent represents. Summary data is not detailed like that in queries. Summary data is supported by column functions, GROUP BY clauses, and HAVING clauses.

Column Functions

Column functions quickly yield very valuable results if you need a statistical report from your data. An article that I recently wrote contained quite a bit of summary data. It was data gathered from an online interview that I created. Respondents were asked 12 questions in the interview and about half of the questions were of the type that could be easily summarized in a statistical fashion. One implicit piece of data was the respondent's country of origin. Through the use of browser data, I gathered the respondent's IP address and loaded that into the database. This information allowed me to summarize the number of people from each country who responded to the interview. I could have further summarized the data into opinions by country but didn't need to, as most of the responses were unanimous and not country specific. In my summary data, I used COUNT(), SUM(), AVG(), MAX(), and MIN().

To get a feel for the column functions for summary queries, you may issue the following statements:

```
SELECT COUNT(Title) FROM Works;
```

Result:

```
+--------------+
| COUNT(Title) |
+--------------+
|            7 |
+--------------+
```

You can receive richer results by using a column alias for COUNT(Title):

```
SELECT COUNT(Title) AS 'Number of Titles' FROM Works;
```

Result:

```
+------------------+
| Number of Titles |
+------------------+
|                7 |
+------------------+
```

Similarly, if you want to find the maximum of a set of numbers, use the column function MAX():

```
SELECT MAX(Sales) FROM Works;
```

Result:

```
+----------------+
|  MAX(Sales)  |
+----------------+
|          600000 |
+----------------+
```

You may also stack the functions similar to the way clauses and other objects are stacked in a query:

```
SELECT MIN(Sales), MAX(Sales), COUNT(Sales), SUM(Sales) AS 'Total Sales' FROM
Works;
```

Result:

```
+------------+------------+--------------+-------------+
| MIN(Sales) | MAX(Sales) | COUNT(Sales) | Total Sales |
+------------+------------+--------------+-------------+
|       2200 |     600000 |            7 |     1247200 |
+------------+------------+--------------+-------------+
```

GROUP BY

The GROUP BY clause is a way of subtotaling numbers to provide interesting reports. Consider the following query using a GROUP BY clause to show pricing data grouped by price:

```
SELECT COUNT(Price), Price FROM Works GROUP BY Price;
```

Result:

```
+--------------+-------+
| COUNT(Price) | Price |
+--------------+-------+
|            1 |  7.99 |
|            1 |  9.99 |
|            1 | 12.95 |
|            2 | 16.99 |
|            1 | 19.99 |
|            1 | 29.99 |
+--------------+-------+
```

The results reveal that of all the works recorded, two are priced at $16.99. You also get a look at the range of pricing from this query.

While these results demonstrate the idea of GROUP BY, they aren't very interesting or terribly useful.

Objective
Produce a report that shows each author and total sales from each author.

Isolate the tables Authors and Works for the query. You need the name of the authors and the total (sum) of sales for each author. A GROUP BY clause is also required because you are mixing summary data (SUM) and non-summary data (First_Name, Last_Name). From those requirements, your query can be constructed to look like this:

```
SELECT Authors.First_Name, Authors.Last_Name, SUM(Works.Sales) AS 'Total Sales'
FROM Works INNER JOIN Authors ON (Works.Author_ID = Authors.Author_ID)GROUP
BY Authors.First_Name, Authors.Last_Name;
```

Result:

```
+------------+-----------+-------------+
| First_Name | Last_Name | Total Sales |
+------------+-----------+-------------+
| Anne       | Cohen     |      600000 |
| Glen       | Harris    |       14000 |
| Lenard     | Dawson    |       14200 |
| Lynn       | Steele    |      400000 |
| Robert     | Balzer    |      219000 |
+------------+-----------+-------------+
```

The tick marks around Total Sales are required because of the space between the words.

HAVING
The HAVING clause is analogous to the WHERE clause for specifying a search condition. Anything that you can put into a WHERE clause can also go into a HAVING clause. HAVING is basically the WHERE for grouping data.

Consider the following query with a HAVING clause using the query from earlier:

```
SELECT Authors.First_Name, Authors.Last_Name, SUM(Works.Sales) AS 'Total Sales'
FROM Works INNER JOIN Authors ON (Works.Author_ID = Authors.Author_ID)GROUP
BY Authors.First_Name, Authors.Last_Name HAVING (SUM(Works.Sales) > 50000);
```

Result:

```
+------------+-----------+-------------+
| First_Name | Last_Name | Total Sales |
+------------+-----------+-------------+
| Anne       | Cohen     |      600000 |
| Lynn       | Steele    |      400000 |
| Robert     | Balzer    |      219000 |
+------------+-----------+-------------+
```

Batch Data Extraction

I am including batch data extraction and batch data loading in this chapter's next section because I consider the methods to be part of MySQL's advanced queries. *Batch data extraction* is the ability to export all, or a subset, of the data in a table to an external file. The external file is a standard text file that is readable by any editor and importable into many programs, such as spreadsheets and other databases. I suggest that you adopt a standard format for exporting data and stick with it. Consistency is very important when exporting and importing data if you wish to maintain data integrity between applications. The following syntax works in MySQL. Each DBMS has its own special syntax for importing and exporting data.

```
SELECT
[<select option> [<select option>...]]
{* | <select list>}
[<export definition>]
[
    FROM <table reference> [{, <table reference>}...]
    [WHERE <expression> [{<operator> <expression>}...]]
    [GROUP BY <group by definition>]
    [HAVING <expression> [{<operator> <expression>}...]]
    [ORDER BY <order by definition>]
    [LIMIT [<offset>,] <row count>]
    [PROCEDURE <procedure name> [(<argument> [{, <argument>}...])]]
    [{FOR UPDATE} | {LOCK IN SHARE MODE}]
]

<export definition>::=
INTO OUTFILE '<filename>' [<export option> [<export option>]]
| INTO DUMPFILE '<filename>'
```

```
<export option>::=
{FIELDS
    [TERMINATED BY '<value>']
    [[OPTIONALLY] ENCLOSED BY '<value>']
    [ESCAPED BY '<value>']}

| {LINES
    [STARTING BY '<value>']
    [TERMINATED BY '<value>']}
```

I will give you the syntax I use for the data extraction that I do on a regular basis. Feel free to adjust it to meet your needs. I find this the most useful method (after a lot of trial and error) for batch data extraction.

For dumping all the data from a table into a file:

```
SELECT * INTO OUTFILE 'Table_Name.txt' FIELDS TERMINATED BY ',' ENCLOSED BY
'"' FROM Table_Name;
```

The '"' is tick, quote, tick.

For your Authors table, the statement would look like this:

```
SELECT * INTO OUTFILE 'Authors.txt' FIELDS TERMINATED BY ',' ENCLOSED BY '"'
FROM Authors;
```

Find the file you just created and open it. You should see the following:

```
"9055","Anne","Cohen","512-555-1555"
"10009","Glen","Harris","512-555-7755"
"10239","Lynn","Steele","512-555-2951"
"10393","Bob","Fischer","512-555-1551"
"12999","Robert","Balzer","512-555-5131"
"23469","Lenard","Dawson","512-555-7055"
```

You may also specify column names, in any order, for a custom extraction:

```
SELECT Column1_Name, Column2_Name INTO OUTFILE 'Table_Name.txt' FIELDS
TERMINATED BY ',' ENCLOSED BY '"' FROM Table_Name;
SELECT Last_Name, First_Name INTO OUTFILE 'Authors1.txt' FIELDS TERMINATED BY
',' ENCLOSED BY '"' FROM Authors;
```

You must use a different filename or you will receive an error for subsequent exports. The output from the preceding statement is shown here:

```
"Cohen","Anne"
"Harris","Glen"
"Steele","Lynn"
"Fischer","Bob"
"Balzer","Robert"
"Dawson","Lenard"
```

You can also use WHERE clauses and multiple tables in your export statements:

```
SELECT Last_Name, First_Name, Works.Sales INTO OUTFILE '/tmp/Authors2.txt'
FIELDS TERMINATED BY ',' ENCLOSED BY '"' FROM Authors, Works WHERE
Authors.Author_ID = Works.Author_ID;
```

Result:

```
"Cohen","Anne","600000"
"Harris","Glen","14000"
"Steele","Lynn","400000"
"Balzer","Robert","9000"
"Balzer","Robert","210000"
"Dawson","Lenard","2200"
"Dawson","Lenard","12000"
```

Using this method, you can only export data. To dump structure or data for a table, multiple tables, a database, or even multiple databases, refer to Appendix B for the use of the mysqldump command. mysqldump is an external shell command for handling these kinds of dumps.

Batch Data Loading

Batch data loading is the inverse of batch data extraction. This is how you get a lot of data into a database quickly. For loading data, I usually use the mysqlimport shell utility described in Appendix B but have, on occasion, used LOAD DATA INFILE. The settings you use for the LOAD are determined by the format in which you have created (or received) the data.

```
LOAD DATA [LOW_PRIORITY | CONCURRENT] [LOCAL] INFILE 'file_name.txt'
    [REPLACE | IGNORE]
    INTO TABLE tbl_name
    [FIELDS
        [TERMINATED BY 'string']
```

```
    [[OPTIONALLY] ENCLOSED BY 'char']
    [ESCAPED BY 'char' ]
]

[LINES
    [STARTING BY 'string']
    [TERMINATED BY 'string']
]

[IGNORE number LINES]
[(col_name_or_user_var,...)]
[SET col_name = expr,...)]
```

To LOAD, or import, data using this method with one of the files you produced with SELECT INTO OUTFILE, you would use the following steps.

Objective
Import the Authors.txt file into the database.

Create a table where the imported data resides or use Authors, if it has been emptied. You have to create the table like the original, adhering to any foreign key constraints, number of columns, and so on in the table. You may rename the columns at this point and change the data order or values in the data file before importing.

```
CREATE TABLE Authors_New (Author_ID integer(4), First_Name char(30),
Last_Name char(40), Phone char(12))ENGINE=INNODB;

LOAD DATA INFILE 'Authors.txt' INTO TABLE Authors_New FIELDS TERMINATED BY
',' ENCLOSED BY '"';

SELECT * FROM Authors_New;
```

Result:

```
+-----------+------------+-----------+--------------+
| Author_ID | First_Name | Last_Name | Phone        |
+-----------+------------+-----------+--------------+
|      9055 | Anne       | Cohen     | 512-555-1555 |
|     10009 | Glen       | Harris    | 512-555-7755 |
|     10239 | Lynn       | Steele    | 512-555-2951 |
|     10393 | Bob        | Fischer   | 512-555-1551 |
```

```
|     12999 | Robert      | Balzer     | 512-555-5131 |
|     23469 | Lenard      | Dawson     | 512-555-7055 |
+-----------+-------------+------------+--------------+
```

The table data has been successfully imported into the database.

Creating your own file is another, but slower, way to import data into a table. For instance, if you want to add some authors into the Authors table, create a new text file like this one:

```
"19555","Bill","Ferris","512-555-1527"
"10909","Janet","Shoals","512-555-7000"
"19001","Clara","Janke","512-555-2196"
```

Save it as New_Authors.txt, though the name doesn't really matter:

```
LOAD DATA INFILE 'New_Authors.txt' INTO TABLE Authors FIELDS TERMINATED BY
',' ENCLOSED BY '"';
```

```
SELECT * FROM Authors;
```

Result:

```
+-----------+-------------+------------+--------------+
| Author_ID | First_Name  | Last_Name  | Phone        |
+-----------+-------------+------------+--------------+
|      9055 | Anne        | Cohen      | 512-555-1555 |
|     10009 | Glen        | Harris     | 512-555-7755 |
|     10239 | Lynn        | Steele     | 512-555-2951 |
|     10393 | Bob         | Fischer    | 512-555-1551 |
|     10909 | Janet       | Shoals     | 512-555-7000 |
|     12999 | Robert      | Balzer     | 512-555-5131 |
|     19001 | Clara       | Janke      | 512-555-2196 |
|     19555 | Bill        | Ferris     | 512-555-1527 |
|     23469 | Lenard      | Dawson     | 512-555-7055 |
+-----------+-------------+------------+--------------+
```

Another handy way of getting data into a new table is by using what is called an INSERT...SELECT statement:

```
CREATE TABLE Authors_Newer (Author_ID integer(4), First_Name char(30),
Last_Name char(40), Phone char(12))ENGINE=INNODB;
```

```
INSERT INTO Authors_Newer (Author_ID, First_Name, Last_Name, Phone) SELECT *
FROM Authors;
```

Result:

```
+------------+-------------+------------+---------------+
| Author_ID  | First_Name  | Last_Name  | Phone         |
+------------+-------------+------------+---------------+
|       9055 | Anne        | Cohen      | 512-555-1555  |
|      10009 | Glen        | Harris     | 512-555-7755  |
|      10239 | Lynn        | Steele     | 512-555-2951  |
|      10393 | Bob         | Fischer    | 512-555-1551  |
|      12999 | Robert      | Balzer     | 512-555-5131  |
|      23469 | Lenard      | Dawson     | 512-555-7055  |
+------------+-------------+------------+---------------+
```

This method of data import is analogous to the SELECT INTO syntax supported by DBMSs like Sybase and Microsoft's SQL Server.

The other SQL data import method is called CREATE...SELECT and works much like the INSERT INTO method with the twist that you create the new table and issue a SELECT statement to import the data from the other table. Depending on the way you create your new table, you may also use a SELECT, in any form, to import data—even from multiple tables. The CREATE and SELECT statements are issued as a single statement separated only by whitespace.

```
CREATE TABLE Authors_Newest (Author_ID integer(4), First_Name char(30),
Last_Name char(40), Phone char(12))ENGINE=INNODB SELECT * FROM Authors;


SELECT * FROM Authors_Newest;
```

Result:

```
+------------+-------------+------------+---------------+
| Author_ID  | First_Name  | Last_Name  | Phone         |
+------------+-------------+------------+---------------+
|       9055 | Anne        | Cohen      | 512-555-1555  |
|      10009 | Glen        | Harris     | 512-555-7755  |
|      10239 | Lynn        | Steele     | 512-555-2951  |
|      10393 | Bob         | Fischer    | 512-555-1551  |
|      12999 | Robert      | Balzer     | 512-555-5131  |
|      23469 | Lenard      | Dawson     | 512-555-7055  |
+------------+-------------+------------+---------------+
```

Batch data loading is my favorite way to gather data from other databases and insert that data into my own databases. I normally use to an external program like Perl to perform these batch extractions and insertions where I select the data I want from another DBMS, write that to a file, then import the data into my database.

Summary

This chapter has covered a great deal of material for advanced queries of many different types. It is by no means an exhaustive review of all of the advanced query types. The query types that I have chosen to leave out are for a more-advanced text such as *SQL Server 2005 for Developers* (Charles River Media). I feel that for an intermediate text, such as this, you have covered a large amount of information on advanced queries. My best advice, when constructing advanced and complicated queries, is to keep your eye on the data you want in the report—the result set. Don't get bogged down in syntax. Draw yourself a picture, if you need to, of a sample report that you want to create with column names and a row of data, so you know exactly what you are looking for in the query. For an exam in this area, you are probably on your own in coming up with a query to fit your needs, but in the "real world" you can go to online forums and other database professionals. Don't feel as if it is a weakness to ask for help from others. Learning from others is how you learn everything, but for some reason people often feel too intimidated to ask for help when it comes to highly technical subject matter.

Chapter Review

Multiple Choice

1. The HAVING clause is analogous to what other kind of clause?

    a) SELECT

    b) FROM

    c) HAVING

    d) WHERE

2. A subquery contains a _____ within a _____.

    a) SELECT, statement

    b) WHERE, statement

    c) HAVING, clause

    d) LOAD, statement

3. Batch data loading with LOAD DATA INFILE is

   a) fast and efficient.

   b) slow and difficult.

   c) costly and inefficient.

   d) not applicable.

4. A summary query is a query that uses

   a) LOAD DATA INFILE.

   b) batch functions.

   c) column functions.

   d) load functions.

5. A GROUP BY clause serves what purpose?

   a) Subtotaling numeric data

   b) Summing data

   c) Averaging data

   d) Subselecting data

6. What is the purpose of a CROSS JOIN?

   a) To give you all unique row possibilities

   b) To aggregate data

   c) To group numeric data by subtotals

   d) To provide a limited subset of data

7. A UNION query is

   a) a method of batch data loading.

   b) a query involving two or more SELECT statements.

   c) a unique subquery method.

   d) a way to extract all unique row possibilities from a table.

8. What is a major rule when using UNIONs?

    a) All tables in the database must have the same number of columns.

    b) You can only use two SELECT statements in a UNION.

    c) The number of columns for each SELECT statement has to match.

    d) You can only UNION numeric data.

9. You may only have one subquery within a query.

    a) True

    b) False

10. A subquery can only return one row of data unless you use the _____ keyword.

    a) UNION

    b) IN

    c) CROSS

    d) SELECT

Concepts

1. Suppose you have a spreadsheet of data to import into your database. Describe the steps that you would take to do this, using SQL if necessary.

2. Construct a query to show the amount of money each author has made so far based on the sales data in the database.

9 Views

Chapter 5 introduced you to the concept of views, but now it is time to get involved with views. *Views*, as stated in Chapter 5, are virtual tables but contain no data of their own. Database administrators love views because they offer a flexible means of allowing access to data without granting access to many tables. Views can, and usually do, consist of data from several tables that users can interact with freely without worrying about creating complex SELECT statements to get at the information they want. The user also needs no knowledge of how the database is constructed to use a view.

Views were an exciting addition to MySQL. I personally anticipated them because I write web applications for end users and views solve a lot of problems in such cases. They are also convenient for the web in that you can put together the data in a readable, organized format for users so reports are easier to generate. Typically, views are *read only*, meaning that the view is constructed via SQL query but information is static within that view and not updatable by the user. Data for the view is updated by having the tables that construct the view updated. This means that the data you see in a view today may be different tomorrow if the data in any underlying table is updated. It is possible, however, to create updatable views. If you recall, one of Edgar F. Codd's rules (Rule #6) was to have updatable views.

In this chapter I cover the syntax of creating, dropping, and using views. Updating views is also covered with demonstrations. The limitations on views are also discussed. You first create some simple views, and then you advance into more-complex ones. The Chapter Review tests your knowledge of the subject matter.

CREATE VIEW

Creating a view is sort of like combining a CREATE TABLE statement with a SELECT statement. You don't have to specify the column types because the view will use the column types from the underlying tables from which the view is derived.

CREATE VIEW syntax follows:

```
CREATE
    [OR REPLACE]
    [ALGORITHM = {UNDEFINED | MERGE | TEMPTABLE}]
    [DEFINER = { user | CURRENT_USER }]
    [SQL SECURITY { DEFINER | INVOKER }]
    VIEW view_name [(column_list)]
    AS select_statement
    [WITH [CASCADED | LOCAL] CHECK OPTION]
```

In its most basic form, a view can be created as simply this:

```
CREATE VIEW Author_Copy AS SELECT * FROM Authors;
```

Result:

```
SELECT * FROM Author_Copy;

+-----------+------------+-----------+--------------+
| Author_ID | First_Name | Last_Name | Phone        |
+-----------+------------+-----------+--------------+
|   9055    | Anne       | Cohen     | 512-555-1555 |
|  10009    | Glen       | Harris    | 512-555-7755 |
|  10239    | Lynn       | Steele    | 512-555-2951 |
|  10393    | Bob        | Fischer   | 512-555-1551 |
|  10909    | Janet      | Shoals    | 512-555-7000 |
|  12999    | Robert     | Balzer    | 512-555-5131 |
|  19001    | Clara      | Janke     | 512-555-2196 |
|  19555    | Bill       | Ferris    | 512-555-1527 |
|  23469    | Lenard     | Dawson    | 512-555-7055 |
+-----------+------------+-----------+--------------+
```

This is an exact virtual copy of the Authors table that is actually a SQL statement. The SQL statement executes when a request is made for the data from the Author_Copy view. The only thing not virtual about a view is its structure, which is kept in a file on disk (Author_Copy.frm). The view takes up no disk space, other than the structure file, in the InnoDB tablespace or as .MYI/MYD files. Views also do not have indexes. They use indexes from the tables from which they are constructed.

❄ ❄ ❄

You can use more-complex queries to create a view, such as the first example from Chapter 8:

```
CREATE VIEW Author_Works AS SELECT First_Name,Last_Name,Works.Title FROM
Authors,Works WHERE Authors.Author_ID = Works.Author_ID;
```

Result:

```
SELECT * FROM Author_Works;
```

```
+------------+------------+------------------------------+
| First_Name | Last_Name  | Title                        |
+------------+------------+------------------------------+
| Lynn       | Steele     | Bruises On My Heart          |
| Robert     | Balzer     | How To Write Great Queries   |
| Lenard     | Dawson     | Topiaries Are Tops           |
| Glen       | Harris     | Good Night, Good Chocolate   |
| Anne       | Cohen      | You Had Me At Shalom         |
| Robert     | Balzer     | You Are Never Your Own Boss  |
| Lenard     | Dawson     | Doodling As Art              |
+------------+------------+------------------------------+
```

You can now query this table like you would any other. Give it a try:

```
SELECT Last_Name, Title FROM Author_Works;
```

Result:

```
+------------+------------------------------+
| Last_Name  | Title                        |
+------------+------------------------------+
| Steele     | Bruises On My Heart          |
| Balzer     | How To Write Great Queries   |
| Dawson     | Topiaries Are Tops           |
| Harris     | Good Night, Good Chocolate   |
| Cohen      | You Had Me At Shalom         |
| Balzer     | You Are Never Your Own Boss  |
| Dawson     | Doodling As Art              |
+------------+------------------------------+
```

Views can also have columns that are calculated values like those you get from a summary query. Consider the following query:

```
CREATE VIEW Sales AS SELECT Authors.First_Name, Authors.Last_Name, SUM
(Works.Sales) * Works.Price AS Total_Sales_$ FROM Works INNER JOIN Authors ON
(Works.Author_ID = Authors.Author_ID) GROUP BY Authors.First_Name,
Authors.Last_Name ORDER BY Total_Sales_$ DESC;
```

Result:

```
SELECT * FROM Sales;
```

```
+------------+----------+---------------+
| First_Name | Last_Name | Total_Sales_$ |
+------------+----------+---------------+
| Robert     | Balzer   |    6567810.00 |
| Anne       | Cohen    |   10194000.00 |
| Lenard     | Dawson   |     141858.00 |
| Lynn       | Steele   |    6796000.00 |
| Glen       | Harris   |     279860.00 |
+------------+----------+---------------+
```

You may notice that though you created the view Sales with an ORDER BY DESC clause, it seems to have no effect on the order in which the data is retrieved from the view. The ORDER BY clause seems to make no difference to the order of data when retrieved with a simple SELECT * statement. You may test this by creating a new view named Sales1 and leaving out the ORDER BY clause:

```
CREATE VIEW Sales1 AS SELECT Authors.First_Name, Authors.Last_Name, SUM
(Works.Sales) * Works.Price AS Total_Sales_$ FROM Works INNER JOIN Authors ON
(Works.Author_ID = Authors.Author_ID) GROUP BY Authors.First_Name,
Authors.Last_Name;
```

Result:

```
SELECT * FROM Sales1;
```

```
+------------+----------+---------------+
| First_Name | Last_Name | Total_Sales_$ |
+------------+----------+---------------+
| Anne       | Cohen    |   10194000.00 |
| Glen       | Harris   |     279860.00 |
| Lenard     | Dawson   |     141858.00 |
```

```
| Lynn       | Steele    |    6796000.00 |
| Robert     | Balzer    |    6567810.00 |
+------------+-----------+---------------+
```

You are seeing the results correctly. The ORDER BY clause, while accepted by the database, has no effect on the order of the data in the view. In fact, it is likely, although not explicitly stated, that the ORDER BY is actually ignored to enhance performance. You may, of course, issue an ORDER BY clause when selecting data from the Sales view for predictable results:

```
SELECT * FROM Sales ORDER BY Total_Sales_$ DESC;
```

```
+------------+-----------+---------------+
| First_Name | Last_Name | Total_Sales_$ |
+------------+-----------+---------------+
| Anne       | Cohen     |   10194000.00 |
| Lynn       | Steele    |    6796000.00 |
| Robert     | Balzer    |    6567810.00 |
| Glen       | Harris    |     279860.00 |
| Lenard     | Dawson    |     141858.00 |
+------------+-----------+---------------+
```

Objective

Create a view that lists the author, the author's works, and the work's publisher.

Isolate the tables and columns that you are interested in for the query: Authors.First_Name, Authors.Last_Name, Works.Title, and Publishers.Company.

Find relationships between the tables: Authors.Author_ID = Works.Author_ID and Works.Publisher_ID = Publishers.Publishers_ID.

The rest is just putting together the query and making it pretty with some AS aliases. Remember that you are creating a view so the data is in a more organized and easier-to-use format for users. While it is reasonable to keep Publishers.Company, the user may be expecting to choose a publisher, not a company.

```
CREATE VIEW Published_Works AS SELECT Authors.First_Name AS First,
Authors.Last_Name AS Last, Works.Title, Publishers.Company AS Publisher FROM
Works INNER JOIN Authors ON (Works.Author_ID = Authors.Author_ID) INNER JOIN
Publishers ON (Works.Publisher_ID = Publishers.Publisher_ID);
```

Use this if you prefer the non-JOIN style query:

```
CREATE VIEW Published_Works AS SELECT Authors.First_Name AS First,
Authors.Last_Name AS Last, Works.Title, Publishers.Company AS Publisher FROM
Authors,Works,Publishers WHERE Works.Author_ID = Authors.Author_ID AND
Works.Publisher_ID = Publishers.Publisher_ID;
```

Result:

```
SELECT * FROM Published_Works ORDER BY Last;
```

```
+--------+--------+------------------------------+-----------------------------+
| First  | Last   | Title                        | Publisher                   |
+--------+--------+------------------------------+-----------------------------+
| Robert | Balzer | You Are Never Your Own Boss  | Publish With Us, LLC.       |
| Robert | Balzer | How To Write Great Queries   | Publish With Us, LLC.       |
| Anne   | Cohen  | You Had Me At Shalom          | Howdy Yall Publishing, Inc  |
| Lenard | Dawson | Topiaries Are Tops           | Huge Publishing House, Inc. |
| Lenard | Dawson | Doodling As Art              | No Newbies Publishing, Inc. |
| Glen   | Harris | Good Night, Good Chocolate   | Huge Publishing House, Inc. |
| Lynn   | Steele | Bruises On My Heart          | Howdy Yall Publishing, Inc  |
+--------+--------+------------------------------+-----------------------------+
```

You can specify the column names to see in the view after the view name instead of using the AS alias syntax. Some prefer this syntax because it makes the query easier to read. Using the preceding example, you see how the syntax is affected:

```
CREATE VIEW Published_Works (First, Last, Title, Publisher) AS SELECT
Authors.First_Name, Authors.Last_Name, Works.Title, Publishers.Company FROM
Authors,Works,Publishers WHERE Works.Author_ID = Authors.Author_ID AND
Works.Publisher_ID = Publishers.Publisher_ID;
```

This is exactly equivalent to the CREATE VIEW statement used in the objective. Feel free to use the syntax that is more comfortable for you, since either is correct.

If you use the OR REPLACE clause when creating a view, you overwrite any view with the same name as the one you are creating. This is especially useful for web programmers because it replaces a view without any errors.

Try out the following CREATE VIEW syntax with the OR REPLACE clause:

```
CREATE OR REPLACE VIEW Published_Works AS SELECT Company, Phone FROM
Publishers;
```

You have just overwritten the Published_Works view with the new view with the same name.

```
SELECT * FROM Published_Works Works;
```

```
+----------------------------+---------------+
| Company                    | Phone         |
+----------------------------+---------------+
| No Newbies Publishing, Inc. | 512-555-9901 |
| Huge Publishing House, Inc. | 408-555-9901 |
| Publish With Us, LLC.      | 512-555-9901 |
| Howdy Yall Publishing, Inc | 512-555-9901 |
+----------------------------+---------------+
```

As you may have noticed, there were no errors from replacing the old view with the new one.

You may also create a view from another view by querying the view as if it were an actual table:

```
CREATE OR REPLACE VIEW Pub_Works AS SELECT First, Last, Publisher FROM
Published_Works:
```

```
SELECT * FROM Pub_Works;
```

```
+--------+--------+----------------------------+
| First  | Last   | Publisher                  |
+--------+--------+----------------------------+
| Lenard | Dawson | No Newbies Publishing, Inc. |
| Lenard | Dawson | Huge Publishing House, Inc. |
| Glen   | Harris | Huge Publishing House, Inc. |
| Robert | Balzer | Publish With Us, LLC.      |
| Robert | Balzer | Publish With Us, LLC.      |
| Lynn   | Steele | Howdy Yall Publishing, Inc |
| Anne   | Cohen  | Howdy Yall Publishing, Inc |
+--------+--------+----------------------------+
```

You can create many "layers" of views this way. One possible scenario for creating *view layers*, or *subviews*, is that you are creating data views for different departments or individuals and you want them to see different information. Creating views of views has no real consequences unless you want them updatable and are overly concerned with performance. If you cascade too deeply with your views, you can complicate things and impede performance. I suggest, for simplicity and manageability, that you only use two levels of views. In other words, creating views and views of those views is probably enough to keep up with. Don't cause yourself unnecessary grief. If you need a table, create a table. If you need a view, create one. Keeping your database simple is not a sign of weakness; it is a sign of wisdom. Databases can quickly get very large and complex and as they do the need for order and simplicity also increases.

The other significant parts of CREATE VIEW syntax have to do with creating the updatable views covered later in this chapter.

ALTER VIEW

ALTER VIEW edits the structure or definition of a view and is similar to other ALTER statements. You can actually redefine the way the view looks by changing the SELECT statement from which it was originally created. This is equivalent to dropping the view and recreating it with the same name.

The syntax for ALTER VIEW is given here:

```
ALTER
    [ALGORITHM = {UNDEFINED | MERGE | TEMPTABLE}]
    [DEFINER = { user | CURRENT_USER }]
    [SQL SECURITY { DEFINER | INVOKER }]
    VIEW view_name [(column_list)]
    AS select_statement
    [WITH [CASCADED | LOCAL] CHECK OPTION]
```

Objective

Change the Published_Works view to include the state. Take a look at the original CREATE statement for Published_Works:

```
CREATE OR REPLACE VIEW Published_Works AS SELECT Company, Phone FROM
Publishers;
```

Now add state to the view with an ALTER VIEW statement:

```
ALTER VIEW Published_Works AS SELECT Company, Phone, State FROM Publishers;
SELECT * FROM Published_Works Works;
```

```
+-----------------------------+---------------+-------+
| Company                     | Phone         | State |
+-----------------------------+---------------+-------+
| No Newbies Publishing, Inc. | 512-555-9901  | TX    |
| Huge Publishing House, Inc. | 408-555-9901  | CA    |
| Publish With Us, LLC.       | 512-555-9901  | TX    |
| Howdy Yall Publishing, Inc  | 512-555-9901  | TX    |
+-----------------------------+---------------+-------+
```

You may also define a completely new SELECT statement when you alter this view.

Objective

Reconstruct the Published_Works view using a new SELECT statement.

You can really do just about anything you want here, but I suggest putting the original Published_Works back together.

```
ALTER VIEW Published_Works AS SELECT Authors.First_Name AS First,
Authors.Last_Name AS Last, Works.Title, Publishers.Company AS Publisher FROM
Works INNER JOIN Authors ON (Works.Author_ID = Authors.Author_ID) INNER JOIN
Publishers ON (Works.Publisher_ID = Publishers.Publisher_ID);
```

Result:

```
SELECT * FROM Published_Works;
```

```
+--------+--------+----------------------------+----------------------------+
| First  | Last   | Title                      | Publisher                  |
+--------+--------+----------------------------+----------------------------+
| Lynn   | Steele | Bruises On My Heart        | Howdy Yall Publishing, Inc |
| Robert | Balzer | How To Write Great Queries | Publish With Us, LLC.      |
| Lenard | Dawson | Topiaries Are Tops         | Huge Publishing House, Inc.|
| Glen   | Harris | Good Night, Good Chocolate | Huge Publishing House, Inc.|
| Anne   | Cohen  | You Had Me At Shalom       | Howdy Yall Publishing, Inc |
| Robert | Balzer | You Are Never Your Own Boss| Publish With Us, LLC.      |
| Lenard | Dawson | Doodling As Art            | No Newbies Publishing, Inc.|
+--------+--------+----------------------------+----------------------------+
```

Performing an ALTER VIEW does not alter any data or underlying tables, so there is no cause for concern when issuing an ALTER VIEW statement. The ALTER VIEW merely reformats the view.

DROP VIEW

DROP VIEW does exactly as you expect; it drops the named view. Like ALTER VIEW, DROP VIEW does not affect any underlying tables or data.

```
DROP VIEW [IF EXISTS]
    view_name [, view_name] ...
    [RESTRICT | CASCADE]
```

You may also drop multiple views at the same time with a single DROP VIEW statement.

SHOW CREATE VIEW

SHOW CREATE VIEW is much like SHOW CREATE TABLE in that it reveals the view's structure and how it was created. It can be a bit hard to read, but I have simplified the results here:

```
SHOW CREATE VIEW view_name
SHOW CREATE VIEW Published_Works;
|| View | Create View |
|| Published_Works | CREATE ALGORITHM=UNDEFINED DEFINER='root'@'localhost' SQL
SECURITY DEFINER VIEW 'Published_Works' AS select 'Authors'.'First_Name' AS
'First','Authors'.'Last_Name' AS 'Last','Works'.'Title' AS
'Title','Publishers'.'Company' AS 'Publisher' from (('Works' join 'Authors' on
(('Works'.'Author_ID' = 'Authors'.'Author_ID'))) join 'Publishers' on
(('Works'.'Publisher_ID' = 'Publishers'.'Publisher_ID'))) |
```

Updating Views

Support for updatable views is one of the original rules listed by Codd in his 12 rules for RDBMSs. *Updatable* means that the underlying data can be edited by means of INSERT, UPDATE, or DELETE statements. Most views are actually updatable provided the user has the proper privileges for the underlying table(s) from which the view is derived.

For instance, if you want to update the name of the author (Lynn Steele) in the Published_Works view to the correct spelling (Lynne), the UPDATE statement would look like the following:

```
UPDATE Published_Works SET First = 'Lynne' WHERE Last = 'Steele';
SELECT * FROM Published_Works;
```

Result:

```
+---------+---------+------------------------------+------------------------------+
| First   | Last    | Title                        | Publisher                    |
+---------+---------+------------------------------+------------------------------+
| Lenard  | Dawson  | Doodling As Art              | No Newbies Publishing, Inc. |
| Lenard  | Dawson  | Topiaries Are Tops           | Huge Publishing House, Inc. |
| Glen    | Harris  | Good Night, Good Chocolate   | Huge Publishing House, Inc. |
| Robert  | Balzer  | How To Write Great Queries   | Publish With Us, LLC.        |
| Robert  | Balzer  | You Are Never Your Own Boss  | Publish With Us, LLC.        |
| Lynne   | Steele  | Bruises On My Heart          | Howdy Yall Publishing, Inc  |
| Anne    | Cohen   | You Had Me At Shalom         | Howdy Yall Publishing, Inc  |
+---------+---------+------------------------------+------------------------------+
```

Lynne's name has been updated in the view Published_Works. The UPDATE actually took place at the table level in the Authors table. You can prove this by issuing a SELECT on the Authors table:

```
SELECT * FROM Authors;
```

Result:

```
+-----------+------------+-----------+---------------+
| Author_ID | First_Name | Last_Name | Phone         |
+-----------+------------+-----------+---------------+
| 9055      | Anne       | Cohen     | 512-555-1555  |
| 10009     | Glen       | Harris    | 512-555-7755  |
| 10239     | Lynne      | Steele    | 512-555-2951  |
| 10393     | Bob        | Fischer   | 512-555-1551  |
| 10909     | Janet      | Shoals    | 512-555-7000  |
| 12999     | Robert     | Balzer    | 512-555-5131  |
| 19001     | Clara      | Janke     | 512-555-2196  |
| 19555     | Bill       | Ferris    | 512-555-1527  |
| 23469     | Lenard     | Dawson    | 512-555-7055  |
+-----------+------------+-----------+---------------+
```

The view appears updated, but it is actually the underlying table that is updated. This also proves that views are dynamic and that they execute anew each time they are called. There is no caching of data in a view.

Views are not updatable if any of the following conditions exist:

- ❈ Aggregate functions: SUM(), MIN(), MAX(), COUNT(), and so forth
- ❈ DISTINCT
- ❈ GROUP BY
- ❈ HAVING
- ❈ UNION or UNION ALL
- ❈ Subquery in the select list
- ❈ JOIN
- ❈ Non-updatable view in the FROM clause
- ❈ A subquery in the WHERE clause referring to a table in the FROM clause
- ❈ Reference only to literal values; in this case, there is no underlying table to update
- ❈ ALGORITHM = TEMPTABLE; use of a temporary table always makes a view non-updatable

Further, a view can only update the underlying tables from which it is derived if there is a one-to-one relationship between its data and the data in the table.

You can insert data into tables via updatable views if the following criteria are met:

* There are no duplicate view column names.
* The view must contain all columns in the base table that do not have a default value.
* The view columns must be simple column references and not derived columns. A *derived column* is one acted upon by a function such as SUM or AVG or is involved in some sort of calculation such as Column1_Name/Column2_Name. You can update the original column.

Multiple tables may be updated via a view in certain circumstances. The view must be created from an INNER JOIN, not from a UNION or an OUTER JOIN. INSERT only works with a single table in a multiple-table–derived view. Deletes are not supported in a multiple-table view. If you attempt a DELETE from a multiple table view, you receive the following error:

```
DELETE FROM Published_Works WHERE First_Name = 'Bill';
ERROR 1395 (HY000): Can not delete from join view 'Books.Published_Works'
```

Limitations of Views

It seems that this entire chapter is made up of limitations placed on views, but the following list summarizes the more significant ones. Note that some of the "limitations" are by design and are limitations of views by definition.

* The SELECT statement cannot contain a subquery in the FROM clause.
* The SELECT statement cannot refer to system or user variables.
* The SELECT statement cannot refer to prepared statement parameters.
* Within a stored routine, the definition cannot refer to routine parameters or local variables.
* Any table or view referred to in the definition must exist. However, after a view has been created, it is possible to drop a table or view that the definition refers to. To check a view definition for problems of this kind, use the CHECK TABLE statement.
* The definition cannot refer to a TEMPORARY table, and you cannot create a TEMPORARY view.
* The tables named in the view definition must already exist.
* You cannot associate a trigger with a view.
* You cannot index a view.

View Security

Views have a very simple security system:

✳ Using a view: Need SELECT permission for the view. This enables read-only access; no permissions necessary for underlying tables for read-only access.

✳ Creating a view: Need at least SELECT privilege on the underlying tables and CREATE VIEW permission in the database in which the view is to be created.

✳ Altering a view: Need CREATE and DROP for the view.

✳ Updating a view: Need access to the underlying tables.

✳ Dropping a view: Need the DROP privilege for the view. To update a view with INSERT, UPDATE or DELETE, the user needs those privileges on the tables from which the view is derived.

Views are inherently secure because your underlying table structure is hidden from the user. If a view is created with ALGORITHM = TEMPTABLE, the view is very secure and cannot be updated regardless of underlying table permissions.

Advanced View Information

ALGORITHM has to do with how the view is processed when executed.

✳ UNDEFINED is the default ALGORITHM for a view. It is not a negative attribute. It simply means that the DBMS will make the decision of which algorithm to use between MERGE and TEMPTABLE. For an UNDEFINED algorithm, either explicitly or implicitly issued, the DBMS first attempts to use a MERGE algorithm.

✳ MERGE means that the view will attempt to *merge* the view's defining SQL statement and any statements that are run against it. This is a good thing if your view is based upon a query that yields a one-to-one relationship between its data and the table data from which it is derived. It is good because MySQL can issue a single SQL query against the tables that are defined in the view plus the new statement rather than one for the view and a separate one for the new query. This makes the query more efficient for you and the database. Where the data in the view and the underlying tables do not have a one-to-one relationship with each other, a MERGE algorithm is not allowed and becomes an UNDEFINED algorithm.

✳ TEMPTABLE is not updatable because the query that defines the view creates a temporary table upon execution and the new query is issued against the data in the temporary table. The temporary table is created each time the view is executed.

DEFINER = CURRENT USER by default, meaning the user who issues the CREATE VIEW statement is the DEFINER. You must have the SUPER privilege to issue a user other than yours in a DEFINER clause. The user defined must be a standard MySQL username, such as 'bob'@'localhost'.

The SQL SECURITY characteristic is issued to tell the parser which account to use when checking access privileges for the view at execution. The default is SQL SECURITY DEFINER. The only other valid value for SQL SECURITY is INVOKER. If SQL SECURITY is set to DEFINER, then the view executes with the permission of the DEFINER, or *creator*, of the view. If SQL SECURITY is set to INVOKER, the view executes with the permissions of the user who invokes the view.

The WITH CHECK OPTION can only be issued on updatable views to prevent updates except for those that are *true* in the WHERE clause of the view's defining SQL statement. The default value is CASCADED if no keyword is given, which means that all underlying views are checked. The keyword LOCAL is specified explicitly to only check the current view.

Summary

This chapter is meant to give you an idea of how important and useful views are to the database administrator. Their role in contemporary databases is one of security as well as convenience. Views allow you to customize and aggregate data for a specific purpose or group of users. They can also be useful in keeping your database design hidden from users, even if you merely create a copy of a table or multiple tables via a UNION query. If you are truly concerned about security and want to keep your database design hidden, you can create a separate database that contains only views. This is a great way to provide a data to a large number of anonymous users—perhaps for use on the Internet. Your data is available in a read-only format for anonymous users while database authenticated users update the information on the actual tables. TEMPTABLES allows this to occur efficiently because the locks on the original data are released and can be updated once the temporary table is created.

I urge you to experiment with views and to consult your users, if possible, to gain an understanding of the types of data collections and aggregations that would make their jobs easier. Databases are supposed to be useful tools that make our lives and jobs richer, easier, and more efficient. Think of it this way: The database, tables, data, procedures, and other database objects are the property of the company and under your control, but views belong to the users and should be designed with them in mind.

Chapter Review

Multiple Choice

1. What is the minimum permission required to use a view?

   a) VIEW

   b) SHOW

   c) CHANGE

   d) SELECT

2. The _____ is the user who created the view, while the _____ is the user who executes the view.

   a) INVOKER, DEFINER

   b) INVOKER, CASCADER

   c) DEFINER, INVOKER

   d) DEFINER, LOCAL

3. A view cannot be made of multiple tables.

   a) True

   b) False

4. A view created with ALGORITHM = TEMPTABLE is

   a) not updatable.

   b) default.

   c) impossible.

   d) possible, but not recommended.

5. The correct syntax for creating a view is

   a) CREATE VIEW View1_Name AS SELECT * FROM Table1_Name;.

   b) CREATE VIEW AS SELECT * FROM Table1_Name;.

   c) CREATE VIEW View1_Name AS Table1_Name;.

   d) CREATE VIEW View1_Name AS READ-ONLY FROM Table1_Name;.

6. Consider the following: You have created a view, View1_Name, as a UNION of two SELECT statements. You also have INSERT, UPDATE, DELETE, and SELECT privileges on all the underlying tables for the view. Which one of the following is true of this scenario?

    a) The view is not updatable but can be queried.

    b) A view cannot be created from a UNION.

    c) The view can be updated and queried.

    d) The view cannot be updated due to insufficient permissions.

7. The correct syntax for deleting a view is

    a) DELETE VIEW View1_Name WHERE VIEW = View1_Name;.

    b) DROP VIEW View1_Name WHERE VIEW = View1_Name;.

    c) DELETE VIEW View1_Name CASCADE WITH CHECK OPTION;.

    d) DROP VIEW View1_Name;.

8. Removing a view also removes all of the underlying tables provided the user has appropriate permissions to do so.

    a) True

    b) False

9. Which permissions must a user have to use ALTER VIEW?

    a) ALTER, CREATE

    b) DROP, CREATE

    c) DROP, ALTER

    d) ALTER, SELECT

10. A view's default algorithm is

    a) SELECT.

    b) UNDEFINED.

    c) MERGE.

    d) TEMPTABLE.

Concepts

1. Why bother with views at all? Wouldn't it be just as easy and secure to use a regular table created with the data needed for the users? Give your arguments for your answer.

2. Explain the steps you take in creating and testing an updatable view.

10 } SQL Optimization

This chapter is provided as an overview of SQL optimization. In it, I cover many different topics and sources of bottlenecks and their resolution. It is true that this book is about SQL. It is also true that you must figure out why your queries are not responding at acceptable speeds. Your database may be choking, sluggish, or running slow for many reasons, and several of them have no relationship to how well your database is designed or SQL statements written. This chapter examines areas that you should investigate prior to rewriting your queries or redesigning your database, as well as things to do to optimize your SQL.

Database administrators are constantly trying to get better throughput, faster access, or quicker data retrieval from their DBMSs. DBAs in larger companies are but one part of an entire team that takes on such tasks. In smaller companies, however, you may be the DBA, the performance expert, the webmaster and CTO—all rolled into one. Discovering the source of performance bottlenecks is not always easy, but it usually only takes someone in a big office to make the determination that the database needs to be faster to get things really moving. This chapter will become very valuable to you when things begin to go wrong.

There isn't sufficient space in this book to make you a performance expert, but it will help you begin troubleshooting and solving performance issues. If you find persistent performance issues with your system(s) that you cannot resolve with this information, you may have to rely on an expert in this field to discover and fix the issues.

Hardware Optimization

Hardware optimization is a good place to start if server responsiveness is not what you, or others, think it should be. IT professionals often think that new hardware is justifiable based on simple "gut" feelings but soon realize that those who hold the checkbook seldom agree. Before you tell someone to spend thousands of dollars on new hardware, you had better do your homework. To do this homework, you need concrete information about your system's performance. You need graphical and numerical information that shows low, standard, and optimal performance compared to your actual data. Replacing hardware on a whim or without concrete data is putting you in treacherous waters. Get a baseline of performance before assessing performance and looking for bottlenecks. I suggest a performance package like Orca (www.orcaware.com) to assist in this process. Orca is a cross-platform performance-monitoring solution that is open source, free, easily installed, and very customizable. This is just a suggestion, as there are many good products, both commercial and open source, for performance monitoring. You will find the installation how-to for Orca in Appendix D.

Four systems require monitoring in order to find potential and actual performance bottlenecks on your database server(s): Disk I/O (Input/Output), CPU (Processor[s]), Memory (RAM and swap), and Network (NIC, switch/hub, router, and connectivity).

Disk I/O

The simple definition of *disk I/O* is the reading and writing of data to and from a disk drive (or *hard drive,* as they are popularly known) by a program. Your disk subsystem should be the first suspect in database sluggishness, as this is where bottlenecks most often occur for database servers. This is because the disk subsystem is the slowest part of the computer. When measuring disk performance, take into account the entire disk subsystem, which is composed of the disk, the controller (which may be a separate card in the case of SCSI drives), and the I/O bus.

What you check and how you check it depend largely on the database server's operating system, but in general check these parameters:

※ Disk reads and/or writes/sec: How often applications are reading from and writing to the disk.

※ Percentage % disk time: How busy the disk is; assessed in conjunction with Disk Queue Length.

※ Disk queue length: Indicates the amount of disk congestion and the number of waiting processes.

※ Disk bytes read: Data transfer rate can indicate random reads versus sequential and level of fragmentation.

I can't look at your system and tell you what kind of parameters you should see, but I can give you some guidelines.

You need to check disk performance on the system when it is quiet and measure your *idle* performance. A quiet system has all services functional except for your dedicated database server. If it is not dedicated, turn off any other user services. Do not turn off any performance-monitoring services. This is your low performance baseline. Then, one at a time, turn on any other disabled services and keep an eye on the disk performance. Finally, start your database server and watch disk performance as users begin to reconnect to the system. You will probably need to watch your performance over a few weeks, noting any trends or patterns.

If your situation is dire, then this monitoring will be of no use to you unless you have performed it in the past and can now compare data. In a drastic situation, the following measures may be taken to relieve the bottlenecks caused from overworked disks. Make backups of data before performing any of these:

- ❄ Turn off any unnecessary services, like indexing, that may be causing your system's disks to be busy.
- ❄ Defragment your drives:
  - ❄ Windows: Run the Disk Defragmenter program.
  - ❄ Unix: Back up and reformat the file systems, then restore the data on those file systems from the backup.
- ❄ Separate your data from other files. Sometimes just adding a separate disk for data will alleviate some of the bottlenecks.
- ❄ Run any repair or optimization programs on your tables. Tables can become fragmented and inefficient over time. This is part of regular maintenance—plan for it.
- ❄ Rework your file systems:
  - ❄ Windows: Always use NTFS. Do not compress the drive or folders that your data is on.
  - ❄ Unix: Create a separate file system for data; use the most efficient type available for your operating system. Never span drives for data.
- ❄ Use a file-system block size appropriate for your data. If your database files are very large, having a block size of 512 bytes is less efficient than 2,048 or 4,096 bytes. You can change your file systems' block size by reformatting the file system and restoring the data to it.
- ❄ Separate logs from data. If possible, have logs written to a different disk than data. Logging is a consistent disk-write process and can severely impact performance based on the logging level. I suggest only logging errors and failures—not warnings or successes—if possible.
- ❄ Replace the disks with newer, faster disks. It is worth the extra cost to go with a 15K rpm disk rather than a 10K rpm or less, if better I/O is what you need. Choose disks with a low seek time. Always purchase the fastest disks you can afford, as disk I/O is very important for file-based applications.
- ❄ RAID configurations generally perform better than single disks if configured correctly. RAID 5 performs better than other RAID types for database servers that perform more reads than writes, which is generally the case. If you have a lot of writes, then you need to investigate RAID 01 or RAID 10 for optimal performance.

❋ Check, upgrade, or add a controller. You may need to upgrade the controller to take full advantage of the disk speed that you already have or add a controller and move some disks to the second controller. If given the choice, move the data to a different controller.

Disks are very inexpensive these days and the technology is always improving. The increase in speed and technology is part of the reason it is very hard to choose between IDE and SCSI disks for a server. The way I have configured database servers in the past on Linux or Windows is to have a mirrored (RAID 1) IDE setup for the system disks and a RAID 5 SCSI setup (three disks) for the data. This pretty nice setup is a real performer and fairly inexpensive. If you have a disk failure, a RAID 5 setup will not suffer much in performance, as many of the other RAID setups do. It is advantageous to purchase disks from different lots when building RAID systems to alleviate failures that occur too closely together. Disks in the same lot tend to have similar failure times. It seems that before I learned this lesson, the time between disk failures was about two weeks.

❋ **YOU WANT RAID WITH THAT?**
Safe. Fast. Cheap. Choose any two. This is the old saying that refers to RAID configurations. Everyone, of course, wants all three but it just isn't possible. The choice of any two of these restrictions always excludes the third.

The bottom line on disk performance for database servers is to buy the best you can afford. Get low seek times (expressed in milliseconds) and high rpms. Get a performance baseline and check regularly on the performance. Don't assume that everything is fine just because you bought the best disks available and set up a RAID 10 configuration. You must maintain constant vigilance over your systems, watching for any anomalies.

CPU

The CPU is the next most popular place to look for performance bottlenecks. CPU bottlenecks are harder to track down and are a bit rare compared to disk problems. It isn't so unusual for the CPU to be 100-percent utilized for certain tasks or queries, but a sustained high CPU utilization may be indicative of a serious problem. Resolving CPU bottlenecks is, or seems, fairly obvious. Once you know you have a CPU bottleneck, you have some options that bring you to a quick resolution:

❋ Turn off server screensavers, especially the 3D ones.

❋ Bind the database process to a CPU or CPUs other than CPU0.

❋ Upgrade the processor(s).

❋ Use a large Level-2 cache.

❋ Examine CPU-bound queries.

If your CPU stays at 80-percent utilization or above, you need to find out why; your users will experience delays in retrieving data. Unlike other problems, a reboot likely will not cure a high CPU usage. Examine Task Manager on Windows or process list data on Unix to find out which process, or processes, are utilizing CPU time. Once you find the process, find out why this process is burning up CPU cycles. Once you determine the process, my suggestion is to upgrade or patch the program that is causing the issue. I have found that checking a product's knowledgebase for such problems is invaluable and time saving. If the patch or upgrade doesn't solve the issue, then you may have to consult the vendor's product information to make sure you have all of the prerequisite components, with the correct versions, installed on your system.

Sometimes, believe it or not, the CPU brand itself can be part of the issue. One of my clients had an issue where their database software kept crashing on their brand-new database server. We, and the vendor, tried everything to resolve it. I even replaced the CPU and RAM on the server. The problem remained. I read all of the information related to the product over a weekend and found that the vendor recommended a particular CPU brand. We, of course, had supplied the other brand. The processor switch subsequently took place and the problems were resolved. There was some issue with a mathematical function with the original processor. I know it is a difficult thing to do, but you should always read the requirements and prerequisites (hardware and software) for your critical applications.

It is possible that you simply need to replace your CPU with a faster one. When purchasing a CPU, always buy the highest amount of cache that you can comfortably afford. DBMSs use this CPU cache. Multiple CPUs are also a performance boost, as you can bind processes to specific CPUs, relieving some of the load on CPU0.

Memory

Memory is consistently the location of most database bottlenecks. This seems to occur more often and with greater severity on Windows than on Unix or Linux. This is not a slam on Windows but just an observation. I have not experienced the memory issues on Windows 2003 Server that I did on previous versions. Generally, on older versions of Windows Server operating systems, a weekly reboot was needed to keep memory fresh and the system running at peak performance. Many systems administrators reboot all servers on a weekly basis, regardless of platform, for this very reason. I do recall however a Solaris server running Oracle with constant connections on very busy database that had an uptime of over 1,200 days. That is impressive to a lot of people and scary to others. It was scary to me and my fears were rewarded with a 2 a.m. page from our network response center engaging me on a priority one incident after a Unix system administrator "accidentally" rebooted the system. This incident made me a fan of periodic system reboots.

Random Access Memory (RAM)

When you think of memory, RAM is what you think of. RAM is one of the defining parts of a computer. Look at any advertisement and you will see the processor, RAM, and disk size mentioned as part of the package's attributes. RAM bottlenecks are bad to have but usually easy to remedy. The simplest thing you can do to remedy a memory bottleneck is buy more RAM for the affected system.

RAM is inexpensive and possibly the one area where people seem to underestimate their needs. Double the recommended RAM for any system that will be even moderately used. This means you need to double the recommended RAM for the operating system and applications that run on it. This may sound extreme but if you don't want to experience problems related to memory, then my suggestion is to spend the extra money now. Typically the minimum and recommended memory requirements for an operating system or an application like a database server are given as guidelines for low to average utilization.

Swap Space or Page File

Swap space is that area on a disk reserved for use when applications need to be paged or swapped to disk. If your swap space, or *page file,* is too small, you experience performance problems on your server. The server seems sluggish and the disk very busy. It is also likely that the amount of available RAM is extremely low. This situation is known as *thrashing* and is an administrator's worst nightmare. The Windows solution is to add more swap space or increase the size of the page file. Occasionally, an undersized Windows page file causes the system to freeze, requiring a reboot and a resizing of the page file.

All kinds of calculations can reveal the ultimate size for your swap space. It is generally accepted to use swap space that is equal to two times the amount of RAM. This is a great place to start and acceptable for a wide range of applications. You should consult your vendor's specifications for swap space if there is any doubt. If you decide that your swap space exceeds three times the amount of RAM, then you should add more RAM to the system. Swap space cannot take the place of RAM. It is only added as a supplement to free RAM for actively running programs.

Network

Network hardware can create a number of interesting and difficult-to-track problems. Interesting because the problems can be intermittent or originate remotely and difficult to track because you may not have the access or the expertise needed to troubleshoot issues with some of the hardware. Aside from hardware, there can also be problems with DNS, WINS, or network information configuration. Generally speaking, most network bottlenecks are due to some hardware failure, but may also originate from faulty drivers. In the following subsections I show you what to look for when you suspect a network problem and how to resolve it.

Network Interface Card (NIC)

The *NIC* is the server's connection to the rest of the network and the outside world. Sustained utilization on your NIC is acceptable at 30–40 percent but if it is much higher, you may not have the capacity to handle traffic spikes.

The solution to network load is to add capacity:

- ❋ A second NIC.
- ❋ An additional server with a load balancer to spread the traffic between the two servers.
- ❋ Move large SQL queries to the database in the form of stored procedures.
- ❋ Upgrade the NIC and switch to multi-speed (10/100 or 10/100/1000). Make sure that the duplexing match on the NIC and the switch.

You can make some other SQL-oriented enhancements to decrease network traffic and improve overall performance, but I discuss those in the "Database Design" section.

Switch/Hub

If you are running a database server on your network, then you need to use a switch instead of a hub. A *switch* is more efficient and intelligent piece of network hardware. Whereas a hub simply forwards signals, a switch provides some traffic and error control for a network. Many people realize they need a switch only after experiencing many database corruptions. These days switches are very inexpensive and very technologically advanced over similar equipment purchased only four or five years ago. The symptoms of a bad switch or hub, or an errant port (on either switch or hub), are easy to diagnose. Troubleshooting is also very simple, as you see in Table 10.1.

Table 10.1   Switch/Hub Troubleshooting

Symptom	Solution
No connectivity	Switch/hub is off or needs to be power cycled.
No or limited connectivity	Move the network cable of interest to another port on the switch/hub.
Intermittent connectivity	Power cycle the switch/hub. If the problem persists, replace the switch/hub.
Intermittent connectivity with link lights flashing in unison	Power cycle. Replace if problem returns.
Data corruption	Replace hub with a switch.
Slow response	Replace hub with a switch.

The symptoms and solutions may seem trivial but you would be surprised at how many times I have used this table in troubleshooting those inexplicable network problems that make users very irritable. To get the best throughput for your data, purchase a multi-speed switch so that any media connected to it works without issue.

Router

A *router* is an intelligent device that connects two dissimilar networks. It routes the packets from one network to another while also providing protection (if properly configured) for an internal network. Bottlenecks due to a faulty router are rare but do occur. If something has been misconfigured in the router, you may experience some *latency* (delay) from or to the outside world. Many routers also provide some firewall capability to keep intruders out of your network. The firewall can also be configured to allow incoming connections to your database server so that you can work remotely or allow remote offices or clients to connect to your data.

Any router bottlenecks are usually attributed to a bad configuration but they could be caused by a faulty software load. First check your version against the latest stable version offered by the router's manufacturer—the manufacturer updates the software with security patches and new features. If you are unsure of what to do, contact a professional who deals with your particular router brand. Router pros also have the network packet sniffers and protocol analyzers that can quickly pinpoint network issues.

Your server, if configured to do so, can also act as a router for your network. In the case of a PC-based router, bottlenecks are possible from a variety of sources (see all of the preceding sections).

Connectivity

Though connectivity can refer to many things, here I am referring to connectivity with your *Internet service provider (ISP)*. The connectivity that you have determines the throughput that remote users experience when working with your data. Connectivity is of no consequence if all of your database users are *local* to the data (on the same LAN). When you pay an ISP for Internet connectivity, the possibilities for bottlenecks are many, and you will likely spend hours on the phone with their technical staff figuring out the issues. To save you some grief, I give you some suggestions for ISP service:

* Choose an ISP that specializes in, or has a significant number of, business users.
* When selecting service, note the upload speed you will be getting, as this number affects your remote users. Make sure there is room for upgrade. (There usually is at a cost.)
* Get a *service-level agreement (SLA)*, which outlines your services, guaranteed uptime, support availability, and so on.
* Do some comparative shopping. Telecommunications companies are sometimes very expensive compared to the smaller, and just as capable, ISPs.

Connectivity-related bottlenecks are typically sensed as slow response for the remote user. This may be in the form of slow or no response to queries, stalled web pages (if a web-based application), or intermittent failures to connect. If the problem is connectivity related, you likely will have remote users who complain about response, yet local users can access the database at full speed. ISPs are like anyone else; they make mistakes. They typically go to any length to get your problem resolved, especially if you feel that it is connectivity related.

Database Software

After hardware, you should next look at the software you are running. Does a newer, stable version resolve some of the issues you are experiencing? You must keep up with your software's new developments. You have to stay aware of patches, updates, security issues, and new versions, and the problems they solve. If you are running a product version that hasn't been patched, updated, or upgraded in the past six months, I strongly suggest contacting your vendor or looking at the support area of their web site to educate yourself and get some updated information.

If you have not yet committed yourself to a particular vendor for a DBMS, then you have the luxury of looking at all of the options that fall within your budget. In Chapter 3, I profiled a number of DBMSs and their attributes. That is a good place to start. Each vendor will, of course, try to convince you that their system is absolutely the best. I am not aware of any really bad ones, but some are better than others for different applications. Make your best educated decision based on your needs and budget.

Operating System

Sometimes the operating system itself can be an issue that affects performance. Just as you need to keep up-to-date on version issues for your DBMS, you need to keep abreast of operating system patches and updates that may affect performance and security. With the exception of Microsoft's SQL Server, most vendors recommend using Unix or Linux as the operating system for their DBMSs. The operating system can have a huge impact on performance. I have read some MySQL benchmarks that show that running MySQL on Windows is 20–30 percent slower than on an equivalent Unix or Linux system. I am not bashing Microsoft but reporting what you will find when you go to choose an operating system for your DBMS server. SQL Server only runs on Windows operating systems so it has no benchmarks for other operating systems.

Many vendors suggest an optimal setup for your DBMS and operating system. I strongly suggest you adhere as closely as possible to it if your budget allows. You will be happier in the long run and you also alleviate any finger pointing when you use the system recommended by the vendor.

Database Design

Now you have come to actual SQL-related information on optimizing SQL. I could have started the chapter with this information but you will find that if you have tested your SQL statements, and I know you will, that most of the time the SQL is already optimized. Having said that, what is the point of the following information? While your SQL statements are fine for a few users, they may not be optimized for many simultaneous users. For example, you may use SELECT * FROM

Authors; for testing purposes but you would never use this statement in production, as it is not optimized. If you don't know why it is not optimized, then read on. By the end of this chapter, you may never use * again in a query.

There is no substitute for good database design. Even the blinding speed of the latest hardware won't make your database perform like it should if it is designed poorly. A poorly designed database is prone to data inconsistencies and low performance and it won't scale well when the data grows. Most database designers don't get it right the first time, so try not to be too rough on yourself. Rarely, if ever, do databases keep the same design over the data's lifetime.

MySQL AB offers the following pointers on database design:

* Use the most efficient (smallest) data types possible. MySQL has many specialized types that save disk space and memory.

* Use the smaller integer types possible to get smaller tables. For example, MEDIUMINT is often a better choice than INT since a MEDIUMINT column uses 25 percent less space.

* Declare columns NOT NULL if possible. It makes everything faster and you save one bit per column. If you really need NULL in your application, you should definitely use it—just avoid having it on all columns by default.

* For MyISAM tables: If you do not have any variable-length columns (varchar, TEXT, or BLOB columns), a fixed-size record format is used. This is faster but, unfortunately, may waste some space. You can hint that you want to have fixed-length rows even if you have varchar columns with the CREATE option ROW_FORMAT=fixed.

* Starting with MySQL/InnoDB 5.0.3, InnoDB tables use a more compact storage format. In earlier versions of MySQL, InnoDB records contain some redundant information, such as the number or length of columns, even for fixed-size columns. By default, tables are created in the compact format (ROW_FORMAT=COMPACT). If you wish to downgrade to older versions of MySQL/InnoDB, you can request the old format with ROW_FORMAT=REDUNDANT.

* The compact InnoDB format also changes the way how char columns containing UTF-8 (8-bit Unicode Transformation Format) is a variable-length character encoding for Unicode created by Ken Thompson and Rob Pike) data are stored. In the ROW_FORMAT=REDUNDANT format, a UTF-8 CHAR(n) occupies 3*n bytes, given that the maximum length of a UTF-8 encoded character is 3 bytes. Since many languages can be written mostly with single-byte UTF-8 characters, a fixed storage length often wastes space. The ROW_FORMAT=COMPACT format allocates a variable amount of n...3*n bytes for these columns by stripping trailing spaces if necessary. The minimum storage length is kept as n bytes to facilitate in-place updates in typical cases.

❋ A table's primary index should be as short as possible. This makes identification of each row easy and efficient.

❋ Create only the indexes that you really need. Indexes are good for retrieval but bad when you need to store data quickly. If you access a table mostly by searching on a combination of columns, make an index on them. The first part of the index should be the column most used. If you always use many columns when selecting from the table, you should use the column with more duplicates first to obtain better compression of the index.

❋ If it is very likely that a column has a unique prefix on the first number of characters, it's better to index only this prefix using MySQL's support for creating an index on the leftmost part of a character column. Shorter indexes are faster not only because they require less disk space, but because they give also you more hits in the index cache, and thus fewer disk seeks.

❋ In some circumstances, splitting an often-scanned table can be beneficial. This is especially true if it is dynamic format. You can use a smaller, static-format table when finding the relevant rows when scanning the table.

In the next chapter, I take you through the process that I use when designing a database. I think you will find it valuable in your own quest for a well-designed database. You will, as you gain experience, come up with a plan that works for you, but for now this is a good way to get started.

I think the following components and attributes are included in a well-designed database that optimizes performance.

❋ A logical separation of entities into tables (Books, Authors, Publishers, and so on).

❋ Narrow tables, limiting width to a maximum of 15 columns.

❋ A primary key for each table (preferably a small numeric one).

❋ Foreign keys.

❋ Views.

❋ Well-formed queries, in some form, for users to use.

❋ Optimized tables.

❋ Indexes on columns that may be used in WHERE clauses.

Including all of these components in your database design does not necessarily mean that it is well designed, but it does guarantee that you have the basis for a good design. You will see, in Chapter 11, how you can bring a design into conformity with a set of standards that complete the picture of a well-designed database.

Indexes

Indexes can speed up database queries by providing a smaller ordered set of data, making them more efficient. Any column in MySQL can be indexed; most table types allow at least 16 indexes per table and each index can be at least 256 bytes in length. Many people still ask me how an index speeds up a search, especially if they have been very careful to sort their data. The answer lies in the way you query the data. If you query the data the same way every single time, then sorting it to your specifications is an index. It just isn't a separate database entity called an index. If you sort your data but query in many different ways, or even unpredictable ways, then multiple indexes are favored, as you can't sort in more than one way if you sort the data yourself. An index is really a way of having a separate collection of sorted data at your disposal. The now-famous example of a library is appropriate at this point.

You go to a library and ask the librarian where books on SQL are located. She looks at you in a puzzled way and says that all books are located in the library, of course. You ask again how to find books on SQL. The librarian points you to the book shelves where the books are not sorted by author, ISBN, title—or any other way. And in this library, there is no Dewey Decimal system. You begin your search and hours later find one book written in 1993. Six hours later you find a second book on SQL in Spanish. Thirty-six hours later you decide to try a more organized library.

The next library is sorted alphabetically by title so you run to the S section to find all of the SQL books. Strangely enough, you only find five books on the subject. But wait. The problem now is that if the book title doesn't begin with S, then you will have the same problem as before. The next library has a better system. Its books are sorted alphabetically by subject and grouped by author. You learn quickly that this library has little advantage over the last one. Frustrated and tired, you seek out another library that has a great system. Its books are sorted by subject and grouped by author. You run to the computer section, find the database books, and filter through those to find ones on SQL. You find all 26 books that you knew existed.

This scenario is somewhat ridiculous but it does illustrate the need for indexes in a database (and a library). You need some way to sort data so it is easy to retrieve via many methods. Indexes provide this sorting, greatly improving the efficiency of searching. Be sure to provide indexes for data that really needs it. As you can read in the library example, the sorting method really does make a difference. It was nice that one of the libraries had its books sorted alphabetical by title, but was that really very useful?

You must be aware not only of how to design a great database and create fantastic SQL statements, but how users will utilize the data and how to make it efficient for them. Index the columns from which they will extract data.

There are some caveats when dealing with indexes, however, as their use can be a detriment to performance. The following list gives examples of when not to use indexes:

- ❋ During updates.
- ❋ On a small table.
- ❋ In the database.
- ❋ On columns that are updated regularly or simply don't need indexing.
- ❋ When multiple-column indexes are the result.

Then there are the times you should use an index:

- ❋ On a large table with many unique values.
- ❋ On multiple-column indexes are advantageous for situations where the column data is naturally oriented toward multiple columns.
- ❋ In columns that have fairly unique values.
- ❋ In a column where mathematical operations will be performed on the data.

First_Name and Last_Name in the Books database is an example when multiple-column indexes are advantageous. First and last names can be repeated but the chances of the combination being repeated is far less than one of the others being repeated individually. A multiple-column index on First_Name and Last_Name can help you search for a last name or all of one last name. Yes, you may use a single column of a multiple-column index in a search. The trade-off, of course, is decreased performance.

Indexes are not used when a column has very few unique values. This is called *low cardinality* regardless of the number of rows. For example, if you have a table where the State column only contains Texas, Wyoming, and Colorado, the need for an index is low because the cardinality of the State column is low. A State column with all 50 states represented would do very well with an index. A column's *high cardinality* is attained by having a large number of unique values. An index on a high-cardinality column would be very efficient and highly recommended. Indexes should only be created on frequently queried columns. If you query columns that are included in WHERE clauses, GROUP BY clauses, ORDER BY clauses, or in JOINS, then indexing will speed the searches. I have seen statistics that indicate a speed increase of anywhere from 100 to 100,000 times than that of non-indexed columns in complex queries where there are hundreds of thousands of records.

Though you can have 15 indexes per table, try to limit yourself to 3 or 4 per table, aside from the primary key and any foreign keys.

Query Optimizer

SELECT queries are the most common of all SQL statements submitted to a database. When you submit a SELECT query, MySQL's query optimizer kicks in, examines the query, and executes it in the most efficient way possible. You don't have to do anything to invoke this built-in MySQL feature—except submit the query. This doesn't mean you can haphazardly submit malformed queries to the database and expect them to be optimized or changed in some way. The database's job is to analyze the query and to use indexes where possible to limit the number of rows in the result set. (The optimizer will always use the most restrictive index in the query.) You still have to do your part creating a reasonable query.

You can actually change the way the optimizer optimizes your queries by using some special SQL keywords and other techniques:

* Use STRAIGHT JOIN. STRAIGHT JOIN tells the query optimizer which order to join the tables for a query. It is preferable to put the table with the least rows first in the JOIN. The first table in the JOIN is used first in a STRAIGHT JOIN. You may want to reverse the order if you feel that there may be a positive result. You should generally try complex queries in multiple ways to see if there is a better choice anyway.

* Use TRUNCATE to empty a table.

* Compare columns with the same data types. In other words, you can compare column A with column B where column A is an integer-type column and column B is text but they both contain numbers. MySQL does do automatic type conversion but it is at a cost to performance; an index can't be used in this situation even if both columns are indexed.

* Use a JOIN instead of a subquery. I discussed this in Chapter 8. Subqueries have to be evaluated separately and the optimizer is generally tuned better for JOIN operations rather than subqueries. It is my opinion that a JOIN is the preferred query method.

* Use LIKE 'string%' over '%string' if possible. Wildcards (%) are necessary but the server takes a performance hit when using them at the beginning of the LIKE in the WHERE clause. Use LIKE '%string%' only when searching for a particular string anywhere in the column, as this always results in a full table scan.

* Only use '%string%' when necessary.

* Check queries with EXPLAIN. This is illustrated in the last section of this chapter.

* Use OPTIMIZE TABLE Table_Name. If you find that your queries are not using indexes properly after examining them with EXPLAIN, try OPTIMIZE TABLE and then do another EXPLAIN to see if there is any improvement.

OPTIMIZE THIS
Every DBMS has a query optimizer, so this information is transferable to the DBMS you use. I discuss the MySQL optimizer but realize that, though subtle differences may exist, the end results will be similar regardless of brand.

You can change the behavior of the MySQL query optimizer a couple of ways. By default, the optimizer prune level is on (optimizer_prune_level = 1). This variable tells the optimizer to disregard, or *prune,* the possible optimization plans that are available to it. According to MySQL AB, the optimizer rarely misses an optimal plan and greatly decreases query compilation time. Consider that even with the optimizer prune-level variable turned on, an exponential number of possibilities are considered for optimal performance. With a large number of tables specified in your query, this can take a long time to complete. If you want the optimizer to do more exhaustive plan searching, turn off the pruning variable.

You can make another behavior adjustment with optimizer_search_depth. High numbers may result in searching for hours or days, and a low number may produce a result within a few seconds. If optimizer_search_depth = 0, then the search depth is set to automatic. I suggest a search depth of 2 or 3. My default search depth was set to 62. I changed it to 3.

optimizer_prune_level and optimizer_search_depth are located in the my.cnf file on Unix/Linux, and in the my.ini file on Windows. These variables should be written under the [mysqld] section of those files. You must restart the MySQL service for the variables to be recognized.

To see these and other MySQL variables, type the following at a MySQL prompt:

```
SHOW VARIABLES;
```

You get a very long list of variables for your MySQL installation. Here is an excerpt from mine showing the optimizer variables.

Linux version:

```
| open_files_limit         | 1024                             |
| optimizer_prune_level    | 1                                |
| optimizer_search_depth   | 3                                |
| pid_file                 | /usr/local/mysql/data/home.pid   |
```

Windows version:

```
| open_files_limit         | 622                                         |
| optimizer_prune_level    | 1                                           |
| optimizer_search_depth   | 3                                           |
| pid_file                 | E:\MySQL\MySQL Server 5.0\Data\megamachine.pid |
```

There is a lot of material available on how MySQL optimizes all types of queries in the MySQL manual. The DBMS you choose is important, but learning your system's advanced features is even more important. By learning the adjustable parameters, you can tune your system for your specific needs.

IF IT AIN'T BROKE
Do your tweaking on a development system, as you don't want some adjustment to affect your general user base unless you know for sure that it is a positive change.

Data Selection

Data selection is another method of enhancing performance of queries. When querying a database, be as specific as possible so that only relevant results are returned. Querying columns that you don't need is inefficient and considered bad form. At some point, you will pass your torch to someone else, so make sure your queries are fine tuned and well formed. You certainly don't want to be the subject of negative water-cooler conversation. Wouldn't you rather have them remembering you fondly and even calling you up, asking for advice? Okay, maybe it's just me.

For whatever reasons that motivate you, use best practices when forming queries and selecting data. Feedback from your users is always your yardstick of success. See them as assets, not liabilities, and you will be far more successful in your career. Design your queries around business rules that make sense for your users. You certainly don't want them using spreadsheets for storing, updating, and passing on important information when there is a perfectly good database (and DBA) that can handle the job. If they are utilizing spreadsheets for such things, it may be time for you to visit with them and find out how you can incorporate their data, their business rules, and their needs into your well-designed database. Ask them about the data and how they need it presented.

There are some key points to remember when selecting data for the users. These are considered best practices for using SQL and you should read and heed them.

SELECT * FROM Table_Name;

Only use SELECT * FROM Table_Name; when testing a table—never in production. Doing so during production selects all data within a table and is not efficient. If you need to select all columns within a table, name each separately, as done in this statement:

```
SELECT First_Name, Last_Name, Phone FROM Authors;
```

Notice that I did not select Authors_ID in this query. This is unnecessary information for this kind of query, which brings up the next point.

Only Select Data Needed for Query

Only select the data that you need for a query. Selecting data that you won't use for a report only makes the query slower and uses unnecessary system and database processing. When selecting data from multiple tables, try to use columns that are related by the primary key/foreign key relationship. For instance, in the following statement, Authors.Author_ID is the primary key for the Authors table, and Works.Author_ID is the foreign key in the Works table:

```
SELECT Authors.First_Name, Authors.Last_Name, Works.Title FROM Authors, Works
WHERE Authors.Author_ID = Works.Author_ID;
```

It is perfectly acceptable to query and requery until you find a comfortable result set. You don't have to get it right the first time. Here is an example that you can relate to when looking for something on your favorite Internet search engine. Type in a single keyword and you are likely to get back more results than you will ever be able to look at. Some search engines limit the number of hits and tell you to refine your search. Refining the search by being very specific limits the result set to a reasonable number of hits. It also performs better than a single-keyword search, both for you and the database you are querying. Conversely, it is possible to receive too few results in a query. If you receive too few results, you may have to take away or change a keyword to broaden the search.

Full Table Scans

Searching through every row of a table, or multiple tables, for a result set is called a *full table scan*. Sometimes a full table scan is more efficient than an indexed scan if the result set is very large. The query optimizer can choose to do a full table scan if it finds that the returned number of rows justify it. A wildcard at the first position in a query will result in a full table scan. For instance, this query would result in a full table scan and find all last names with "man" at the end of them. Possible matches include Herman, Kingman, Perlman, Amman, and so on:

```
SELECT First_Name, Last_Name FROM Authors WHERE Last_Name LIKE '%man';
```

You can't avoid full table scans altogether but you should try to avoid them when possible. Don't stress your DBMS or its host server any more than is necessary. Too many full table scans result in a low-performing database and associated applications.

Be especially cautious on shared systems such as an ISP or other hosted service; you may end up paying extra money for the performance hits. You should be cautious, as well, on shared systems in your internal network, as users and systems administrators will become frustrated. Don't get yourself booted from a shared system due to laziness when creating queries that perform unnecessary full table scans. Poor design is easy in the short term but you end up paying the price for it eventually.

EXPLAIN

EXPLAIN is an SQL keyword used in two ways: as a synonym for DESCRIBE Table_Name or SHOW COLUMNS FROM Table_Name or—the way you are most interested in—related to how a SELECT query will be executed.

```
EXPLAIN tbl_name
```

```
EXPLAIN [EXTENDED] SELECT select_options
```

To use EXPLAIN, enter it before a SELECT statement:

```
EXPLAIN SELECT First_Name, Last_Name, Phone FROM Authors;
```

id	select_type	table	type	possible_keys	key	key_len	ref	rows	Extra
1	SIMPLE	Authors	ALL	NULL	NULL	NULL	NULL	9	

Since this is a single-table query, this is not very useful. Another query yields much more interesting results:

```
SELECT Authors.First_Name, Authors.Last_Name, Works.Title FROM Authors, Works
WHERE Authors.Author_ID = Works.Author_ID;
```

id	select_type	table	type	possible_keys	key	key_len	ref	rows	Extra
1	SIMPLE	Works	ALL	author_idx	NULL	NULL	NULL	7	
1	SIMPLE	Authors	eq_ref	PRIMARY	PRIMARY	4	Books.Works.Author_ID	1	

Table 10.2 gives an explanation of the output from EXPLAIN.

Table 10.2   Explain Output

Output	Description
id	The SELECT identifier. This is the sequential number of the SELECT within the query.
select_type	The type of SELECT, which can be any of the following:
	• SIMPLE
	• Simple SELECT (not using UNION or subqueries)
	• PRIMARY
	• Outermost SELECT
	• UNION
	• Second or later SELECT statement in a UNION
	• DEPENDENT UNION
	• Second or later SELECT statement in a UNION, dependent on outer query
	• UNION RESULT

Output	Description
	• Result of a UNION
	• SUBQUERY
	• First SELECT in subquery
	• DEPENDENT SUBQUERY
	• First SELECT in subquery, dependent on outer query
	• DERIVED
	• Derived table SELECT (subquery in FROM clause)
table	The table to which the row of output refers.
type	The JOIN type. The different JOIN types are explained after this table, ordered from most efficient to least efficient.
possible_keys	Indicates which indexes MySQL could use to find rows in this table. Totally independent of the table order as displayed in the output from EXPLAIN; some of the keys might not be usable in practice with the generated table order. If this column is NULL, there are no relevant indexes. In this case, you may be able to improve query performance by examining the WHERE clause to see whether it refers to some column(s) suitable for indexing. If so, create an appropriate index and check the query with EXPLAIN again. To see what indexes a table has, use SHOW INDEX FROM tbl_name.
key	Indicates the key (index) that MySQL actually decided to use. The key is NULL if no index was chosen. To force MySQL to use or ignore an index listed in the possible_keys column, use FORCE INDEX, USE INDEX, or IGNORE INDEX in your query. For MyISAM and BDB tables, running ANALYZE TABLE helps the optimizer choose better indexes. For MyISAM tables, myisamchk –analyze does the same.
key_len	Indicates the length of the key that MySQL decided to use. The length is NULL if the key column says NULL. key_len value allows you to determine how many parts of a multiple-part key MySQL actually uses.
ref	Shows which columns or constants are used with the key to select rows from the table.
rows	Indicates the number of rows MySQL believes it must examine to execute the query.
Extra	Contains additional information about how MySQL resolves the query. Table 10.3 explains the different text strings that can appear in this column.

Table 10.3   Text Strings That Can Appear In The Extra Column

String	Description
Distinct	MySQL stops searching for more rows for the current row combination after it has found the first matching row.
Not exists	MySQL did a LEFT JOIN optimization on the query and does not examine more rows in this table for the previous row combination after it finds one row that matches the LEFT JOIN criteria.
range checked for each record (index map: #)	MySQL found no good index to use, but found that some of indexes might be used once column values from preceding tables are known. For each row combination in the preceding tables, MySQL determines whether it can use a range or index_merge access method to retrieve rows with the exception that all column values for the preceding table are known and considered constants. This is not very fast, but is faster than performing a JOIN with no index at all.
Using filesort	MySQL needs to do an extra pass to find out how to retrieve the rows in sorted order. The sort is done by going through all rows according to the JOIN type and storing the sort key and pointer to the row for all rows that match the WHERE clause. The keys then are sorted and the rows retrieved in sorted order.
Using index	The column information is retrieved from the table using only information in the index tree without having to do an additional seek to read the actual row. Use this strategy when the query uses only columns that are part of a single index.
Using temporary	To resolve the query, MySQL needs to create a temporary table to hold the result. This typically happens if the query contains GROUP BY and ORDER BY clauses that list columns differently.

String	Description
Using where	A WHERE clause restricts which rows to match against the next table or send to the client. Unless you specifically intend to fetch or examine all rows from the table, you may have something wrong in your query if the Extra value is not Using where and the table JOIN type is ALL or index. If you want to make your queries as fast as possible, look out for Extra values of Using filesort and Using temporary.
Using sort_union(...), Using union(...), Using intersect (...)	These indicate how index scans are merged for the index_merge JOIN type.
Using index for group-by	Similar to Using index for accessing a table, Using index for group-by indicates that MySQL found an index that can be used to retrieve all columns of a GROUP BY or DISTINCT query without any extra disk access to the actual table. Additionally, the index is used in the most efficient way so that for each group, only a few index entries are read.

JOIN TYPES

The following is a list of the JOIN types output from the EXPLAIN statement and their explanation. They are ordered from most efficient to least efficient.

system

The table has only one row (= system table). This is a special case of the const JOIN type.

const

The table has, at most, one matching row, which is read at the start of the query. Because there is only one row, values from the column in this row can be regarded as constants by the rest of the optimizer. const tables are very fast because they are read only once. Use const when you compare all parts of a primary key or unique index with constant values. In the following queries, tbl_name can be used as a const table:

```
SELECT * FROM tbl_name WHERE primary_key=1;
```

```
SELECT * FROM tbl_name
```

```
WHERE primary_key_part1=1 AND primary_key_part2=2;
```

eq_ref

One row is read from this table for each combination of rows from the previous tables. Other than the const types, this is the best possible JOIN type. Use eq_ref when all parts of an index are used by the JOIN and the index is a PRIMARY KEY or UNIQUE index, or for indexed columns that are compared using the = operator. The comparison value can be a constant or an expression that uses columns from tables that are read before this table. In the following examples, MySQL can use an eq_ref join to process ref_table:

```
SELECT * FROM ref_table,other_table

WHERE ref_table.key_column=other_table.column;

SELECT * FROM ref_table,other_table

WHERE ref_table.key_column_part1=other_table.column AND
ref_table.key_column_part2=1;
```

ref

All rows with matching index values are read from this table for each combination of rows from the previous tables. Use ref if the JOIN uses only the key's leftmost prefix, if the key is not a primary key, or if the key is not a unique index (in other words, if the JOIN cannot select a single row based on the key value). If the used key matches only a few rows, this is a good JOIN type. Use ref for indexed columns that are compared using the = or <=> operator. In the following examples, MySQL can use a ref JOIN to process ref_table:

```
SELECT * FROM ref_table WHERE key_column=expr;

SELECT * FROM ref_table,other_table

WHERE ref_table.key_column=other_table.column;

SELECT * FROM ref_table,other_table

WHERE ref_table.key_column_part1=other_table.column

AND ref_table.key_column_part2=1;
```

ref_or_null

This JOIN type is like ref, but with the addition that MySQL does an extra search for rows that contain NULL values. This JOIN type optimization is used most often in resolving subqueries. In the following examples, MySQL can use a ref_or_null JOIN to process ref_table:

```
SELECT * FROM ref_table

WHERE key_column=expr OR key_column IS NULL;
```

index_merge

This JOIN type indicates that the index merge optimization is used. In this case, the key column contains a list of indexes used, and key_len contains a list of the longest key parts for the indexes used.

unique_subquery

This type replaces ref for some IN subqueries of the following form:

```
value IN (SELECT primary_key FROM single_table WHERE some_expr)
```

unique_subquery is just an index lookup function that replaces the subquery completely for better efficiency.

index_subquery

This JOIN type is similar to unique_subquery. It replaces IN subqueries, but it works for non-unique indexes in subqueries of the following form:

```
value IN (SELECT key_column FROM single_table WHERE some_expr)
```

range

Only rows that are in a given range are retrieved, using an index to select the rows. The key column indicates which index is used. The key_len contains the longest key part that was used. The ref column is NULL for this type. You can use range when a key column is compared to a constant using any of the =, <>, >, >=, <, <=, IS NULL, <=>, BETWEEN, or IN operators:

```
SELECT * FROM tbl_name

WHERE key_column = 10;

SELECT * FROM tbl_name

WHERE key_column BETWEEN 10 and 20;

SELECT * FROM tbl_name
```

```
WHERE key_column IN (10,20,30);

SELECT * FROM tbl_name

WHERE key_part1= 10 AND key_part2 IN (10,20,30);
```

index

This JOIN type is the same as ALL, except that only the index tree is scanned. This usually is faster than ALL, because the index file usually is smaller than the data file. MySQL can use this JOIN type when the query uses only columns that are part of a single index.

ALL

A full table scan is done for each combination of rows from the previous tables. This is normally not good if the table is the first table not marked const, and usually very bad in all other cases. Most often you can avoid ALL by adding indexes that allow row retrieval from the table based on constant values or column values from earlier tables.

Examining the Query

Now examine the query that referenced two different tables from earlier in this chapter:

* The id column is the SELECT number, which is 1, since you only have a single SELECT.
* The select_type is SIMPLE because there are no UNIONs or subqueries.
* The table column gives the names of the tables involved in the query.
* The type column is the JOIN type used in the query. The eq_ref JOIN type can index columns that are compared using the = operator. eq_ref is used when all parts of an index are used by the JOIN and the index is a primary key or unique index. The ALL designation is for a full table scan.
* The possible_keys column shows the indexes that are involved in the query that could be used.
* The key column tells you which key MySQL decided to use from each table. NULL means that no key was used. PRIMARY means that the primary key from the Authors table was utilized.
* The key_len column shows the length of the key used. NULL means no key was used and the 4 is the length of the key from the Authors table that was used.
* The ref column shows which columns or constants are used with the key to select rows from the table.
* The rows column indicates the number of rows MySQL believes it must examine to execute the query.

For me, the most important columns to look at are type, key, ref, and rows. These give a pretty good picture of how well the query works based on the number of rows affected in the rows column. The optimizer should use the smaller of the two numbers when executing the query, but there is no guarantee of this—especially if no keys are involved in the query.

If you have a slow-running query, using EXPLAIN may give some insight into it. Check to see if your indexes are being used by looking first at the key column. If that column is filled with NULL, either redo the query or create some indexes. The other possibility is that full table scans were the best way to go for the optimizer, in which case you will most likely see a 'Using where' in the Extra column. In the case of the key column being filled with NULL and the Extra column does not say 'Using where', then you may have a problem and I suggest rewriting the query from scratch.

Summary

I think sometimes that DBMS optimization is an arcane science more akin to alchemy than a concrete process that follows a protocol of any discernable kind. Though I have given you quite a bit to think about in this chapter, I have to be honest and say that the most profound solutions are the simplest. My best example is the one I gave where I ended up changing out a hub for a switch. And as I stated in this chapter's introduction, I know this is a book on SQL but I feel that I also have a duty to make this book a true teaching tool. I would only be giving you part of the story if I focused entirely on SQL solutions to problems that may not have a basis in SQL. Hopefully, now you have the tools necessary to troubleshoot DBMS performance issues whether they are related to hardware, software, database design, or query optimization.

The choices you make in hardware, design, and implementation have far-reaching consequences. If you have influence in the decision-making process, make choices that will benefit your users, protect your data, and be financially palatable to your corporate check writers.

Install and use Orca to keep track of performance of your systems. It is easier to justify upgrades and replacements later if you gather hard data to support your claims. Your intuition may be right on, but graphs and numbers are far more concrete and will support your opinions.

Chapter Review

Multiple Choice

1. Using EXPLAIN does what for you?

    a) Explains the need for a software upgrade

    b) Sets the database into standby mode

    c) Optimizes the database

    d) Shows the execution plan for a query

2. When selecting data, you should

   a) get as much as possible; more is always better.

   b) be selective to narrow the results.

   c) join at least three tables.

   d) use SELECT * FROM Table_Name;.

3. A full table scan is always bad.

   a) True

   b) False

4. Which of the following is generally the most efficient?

   a) A query using SELECT *

   b) A JOIN

   c) A subquery

   d) An UPDATE that includes three indexed columns

5. Indexes always speed queries.

   a) True

   b) False

6. Indexes should be placed on columns that

   a) are queried frequently.

   b) are updated often.

   c) have a lot of unique values.

   d) include both a and c.

7. Indexes should not be placed on columns that are

   a) queried frequently.

   b) involved in JOINs.

   c) updated often.

   d) include both a and c.

8. When looking for performance bottlenecks, which of the following should you look at first?

   a) Memory

   b) Vendor

   c) Power

   d) NIC

9. What is the probable culprit if you experience a network bottleneck and a lot of database corruption?

   a) NIC

   b) Memory

   c) CPU

   d) Hub

10. Related to question 9: How would you resolve this issue?

   a) Replace the NIC.

   b) Replace or add more memory.

   c) Replace a CPU.

   d) Replace the hub with a switch.

Concepts

1. Local database users can operate as usual with no reported issues. Remote users, at the same time, are experiencing sluggish response from the database. What would you check to resolve this issue?

2. Your database server and databases are approximately two years old. Your database seems to be going slower and slower and needs to be restarted about once a week to keep it somewhat responsive. What would you check on this server or in the DBMS? How would you attempt to resolve this issue?

11} Normalization

Normalization is the process of eliminating duplicate data from a database. You relate data together instead of storing the same data in multiple tables. Originally, E.F. Codd introduced three normal forms: First Normal Form (1NF), Second Normal Form (2NF), and Third Normal Form (3NF). Even today, most database experts consider 3NF adequate in most circumstances. Normalization and *normal forms* are theoretical database models meant to guide database and relationship design. A well-normalized database is designed such that its data can be updated quickly and with little opportunity for introducing inconsistencies. Normalization makes a database more efficient, more easily maintained, more consistent, and often better performing than a non-normalized one. It also makes a database more scalable by removing redundancies and inconsistencies in the data.

Having said all of this, it is possible to overnormalize a database, making it inefficient and poorly performing. When this happens, you must go through the process of *denormalization,* where some data is recombined into common tables.

Normalization is a progressive task. That is to say, you can't have a 3NF normalized database until you have a 1NF normalized database that is also 2NF normalized. This chapter takes you through the theoretical definitions of each normal form and then explains how and when to apply each.

Before any attempt at normalization can be successful, your tables have to satisfy the requirements for a relation. To meet the requirements of a relation, your tables must meet the following criteria:

* Column order doesn't matter.
* Row order doesn't matter.
* All rows are unique and contain a unique identifier.
* The data in a table is for a single entity.

If those criteria are met, the tables are relations and are considered to be in Zero Normal Form. Consider the following database, Chapter11, and table Authors:

```
CREATE DATABASE Chapter11;

USE Chapter11;

CREATE TABLE Authors (ID integer(4) NOT NULL PRIMARY KEY AUTO_INCREMENT,
FirstName char(40), LastName char(60), Author_Phone char(20), Book_Title char
(80), ISBN CHAR(20), Publisher CHAR(80), Publisher_Phone char(20));
```

Now insert some data into the table. You only need a few records to illustrate:

```
INSERT INTO Authors VALUES ('', 'Bob', 'Shaw', '512-555-1555', 'Hello Back',
'1001100110', 'Giant House', '512-555-1000');

INSERT INTO Authors VALUES ('', 'Jim', 'Jaske', '512-555-1501',
'Commonalities', '1001100500', 'Serial Publishers', '512-555-2000');

INSERT INTO Authors VALUES ('', 'Paul', 'Fox', '512-555-1541', 'The Bend',
'1044400500', 'Giant House', '512-555-1000');

INSERT INTO Authors VALUES ('', 'Dan', 'Brown', '512-555-1533', 'Mouse Pad',
'1044400655', 'Tek House', '512-555-3000');

INSERT INTO Authors VALUES ('', 'Jim', 'Jaske', '512-555-1501',
'Tranquilities', '1001100610', 'Serial Publishers', '512-555-2000');
```

```
+----+-----------+----------+--------------+---------------+------------+-
----------------+----------------+
| ID | FirstName | LastName | Author_Phone | Book Title    | ISBN
Publisher         Publisher_Phone |
+----+-----------+----------+--------------+---------------+------------+-
----------------+----------------+
|  1 | Bob       | Shaw     | 512-555-1555 | Hello Back    | 1001100110 |
Giant House       | 512-555-1000   |
|  2 | Jim       | Jaske    | 512-555-1501 | Commonalities | 1001100500 |
Serial Publishers | 512-555-2000   |
|  3 | Paul      | Fox      | 512-555-1541 | The Bend      | 1044400500 |
Giant House       | 512-555-1000   |
|  4 | Dan       | Brown    | 512-555-1533 | Mouse Pad     | 1044400655 |
Tek House         | 512-555-3000   |
```

```
|  5 | Jim         | Jaske      | 512-555-1501 | Tranquilities | 1001100610 |
Serial Publishers | 512-555-2000 |
+----+----------+----------+-------------+-------------+------------+-
---------------+--------------+
```

I could have added agent and editor information but I think you get the idea. This table fulfills all the requirements for a relation. The order of the columns and rows doesn't matter, each row is unique, and the table holds information for a single entity: Authors. Now you can begin normalizing this database.

❊ **WHAT'S IN A NAME?**

When putting names of people into a table, put first names into a separate column from last names. Putting them together into a single column makes searching or ordering on last name almost impossible. No internal split function does this in SQL (normally), so if you make the mistake of using one column, you have to use a third-party program to split the names and alter your table, and then enter the names into the table. Save yourself some time and just create a FirstName and a LastName column.

First Normal Form

The first normal form requires these things:

❊ There are no repeating groups.

❊ Each field is atomic or indivisible.

For a field to be *atomic,* it must have only one type of data in it—not multiple types or arrays. To put the Chapter11 database in first normal form, you must examine your Authors table and look for repeating groups of data and fields that contain data that is not atomic.

You may notice that there are repeating groups. The author's name can be repeated though the record is unique, book titles may be repeated, and publishers certainly are repeated. A hint about separating data into individual tables: If you see repeating data, that column and related columns can be split into their own tables. In other words, if a column that contains the names of publishers whose names are repeated, publishers should have a separate table. The same goes for authors and books.

So now you have the potential for three tables from this original one: Authors, Publishers, and Books. Go ahead and split the Authors table into the three that I identified:

```
CREATE TABLE Publishers SELECT DISTINCT Publisher, Publisher_Phone from
Authors;
```

This creates the table with data, but you need to also add a primary key and an auto-increment field:

```
ALTER TABLE Publishers ADD COLUMN ID integer(4) AUTO_INCREMENT PRIMARY KEY
FIRST;

SELECT * FROM Publishers;
```

```
+----+-------------------+-----------------+
| ID | Publisher         | Publisher_Phone |
+----+-------------------+-----------------+
|  1 | Giant House       | 512-555-1000    |
|  2 | Serial Publishers | 512-555-2000    |
|  3 | Tek House         | 512-555-3000    |
+----+-------------------+-----------------+
```

When creating the table Books, you must be cautious: Each author may have more than one book. An author identifier is needed in the Books table to identify the author without putting in the author's name. The Authors table would be made smaller by only having unique author listings. Create the Books table as shown here:

```
CREATE TABLE Books SELECT DISTINCT ISBN, ID AS Author_ID, ID AS Publisher_ID,
Book_Title FROM Authors;
```

Since ISBN is unique, you can use it as a primary key:

```
ALTER TABLE Books ADD PRIMARY KEY (ISBN);
SELECT * FROM Books;
```

```
+------------+-----------+--------------+---------------+
| ISBN       | Author_ID | Publisher_ID | Book_Title    |
+------------+-----------+--------------+---------------+
| 1001100110 |         1 |            1 | Hello Back    |
| 1001100500 |         2 |            2 | Commonalities |
| 1044400500 |         3 |            3 | The Bend      |
| 1044400655 |         4 |            4 | Mouse Pad     |
| 1001100610 |         5 |            5 | Tranquilities |
+------------+-----------+--------------+---------------+
```

Notice that you still have multiple problems. According to this table, you have five distinct authors and five distinct publishers. You know that this isn't the case: You actually have four authors and three publishers. The author for *Commonalities* and *Tranquilities* is the same, so you need to make that change. This change is easy on your little table, but imagine having hundreds or thousands of records. Good database design makes sense. You may not make it perfect the first time but you can avoid some common pitfalls by making some good decisions at the beginning.

You also need to make the publisher changes for the books. Looking at the original Authors table, you see that you need to set the Publisher_ID correctly for the two books that are from repeat publishers:

```
UPDATE Books SET Author_ID = '2' WHERE Book_Title = 'Tranquilities';

UPDATE Books SET Publisher_ID = '1' WHERE Book_Title = 'The Bend';

UPDATE Books SET Publisher_ID = '2' WHERE Book_Title = 'Tranquilities';

SELECT * FROM Books;
```

```
+------------+-----------+--------------+---------------+
| ISBN       | Author_ID | Publisher_ID | Book_Title    |
+------------+-----------+--------------+---------------+
| 1001100110 |         1 |            1 | Hello Back    |
| 1001100500 |         2 |            2 | Commonalities |
| 1044400500 |         3 |            1 | The Bend      |
| 1044400655 |         4 |            4 | Mouse Pad     |
| 1001100610 |         2 |            2 | Tranquilities |
+------------+-----------+--------------+---------------+
```

Now there is a relationship between the Publishers table and the Books table, and there is a relationship between the Authors table and the Books table. Since the publisher is a book attribute, like the author, reference it in the Books table. The Author_ID column cannot be set to UNIQUE because there may be multiple titles by a single author. This table is complete for now. Strangely enough, you may find that getting your database into first normal form actually propels your database into higher normal forms as well.

You need to clean up the Authors table so that it only contains author information. You can do this many ways but for our purposes this seems the most direct:

```
ALTER TABLE Authors DROP COLUMN Book_Title, DROP COLUMN ISBN, DROP COLUMN
Publisher, DROP COLUMN Publisher_Phone;
```

Get rid of the repeat author entry, Jim Jaske:

```
DELETE FROM Authors WHERE ID = 5;

SELECT * FROM Authors;
```

```
+----+-----------+----------+--------------+
| ID | FirstName | LastName | Author_Phone |
+----+-----------+----------+--------------+
|  1 | Bob       | Shaw     | 512-555-1555 |
|  2 | Jim       | Jaske    | 512-555-1501 |
|  3 | Paul      | Fox      | 512-555-1541 |
|  4 | Dan       | Brown    | 512-555-1533 |
+----+-----------+----------+--------------+
```

You now have three tables, separated appropriately, complete with data. The tables are now in first normal form.

Second Normal Form

Second normal form requires these things:

* A database in first normal form.
* Each table column must depend on the whole key.
* No partial dependencies are included.

You usually get into trouble with the second normal form if the table contains data from more than one entity. This creates partial dependencies, which violate the second normal form. Work around partial dependencies by splitting the tables into smaller tables that only contain single-entity data; create foreign key relationships between the tables. Sometimes you can get into trouble with the second normal form by having a column that depends on only one column of a multiple-column key. In that case, you have to split your table again, removing the column (and possibly others) that have this type of dependency.

Verify that each table has a primary key and each column in a table depends on the primary key. You can verify that each table has a primary key by looking at the CREATE TABLE statement for each:

```
SHOW CREATE TABLE Authors;

| Authors | CREATE TABLE `Authors` (
  `ID` int(4) NOT NULL auto_increment,
  `FirstName` char(40) default NULL,
  `LastName` char(60) default NULL,
  `Author_Phone` char(20) default NULL,
  PRIMARY KEY  (`ID`)
) ENGINE=MyISAM DEFAULT CHARSET=latin1 |
```

```
SHOW CREATE TABLE Books;

| Books | CREATE TABLE `Books` (
  `ISBN` char(20) NOT NULL default '',
  `Author_ID` int(4) NOT NULL default '0',
  `Publisher_ID` int(4) NOT NULL default '0',
  `Book_Title` char(80) default NULL,
  PRIMARY KEY (`ISBN`)
) ENGINE=MyISAM DEFAULT CHARSET=latin1 |

SHOW CREATE TABLE Publishers;

| Publishers | CREATE TABLE `Publishers` (
  `ID` int(4) NOT NULL auto_increment,
  `Publisher` char(80) default NULL,
  `Publisher_Phone` char(20) default NULL,
  PRIMARY KEY (`ID`)
) ENGINE=MyISAM DEFAULT CHARSET=latin1 |
```

All of the tables have primary keys. You need to check dependencies on the primary key. Figure 11.1 shows the tables in graphical format for easy comparison. As you examine each table, try to find any columns that contain repeated data. I believe you will find the database complies with second normal form. Another way to test for second normal form is to check for many-to-many relationships between tables. Relationships should be one-to-many; otherwise the database may still need work.

Third Normal Form

The two main rules for third normal form are thus:

❋ The database must comply with second normal form.

❋ The table should contain no *transitive dependencies*—that is, no column may have a dependency on any other non-key column.

You also may not have calculated values in a column because that creates dependencies on other columns. Calculated values can be retrieved via a query. Therefore, columns that have totals, averages, or any other calculated data need to be split into their raw data forms (if the raw data also exists in the database). Only store the raw numbers in the table unless the data itself is inserted into the table as a total or sum and the raw data does not exist elsewhere in the database.

Examine the tables again to see if any column in any table depends on the value (or existence) of any other. It is appropriate for columns to depend on the primary key column(s). I suppose

Figure 11.1

Chapter11 database tables.

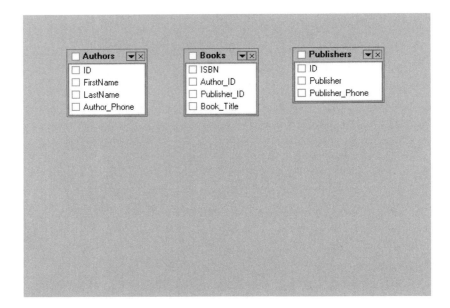

you could argue that the Phone_Number column from each table could be moved to its own table and add foreign keys for Author_ID and Publisher_ID, but I don't see any real advantage to that. From my observations, your database is already in third normal form without making any changes. Good design has its advantages.

The third normal form is really the highest practical of the normal forms, although some designers make their databases conform to the Boyce-Codd normal form discussed in the next section. I usually stop at 3NF because at this point you have referential integrity (if you enforce those foreign key constraints) and very narrow, focused tables. And as I stated in the introduction to this chapter, most database experts consider 3NF to be adequate normalization. A table is designed well if you can't divide it any further. That means any *reasonable* division. I suppose you could divide an entire database into two-column tables but that wouldn't be very practical.

Boyce-Codd Normal Form

The Boyce-Codd normal form is just an extension of the third normal form. The formal definition of the *Boyce-Codd normal form (BCNF)* determines that every determinant in the table be a candidate key. A *determinant* is any attribute whose value determines other values with a row. A *candidate key* is any set of one or more columns whose combined values are unique among all occurrences. If a table contains only one candidate key, the 3NF and the BCNF are equivalent. By the time you put your tables in third normal form, you usually also comply with Boyce-Codd normal form.

Examine the three tables in your database. Do they qualify as Boyce-Codd normalized? They do because even though two authors may have the same name, they will not have the same phone number. In the Books table, two books could have the same title and Publisher_ID (though unlikely) but will never have the same ISBN or Author_ID.

Some database researchers and administrators believe that BCNF should replace the definition of third normal form. These are theoretical definitions that aid in design but I caution you against being bound by the strict rules of normal form compliance. The section on denormalization explains further.

Advanced Normal Forms

Those who design databases for a living rarely go beyond third normal form. It is the de facto standard of normalization. There are fourth, fifth, and even sixth normal form standards written. If you are interested in them beyond this brief introduction, I suggest obtaining a copy of an advanced database text that discusses theoretical relational design. I think for an intermediate text, such as this, you should be aware of the theoretical definitions, but mostly you need to know how to implement a well-designed database. For those of you who want to see the definitions of the advanced normal forms, here they are:

✳ Fourth normal form: Complies with third normal form and additionally states that no column may depend on any other column except the primary key and it must depend on the whole primary key in the case of multiple-column primary keys.

✳ Fifth normal form: Complies with fourth normal form and addresses the situation where a table may lose information if split in two, but the table may be split into more than two tables.

✳ Sixth normal form: This form is mostly theoretical in nature and is very ambitious. Data is synchronized throughout the database (where appropriate) and there is no possibility of errors resulting from modification (*modification anomalies*) being injected into the database.

Denormalization

Denormalization is the normalization "undo," in a manner of speaking. The need for denormalization comes when normalization efforts have paid off in the form of very long SQL statements that decrease performance so much that you need to *dirty* the system a bit to get things going again, recombining tables into less normalized but more efficient and usable formats. I have seen valiant efforts by database administrators who go to extreme lengths to build the totally normalized database. They are so proud of themselves. Sometime in the not-too-distant future, they must scramble to redesign and denormalize their once brilliant creation. As the amount of data increases, performance will suffer greatly. This usually happens when normalization is taken past third normal form. This is the main reason why really good database designers strive for third normal form in their designs.

You won't necessarily need to denormalize your databases. It is not a normal (pardon the accidental pun) part of database design. Denormalization is a fix for design that has been taken to the extreme. There are trade-offs in design, data integrity, and performance to achieve a database that is scalable, reasonably fast, and less prone to anomalies than one designed haphazardly.

A Database Design How-To

This section is an excerpt from my experience in building databases. This is the way I do it. There are many correct ways to go about it but this one seems to work for me.

Sketch It Out

I start with my design on paper. I actually write out what I want to put into a database without regard for any normalization. I just want to create a database and put data into it so I can get it out quickly and easily later.

For the Chapter11 database in this chapter's examples, I got out some blank paper and started writing down possibilities for tables. I didn't think of them as tables at the time but that is what they became. These are the things I need in a database for Chapter11: Authors, Publishers, Books, Editors, and Agents. To make the example easier to use, I shortened it to Authors, Publishers, and Books. For each author, I thought, I will need the author's contact information. For the contact information, I chose name and phone number. I could have added email address, also a unique value. For books, I need the ISBN and title. The publisher data I need is the name of the company and a phone number. In real life, you would need more information, but for the examples I didn't want to get carried away.

In the example, I put all of the information into one large table. I would not ordinarily do this. It worked for the example but in real life I would just start writing down what I want in the database in a table-and-column–type arrangement. The major subjects that I want in the database become tables and their attributes become the columns. This is a natural progression of design in my world. For example, you probably will want to write down all of the major subjects you want in the database before you start adding attributes: Write down authors before writing down author phone numbers, addresses, or zip codes.

Under each major subject (table), you write the attributes (columns) that you want for each subject. Do this without regard for primary keys, foreign keys, or normalization. It is too early to start that kind of analysis. Also, don't worry about subject or attribute naming. This is a brainstorming session. Get your ideas down while you are thinking of them. Add major subjects at any time as you go through the process. It is never too late to add another table. Figure 11.2 is my brainstorming session for the Chapter11 database.

This is my original preliminary sketch for the Chapter11 database though it looks very different now. I want to take you through the rest of the process of turning this concept into a functional database so, for this example, let's assume you haven't already seen the Chapter11 database.

```
Authors     Books       Publishers
Name        Title       Company
Address     ISBN        Address
City        Publisher   City
State       Pages       State
Zip                     Zip
Phone                   Phone
Email                   Contact
                        Email
```

Figure 11.2
Database design: The first steps.

Check for Redundancies

My next step is to check for potential redundancies so that I may create a new table if needed. For the author's table, I have name, address, city, state, zip, phone, and email. The first column, Name, may give some trouble, as more than one author could have the same name. To alleviate this issue, it is necessary to split that column into three others: First, Middle, and Last. If further distinction is required at some point, other unique attributes will be used—such as an author identification number. Address will more than likely be unique, but city, state, and zip could be repeated so they need an X to remind me to reevaluate that situation. Phone and email will be unique to each author.

A look at the Books table's attributes yields the following column possibilities: Title, ISBN, Publisher, and Pages. Title will probably be unique with the same argument as the author name. ISBN is a unique identifier. Publisher will definitely repeat and number of pages may repeat. An author may have more than one book in the Books table. Place an X by Publisher, Pages, and Author. The Publishers table is composed of Company, Address, City, State, Zip, Phone, Contact, and Email. The Company name is a repetitive data column but, as I have shown before in Authors and Books, good design deals with that issue. Address will be unique per publisher but city, state, and zip are very likely be repeated values. Phone, contact, and email will be unique per contact at a particular publisher. Place an X by City, State, and Zip under Publishers. As I now look at the original design, this is what I see as the issues to address for this database. Figure 11.3 shows the current status in the stepwise database design.

I now examine the potential redundancies and begin to deal with them. City, state, and zip are redundant columns in the Authors table and in the Publishers table. These attributes need to be split out as a separate table, which I am calling Location. Figure 11.4 is the result of moving the repetitive columns out to the new table.

The remaining Xs in the Books table remind me to deal with them, too. I think that since the number of pages can vary so much that this should stay in the table as is. I may have a few redundancies but not enough to justify another table for pages. Each book has a publisher and an author but the database also has a Publisher and an Author table, so I think I can retain those columns; they

Figure 11.3

Database design:
Redundant data check—
first pass.

```
Authors    Books        Publishers
Name       Title        Company
Address    ISBN         Address
x City     x Publisher  City  x
x State    x Pages      State x
x Zip      x Author     Zip   x
Phone                   Phone
Email                   Contact
                        Email

      Name = First, Middle, Last
```

Figure 11.4

Database design:
Reducing redundancies.

```
Authors   Books       Publishers   Location
First     Title       Company      City
Middle    ISBN        Address      State
Last      x Publisher Phone        Zip
Address   x Pages     Contact
Phone     x Author    Email
Email
```

will be references to the respective publisher and author for each book. I mark the Publisher and Author columns in the Books table with a lowercase r to remind me that this is a reference to another table. Figure 11.5 catches me up to this point.

Figure 11.5

Database design: Making
adjustments.

```
Authors   Books       Publishers   Location
First     Title       Company      City
Middle    ISBN        Address      State
Last      r Publisher Phone        Zip
Address   Pages       Contact
Phone     r Author    Email
Email
```

Now I have to step back and take a look at what I have. I check again for redundancies. The Authors table looks good, Books looks good since I decided to use Publishers and Authors as references but Publishers presents a bit of a problem. The problem is if there is more than one contact at a publisher. If I stay with my current design, I will have multiple entries for the publisher information to be able to enter a new contact name, phone, and email. My solution is to split out Contact, Phone, and Email into a separate table called Pub_Contacts and leave a reference column in Publishers. A scan of the Location table yields no redundancies. Figure 11.6 reflects the changes I have made.

Figure 11.6
*Database design:
Redundant data check—
second pass.*

Assign Primary Keys

Now it is finally time to get down to some real database work. I need to assign primary keys for each table. This is relatively easy for me since I most often name part of the column from the table and ID. Sometimes I just use ID but using the table name with ID is more prudent for easy foreign key locating. In the case of the Books table, I use ISBN as the primary key because it is already unique and a number so it fits very well into my scheme for a primary key. Figure 11.7 is the result of my primary key magic.

Figure 11.7
Database design: Assign primary keys.

Assign Foreign Keys

The next step is easy since I have already identified some reference columns in my tables. In case you didn't catch it, those reference columns are my foreign keys. I assign foreign keys by simply renaming those reference columns to the column they reference in the other table. I also need to add Location_ID to the Authors and the Publishers tables because I removed the city, state, and zip from those two. Figure 11.8 is the result of these changes.

Once the foreign keys are assigned, my efforts look like an actual database. The only potential problem I see in the database is very subtle: Look at the Location table. The Zip column may be a problem because many larger towns have multiple zip codes; there is possibility for redundancy. You may choose to ignore this or you may be a good DBA and split it into its own table.

Figure 11.8

Database design: Assign foreign keys.

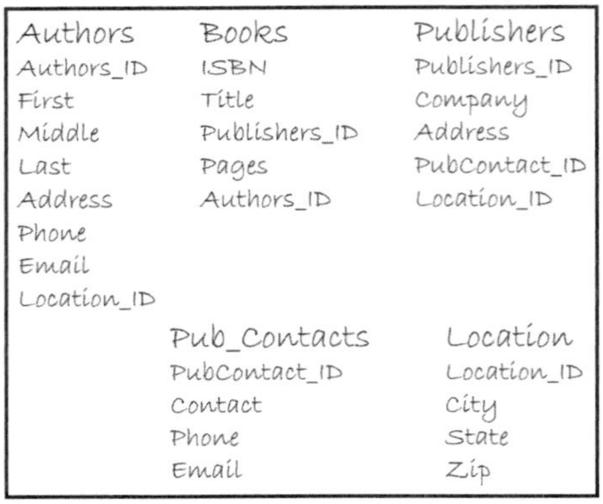

Authors	Books	Publishers
Authors_ID	ISBN	Publishers_ID
First	Title	Company
Middle	Publishers_ID	Address
Last	Pages	PubContact_ID
Address	Authors_ID	Location_ID
Phone		
Email		
Location_ID		

Pub_Contacts	Location
PubContact_ID	Location_ID
Contact	City
Phone	State
Email	Zip

Once the foreign keys are assigned, my efforts look like an actual database. The only potential problems I see in the database are very subtle: Look at the Location table. The City, State, and Zip columns are all going to experience redundancy. Think about it: Every time you enter a new author, a city, state, and zip are associated with his address. Every time you enter a new publisher, a city, state, and zip are associated. If you add an Agents table and an Editors table, each will have a city, state, and zip as well. Instead of having a Location table, it may be wiser to have a City table, a State table, and a Zip table, and then connect them via foreign keys to the tables that need those attributes. You have to decide for yourself if having three new tables with no redundancy or one table with many redundancies is the better trade-off. If I were actually building this database for use, I would split the Location table into the three. I think it would be wise to do so in the long run. Figure 11.9 shows what the database would look like after making those changes.

Figure 11.9

Database design: Further normalization.

Authors	Books	Publishers
Authors_ID	ISBN	Publishers_ID
First	Title	Company
Middle	Publishers_ID	Address
Last	Pages	PubContact_ID
Address	Authors_ID	City_ID
Phone		State_ID
Email		Zip_ID
City_ID		
State_ID		
Zip_ID		

Pub_Contacts	City	State	Zip
PubContact_ID	City_ID	State_ID	Zip_ID
Contact	City_Name	State_Name	Zip_Code
Phone			
Email			

I now have a third normal form database without ever thinking about the normal forms or even mentioning them to this point. Test it for yourself against the standards. At this point, I would connect to my DBMS and create my tables as shown. Since the data in the City, State, and Zip tables would be relatively stable, this database would be very efficient as the data grows in the other tables. You will only have 50 states, a probable maximum of 100 or so cities, and maybe 500 zip codes. This is very little data for a database server to sift through in a query. You will also have a few dozen publishers, agents, and editors in those tables should you decide to add the other tables. My point is that this is a very well-designed database and will scale very well. It will continue to perform well over the long haul.

Summary

The goal of normalization is to create databases that are resistant to anomalies. There is practically no way to design an anomaly-proof database that performs with acceptable speed. As you have seen, it is possible to overnormalize a database to the point where performance suffers. The process of addressing those performance issues is called denormalization. Once you have designed your database, you should analyze it for performance issues. You can't predict everything but you should look at the level of normalization, the amount of data in the tables, and which tables will experience the most growth.

It is okay to create a table design like the original Authors table with all of the possible information you want in your database. I suggest putting it down on paper. Just remember to analyze the design before putting a lot of—or any—data into it. It is far easier to change a database design without data in it. As I said before, you are likely to change the structure at some point but having the database in a standardized form allows you to make the changes more easily. You made many revisions on a database that started with a simple concept and three tables, and ended up with a database with seven tables.

Here are the major points to remember when building databases for public use: Create tables with useful, necessary information, which means leave out superfluous data that adds no value. Every table needs a primary key. Make your tables narrow, with the fewest number of columns possible. Use foreign keys to maintain referential integrity. Get rid of redundancies in your tables. Analyze your table design for growth and performance. Create as many small, static tables (like State in our example) that you need.

Don't be afraid to go back and edit your database structure if you find anomalies, inconsistencies, or something that just doesn't work. Normalize your tables to an efficient point but don't get so wrapped up in hitting BCNF just as a brag point. Your database's performance and integrity are the true yardsticks of success, not the fact that you have achieved fifth normal form.

Chapter Review

Multiple Choice

1. What is the requirement of a database before starting the normalization process?

   a) The tables have to contain data.

   b) The tables have to be relations.

   c) The tables have to have foreign keys.

   d) The tables have to be in ascending sort order.

2. Third normal form is considered

   a) the ultimate goal in database design.

   b) adequate normalization.

   c) an advanced normalized form.

   d) A theoretical normal form.

3. The Boyce-Codd normal form is actually

   a) another way of saying *fully normalized*.

   b) a theoretical normal form.

   c) the same as second normal form.

   d) an extension of third normal form.

4. The main reason for denormalization is

   a) increasing performance.

   b) decreasing latency.

   c) minimizing dependencies.

   d) maximizing data integrity.

5. Every database must be normalized to the highest possible degree.

   a) True

   b) False

6. From a user's perspective, what is a database's most important attribute?

    a) The variety of data.

    b) The extent of normalization.

    c) Cleverly named columns.

    d) Performance.

7. In going through the normalization process, your goals are to

    a) minimize table size and maximize SQL purity.

    b) minimize table width and maximize performance.

    c) maximize data integrity and maximize performance.

    d) maximize normalization and maximize table width.

8. Which of the following is the strictest normal form?

    a) BCNF

    b) 3NF

    c) 2NF

    d) 1NF

9. Complying with first normal form involves which of the following?

    a) Combining data into arrays.

    b) Removing bad data.

    c) Eliminating repeated groups of data.

    d) Creating foreign keys.

10. To comply with any normal form, you must first

    a) comply with the previous normal form.

    b) create new tables.

    c) do a performance analysis.

    d) remove redundant tables of data.

Concepts

1. Define normalization and explain why it is necessary to any scalable database.

2. Users report that a two-year-old database is running slower and slower. What would you do to remedy the problem?

12 } Embedded SQL

Embedded SQL results in using SQL statements inside of another host language to enhance and extend the power of both languages. When people think of embedded SQL, they generally think of C or C++ as the host language, but many languages can host SQL: Python, Ruby, Java, C, .NET technologies, PHP, and Perl, to name the most popular. I prefer to use PHP for my embedded SQL work so that is what I spend most of the time discussing in this chapter.

I am going to show you how to use PHP to work with MySQL via web pages and at the command line. I feel that both of these methods are very powerful and can truly enhance your users' database experience. Through the use of PHP, you will find that your experiences may be equally enhanced. The information that I teach you in this chapter is applicable to other DBMSs as well. It is very easy, in fact, to utilize PHP for working with Microsoft's SQL Server. I have written web database applications in PHP for use with a MySQL server and within an hour or two converted the application for use with SQL Server. It is truly impressive to do something like that—unfortunately, never impressive enough for a large monetary bonus or raise, but it certainly elicited some smiles from my management and smirks of disbelief from some of my peers.

This is not an attempt at teaching you how to be a programmer but if you have a desire to get data into and out of a database in a more elegant way than typing it into a command-line interface, or a even graphical tool, then stay tuned. You learn how to use the host languages to embed SQL, manipulate data, and even present it in a readable fashion but it won't be pretty, secure, or recommended for public consumption. I leave the bells, whistles, and security to those of you who want to learn more about these host languages. Plenty of books on the market will teach you the higher points of the languages, and a good book on HTML will show you how to make it pretty.

PHP for the Web

PHP stands for *PHP: Hypertext Preprocessor*, which is a recursive acronym like pine (pine is not elm) or GNU (GNUs not Unix). I know it's pretty geeky, huh? Well, I didn't get to name it but

PHP is one of those roses by any other name, if you get my drift. PHP is my web language of choice. It is open source, well documented, and easy to use. It has a C-like syntax, which means that if you know another language like C, Java, or Perl then you will have no trouble learning PHP. It is a full language with looping, object-oriented programming support, many built-in functions, operating system interaction support, and so on.

I use PHP for all kinds of crazy things like automated FTP, performing backups, creating directories, creating web pages on-the-fly, creating htaccess files for user authentication, and even editing the Apache httpd.conf config file. I have yet to be disappointed by PHP in any way. I have done some really fun and interesting things with it. I hope you enjoy it and become addicted to it the same way I have.

The web site for PHP and those who support it is at www.php.net. Here you may download different versions, obtain source code, browse documentation, and search for solutions to your questions or problems. If you do not have PHP on a Windows or Linux computer, as well as a functional web server that supports PHP, please refer to the instructions in Appendix E of this book.

THINK GLOBALLY

It is considered less than desirable, for security reasons, to operate with global variables enabled when using PHP. I, however, like using register_globals=On in the php.ini file. The programming in this chapter assumes register_globals=On. It is not register_globals being enabled that causes a problem, but rather the practice of not declaring variables before using them.

Testing

If you have just started using PHP and would like to test your installation, here is the easiest way to do that.

1. In the directory where your index.htm or index.html file is, create a new text file called test.php.
2. Enter the following code into it:
   ```
   <? phpinfo(); ?>
   ```
3. Save the file.
4. Open a browser and point it to http://yourserver/test.php.
   You should see something like the page in Figure 12.1. This figure does not show the full page. The phpinfo page has a lot of great information about your installation. This makes it a nice way for intruders to get at your system information. If you want a phpinfo page to look at occasionally, put it somewhere off the beaten path.

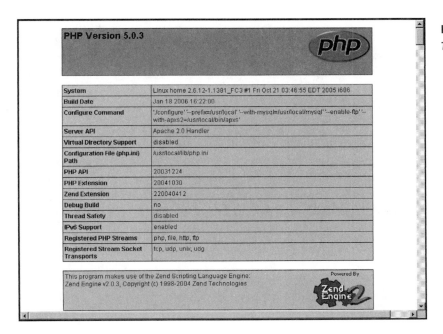

Figure 12.1
The phpinfo page.

Assuming that the phpinfo test went well, move on to another interesting test, incorporating some HTML, to show you just how simple and powerful PHP is:

1. Create a new text file and name it first.php.

2. In this file type the following code:

```
<?
echo '
<FORM METHOD=POST ACTION="second.php">
Enter your First Name: <INPUT TYPE="TEXT" NAME="FIRST" VALUE="" SIZE=20
MAXLENGTH=20>
<P>
<INPUT TYPE="SUBMIT" NAME="Submit" VALUE="Enter">
</FORM>
';
?>
```

The first and last lines are PHP script tags. In the second line (echo '), the ' is a single quote mark, not a back tick.

3. Create another text file and name it second.php.

247
❄ ❄ ❄

4. Enter this code in the file:

```
<?
echo $FIRST;
?>
```

5. Point your browser to http://yourserver/first.php.

6. Type your name into the blank and click Submit.

   You are directed to second.php and your name should show up on the page just as you typed it. Can you figure out what is going on here? In the form, first.php, a variable called FIRST was set up for you. When the second form receives the variable, it is received as $FIRST. The $ sign is the traditional designation for a variable. You could have used any word with any case (First, first, fiRst, Blah, blahblah) for the variable but the words have to match in the form and in the receiving page. Give it a try.

Embedded SQL Examples

Now look at some more interesting examples involving embedded SQL, since that is the subject at hand. This example is fairly complex but I explain each part of it along the way. I hope that you kept the Books database with the Authors, Works, Agents, and Editors tables in it because you are going to use it now for the examples.

1. Log in to MySQL at the command line.

2. Create a new user with SELECT, INSERT, and UPDATE privileges on the Books database. In case you have forgotten, here is the syntax:

```
GRANT SELECT, INSERT, UPDATE ON Books.* TO 'sqluser'@'localhost'
IDENTIFIED BY 'secret';
```

   This creates a local user, sqluser, so that you may connect to the database via PHP. If your web server runs *locally* (on the same computer with the database), then this setup is fine. If the web server is remote to the database server (on a different computer) then name that host in the GRANT statement, replacing localhost with the hostname or IP address of the web server.

3. Create a new text file and name it sqlfirst.php.

4. Enter the following code into the file (without the line numbers; it is indented for clarity):

```
1    <?
2    $connect = mysql_connect("localhost", "sqluser", "secret");
3    $db = mysql_select_db("Books", $connect);
4    $GETDATA = "SELECT First_Name, Last_Name FROM Authors";
5    $result_set = mysql_query($GETDATA, $connect);
```

```
6      while ($row = mysql_fetch_array($result_set)) {
7              $first  = $row["First_Name"];
8              $last = $row["Last_Name"];
9      echo "$first $last";
10     echo "<BR>";
11     }
12     ?>
```

5. Save this file and point your browser to http://yourserver/sqlfirst.php to display the following:

```
Anne Cohen
Glen Harris
Lynne Steele
Bob Fischer
Janet Shoals
Robert Balzer
Clara Janke
Bill Ferris
Lenard Dawson
```

Do you see the embedded SQL statement?

`SELECT First_Name, Last_Name FROM Authors`

Take a look at what is going on in our little 12-line wonder, sqlfirst.php:

❊ Lines 1 and 12 are the opening and closing PHP script tags. From now on, I won't mention them because they are always there.

❊ Line 2 is called the *connect string* and I set that whole string equal to $connect. mysql_connect(...) is a PHP function that allows me to put in a hostname, a username, and a password for a user connecting to the MySQL server.

❊ Line 3 selects the database you want to use. This, along with the connect string, connects to the Books database. At the command line you use the following to connect to the database: mysql –usqluser –psecret Books.

❊ Line 4 is the cleverly, properly formed embedded SQL statement. Notice how each line is set equal to a variable, shortening the amount of typing later in the script.

❊ Line 5 submits the query to the database via mysql_query(...), a mysql function whose arguments are the SQL statement $GETDATA and the connect string $connect.

※ Line 6 sets up a loop to go through the data being pulled from the database. If you type that statement in the MySQL command-line interface, you get the list of names that you saw in the browser earlier. This is the result set that I called $result_set in line 5. This data comes from the database in an array, but thanks to the magic of PHP you can extract the individual array members with the next few lines of code. So, line 6 is saying that while there are items in the array called $result_set, I want to extract them. Do you see the $row variable? That variable holds one row of data at a time in the loop. You extract one row of data each time through the loop.

※ Lines 7 and 8 are further extracting the array of First_Name Last_Name into the individual First_Name and Last_Name columns. I set $row["First_Name"] to the variable $first and $row["Last_Name"] to $last so that I can use them.

※ Line 9 is an echo statement that sends those values to the screen. *Echo* means echo to the screen. In your case, the screen is a browser.

※ Line 10 is just the HTML tag for a line break that is echoed to the screen.

※ Line 11, with a closing bracket, ends the loop that began on line 6 with the while statement. Anything inside the loop is iterated as long as the loop is going. Anything outside the loop only shows up one time.

And that is basically how you embed SQL into a host language like PHP. You have to maintain the syntax and respect the rules for both—and in this case, all three—languages: HTML, PHP and SQL. Yes, you can put tables into PHP pages, multiple SQL statements, even attach to multiple databases, use any query you wish, connect as multiple users with separate connect strings, create drop-down boxes with result sets, and a host of other possibilities. Once you get the hang of using PHP with embedded SQL, you may become obsessed with the things you can do.

Here's another example that will be of interest if you are true visionary of possibilities. This example requires a bit more HTML but it is no more complex than the first example.

1. Make a copy of sqlfirst.php and call it sqlsubmit.php.

2. Make the following changes to sqlsubmit.php:
   ```
   <?
   $connect = mysql_connect("localhost", "sqluser", "secret");
   $db = mysql_select_db("Books", $connect);
   $GETDATA = "SELECT First_Name, Last_Name FROM Authors";
   $result_set = mysql_query($GETDATA, $connect);
   echo "<FORM METHOD=POST ACTION='sqlreceive.php'>";
   echo "<SELECT NAME='Writer'>";
   while ($row = mysql_fetch_array($result_set)) {
   ```

```
        $first  = $row["First_Name"];
        $last = $row["Last_Name"];
echo "<OPTION>$first $last</OPTION>";
}
echo "</SELECT>";
echo "<P>";
echo "<INPUT TYPE='SUBMIT' NAME='Submit' VALUE='Enter'>";
echo "</FORM>";
?>
```

3. Once you have added those lines and removed the <BR> line inside the loop, save sqlsubmit.php.

4. Make a copy of second.php and make the following change:

```
<?
echo $Writer;
?>
```

This file reflects the name of the author you choose on sqlsubmit.php. The $Writer variable comes from the SELECT tag in the drop-down.

5. Point your browser to http://yourserver/sqlsubmit.php, choose an author, and then click Enter.
   If all went well, you should see the name of the author on the sqlreceive.php page. If you get an error, make sure you typed exactly as shown and included the semicolons at the end of each line.

This example should have you wondering if you could submit this author name to the receiving page and have a query run from that information. Yes, you could. That is exactly how web database applications work. When you select from a drop-down and click Submit, you are probably submitting a variable into a query. Isn't that exciting? If that fact doesn't have you scrambling to use PHP, I am not sure you are convinced yet of its true power.

In the final PHP example, you do just that with one small change to the sqlsubmit.php file:

1. Make a copy of the sqlsubmit.php file and name it sqlquery.php.

2. Edit the file and make the following change to line 10:
   ```
   echo "<FORM METHOD=POST ACTION='sqlvision.php'>";
   ```

3. To create the receiving page, sqlvision.php, make a copy of sqlfirst.php and name the copy sqlvision.php.

4. Make the following changes in sqlvision.php. The line numbers and indentations are for clarity; you don't need them in your code.

```
1    <?
2    $connect = mysql_connect("localhost", "sqluser", "secret");
3    $db = mysql_select_db("Books", $connect);
4    $name = explode(" ", $Writer);
5    $GETDATA = "SELECT Author_ID FROM Authors WHERE Last_Name =
     '$name[1]'";
6    $result_set = mysql_query($GETDATA, $connect);
7    while ($row = mysql_fetch_array($result_set)) {
8            $authorid  = $row["Author_ID"];
9    }
10    $SHOWDATA = "SELECT Authors.First_Name, Authors.Last_Name, Works.
      Title FROM Authors, Works WHERE Authors.Author_ID = $authorid AND
      Works.Author_ID =$authorid";
11    $result_set2 = mysql_query($SHOWDATA, $connect);
12    while ($row = mysql_fetch_array($result_set2)) {
13            $first  = $row["First_Name"];
14            $last   = $row["Last_Name"];
15            $title  = $row["Title"];
16    echo "Book: $title by $first $last";
17    }
18    ?>
```

Here is the explanation of this page:

✻ Line 4 is a way of splitting a combined variable into its component parts. In sqlquery.php, I have the first names and last names combined into a single variable, $Writer. When I send that variable to sqlvision.php, I don't have a way of querying with the combined first and last name so I have to explode that variable with the PHP function explode(...). The explode function takes two arguments: the separator you want to split on and the name of the variable to split. You want to split $Writer where the space is between the names. Since you have a first and last name, the first becomes $name[0] and the last becomes $name[1].

✻ Line 5 is the query. Notice that I used the last name variable $name[1]. Strings must have single quotes around them in a query.

✻ Line 10 is the query you need to get the author's name and the book title(s) from that author.

✻ Lines 1–3, 6–9, and 11–18 are explained in the previous examples.

This was a brief but hopefully interesting introduction to web-based embedded SQL using PHP for you. You see how to use the results of a choice from one query, submit that choice to another query, and have those results used for other queries. The possibilities are virtually unlimited and I hope you pursue using PHP for yourself, at least, and maybe you end up building some very nice web applications with PHP and the database of your choice.

Command-Line PHP

I also use PHP at the command line when a web-oriented approach doesn't really work for a particular task. Using PHP at the command line is simple and writing a command-line interface script is much more streamlined than one written with HTML code for the web included. Command-line PHP is also more flexible than just shell scripting alone, plus I haven't found a way to embed SQL into a shell script yet.

Command-Line PHP Examples

For the first example, follow these steps:

1. Copy sqlfirst.php to sqlcmd.php and open it to make the following changes:
   Originally:
   ```
   echo "$first $last";
   echo "<BR>";
   ```

   Change to:
   ```
   echo "$first $last\n";
   ```

   This is the command-line version of the original two lines, where \n means newline.

2. Save the file.

3. Type the following at a command line:
   ```
   php sqlcmd.php
   ```

   You should see the following response:
   ```
   Content-type: text/html
   X-Powered-By: PHP/5.0.3


   Anne Cohen
   Glen Harris
   Lynne Steele
   Bob Fischer
   Janet Shoals
   Robert Balzer
   ```

Clara Janke

Bill Ferris

Lenard Dawson

The next example requires some SQL work:

1. Perform the following logged in to your MySQL as root, using the Books database:

```
CREATE TABLE Authors1 SELECT * FROM Authors;
```

2. Empty the table:

```
TRUNCATE TABLE Authors1;
```

3. Copy sqlcmd.php to grabnfill.php.

4. Open grabnfill.php to make it look like this. The line numbers and indentations are for clarity; you don't need them in your code.

```
1  <?
2  $connect = mysql_connect("localhost", "sqluser", "secret");
3  $db = mysql_select_db("Books", $connect);
4  $GRAB = "SELECT Author_ID, First_Name, Last_Name, Phone FROM Authors";
5  $result_set = mysql_query($GRAB, $connect);
6  while ($row = mysql_fetch_array($result_set)) {
7          $id   = $row["Author_ID"];
8          $first  = $row["First_Name"];
9          $last = $row["Last_Name"];
10         $phone = $row["Phone"];
11 $FILL = "INSERT INTO Authors1 VALUES ($id, '$first', '$last',
   '$phone')";
12 $do_the_fill = mysql_query($FILL, $connect);
13 }
14 ?>
```

Here is the explanation:

✱ Line 4 includes the changed variable name, which illustrates what is going on with each step. You added all the fields in the Authors table. Notice that you did not use SELECT * when creating the grab query.

✱ Line 5 reflects the change of the variable name from line 4.

✱ Lines 7–10 reflect the four columns you are grabbing out of the Authors table.

❋ Line 11 is the fill query to put data into the Authors1 table. The fill query has to go inside the loop to insert each row into the Authors1 table as it is pulled from the Authors table.

❋ Line 12 executes the $FILL query in line 11.

5. At a command prompt, type the following:

```
php grabnfill.php
```

You should receive the following response:

```
Content-type: text/html
X-Powered-By: PHP/5.0.3
```

This really doesn't tell you much but at least there are no errors. The only way you can ensure it worked successfully is to check the table Authors1.

Be daring and use this:

```
SELECT * FROM Authors1;
```

Author_ID	First_Name	Last_Name	Phone
9055	Anne	Cohen	512-555-1555
10009	Glen	Harris	512-555-7755
10239	Lynne	Steele	512-555-2951
10393	Bob	Fischer	512-555-1551
10909	Janet	Shoals	512-555-7000
12999	Robert	Balzer	512-555-5131
19001	Clara	Janke	512-555-2196
19555	Bill	Ferris	512-555-1527
23469	Lenard	Dawson	512-555-7055

This is an interesting example but it isn't extremely useful since you can just copy the table without truncating it and have the same results. The true beauty of this example lies not in how great this particular one is but in the expansion of this idea to include two different database servers. Though I can't demonstrate directly for you the output you would get, I can give you the code that would make it work.

Objective

Query a MySQL database on a remote host (10.0.1.250) and put the data into your local MySQL database. I am using familiar examples for the SQL statements so you can better visualize what is happening. If you choose not to do the actual exercise, it is okay just to watch what I am doing since you won't be able to actively participate in this one.

1. Copy grabnfill.php to rem2loc.php.

2. Open rem2loc.php to see the following:

```php
<?
// Connect to both databases
$remote_connect = mysql_connect("10.0.1.250", "sqluser", "secret");
$local_connect = mysql_connect("localhost", "sqluser", "secret");

// Select the Databases from each server
$remote_db = mysql_select_db("Publishing", $remote_connect);
$local_db = mysql_select_db("Books", $local_connect);

// Issue the remote SQL query to get the data
$remote_select = "SELECT Authors.Author_ID, Authors.First_Name,
Authors.Last_Name, Authors.Phone, Works.Title FROM Authors, Works WHERE
Authors.Author_ID = Works.Author_ID";

// Execute the query on the remote database
$remote_result_set = mysql_query($remote_select, $remote_connect);

// Iterate through the rows of data
while ($row = mysql_fetch_array($remote_result_set)) {

        $id    = $row["Author_ID"];
        $first  = $row["First_Name"];
        $last = $row["Last_Name"];
        $phone  = $row["Phone"];
        $title  = $row["Title"];

// Insert the data into our local database
$local_insert = "INSERT INTO Authors VALUES ($id, '$first', '$last',
'$phone', 'title')";

// Execute the insert query on our database
$local_fill = mysql_query($local_insert, $local_connect);
}
?>
```

I provided standard comments in this file so that you know for what each step is. The one thing you may notice is that I do not use the fully qualified Table_Name.Column_Name when I pull the individual columns out of the result set array. That is because PHP doesn't use the dot notation for those variables. If you have multiple columns named the same in different tables (which you don't here), you can work around this issue by using an AS alias for the column name and using the alias in the array variable. Here is an example of what I mean:

```
$GETDATA = "SELECT Authors.First_Name, Authors.Last_Name, Agents.First_Name,
Agents.Last_Name FROM Authors, Agents WHERE Authors.Authors_ID =
Agents.Authors_ID";
```

In a regular SELECT, this is not a problem because all columns are uniquely identified, but in PHP you need to do the following to this $GETDATA query:

```
$GETDATA = "SELECT Authors.First_Name, Authors.Last_Name, Agents.First_Name
AS Agents_First, Agents.Last_Name AS Agents_Last FROM Authors, Agents WHERE
Authors.Author_ID = Agents.Author_ID";
```

This solves the column names looking the same to PHP. The array extraction would look like this:

```
$Au_first  = $row["First_Name"];
$Au_last   = $row["Last_Name"];
$Ag_first  = $row["Agents_First"];
$Ag_last = $row["Agents_Last"];
```

You may try that one yourself to prove that it works. I copied sqlcmd.php to a new file and made the adjustments to the new file. Here is the output:

```
Content-type: text/html
X-Powered-By: PHP/5.0.3
Glen Harris - Paul Jones
Lenard Dawson - Lee Smith
Anne Cohen - Ed Trumbull
Robert Balzer - LeeAnn Evans
Lynne Steele - Tom Rosen
```

You always get the first two lines (header info) when using PHP at the command line because PHP thinks it is a web-oriented language.

That should be enough to whet your appetite for learning more about PHP and its command-line scripting capabilities. You can see how useful embedded SQL is for a host language. Being able to embed one language within another expands them both beyond their uses as separate, distinct entities.

Other Languages

I am including this section on using embedded SQL in other languages for your edification. Though I really love PHP, I know that it is not the only way to do it. Any language you choose to use will work. I don't know that any are really any better than any of the others. They all have their own limitations, quirks, and high points. You will ultimately have to make the decision which language or languages you choose to work with in your environments. The languages that I am including here are also not the only players in the field of scripting or host languages in which you can embed SQL.

I cover Perl, Python, and Ruby in this section. The choice to include these is fairly straightforward; I prefer the newer open-source languages. Java, to me, is too large and clunky to be useful in the capacity in which I use a language like this. C and C++ have to be compiled and are therefore too troublesome for me. I don't want to spend a lot of time writing, compiling, testing, then re-peating. I like to see my code, see what it is doing, perform quick edits, and get on with the task at hand. The Microsoft .NET realm is really not my cup of tea. Some innovative individuals out there have ported most of the .NET technology to Unix/Linux, but I prefer to keep my distance. The technology is fine but the programming concepts are the opposite of the way I think. It is merely a personal preference and I remain dedicated to cross-platform, open-source solutions.

I am not including installation for these languages in this section but name the resources available to do so. Under each language, I supply resources that, in turn, provide documentation and downloads. The example given in each section is a derivative of the familiar sqlfirst.php that I used when you looked at PHP. I did this on purpose so you can directly compare the languages and the output.

Perl

Perl is the granddaddy of all scripting languages. It is very mature, widely used, well documented, and has been extended to the nth degree with modules that make it still one of today's heavy-weight contenders in the world of scripting languages. Perl should really be written PERL because it is an acronym for Practical Extraction and Report Language. It is now so much more than that; I am unsure the acronym still applies. Well, except for the story I am about to relate.

My first exposure to Perl was in 1997 when I had a database project converting an old DOS-based database to Microsoft Access. The database had been around for several years so it had anomalies of every kind. It had been passed from user to user and was poorly maintained. I was very frustrated trying to export the data to Excel or a comma-separated text file so it could be easily converted to Microsoft Access. After many hours, I gave up. I thought would have to enter all 15,000 records into Access myself, then do the conversion into tables, and so on. Several beers later, a friend of mine and I were talking and I brought up the problem to him, a Java programmer by trade. He told me about Perl and said he would take a look at the data. I was thrilled. The next day he came in, sat down at my desk, and began tapping away at some strangely mangled mess on the screen that made me dizzy. No, it wasn't the beer. In about 15 minutes, he had completely extracted the data from the old DOS database and successfully inserted all 15,000 records into a new Microsoft Access table for me. As he walked away he said, "No charge." I sneaked up on my computer and nervously took a look, and there it was: a table full of beautiful data with column headings and everything. I couldn't believe it. After all I had been through, he just came in and whipped up a quick solution with such little effort. He used the power of Perl's ability to extract data quickly and efficiently using regular expressions. *Regular expressions* are bits of code used to match patterns. To find out more about regular expressions, read a good book on Perl. Have a caffeinated beverage handy when you do.

It has been a long time since that fateful day but I have never forgotten the power of Perl. I began gobbling up impossibly thick books and trying everything I could ever want something this magical to do for me. You are probably thinking that this story will end with me landing hard after Perl somehow let me down, but it doesn't. My love for Perl may have waned some since then but I still use it for those times when I need to push or pull a lot of data in a short amount of time from one database to another. In fact, I used to pull a large quantity of data from an Oracle database and insert it into a MySQL database every day via an automated task that I set up. Perl works pretty much the same as PHP for building web-type applications but I find it too cumbersome for those kinds of tasks. To me, PHP is a better fit for web-oriented projects. Perl is more like the big hammer in the toolbox. You use it sparingly but it certainly gets the job done.

For all of its positive attributes, Perl does have some drawbacks that bear mentioning at this point if you are considering it as part of your toolbox:

❋ Can be difficult to read.

❋ Requires installation.

❋ Can be difficult to maintain between programmers.

❋ Many ways to do the same thing.

❋ May be difficult for newcomers to learn.

❋ Must use modules for many of the more interesting capabilities.

To speak to, but not necessarily refute, these disadvantages, I can say that Perl was a little difficult for me to learn at first. I must also confess that I still refer to my Perl library of books when doing almost anything. Perl's syntax is C-like but is certainly non-trivial in nature. Its code can even be difficult for another Perl programmer to read since there are so many different ways to do things in Perl. This can be advantageous if you are trying to get something to work, but a serious disadvantage if you are looking for consistency and the ability to maintain the code, especially between programmers. I see installation as a necessary evil but not necessarily a serious disadvantage to using it. Many things require installation but Microsoft's support for Perl has a very low status.

Please don't get the impression that I don't like Perl; I do. I personally think the advantages far outweigh any listed disadvantages. As a matter of fact, one of the best programs I have ever seen for administering Unix and Linux type operating systems is written in Perl. The program is Webmin (www.webmin.com) and if you haven't tried it for your Unix or Unix-type operating system, you need to.

Perl Resources

The three main resources for Perl, Perl modules, and Perl-related information follow:

* ActiveState at www.activestate.com

* Comprehensive Perl Archive Network (CPAN) at www.cpan.org

* Perl.org at www.perl.org

If you are looking for something to do with Perl and can't find it at one of these places, it may not exist. ActiveState is the place for Perl for Windows. They have other languages and Perl for other operating systems but these folks actively maintain these open-source languages and provide them for free. They also have an array of commercial offerings that enhance your experience with these languages.

Perl Example

Now we jump into an example of using Perl as a host language for embedded SQL.

1. Open a text file and name it sqlfirst.pl.

2. Type the following lines of code into it:

```
use DBI;
$connect = DBI->connect("dbi:mysql:Books:localhost", "sqluser",
"secret");
$GETDATA = "SELECT First_Name, Last_Name FROM Authors";
$result_set = $connect->prepare($GETDATA);
$result_set->execute;
 while (@row = $result_set->fetchrow_array) {
        print "@row\n";
  }
```

I used the same variable names so that you can do a direct comparison between PHP and Perl.

3. To execute this script, type the following:

```
perl sqlfirst.pl
```

You should see these results:

```
Anne Cohen
Glen Harris
Lynne Steele
Bob Fischer
Janet Shoals
Robert Balzer
Clara Janke
Bill Ferris
Lenard Dawson
```

Python

Python is a language I think is hard to get to know. I feel its cryptic nature keeps me at bay and I just can't bring myself to embrace it. Many people, however, are extremely adept at its use and have built some very powerful programs with it. I have a friend who is a Python programmer and he absolutely swears by it, preferring it over Perl, and when he teaches Python he uses Perl as a transitional language between the two.

I have almost no experience with Python and could only tell you what others have told me about it; there are plenty of good books available on the subject. My personal opinion is that Python is ready for prime time. It is such a robust language that, if you don't want to learn C, it would or should be next on the list. In any case, if you are looking for a scripting language, then you should probably give Python a try.

Python Resource

For more information on python, go to www.python.org.

Python Example

The following is a code listing for the equivalent for the sqlfirst.php file created in the PHP section.

1. Install Python.

2. Install the MySQLdb module for accessing a MySQL database.

3. Create the script as sqlfirst.py.

4. Type the following to invoke the script:

```
python sqlfirst.py
import MySQLdb
```

```
db=MySQLdb.connect("localhost", "sqluser", "secret", "Books")
dbbrowser=db.cursor()
dbbrowser.execute('SELECT First_Name, Last_Name FROM Authors')
print dbbrowser.fetchall()
```

You should see this output from the script:

```
(('Anne', 'Cohen'), ('Glen', 'Harris'), ('Lynne', 'Steele'), ('Bob',
'Fischer'), ('Janet', 'Shoals'), ('Robert', 'Balzer'), ('Clara',
'Janke'), ('Bill', 'Ferris'), ('Lenard', 'Dawson'))
```

Ruby

Ruby has been slow to catch on in many parts of the world, including the U.S., but has quickly overtaken Python in Japan. Ruby is a 100-percent object-oriented programming language. It is said to be easy, transparent, small, and very powerful. It is also free and open source. I have no real experience with Ruby but I was able to install it on my Linux server, install the MySQL module for it, and adapt an existing program to fit the sqlfirst format.

Ruby Resources

For more information visit these sites:

* RubyCentral at www.rubycentral.com
* Ruby: Programmer's Best Friend at www.ruby-lang.org
* Ruby Garden at www.rubygarden.org

Ruby Example

1. Install Ruby.
2. Install the MySQL module for accessing a MySQL database.
3. Create the script as sqlfirst.rb:

```
#!/usr/local/bin/ruby -w
require "mysql"
dbname = "Books"
connect = Mysql.new("localhost", "sqluser", "secret")
connect.select_db("Books")
result = connect.query("SELECT First_Name, Last_Name FROM Authors")
result.each do |array|
    array.each do |value|
        puts value
```

```
        end
        puts
    end
connect.close
```

4. Type the following to invoke the script:

```
ruby sqlfirst.rb
```

This is the output:

```
Anne
Cohen

Glen
Harris

Lynne
Steele

Bob
Fischer

Janet
Shoals

Robert
Balzer

Clara
Janke

Bill
Ferris


Lenard
Dawson
```

Summary

Embedded SQL is a great tool for DBAs, systems administrators, developers, and a few others who just want an easier, more intuitive way to interact with a database and data. I like the flexible nature of the host languages so that I can work with them either at the command line or in a web browser. I still get excited when I program a query or solution using a language like PHP or Perl. I still have that same thrill every time I see the data spilling out into the web browser or into my command-line interface. There is a strange sense of accomplishment. Programming with these newer languages is not only productive but it is also a lot of fun. Enabling users to be more efficient and to take their wish lists and make them a reality is extremely gratifying.

If you haven't tried one of the many host languages available, you should. Try two or three to see which one you connect with and then see how far you can go with your ideas. Embedded SQL is here to stay until someone develops a new integrated language. I strongly urge you to try out a tool like Webmin, for instance, that uses embedded SQL. I hope this chapter has sparked your curiosity and motivates you to look deeper into the subject.

Chapter Review

Multiple Choice

1. Embedded SQL is "embedded" into what?

    a) A host programming language

    b) A database

    c) An SQL statement

    d) Nothing

2. Most of the new programming languages have what type of syntax?

    a) Complex

    b) Simplified

    c) C-like

    d) COBOL-like

3. PHP is an acronym for what?

    a) Private Hypertext Protocol

    b) Persistent Hypertext Protocol

    c) PHP: Hypertext Preprocessor

    d) Partitioned Hash Protocol

4. PERL is an acronym for what?

    a) Practical Enhanced Regular Language

    b) Practical Extraction and Report Language

    c) Practically Everything Report Language

    d) Protocol Extraction and Reboot Language

5. Data, when queried from a database using embedded SQL, is initially extracted as

    a) a random number.

    b) compiled and obfuscated characters.

    c) an array.

    d) a disarray.

6. In embedded SQL, the SQL statements are used by the host language as

    a) variables.

    b) results.

    c) directives.

    d) reports.

7. Perl is a poorly maintained and documented language.

    a) True

    b) False

8. The mechanism by which a language pulls data from a result set one row at a time is called what?

    a) An array

    b) A loop

    c) A relation

    d) An extraction

9. Ruby is what kind of language?

    a) Extractional

    b) Object-oriented

    c) Object-extractional

    d) Temporal

10. All of these host languages share one disadvantage:

    a) They are difficult to learn.

    b) They require a database.

    c) They have to be installed.

    d) They are obfuscated.

13 } Stored Procedures

MySQL has made the great leap into the realm of true enterprise-level database systems with the long-awaited addition of stored procedures in version 5.x. A *stored procedure* is a collection of SQL statements that are permanently stored within the database. Stored procedures are executed by the database engine without the need for data being sent back and forth via the network or any client. Theoretically, stored procedures execute faster since they are server side, not client-server. They are not compiled or precompiled in any way, so I can bust that myth for you up front. Like any query, they are passed through the query optimizer and therefore are optimized—but there is no compilation. If you experience some perceived speed increase, it is due to the location of the query (inside the database), not as a result of code manipulation of any kind.

Many users of other DBMSs had, for some time, criticized MySQL for not implementing stored procedures. Now that stored procedures are available, there is little reason not to try MySQL for any size environment. Though stored procedures were much anticipated, many major sites are running on MySQL 4.x, which does not have stored procedures. The use of stored procedures is highly debated and somewhat controversial. I, personally, do not like stored procedures in any DBMS. I don't refuse to use them because sometimes they are appropriate. I rarely use them and there are many reasons, but the one that comes to mind right off is that they are difficult to maintain. The added layer of complexity makes maintenance and debugging difficult; that slows the process of application development. I am looking at stored procedures from a developer's point of view, not a DBA's.

My goal is to educate you about stored procedures, not to sway your opinion about using them. Use them or don't use them, but be aware of their presence and recognize that they are part of most DBMSs. To be completely balanced in this presentation, I am providing the advantages and disadvantages of that the database community generally accepts. Because of the relative youth of stored procedures in MySQL, and the fact that I think stored procedures are an advanced topic, this chapter is a very brief introduction to them. I give enough information to get you started with stored procedures, but by no means take a complete look at them.

Advantages of stored procedures:

* Move SQL management to the database, providing a central location for DBMS management.
* Lower network traffic in client-server systems by using a simple call statement from the client.
* Provide greater control over query design and optimization.
* Provide greater security by allowing access to execute a procedure to a user but requiring no user access to a database or table.
* Make for cleaner code by not embedding SQL in HTML/PHP/Perl/etc. pages.
* Using stored procedures, like using views, can hide the database structure from everyone but the database administrators.

Disadvantages of stored procedures:

* May be difficult to maintain and debug.
* Very limiting for multiple or custom circumstances.
* Passing parameters via variables to a database can get rather cumbersome and make any application less maintainable when things change.
* Developers and DBAs in many companies are in different groups, which make changes, testing, and data management more difficult.
* Not necessarily more efficient or faster than sending the query via embedded SQL.
* Syntax differs from vendor to vendor, so your stored procedures are unlikely to be portable to other DBMSs and vice versa.

DELIMITER

DELIMITER is not really part of the stored procedure language. However, it is useful in the creation of stored procedures because it changes the symbol that concludes an SQL statement. The standard semicolon has to be changed because many statements within a stored procedure are terminated by a semicolon. To create a stored procedure, issue the DELIMITER keyword followed by the delimiter to be set. The stored procedure is written with individual statements within it that are terminated by the familiar semicolon. The procedure is terminated with the delimiter. Using this method, the stored procedure is executed and all of the SQL statements within it are executed as individual statements, as if they were executed interactively.

```
DELIMITER //
    Stored Procedure
//
```

When finished with the procedure, you will probably want to use the standard delimiter again. To do this, issue the following command:

```
DELIMITER ; //
```

Remembering to set and unset the delimiter is sometimes difficult.

CREATE PROCEDURE

This command creates stored procedures. Each stored procedure must have a unique name. The naming convention generally used is sp_*Name_Description* or some variation thereof. When working, I most often use the convention sp_*Table(s)_Description*, and this is the convention for this book. Although stored procedure names are not case sensitive, I still prefer to stay with a particular naming convention.

Just about any legal SQL statement is allowed in the body of the procedure. You may use SELECT, INSERT, UPDATE, DELETE, CREATE, DROP, and so on. You can't use CREATE PROCEDURE within a procedure nor can you use the USE keyword; MySQL assumes that the procedure uses the current database.

```
CREATE PROCEDURE sp_name ([proc_parameter[,...]])
    [characteristic ...] routine_body
type:
    Any valid MySQL data type
characteristic:
    LANGUAGE SQL
  | [NOT] DETERMINISTIC
  | { CONTAINS SQL | NO SQL | READS SQL DATA | MODIFIES SQL DATA }
  | SQL SECURITY { DEFINER | INVOKER }
  | COMMENT 'string'
routine_body:
    Valid SQL procedure statement or statements
```

Objective

Create a stored procedure to show authors and their works.

First, get the correct SQL statement to get the required information. In this case, you can use this familiar query:

```
SELECT Authors.First_Name, Authors.Last_Name, Works.Title FROM Authors, Works
WHERE Authors.Author_ID = Works.Author_ID;
```

Next, create the stored procedure.

Set the delimiter to something other than a semicolon:

```
DELIMITER //
```

Create the procedure using the SELECT statement from before:

```
CREATE PROCEDURE sp_AuthorWorks () SELECT Authors.First_Name, Authors.Last_Name,
Works.Title FROM Authors, Works WHERE Authors.Author_ID = Works.Author_ID;
```

End with the delimiter:

```
//
```

Set the delimiter back to the standard semicolon:

```
DELIMITER ;
```

The parentheses after the procedure name are for passing parameters to the stored procedure. To do this, you have to employ variables in your stored procedure, which is covered later in this chapter.

CALL

The CALL keyword is used to invoke a stored procedure. CALL can pass back values to its caller using parameters that are declared as OUT or INOUT parameters. It also returns the number of rows affected, which a client program can obtain at the SQL level by calling the ROW_COUNT() function.

```
CALL sp_name([parameter[,...]])
```

Result:

```
CALL sp_AuthorWorks();
```

```
+------------+-----------+----------------------------+
| First_Name | Last_Name | Title                      |
+------------+-----------+----------------------------+
| Lynne      | Steele    | Bruises On My Heart        |
| Robert     | Balzer    | How To Write Great Queries |
| Lenard     | Dawson    | Topiaries Are Tops         |
| Glen       | Harris    | Good Night, Good Chocolate |
| Anne       | Cohen     | You Had Me At Shalom       |
| Robert     | Balzer    | You Are Never Your Own Boss|
| Lenard     | Dawson    | Doodling As Art            |
+------------+-----------+----------------------------+
```

Notice that you did not have to specify the database or any other parameter to invoke the procedure. This is because MySQL assumes that the current database holds the stored procedure that you are calling.

SHOW CREATE PROCEDURE

Once you have created a procedure, you may want to take a look at it—especially if it has been some time since you created it.

```
SHOW CREATE PROCEDURE sp_name
```

Result:

```
SHOW CREATE PROCEDURE sp_AuthorWorks;
```

```
+------------------+----------+-------------------------------------------+
| Procedure        | sql_mode | Create Procedure                          |
+------------------+----------+-------------------------------------------+
| sp_AuthorWorks   |          | CREATE PROCEDURE `sp_AuthorWorks`()       |
 SELECT Authors.First_Name, Authors.Last_Name,Works.Title FROM Authors,Works
 WHERE Authors.Author_ID = Works.Author_ID |

+------------------+----------+-------------------------------------------+
```

ALTER PROCEDURE

ALTER PROCEDURE does not work like other ALTER commands. You can change few things with the ALTER PROCEDURE command, as you can see from the syntax. You can add a comment, change characteristics, and alter security information. You cannot edit the code of a stored procedure. To do that, you have to DROP and CREATE the procedure again from scratch.

```
ALTER PROCEDURE sp_name [characteristic ...]
characteristic:
    { CONTAINS SQL | NO SQL | READS SQL DATA | MODIFIES SQL DATA }
  | SQL SECURITY { DEFINER | INVOKER }
  | COMMENT 'string'
```

Objective

Add a comment to the stored procedure sp_AuthorWorks to describe its function.

```
ALTER PROCEDURE sp_AuthorWorks COMMENT 'Selects Authors and Works via Join on
Author_ID';
```

You may change the comment that you have just added by issuing another ALTER PROCEDURE command with the new comment. To see your comment, use the SHOW CREATE PROCEDURE command:

```
SHOW CREATE PROCEDURE sp_AuthorWorks;
```

```
+-----------------+----------+-------------------------------------------+
| Procedure       | sql_mode | Create Procedure                          |
+-----------------+----------+-------------------------------------------+
| sp_AuthorWorks  |          | CREATE PROCEDURE `sp_AuthorWorks`()       |
   COMMENT 'Selects Authors and Works via Join on Author_ID'
 SELECT Authors.First_Name, Authors.Last_Name,Works.Title FROM Authors,Works
 WHERE Authors.Author_ID = Works.Author_ID

+-----------------+----------+-------------------------------------------+
```

DROP PROCEDURE

The DROP PROCEDURE command removes a named procedure from the database.

```
DROP PROCEDURE [IF EXISTS] sp_name
```

```
DROP PROCEDURE sp_AuthorWorks;
```

The procedure has been removed permanently.

BEGIN...END

The BEGIN...END compound statement contains many SQL statements, all terminated with a semicolon. The BEGIN and END statements may have a label. Within a specific BEGIN...END compound statement, the labels must be the same. A procedure with multiple SQL statements must have a BEGIN and END statement.

```
 [begin_label:] BEGIN
     [statement_list]
 END [end_label]

Procedure1: BEGIN
SQL statement1;
SQL statement2;
END Procedure1;
```

DECLARE

DECLARE is used to declare local variables within a procedure. To provide a default value for the variable, include a DEFAULT clause. The default value may be specified as an expression instead of a constant. If you don't specify a default value, then NULL is assigned.

```
DECLARE var_name[,...] type [DEFAULT value]
```

The scope of a local variable is within the BEGIN...END block where it is declared. You can use it in nested blocks except those that declare a variable with the same name.

```
DECLARE Sum int DEFAULT 0;

DECLARE Title VARCHAR (60);
```

SHOW PROCEDURE STATUS

SHOW PROCEDURE STATUS returns information about all procedures contained within the MySQL server installation. To get information on a specific procedure or family of procedures, use the LIKE clause with a naming pattern.

```
SHOW {PROCEDURE | FUNCTION} STATUS [LIKE 'pattern']

SHOW PROCEDURE STATUS LIKE 'sp_Authors';
```

Db	Name	Type	Definer	Modified	Created	Security_type	Comment
Books	sp_Authors	PROCEDURE	root@local-host	2006-04-04 20:42:58	2006-04-04 20:58	DEFINER	
Books	sp_Author_Select	PROCEDURE	root@local-host	2006-04-10 10:41:07	2006-04-10 10:41:07	DEFINER	

Programming Constructs

The stored procedure implementation in MySQL contains many programming capabilities that you will find useful. Among them are the branching, looping, and error-handling constructs described in this section. These constructs are also called *control flow constructs* because they control the flow of a program or procedure. The IF, CASE, LOOP, WHILE, ITERATE, and LEAVE constructs are fully implemented. Without these constructs, it is almost impossible to fully enjoy the power of stored procedures and the decision-making capability they provide.

Branching

Branching is that part of programming that deals with making decisions and then dealing with the results. You have probably seen an old-fashioned flow chart diagram with Yes and No conditionals (diamond-shaped figures) on it. If you have seen one of those diagrams, then you are already familiar with branching. The conditional (diamond shape) is the point at which the diagram is branched depending on the answer to the question inside it.

IF...THEN...ELSE

Most often this branching is in the form of an IF...THEN...ELSE statement where if a certain condition exists, then one or another thing happens. The syntax, shown here, illustrates the possibilities:

```
IF search_condition THEN statement_list

    [ELSEIF search_condition THEN statement_list] ...

    [ELSE statement_list]


END IF
```

The IF...THEN...ELSE implementation is the basic conditional construct that programmers are familiar with where if a search condition evaluates to true, then one or more SQL statements is executed. If the condition is false, then the ELSE statement is executed.

You may use this IF...THEN...ELSE syntax within WHERE or HAVING clauses in SELECT statements. Also look at the IF() function in Appendix F for similar functionality.

CASE

The CASE construct is a complex conditional used with multiple conditions that depend on single values or when you need greater branching flexibility than an IF...THEN...ELSE conditional can provide.

```
CASE case_value
    WHEN when_value THEN statement_list
    [WHEN when_value THEN statement_list] ...
    [ELSE statement_list]
END CASE

CASE
    WHEN search_condition THEN statement_list
    [WHEN search_condition THEN statement_list] ...
    [ELSE statement_list]
END CASE
```

Unlike a standard programming CASE construct, this implementation ends with END CASE instead of END or ESAC. There is also a CASE function, described in Appendix F, that has an ELSE NULL clause possible.

Looping

Looping is an important part of programming when you need to repeat a particular statement or sequence of statements until a certain condition is met or a specific number of iterations are complete.

LOOP

The syntax for looping with the keyword LOOP is given here:

```
[begin_label:] LOOP
    statement_list
END LOOP [end_label]
```

LEAVE

The LEAVE statement exits a looping construct. It can also be used with BEGIN...END blocks.

```
LEAVE label
```

ITERATE

ITERATE can only appear within a looping construct and it literally means to repeat.

```
ITERATE   label
```

REPEAT

The REPEAT statement sets up a loop that repeats a statement or set of statements until a condition is met.

```
[begin_label:] REPEAT
    statement_list
UNTIL search_condition
END REPEAT [end_label]
```

Result:

```
DELIMITER //

CREATE PROCEDURE sp_Repeat(dat1 INT)
BEGIN
SET @counter = 0;
REPEAT SET @counter = @counter + 1; UNTIL @counter > dat1 END REPEAT;
END
//

CALL sp_Repeat(50)//
```

```
SELECT @counter//

+----------+
| @counter |
+----------+
| 51       |
+----------+
```

WHILE

WHILE has the opposite function of REPEAT: It continues looping until the condition is false.

```
[begin_label:] WHILE search_condition DO
    statement_list
END WHILE [end_label]

DELIMITER //
CREATE PROCEDURE sp_While()
BEGIN
  DECLARE var1 INT DEFAULT 10;

  WHILE var1 > 0 DO
    SELECT * FROM DEMO;
    SET var1 = var1 - 1;
  END WHILE;
END
//

CALL sp_While()//
```

You should see 10 results of SELECT * FROM DEMO in the window.

Summary

Stored procedures are a great way to streamline code and to alleviate some of the network traffic generated by web-based applications. They are probably most useful and maintainable in situations where an application's developer has access to write her own stored procedures. Stored procedures can be difficult to manage and maintain between personnel changes. The key to any successful implementation is dedication to a naming convention and documentation. My best advice for using stored procedures is to only implement them when you think that using them will offer some significant advantage over not using them.

You needn't feel compelled to use stored procedures just because they exist. My experience with stored procedures has been tainted by having to take over DBMSs where they have been used extensively and during a conversion of one type of DBMS to MySQL; not only do you have to edit the code in the application, but you also have to edit every stored procedure or get rid of them by transferring that logic to embedded SQL.

MySQL uses its own language for stored procedures. Other DBMSs use PL/SQL, Transact-SQL, or some other procedural language that adheres (at least in part) to the SQL2003 standard. Transact-SQL (T-SQL) is used in Sybase and Microsoft SQL Server. Oracle uses PL/SQL. While MySQL's procedure language seems to be a mix of PL/SQL and Transact-SQL—taking the best of both worlds—it was actually developed solely from the SQL2003 standard.

Chapter Review

Multiple Choice

1. To look at all of the stored procedures in a database, you would use

   a) SHOW STORED PROCEDURE.

   b) SHOW PROCEDURES.

   c) SHOW PROCEDURE STATUS.

   d) SHOW PROCEDURES LIKE '%'.

2. When calling a stored procedure, it is necessary to specify

   a) the procedure.

   b) the database.

   c) a character set.

   d) a language.

3. Which of these is the branching construct used most often?

   a) LOOP

   b) DELIMITER

   c) IF...THEN...ELSE

   d) CASE

4. Using stored procedures can decrease

   a) network traffic.

b) speed.

c) efficiency.

d) salability.

5. What is the purpose of using DELIMITER //?

a) To increase speed.

b) To start a stored procedure.

c) To simply declare a variable.

d) To use a semicolon in the stored procedure.

6. If you make a mistake in a stored procedure, you would use ALTER PROCEDURE to change it.

a) True

b) False

7. A stored procedure that contains multiple SQL statements must also contain a(n)

a) ALTER statement.

b) BEGIN...END block.

c) variable.

d) loop.

8. Stored procedures are

a) precompiled for efficiency.

b) a discontinued part of SQL.

c) optimized like any other query.

d) A misrepresented part of SQL.

9. Which of the following is the correct syntax for creating a stored procedure?

a) CREATE PROCEDURE sp_Names () SELECT * FROM Names //

b) CREATE PROCEDURE sp_Names SELECT * FROM Names //

c) CREATE PROCEDURE sp_Names () SELECT * FROM Names; //

d) CREATE NEW PROCEDURE sp_Names () SELECT * FROM Names; //

10. To add a comment to a stored procedure, which keyword would you use?

    a) SELECT

    b) ALTER

    c) DELETE

    d) COMMENT

Concepts

1. Discuss the advantages of using a stored procedure versus an embedded SQL statement.

2. Discuss what is meant by "A stored procedure can decrease network traffic associated with a web-based application."

14 } Data Warehousing

Perhaps it is just the phrase *data warehousing* that brings to mind a huge, glassed-in data center kept at a cozy 55 degrees Fahrenheit with a raised floor, fluorescent lighting (always a few flickering ones), and the ever-present hum of power supplies. Somewhere hidden in the racks and aisles of that fictitious data center may very well be a data warehouse—possibly even several dozen. The truth is that data warehouses come in all sizes and configurations and can actually reside on a single computer (hopefully one that is backed up every night). Data warehouses and data warehousing are not something dark and mysterious, but rather very simple concepts easily illustrated with some familiar terms and examples.

Data warehousing is simply storing historical data in a database and using some sort of interface to extract relevant data. There are many more-complex definitions, but in a nutshell that is it. There is no magic in a data warehouse. It is simply data that is of sufficient volume that you need to separate it from daily use, or *transactional*, data.

In this chapter you learn about the different types of database processing along with the associated terminology. You also learn the difference between a data warehouse, a data mart, and an operational database. At the end of the chapter, you learn the steps in constructing a data warehouse. Data warehousing is a huge subject area in the database world and this chapter is a mere introduction to it.

OLTP

OLTP is the acronym for *Online Transaction Processing*.

OLTP is a term thrown about in conversation, meetings, and in written communications with minimal regard for its true meanings. One definition is a data transaction that is interactive, real time, and rapid feedback in nature. A transaction may or may not actually include the SQL meaning of a transaction. Many people confuse OLTP with ACID transactions in a database. A transaction may simply consist of submitting your name and other contact information to a database via a web-based application. This is an OLTP action whether or not it includes an actual transactional block with COMMIT and ROLLBACK capabilities.

OLTP is the querying, inserting, deleting, and updating of data on a daily basis. Its focus is on current data and processing of specific queries usually returning only a few records at a time. All of the databases dealt with in this book are of this type. A database that employs OLTP is considered operational.

OLAP

OLAP is a another term bandied about with little regard for its true meanings. *Online Analytical Processing (OLAP)* is generally synonymous with data warehousing. In contrast to OLTP, OLAP is 99-percent data read. Rarely are any data changed once they are in the data warehouse, except possibly to correct errors or to update significantly changed data. OLAP is, as the name implies, for business analysis and looking at trends in business data.

The Operational Database

The *operational database* is the type you are most familiar with. It handles your business data, returns your queries with great speed, it is constantly involved in inserts, updates, deletes, and regular queries. The operational database is where your critical current data resides. It is highly normalized with many small (narrow) tables all of which are in *3NF (Third Normal Form)* or *BCNF (Boyce-Codd Normal Form)*.

The operational database is where the bulk of this book has been focused. Operational databases far outnumber data warehouses in businesses of all sizes. Data warehouses were born out of the unrestrained growth of operational databases in the enterprise. The problem presented is that all of a business' data is important and can't be archived into oblivion, but it also can't remain in the operational database due to decreasing performance. The problem is resolved by splitting out all non-current data from the operational database and creating a new database to house the historical data. This is how the data warehouse came to be. I am sure, with no real proof, that data warehouses existed long before anyone actually coined the term. Once the historical data is excised from the operational database, the operational database's performance returns to the snappy, agile speeds with which users have become accustomed. Just remember that once the data has been removed from the operational database, you must repair and optimize the tables so the data that remains in the operational database will perform as expected.

The Data Warehouse

The *data warehouse* is a collection of a business' historical data that is specifically set up to be extensively analyzed by its users. The database is designed with analysis as its primary focus.

Two major *schemas*, or designs, are used in data warehousing: star and snowflake. These designs make the data warehouse more efficient and easier to maintain over time.

Data warehouses are focused on summary data, comparisons, and aggregations. For example, sales figures are usually projected incrementally by quarter, year, and maybe over five years. A data warehouse is the perfect solution to these needs. It is generally accepted that a data warehouse should be an actual data warehouse rather than a virtual one. That is to say, the data warehouse needs to house its own data within its own tables and have its own life cycle rather than depend on querying multiple data sources for its contents. The main reasons for this rule are performance and reliability. If data is uploaded to the data warehouse on a periodic basis rather than on demand, its contents are stable and reliable. There may be times, if using a virtual data warehouse, that data is unavailable for a variety of reasons.

Star Schema

The *star schema* is the simplest and by far the most popular data warehouse schema in use today. The star schema is characterized by a central fact table connected to dimension tables. The fact table is generally normalized to 3NF, while the dimension tables are denormalized to 2NF. This design is to ensure performance, as data integrity is no longer an issue for read-only data. The integrity was already maintained during the creation of the original data.

When possible, use the star schema for your data warehouse implementations. The main concerns are performance and access to analytical data, and the star schema provides these.

The central fact table is connected to the dimension tables by foreign keys. The fact table is composed of facts and foreign keys. The primary key is usually comprised of all of the foreign keys.

Snowflake Schema

The *snowflake schema* is designed more like an operational database with the central fact table and more normalized dimension tables. By using this kind of schema, performance suffers and applications that access the warehouse have to be designed so users can easily choose reports and analytical data.

Do not expect users to understand star and snowflake schemas or anything about database design; that is your job. Create analytical applications such that they are simple and flexible and provide data that users need. It is more difficult to create a simple application than one designed for database professionals, but it is well worth the effort in cost savings to your company. The cost savings are realized in saving time when generating reports and analyzing data.

The Data Mart

A *data mart* is a specialized subset of a data warehouse. It has been separated from the data warehouse based on business criteria for a specific purpose. There are many reasons to create a data mart, but perhaps the most widely given, and compelling, reason is that it yields increased performance for a subset of data. A data warehouse can become very large and somewhat unwieldy, so sometimes it is advisable to create a data mart to offload certain subsets. For instance, the financial department in a large manufacturing company may request to have the financial data offloaded into a data mart (though they may not call it that) because the data warehouse is too slow in extracting the data they need for reporting.

To create this example of a financial data mart, select out all of the relevant finance-related information in the data warehouse and create a new database out of it. Select this information by visiting with members of the financial department to determine needs and wants for reporting. Get as specific as possible when asking what data the department needs. Selecting too much data will result in continued poor performance, and selecting too little will result in redoing the job amidst complaints and deadlines.

A data mart may consist of several fact tables and many dimension tables. There are really no hard and fast rules as yet, although I think that many would agree that like data warehouses, data marts should be actual entities rather than virtual ones.

Building a Data Warehouse

There are a few key points to remember when building or designing a data warehouse. First and foremost, you have to realize that it will be very large compared to your operational database. You also have to determine what is considered historical data and what is considered current data, as this varies from one implementation to another.

When you build a data warehouse, all of the information you have gleaned from your experience, this book, other books, and people on your team will be invaluable. Database normalization and optimization are the two most important concepts during the design and construction phases. Do not minimize this effort. Keep in mind the level of normalization for a data warehouse is very different than that of an operational database.

My own experience in building a data warehouse was an impromptu one. I had built a reporting database for the group I was working in at the time. The database grew rapidly over a few months and I realized then that we had to do something quickly because performance was suffering. I knew that the performance rested solely with me since I designed it and the applications that accessed it. Performance was a great concern because, aside from regular users, I happened to be working in a group that did performance analysis for the rest of the company. I had also gone out on a limb by stating, rather vigorously, that database and web-based applications were the way to go versus the text documents and spreadsheets that were currently being used to do the same job. I had to make everything work smoothly, quickly, and without flaw or we would go back to the primitive culture of passing around spreadsheets and text documents.

I won't make you relive the whole exhausting process of the several revisions of my work, complaints from co-workers about my unwieldy application, or the high-profile executive murmurings that liked the idea but decided that perhaps our team just couldn't pull it off. I had to sit back and revise my thinking on the whole thing. I also had to reconsider my original design. There were many team meetings to determine what my audience needed from the operational database and the data warehouse. There were also meetings and emails from the other data consumers as to what kind of business intelligence needed to be included in the reporting applications. The end product ended up like this: I completely redesigned the operational database and normalized it to 3NF. The operational database only contained current data defined as data pertaining to the current month. At the end of every month, the data is extracted and transferred to the data warehouse. The application was built such that all of this is automated. I haven't touched the basic configuration or operation in over two years. The operational database is small and fast. The data warehouse grows each month but performance hasn't suffered because of the table design. It is about time for another revision of the data warehouse due to its age and increased usage.

Yes, a data warehouse has to be updated and maintained just like any other database. The data is read only to the user but not to the administrator. A vendor changes phone number, a member of the team leaves, a new member comes into the team: Those changes have to be reflected in the data warehouse. A data warehouse is not a static entity. Although it is not as dynamic as an operational database, it is still dynamic.

When creating a data warehouse remember these key points:

- ❋ Define and remember your audience (user).
- ❋ Ensure proper normalization.
- ❋ Determine what is defined as historical data.
- ❋ Determine what is defined as operational data.
- ❋ Maintain a dialog with your audience to make sure the data warehouse is meeting its needs.
- ❋ Automate, as much as possible, data extraction, transformation, and loading into the data warehouse.
- ❋ A database, even a data warehouse, is a dynamic entity.

It is very difficult to teach someone how to build a data warehouse because every situation is different. The culture at a particular company alters the way data is used and interpreted. Whether you are an in-house support person or a work-for-hire consultant, you need to focus on the end user and the corporate culture. You can't go in and just create a data warehouse without understanding a company's or department's business needs.

Summary

Data warehousing is an important aspect of database technology. Every DBA should know something about it. At some point, almost every DBA will be asked to participate on a data warehousing project. It will be too late to figure out a strategy when you are asked to assist. Once you have mastered the SQL statements and applications contained in an introductory SQL book and this one, you will no doubt want to delve into more-advanced projects like data warehousing or the creation of a data mart.

I think that the creation of a data mart is far more difficult than creating a data warehouse because of the high level of specificity that goes into the logic. Data marts are a road currently far less traveled than data warehousing, but you will see more occurrences in the future as data warehouses become so large and complex that they're impractical. An example of this is a keyword search in an Internet search engine: You type a keyword into the search field and get a return of more than 50,000 hits. Chances are you will never look through them all, as it is too impractical and time consuming. A solution is to construct data marts on specific areas of interest that returns fewer results with a higher relevance ratio.

For those of you who want to know more about data warehousing, I suggest picking up a good book on the subject perhaps starting with an introductory one then moving on to a larger more advanced one after really digesting the primer.

Chapter Review

Multiple Choice

1. OLAP is synonymous with

    a) operational databases.

    b) holistic data.

    c) in-memory databases.

    d) data warehousing.

2. Operational databases are typified by

    a) OLAP

    b) OLTP

    c) OLGP

    d) RTFM

3. Data warehouses are normalized to what degree?

   a) 1NF

   b) 2NF

   c) 3NF

   d) A combination of 2NF and 3NF

4. Operational databases are the most plentiful type of database in use.

   a) True

   b) False

5. A data mart is a

   a) subset of a data warehouse.

   b) subset of an operational database.

   c) superset of a data warehouse.

   d) superset of an operational database.

6. The role of the user in data warehouse design is

   a) minimal.

   b) irrelevant.

   c) administrative.

   d) essential.

7. The star schema is the simplest design for which of the following?

   a) An operational database.

   b) A data warehouse.

   c) A dimension table.

   d) A fact table.

8. The construction of a data mart is advisable when what situation arises?

   a) Users complain too much.

   b) Business productivity dictates it.

c) The operational database isn't adequate.

d) The data warehouse isn't normalized.

9. A data warehouse is comprised of

a) current operational data.

b) financial data.

c) highly transactional and volatile data.

d) historical data.

10. Operational databases focus on transactional data, while data warehouses focus on

a) process data.

b) symbiotic data.

c) analytical data.

d) outdated data.

Concepts

1. When confronted with the task of creating a data warehouse, what is the most important thing to consider in the database design? Explain.

2. Considering question 1, what could happen if you didn't consider this very important aspect of design?

Database Administrator Utilities

The following is a list of DBA commands and syntax. Some of these will only work with MySQL but they are worth the time to become familiar with. For MySQL and other DBMSs, there are graphical equivalents of some of these commands.

Account Management Statements

CREATE USER
```
CREATE USER user [IDENTIFIED BY [PASSWORD] 'password']
    [, user [IDENTIFIED BY [PASSWORD] 'password']] ...
```

DROP USER
```
DROP USER user [, user] ...
```

GRANT and REVOKE
```
GRANT priv_type [(column_list)] [, priv_type [(column_list)]] ...
    ON [object_type] {tbl_name | * | *.* | db_name.*}
    TO user [IDENTIFIED BY [PASSWORD] 'password']
        [, user [IDENTIFIED BY [PASSWORD] 'password']] ...

    [REQUIRE
        NONE |
```

```
        [{SSL| X509}]
        [CIPHER 'cipher' [AND]]
        [ISSUER 'issuer' [AND]]
        [SUBJECT 'subject']]
    [WITH with_option [with_option] ...]

object_type =
        TABLE
    | FUNCTION
    | PROCEDURE

with_option =
        GRANT OPTION
    | MAX_QUERIES_PER_HOUR count
    | MAX_UPDATES_PER_HOUR count
    | MAX_CONNECTIONS_PER_HOUR count
    | MAX_USER_CONNECTIONS count

REVOKE priv_type [(column_list)] [, priv_type [(column_list)]] ...
        ON [object_type] {tbl_name | * | *.* | db_name.*}
        FROM user [, user] ...

REVOKE ALL PRIVILEGES, GRANT OPTION FROM user [, user] ...
```

RENAME USER

```
RENAME USER old_user TO new_user
    [, old_user TO new_user] ...
```

SET PASSWORD

```
SET PASSWORD = PASSWORD('some password')
SET PASSWORD FOR user = PASSWORD('some password')
```

Table Maintenance Statements

ANALYZE TABLE

```
ANALYZE [LOCAL | NO_WRITE_TO_BINLOG] TABLE tbl_name [, tbl_name] ...
```

BACKUP TABLE

```
BACKUP TABLE tbl_name [, tbl_name] ... TO '/path/to/backup/directory'
```

CHECK TABLE

```
CHECK TABLE tbl_name [, tbl_name] ... [option] ...
option = {QUICK | FAST | MEDIUM | EXTENDED | CHANGED}
```

CHECKSUM TABLE

```
CHECKSUM TABLE tbl_name [, tbl_name] ... [ QUICK | EXTENDED ]
```

OPTIMIZE TABLE

```
OPTIMIZE [LOCAL | NO_WRITE_TO_BINLOG] TABLE tbl_name [, tbl_name] ...
```

REPAIR TABLE

```
REPAIR [LOCAL | NO_WRITE_TO_BINLOG] TABLE
     tbl_name [, tbl_name] ... [QUICK] [EXTENDED] [USE_FRM]
```

RESTORE TABLE

```
RESTORE TABLE tbl_name [, tbl_name] ... FROM '/path/to/backup/directory'
```

SHOW Syntax

SHOW CHARACTER SET

```
SHOW CHARACTER SET [LIKE 'pattern']
```

SHOW COLLATION

```
SHOW COLLATION [LIKE 'pattern']
```

SHOW COUMNS

```
SHOW [FULL] COLUMNS FROM tbl_name [FROM db_name] [LIKE 'pattern']
```

SHOW CREATE DATABASE

```
SHOW CREATE {DATABASE | SCHEMA} db_name
```

SHOW CREATE TABLE

```
SHOW CREATE TABLE tbl_name
```

SHOW DATABASES

```
SHOW {DATABASES | SCHEMAS} [LIKE 'pattern']
```

SHOW ENGINE

```
SHOW ENGINE engine_name {LOGS | STATUS }
```

SHOW ENGINES

```
SHOW [STORAGE] ENGINES
```

SHOW ERRORS

```
SHOW ERRORS [LIMIT [offset,] row_count]
SHOW COUNT(*) ERRORS
```

SHOW GRANTS

```
SHOW GRANTS FOR user
```

SHOW INDEX

```
SHOW INDEX FROM tbl_name [FROM db_name]
```

SHOW INNODB STATUS

```
SHOW INNODB STATUS (Deprecated form of SHOW ENGINE INNODB STATUS)
```

SHOW LOGS

```
SHOW [engine_name] LOGS (Deprecated form of SHOW ENGINE engine_name LOGS)
```

SHOW OPEN TABLES

```
SHOW OPEN TABLES [FROM db_name] [LIKE 'pattern']
```

SHOW PRIVILEGES

```
SHOW PRIVILEGES
```

SHOW PROCESSLIST

```
SHOW [FULL] PROCESSLIST
```

SHOW STATUS

```
SHOW [GLOBAL | SESSION] STATUS [LIKE 'pattern']
```

SHOW TABLE STATUS

```
SHOW TABLE STATUS [FROM db_name] [LIKE 'pattern']
```

SHOW TABLES

```
SHOW [FULL] TABLES [FROM db_name] [LIKE 'pattern']
```

SHOW TRIGGERS

```
SHOW TRIGGERS [FROM db_name] [LIKE expr]
```

SHOW VARIABLES

```
SHOW [GLOBAL | SESSION] VARIABLES [LIKE 'pattern']
```

SHOW WARNINGS

```
SHOW WARNINGS [LIMIT [offset,] row_count]
SHOW COUNT(*) WARNINGS
```

Miscellaneous Administrative Statements

SET

```
SET variable_assignment [, variable_assignment] ...

variable_assignment:
      user_var_name = expr
    | [GLOBAL | SESSION] system_var_name = expr
    | @@[global. | session.]system_var_name = expr
```

CACHE INDEX

```
CACHE INDEX
      tbl_index_list [, tbl_index_list] ...
      IN key_cache_name

tbl_index_list:
      tbl_name [[INDEX|KEY] (index_name[, index_name] ...)]
```

DESCRIBE

```
{DESCRIBE | DESC} tbl_name [col_name | wild]
```

FLUSH

```
FLUSH [LOCAL | NO_WRITE_TO_BINLOG] flush_option [, flush_option] ...
```

KILL

```
KILL [CONNECTION | QUERY] thread_id
```

LOAD INDEX INTO CACHE

```
LOAD INDEX INTO CACHE
      tbl_index_list [, tbl_index_list] ...

tbl_index_list:
      tbl_name
```

```
    [[INDEX|KEY] (index_name[, index_name] ...)]
    [IGNORE LEAVES]
```

RESET

```
RESET reset_option [, reset_option] ...
```

USE

```
USE db_name
```

Appendix B }

MySQL Maintenance

Each DBMS provides utilities and commands for maintenance, but since this book uses MySQL, I feel compelled to provide you with its specific maintenance model. MySQL provides some great utilities for the DBA to maintain and optimize tables. These utilities have been built into MySQL using SQL statements, and external programs have also been provided so you can perform maintenance tasks outside MySQL. You should always make a backup before performing any table maintenance. The internal tools are considered safer than the external tools. For the sake of clarity, I will give you the internal maintenance statements first then the equivalent external maintenance commands.

※ **CHECK MATE**

The very versatile utility, myisamchk, is so versatile that it has the ability to check, repair, recover, and analyze tables that in each section in which myisamchk is used, I designate its use explicitly. Here is an example:

myisamchk (Check Tables)

Do not use myisamchk when the mysql server is running.

Checking Tables for Errors
CHECK TABLE, myisamcheck, and mysqlcheck are explained here.

CHECK TABLE

The CHECK TABLE Table_Name without any option defaults to MEDIUM.

```
CHECK TABLE tbl_name [, tbl_name] ... [option] ...
option = {QUICK | FAST | MEDIUM | EXTENDED | CHANGED}
```

CHECK TABLE returns a table of information in the manner given in Table B.1.

Table B.1   Check Table Table_Name;

Column	Value
Table	Table name
Op	Always analyze
Msg_type	One of status, info, error, or warning
Msg_text	The message

Normally the Msg_type should be OK. If the status is not OK or "Table is already up to date", then you should repair the table. Table B.2 shows the different options and their meanings.

Table B.2   Check Table Options

Type	Meaning
QUICK	Do not scan the rows to check for incorrect links.
FAST	Check only tables that have been closed improperly.
CHANGED	Check only tables that have been changed since the last check or that have been closed improperly.
MEDIUM	Scan rows to verify that deleted links are valid. This also calculates a key checksum for the rows and verifies this with a calculated checksum for the keys.
EXTENDED	Do a full key lookup for all keys for each row. This ensures that the table is 100-percent consistent, but takes a long time.

You may combine options to customize your table checks:

```
CHECK TABLE Table_Name FAST QUICK;
```

If an error is found with a table, it cannot be used until a repair has been completed successfully. You should only run EXTENDED after a regular check has been run and you receive some errors.

myisamchk (Check Tables)

The myisamchk utility either gets information about your database tables or checks, repairs, or optimizes them. myisamchk works with MyISAM tables: those with .MYI and .MYD files.

```
# myisamchk [options] Table_Name.MYI
```

POUND NOTE

When you see the # sign, this means you are using the operating system at the command line. Using # or $ is traditional in the Unix world to show that you are at a prompt. If you are a Windows user, it is C:\>.

Table B.3 shows you the myisamchk Check options.

Table B.3 Myisamchk Check Options

Type	Meaning
-c, –check	Check table for errors.
-e, –extend-check	Check the table very thoroughly. Only use this in extreme cases, as myisamchk should normally determine if the table is okay, even without this switch.
-F, –fast	Check only tables that have been closed improperly.
-C, –check-only-changed	Check only tables that have changed since last check.
-f, –force	Restart with -r if there are any errors in the table. States will be updated as with –update-state.
-i, –information	Print statistics information about checked table.
-m, –medium-check	Faster than extend-check, but only finds 99.99 percent of all errors. Should be good enough for most cases.
-U, –update-state	Mark tables as crashed if you find any errors.
-T, –read-only	Don't mark table as checked.

The SQL check and the external utility, myisamchk, give similar results but there is much more detail in myisamchk's information. You *must not* allow access to your tables while performing a myisamchk on them. Data can be corrupted if myisamchk is running a check while a user accesses them.

To check a single table, use this:

```
#  myisamchk [option] Table_Name.MYI
```

To check all tables, use this:

```
#   myisamchk [option]  *.MYI
```

mysqlcheck

This utility is hard to classify as internal or external to MySQL because it is an external utility, yes, but it logs in to the MySQL server and performs its operations with SQL. Unlike myisamchk, you must use mysqlcheck while the MySQL Server is running. I really like this utility because it saves a lot of time for a DBA. You can check entire, or even multiple, databases with one command. The syntax is also very simple:

```
#   mysqlcheck [options] –uroot –ppassword Database_Name
#   mysqlcheck [options] –uroot –ppassword Database_Name Table1_Name
    [Table2_Name…]
#   mysqlcheck [options] –uroot –ppassword --databases Database1_Name
    [Database2_Name…]
#   mysqlcheck [options] –uroot –ppassword --all-databases
```

The mysqlcheck options are given in Table B.4.

Table B.4   Mysqlcheck Options

Type	Meaning
–print-defaults	Print the program argument list and exit.
–no-defaults	Don't read default options from any options file.
–defaults-file=#	Only read default options from the given file named #.
–defaults-extra-file=#	Read this file after the global files are read.
-A, –all-databases	Check all the databases. This is the same as –databases with all databases selected.
-a, –analyze	Analyze given tables.
-1, –all-in-1	Instead of issuing one query for each table, use one query per database, naming all tables in the database in a comma-separated list.
–auto-repair	If a checked table is corrupted, automatically fix it. Repairing is done after all tables have been checked, if corrupted ones were found.
–character-sets-dir=name	Directory where character sets are.
-c, –check	Check table for errors.
-C, –check-only-changed	Check only tables that have changed since last check or have been closed improperly.

Type	Meaning
–compress	Use compression in server/client protocol.
-B, –databases	Check several databases. Note the difference in usage; in this case no tables are given. All name arguments are regarded as database names.
-#, –debug[=#]	This is a non-debug version. Catch this and exit.
–default-character-set=name	Set the default character set.
-F, –fast	Check only tables that haven't been closed properly.
-f, –force	Continue even if you get an sql-error.
-e, –extended	If you are using this option with CHECK TABLE, it ensures that the table is 100-percent consistent, but takes a long time. If you are using this option with REPAIR TABLE, it forces using old, slow repair with keycache method, instead of much faster repair by sorting.
-?, –help	Display this help message and exit.
-h, –host=name	Connect to host.
-m, –medium-check	Faster than extended-check, but only finds 99.99 percent of all errors. Should be good enough for most cases.
-o, –optimize	Optimize table.
-p, –password[=name]	Password to use when connecting to server. If password is not given, it's solicited on the tty.
-P, –port=#	Port number to use for connection.
–protocol=name	The protocol of connection (tcp, socket, pipe, memory).
-q, –quick	If you are using this option with CHECK TABLE, it prevents the check from scanning the rows to check for wrong links. This is the fastest check. If you are using this option with REPAIR TABLE, it tries to repair only the index tree. This is the fastest repair method for a table.
-r, –repair	Can fix almost anything except unique keys that aren't unique.
-s, –silent	Print only error messages.
-S, –socket=name	Socket file to use for connection.
–tables	Overrides option –databases (-B).
-u, –user=name	User for login if not current user.
–use-frm	When used with REPAIR, get table structure from .frm file, so the table can be repaired even if .MYI header is corrupted.
-v, –verbose	Print info about the various stages.
-V, –version	Output version information and exit.

An interesting mysqlcheck feature is that you can sort of create your own custom utilities with it by simply copying mysqlcheck to a new filename. By copying mysqlcheck to mysqlrepair, you automatically have created a utility that repairs your tables. The utility mysqlrepair is equivalent to using the mysqlcheck utility with the −r or −repair option. You can also copy mysqlcheck to mysqlanalyze and to mysqloptimize for similar results.

Repairing Errors

REPAIR TABLE is the SQL syntax that fixes corrupted tables. myisamchk is an external utility that is useful for repairing and recovering tables that have been corrupted in some way.

REPAIR TABLE

This command has the same effect myisamchk has: recover Table_Name. It is possibly the only way to retrieve all of your information from a MyISAM table that has been corrupted. You hopefully will never have to run this command.

```
REPAIR [LOCAL | NO_WRITE_TO_BINLOG] TABLE
    tbl_name [, tbl_name] ... [QUICK] [EXTENDED] [USE_FRM]
```

SQL syntax to repair possibly corrupted MyISAM or Archive tables. The QUICK option only repairs index tables. The EXTENDED option recreates the index row by row and the USE_FRM will recreate the .MYI file from the .frm file if the .MYI file is missing or corrupt.

myisamchk (Repair Tables)

myisamchk may be called the MySQL DBA's best friend when things go wrong. To perform a repair on a table, first stop the MySQL Server. Issue the myisamchk command with options on the table index file (.MYI). To use myisamchk for repairs, you must at least use−r, which stands for *recover* and can fix most problems encountered. If you get a message that says the data file cannot be fixed, try the −o option (safe recover). See Table B.5 for more information.

```
# myisamchk -r [options] Table_Name.MYI
```

Table B.5   Mysqlcheck Options

Type	Meaning
Repair options (When using -r or -o)	
-B, –backup	Make a backup of the .MYD file as 'filename-time.BAK'.
-D, –data-file-length=#	Max length of data file (when recreating data file when it's full).
-e, –extend-check	Try to recover every possible row from the data file. Normally finds a lot of garbage rows. Recommended that you not use this option unless you are totally desperate.

Type	Meaning
-f, –force	Overwrite old temporary files.
-k, –keys-used=#	Tell MyISAM to update only specific keys. # is a bit mask of which keys to use. Can be used to get faster inserts!
-l, –no-symlinks	Do not follow symbolic links. Normally myisamchk repairs the table at which a symlink points.
-r, –recover	Can fix almost anything except unique keys that aren't unique.
-n, –sort-recover	Force recovering with sorting even if the temporary file would be very big.
-o, –safe-recover	Uses old recovery method; slower than '-r' but can handle a couple of cases where '-r' reports that it can't fix the data file.
–character-sets-dir=...	Directory where character sets are.
–set-character-set=name	Change the character set used by the index.
-t, –tmpdir=path	Path for temporary files.
-q, –quick	Faster repair by not modifying the data file. One can give a second '-q' to force myisamchk to modify the original data file in case of duplicate keys.
-u, –unpack	Unpack file packed with myisampack.

myisamchk has some miscellaneous options that are extremely valuable to a DBA. Pay particular attention to analyze (-a) and sort (-S). Table B.6 lists other actions.

Table B.6   Myisamchk Options

Type	Meaning
-a, –analyze	Analyze distribution of keys. Makes some joins in MySQL faster. Check the calculated distribution by using '–describe –verbose table_name'.
-d, –description	Prints table information.
-A, –set-auto-increment[=value]	Force auto_increment to start at this or higher value. If no value is given, then sets the next auto_increment value to the highest used value for the auto key + 1.
-S, –sort-index	Sort index blocks. Speeds up 'read-next' in applications.
-R, –sort-records=#	Sort records according to an index. Localizes your data and may speed up things; it may be very slow to do a sort the first time.

myisampack

The myisampack utility compresses MyISAM tables and makes them read only. The compression is usually in the range of 40–70 percent. MySQL AB will make compressed tables writable in the future, but this feature is not high on the to-do list. After running myisampack, you need to run myisamchk to recreate the indexes.

If you need to unpack a packed (compressed) table, use myisamchk with the –unpack option. The myisampack utility is invoked by issuing this command:

```
# myisampack [options] filename.MYI ...
```

The options for myisampack are listed in Table B.7.

Table B.7   Myisampack Options

Type	Meaning
-b, –backup	Make a backup of the table as table_name.OLD.
-f, –force	Force packing of table even if it gets bigger or if tempfile exists.
-j, –join='new_table_name'	Join all given tables into 'new_table_name'. All tables *must* have identical layouts.
-s, –silent	Be more silent.
-t, –test	Don't pack table, only test packing it.
-v, –verbose	Write info about progress and packing result.
-w, –wait	Wait and retry if table is in use.
-T, –tmpdir=...	Use temporary directory to store temporary table.
-#, –debug=...	Output debug log. Often this is 'd:t:o,filename'
-?, –help	Display this help and exit.
-V, –version	Output version information and exit.

mysql

The mysql command is the SQL shell or CLI for the MySQL Server. To use mysql, use the following syntax:

```
# mysql -u username -p password [Database_Name]
```

The default prompt you see is mysql>. At this prompt, you may enter SQL statements. Results are returned in ASCII text. This is the utility used throughout the entire book. It is the handiest interface because you know that it always exists in every MySQL installation. The downside is that it is probably the least efficient interface of all. Compared to the available graphical tools, this ones seems very primitive.

mysqlaccess

This script checks the access privileges for a hostname, username, and database combination. See Table B.8.

```
mysqlaccess [host [user [db]]] OPTIONS
```

You must supply the user and database to get this utility to work. You may use wildcards. Here is a sample output from one of the book's examples:

```
# mysqlaccess bjones Books

mysqlaccess Version 2.06, 20 Dec 2000
By RUG-AIV, by Yves Carlier (Yves.Carlier@rug.ac.be)
Changes by Steve Harvey (sgh@vex.net)
This software comes with ABSOLUTELY NO WARRANTY.


Access-rights
for USER 'bjones', from HOST 'localhost', to DB 'BOOKS'
    +-----------------+---+ +-----------------+---+
    | Select_priv     | N | | Lock_tables_priv | N |
    | Insert_priv     | N | | Execute_priv     | N |
    | Update_priv     | N | | Repl_slave_priv  | N |
    | Delete_priv     | N | | Repl_client_priv | N |
    | Create_priv     | N | | Create_view_priv | N |
    | Drop_priv       | N | | Show_view_priv   | N |
    | Reload_priv     | N | | Create_routine_priv | N |
    | Shutdown_priv   | N | | Alter_routine_priv | N |
    | Process_priv    | N | | Create_user_priv | N |
    | File_priv       | N | | Ssl_type        | ? |
    | Grant_priv      | N | | Ssl_cipher      | ? |
    | References_priv | N | | X509_issuer     | ? |
    | Index_priv      | N | | X509_subject    | ? |
    | Alter_priv      | N | | Max_questions   | 0 |
    | Show_db_priv    | N | | Max_updates     | 0 |
    | Super_priv      | N | | Max_connections | 0 |
```

```
    | Create_tmp_table_priv | N |    | Max_user_connections | 0 |
    +------------------+---+ +------------------+---+
NOTE: A password is required for user 'bjones' :-(

The following rules are used:
db : 'No matching rule'
host : 'Not processed: host-field is not empty in db-table.'
user : 'localhost','bjones','*2470C0C06DEE42FD1618BB99005ADCA2EC9D1E19',
'N','N','N','N','N','N','N','N','N','N','N','N','N','N','N','N','N','N','N',
'N','N','N','N','N','N','N','','','','','0','0','0','0'


BUGs can be reported by email to bugs@mysql.com
```

Table B.8   Mysqlaccess Options

Type	Meaning
-?, –help	Display this help screen and exit.
-v, –version	Print information on the program mysqlaccess.
-u, –user=#	Username for logging in to the database.
-p, –password=#	Validate password for user.
-h, –host=#	Name or IP number of the host.
-d, –db=#	Name of the database.
-U, –superuser=#	Connect as superuser.
-P, –spassword=#	Password for superuser.
-H, –rhost=#	Remote MySQL Server to connect to.
–old_server	Connect to old MySQL Server (before v3.21) that does not yet know how to handle full WHERE clauses.
-b, –brief	Single-line tabular report.
-t, –table	Report in table format.
–relnotes	Print release notes.
–plan	Print suggestions/ideas for future releases.
–howto	Some examples of how to run mysqlaccess.
–debug=N	Enter debuglevel N (0...3).
–copy	Reload temporary grant tables from original ones.
–preview	Show differences in privileges after making changes in (temporary) grant tables.

Type	Meaning
–commit	Copy grant rules from temporary tables to grant tables. Don't forget to do a mysqladmin reload.
–rollback	Undo the last changes to the grant tables.

Note the following:

- ✳ At least the user and the db must be given (even with wildcards).
- ✳ If no host is given, localhost is assumed.
- ✳ Wildcards (*,?,%, and _) are allowed for host, user, and database, but be sure to escape them from your shell...type * or '*'.

To escape the wildcards from your shell, enter a command like one of the following:

```
# mysqlaccess bjones \*
```

```
# mysqlaccess bjones '*'
```

Using wildcards with mysqlaccess returns a lot of information, so I suggest redirecting the output to a file and then opening the file with a text editor to examine it.

```
# mysqlaccess bjones \* > bjones.txt
```

mysqladmin

This client performs administrative operations, such as creating or dropping databases, reloading the grant tables, flushing tables to disk, and reopening log files. This utility gets my vote as the most valuable command-line program that I have ever used with MySQL. I like it because I can automate database creation, changing passwords, reloading grant tables, flushing privileges, getting a server status, and much more.

```
mysqladmin [OPTIONS] command command....
```

The very long list of mysqladmin's options appears in Table B.9.

Table B.9   Mysqladmin Options

Type	Meaning
-c, –count=#	Number of iterations to make. This works with -i (–sleep) only.
-#, –debug[=name]	Output debug log. Often this is 'd:t:o,filename'.

Type	Meaning
-f, –force	Don't ask for confirmation on drop database; with multiple commands, continue even if an error occurs.
-C, –compress	Use compression in server/client protocol.
–character-sets-dir=name	Directory where character sets are.
–default-character-set=name	Set the default character set.
-?, –help	Display this help and exit.
-h, –host=name	Connect to host.
-p, –password[=name]	Password to use when connecting to server. If password is not given, it's asked from the tty.
-P, –port=#	Port number to use for connection.
–protocol=name	The protocol of connection (tcp, socket, pipe, memory).
-r, –relative	Show difference between current and previous values when used with -i. Currently works only with extended status.
-O, –set-variable=name	Deprecated. Set variables directly with –variable-name=value.
-s, –silent	Silently exit if you can't connect to server.
-S, –socket=name	Socket file to use for connection.
-i, –sleep=#	Execute commands again and again with a sleep between.
-u, –user=name	User for login if not current user.
-v, –verbose	Write more information.
-V, –version	Output version information and exit.
-E, –vertical	Print output vertically. Similar to –relative, but prints output vertically.
-w, –wait[=#]	Wait and retry if connection is down.
–connect_timeout=#	
–shutdown_timeout=#	
Variables (–variable-name=value) and boolean options {FALSE	TRUE} Value (after reading options)	

Type	Meaning
count	0.
force	FALSE.
compress	FALSE.
character-sets-dir	No default value.
default-character-set	No default value.
host	No default value.
port	0.
relative	FALSE.
socket	No default value.
sleep	0.
user	No default value.
verbose	FALSE.
vertical	FALSE.
connect_timeout	43200.
shutdown_timeout	3600.

Default options are read from the following files in the given order:

`/etc/my.cnf ~/.my.cnf`

The groups in Table B.10 are read: mysqladmin client. The following options may be given as the first argument.

Table B.10   Mysqladmin Options As First Argument

Type	Meaning
–print-defaults	Print the program argument list and exit.
–no-defaults	Don't read default options from any options file.
–defaults-file=#	Only read default options from the give file named #.
–defaults-extra-file=#	Read this file after the global files are read. Where command is one or more of: Commands may be shortened.
create databasename	Create a new database.
debug	Instruct server to write debug information to log.
drop databasename	Delete a database and all its tables.
extended-status	Give an extended status message from the server.

Type	Meaning
flush-hosts	Flush all cached hosts.
flush-logs	Flush all logs.
flush-status	Clear status variables.
flush-tables	Flush all tables.
flush-threads	Flush the thread cache.
flush-privileges	Reload grant tables (same as reload).
kill id,id,...	Kill mysql threads.
password new-password	Change old password to new password, MySQL 4.1 hashing.
old-password new-password	Change old password to new password in old format.
ping	Check if mysqld is alive.
processlist	Show list of active threads in server.
reload	Reload grant tables.
refresh	Flush all tables and close and open log files.
shutdown	Take server down.
status	Retrieve a short status message from the server.
start-slave	Start slave.
stop-slave	Stop slave.
variables	Print variables available.
version	Get version information from server.

mysqlbinlog

Use this utility for reading statements from a binary log. The log of executed statements contained in the binary log files can be used to help recover from a crash. See Table B.11 for options.

```
mysqlbinlog [options] log-files
```

Table B.11   Mysqlbinlog Options

Type	Meaning
--character-sets-dir=name	Directory where character sets are.
-d, --database=name	List entries for just this database; local log only.

Type	Meaning
-D, –disable-log-bin	Disable binary log. Useful if you enabled –to-last-log and are sending the output to the same MySQL server. This way you could avoid an endless loop. Also use when restoring after a crash to avoid duplication of statements. You need a SUPER privilege to use this option.
-f, –force-read	Force reading unknown binlog events.
-?, –help	Display this help and exit.
-H, –hexdump	Augment output with hexadecimal and ASCII event dump.
-h, –host=name	Get the binlog from server.
-o, –offset=#	Skip the first *N* entries.
-p, –password[=name]	Password to connect to remote server.
-P, –port=#	Use port to connect to the remote server.
-j, –position=#	Deprecated. Use –start-position instead.
–protocol=name	The connection protocol (tcp, socket, pipe, memory).
-r, –result-file=name	Direct output to a given file.
-R, –read-from-remote-server	Read binary logs from a MySQL server.
–open_files_limit=#	Reserve file descriptors for usage by this program.
-s, –short-form	Just show the queries, no extra info.
-S, –socket=name	Socket file to use for connection.
–start-datetime=name	Start reading the binlog at first event having a datetime equal or posterior to the argument; the argument must be a date and time in the local time zone, in any format accepted by the MySQL Server for DATETIME and TIMESTAMP types. For example: 2004-12-25 11:25:56. You should probably use quotes to properly set your shell.
–stop-datetime=name	Stop reading the binlog at first event having a datetime equal or posterior to the argument; argument must be a date and time in the local time zone, in any format accepted by the MySQL Server for DATETIME and TIMESTAMP types. For example: 2004-12-25 11:25:56. You should probably use quotes to properly set your shell.
–start-position=#	Start reading the binlog at position *N*. Applies to the first binlog passed on the command line.
–stop-position=#	Stop reading the binlog at position *N*. Applies to the last binlog passed on the command line.

Type	Meaning
-t, --to-last-log	Requires -R. Will not stop at the end of the requested binlog but rather continue printing until the end of the last binlog of the MySQL Server. Sending the output to the same MySQL Server may lead to an endless loop.
-u, --user=name	Connect to the remote server as username.
-l, --local-load=name	Prepare local temporary files for LOAD DATA INFILE in the specified directory.
-V, --version	Print version and exit.

mysqldump

This client dumps a MySQL database into a file as SQL statements or as tab-separated text files. mysqldump is an exciting utility that allows some great flexibility in making database and table backups. I often use it to dump the structure and data to a file so that it can easily be loaded into another server or just kept as a snapshot for backup purposes.

```
mysqldump [OPTIONS] database [tables]

mysqldump [OPTIONS] --databases [OPTIONS] DB1 [DB2 DB3...]

mysqldump [OPTIONS] --all-databases [OPTIONS]
```

In its simplest form, mysqldump can be used to create a .sql file that, when loaded into another MySQL server, is an exact copy of the databases, tables, and so on at the time of the dump. This is a very quick way of getting a good backup of your database structure and data. I use this syntax:

```
# mysqldump Books Customers > Customers.sql
```

If you use mysqldump without the redirect to a filename, it dumps the information to the screen. To back up an entire database and all of its entities, use this:

```
# mysqldump Books > Books.sql
```

To get an idea of how to back up and restore a whole database, use the following example:

```
# mysqldump Books > Books.sql

# mysqladmin create Books_New

# mysql -uroot -ppassword Books_New < Books.sql
```

You now have an exact copy of the whole Books database including the data. Table B.12 lists mysqldump command-line options.

Table B.12   Mysqldump Options

Type	Meaning
–print-defaults	Print the program argument list and exit.
–no-defaults	Don't read default options from any options file.
–defaults-file=#	Only read default options from the given file named #.
–defaults-extra-file=#	Read this file after the global files are read.
-a, –all	Deprecated. Use –create-options instead.
-A, –all-databases	Dump all the databases. The same as –databases with all databases selected.
–add-drop-database	Add a DROP DATABASE before each create.
–add-drop-table	Add a DROP TABLE before each create.
–add-locks	Add locks around INSERT statements.
–allow-keywords	Allow creation of column names that are keywords.
–character-sets-dir=name	Directory where character sets are.
-i, –comments	Write additional information.
–compatible=name	Change the dump to be compatible with a given mode. By default, tables are dumped in a format optimized for MySQL. Legal modes are ansi, mysql323, mysql40, postgresql, oracle, mssql, db2, maxdb, no_key_options, no_table_options, and no_field_options. Use several modes separated by commas. Requires MySQL server version 4.1.0 or higher; earlier server versions ignore this option.
–compact	Give less-verbose output (useful for debugging). Disables structure comments and header/footer constructs. Enables options –skip-add-drop-table, –no-set-names, and –skip-disable-keys –skip-add-locks.
-c, –complete-insert	Use complete INSERT statements.
-C, –compress	Use compression in server/client protocol.
–create-options	Include all MySQL-specific CREATE options.
-B, –databases	Dump several databases. Note the difference in usage: In this case no tables are given. All name arguments are regarded as database names. 'USE db_name;' is included in the output.
-#, –debug[=#]A	non-debug version. Catch this and exit.
–default-character-set=name	Set the default character set.
–delayed-insert	Insert rows with INSERT DELAYED;.

Type	Meaning
–delete-master-logs	Delete logs on master after backup. Automatically enables –master-data.
-K, –disable-keys	'/*!40000 ALTER TABLE tb_name DISABLE KEYS */; and '/*!40000 ALTER TABLE tb_name ENABLE KEYS */; is in the output.
-e, –extended-insert	Allows utilization of the new, much-faster INSERT syntax.
–fields-terminated-by=name	Fields in the text file are terminated by ....
–fields-enclosed-by=name	Fields in the import file are enclosed by ....
–fields-optionally-enclosed-by=name	Fields in the infile are optionally enclosed by ....
–fields-escaped-by=name	Fields in the infile are escaped by ....
-x, –first-slave Deprecated.	Use –lock-all-tables.
-F, –flush-logs	Flush logs file in server before starting dump. If you dump many databases at once (using –databases= or –all-databases), the logs are flushed for each database dumped. The exception is when using –lock-all-tables or –master-data: These logs are flushed only once, corresponding to the moment all tables are locked. If you want your dump and the log flush to happen at the same moment, use –lock-all-tables or –master-data with –flush-logs.
-f, –force	Continue even if you get an sql-error.
-?, –help	Display this help message and exit.
–hex-blob	Dump binary strings (BINARY, VARBINARY, BLOB) in hexadecimal format.
-h, –host=name	Connect to host.
–ignore-table=name	Do not dump the specified table. To specify more than one table to ignore, use the directive once for each table. Each table must be specified with both database and table names (for example, –ignore-table=database.table, –insert-ignore). Insert rows with INSERT IGNORE.
–lines-terminated-by=name	Lines in the infile are terminated by .....
-x, –lock-all-tables	Locks all tables across all databases by taking a global read lock for the duration of the whole dump. Automatically turns off –single-transaction and –lock-tables.
-l, –lock-tables	Lock all tables for read.

Type	Meaning
–master-data[=#]	Appends the binary log position and filename to the output. If equal to 1, prints it as a CHANGE MASTER command; if equal to 2, that command is prefixed with a comment symbol. Turns on –lock-all-tables, unless –single-transaction is specified too (in which case a global read lock is only taken a short time at the beginning of the dump; don't forget to read about –single-transaction later). In all cases any action on logs happen at the exact moment of the dump. Option automatically turns off –lock-tables.
–max_allowed_packet=#	
–net_buffer_length=#	
–no-autocommit	Wrap tables with autocommit/commit statements.
-n, –no-create-db	'CREATE DATABASE /*!32312 IF NOT EXISTS*/ db_name;' is not in the output. The above line is added otherwise, if –databases or –all-databases option was given.
-t, –no-create-info	Don't write table creation information.
-d, –no-data	No row information.
-N, –no-set-names	Deprecated. Use –skip-set-charset instead.
–opt	Same as –add-drop-table, –add-locks, –create-options, –quick, –extended-insert, –lock-tables, –set-charset, and –disable-keys. Enabled by default; disable with –skip-opt.
–order-by-primary	Sort each table's rows by primary key, or first unique key, if such a key exists. Useful when dumping a MyISAM table to be loaded into an InnoDB table, but makes the dump itself take considerably longer.
-p, –password[=name]	Password to use when connecting to server. If password is not given, it's solicited on the tty.
-P, –port=#	Port number to use for connection.
–protocol=name	The connection protocol (tcp, socket, pipe, memory).
-q, –quick	Don't buffer query; dump directly to stdout.
-Q, –quote-names	Quote table and column names with backticks (`).
-r, –result-file=name	Direct output to a given file. Should be used in MSDOS, because it prevents new line \n from being converted to \r\n (carriage return + line feed).
-R, –routines	Dump stored routines (functions and procedures).

Type	Meaning
–set-charset	Add SET NAMES default_character_set to the output. Enabled by default; suppress with –skip-set-charset.
-O, –set-variable=name	Deprecated. Set variables directly with –variable-name=value instead.
–single-transaction	Creates a consistent snapshot by dumping all tables in a single transaction. Works *only* for tables in storage engines that support multiversioning (currently only InnoDB does); the dump is *not* guaranteed to be consistent for other storage engines. Automatically turns off –lock-tables.
–skip-opt	Disable –opt. Disables –add-drop-table, –add-locks, –create-options, –quick, –extended-insert, –lock-tables, –set-charset, and –disable-keys.
-S, –socket=name	Socket file to use for connection.
-T, –tab=name	Creates tab-separated text file for each table to given path. Creates .sql and .txt files. Only works if mysqldump is run on the same machine as the mysqld daemon.
–tables	Overrides option –databases (-B).
–triggers	Dump triggers for each dumped table.
–tz-utc	SET TIME_ZONE='+00:00' at top of dump to allow dumping of TIMESTAMP data when a server has data in different time zones or data is being moved between servers with different time zones.
-u, –user=name	User for login if not current user.
-v, –verbose	Print info about the various stages.
-V, –version	Output version information and exit.
-w, –where=name	Dump only selected records; quotes mandatory.
-X, –xml	Dump a database as well-formed XML.

mysqlhotcopy

This utility quickly makes backups of MyISAM or ISAM tables while the server is running.

```
# mysqlhotcopy db_name[./table_regex/] [new_db_name | directory]
```

This is great for making quick backups. It performs all the steps that you did earlier with mysqldump, mysqladmin, and mysql to dump a database, create a new one, and load all your data into it. Here's the simple syntax for doing this:

```
# mysqlhotcopy Books Books_Backup
```

All of the available mysqlhotcopy command-line options are given in Table B.13.

Table B.13   Mysqlhotcopy Options

Type	Meaning
-?, –help	Display this help screen and exit.
-u, –user=#	User for database login if not current user.
-p, –password=#	Password to use when connecting to server (if not set in my.cnf, which is recommended).
-h, –host=#	Hostname for local server when connecting over TCP/IP.
-P, –port=#	Port to use when connecting to local server with TCP/IP.
-S, –socket=#	Socket to use when connecting to local server.
–allowold	Don't abort if target directory already exists (rename it _old).
–addtodest	Don't rename target directory if it exists, just add files to it.
–keepold	Don't delete previous (now renamed) target when done.
–noindices	Don't include full index files in copy.
–method=#	Copy method; only "cp" currently supported.
-q, –quiet	Be silent except for errors.
–debug	Enable debug.
-n, –dryrun	Report actions without doing them.
–regexp=#	Copy all databases with names matching regexp.
–suffix=#	Suffix for names of copied databases.
–checkpoint=#	Insert checkpoint entry into specified db.table.
–flushlog	Flush logs once all tables are locked.
–resetmaster	Reset the binlog once all tables are locked.
–resetslave	Reset the master.info once all tables are locked.
–tmpdir=#	Temporary directory (instead of /tmp).
–record_log_pos=#	Record slave and master status in specified db.table.
–chroot=#	Base directory of chroot jail in which mysqld operates.

mysqlimport

This client imports text files into their respective tables using LOAD DATA INFILE.

```
mysqlimport [options] db_name textfile1 [textfile2 ...]
```

The command-line options for mysqlimport are in Table B.14.

Table B.14   Mysqlimport Options

Type	Meaning
–print-defaults	Print the program argument list and exit.
–no-defaults	Don't read default options from any options file.
–defaults-file=#	Only read default options from the given file named #.
–defaults-extra-file=#	Read this file after the global files are read.
–character-sets-dir=name	Directory where character sets are.
–default-character-set=name	Set the default character set.
-c, –columns=name	Use only these columns to import the data to. Give the column names in a comma-separated list. Same as giving columns to LOAD DATA INFILE.
-C, –compress	Use compression in server/client protocol.
-#, –debug[=name]	Output debug log. Often this is d:t:o,filename.
-d, –delete	First delete all rows from table.
–fields-terminated-by=name	Fields in the text file are terminated by ....
–fields-enclosed-by=name	Fields in the import file are enclosed by ....
–fields-optionally-enclosed-by=name	Fields in the infile are opt. enclosed by ....
–fields-escaped-by=name	Fields in the infile are escaped by ....
-f, –force	Continue even if you get an sql-error.
-?, –help	Display this help and exit.
-h, –host=name	Connect to host.
-i, –ignore	If duplicate unique key was found, keep old row.
–ignore-lines=#	Ignore first N lines of data infile.
–lines-terminated-by=name	Lines in the infile are terminated by ....
-L, –local	Read all files through the client.
-l, –lock-tables	Lock all tables for write.
–low-priority	Use LOW_PRIORITY when updating the table.
-p, –password[=name]	Password to use when connecting to server. If password is not given, it's asked from the tty.
-P, –port=#	Port number to use for connection.
–protocol=name	The protocol of connection (tcp, socket, pipe, memory).
-r, –replace	If duplicate unique key was found, replace old row.
-s, –silent	Be more silent.
-S, –socket=name	Socket file to use for connection.

Type	Meaning
-u, –user=name	User for login if not current user.
-v, –verbose	Print info about the various stages.
-V, –version	Output version information and exit.

mysqlshow

This client displays information about databases, tables, columns, and indexes.

```
mysqlshow [OPTIONS] [database [table [column]]]
```

perror

This utility displays the meaning of system or MySQL error codes. Table B.15 details its options.

```
perror [OPTIONS] [ERRORCODE [ERRORCODE...]]
```

Table B.15   Perror Options

Type	Meaning
-?, –help	Display this help and exit.
-I, –info	Synonym for the -?.
-s, –silent	Only print the error message.
-v, –verbose	Print error code and message (default).
-V, –version	Display version information and exit.

```
# perror 12

Error code 12: Cannot allocate memory
```

Valid error codes are numbers between 0 and 149 and can be listed one after the other separated by spaces. See the example:

```
# perror 12 60 99 32

Error code 12: Cannot allocate memory
Error code 60: Device not a stream
Error code 99: Cannot assign requested address
Error code 32: Broken pipe
```

replace

This utility program changes strings in place in files or on the standard input.

```
replace a b b a -- file1 file2 ...
```

This utility can be useful for replacing strings in files without going into each one with an editor and searching and replacing by hand.

Create a file with your favorite text editor with the following sentence in it:

```
It's bean a long time since I have been to Europe.
```

Save and exit. My file is called test.txt.

```
# replace bean been -- test.txt

test.txt converted
```

Check the file and see that bean has been replaced with been.

Appendix C {

MySQL Installation

I am providing installation instructions for the Windows platform and for Unix/Linux in binary format. There are far too many options for compiling MySQL and I consider it to be a topic that is too advanced for this book. For compilation options, please refer to the MySQL web site at www.mysql.com.

Windows

I suggest downloading and installing the complete binary distribution for Windows. For the current version, in this book, the link is dev.mysql.com/downloads/mysql/5.0.html. At this time there are three downloads for MySQL 5.0.XX for Windows. The current choices on the site are

- Windows Essentials (x86)
- Windows (x86)
- Without installer (unzip in C:\)

I always download and install the Windows (x86) version that comes with the installer. I find that all of the necessary components go to the right places, my path gets updated, and so on. It is the largest of the Windows distributions, but it is also the easiest to deal with. The 35MB file that I downloaded is mysql-5.0.18-win32.zip. After unzipping, I ended up with a single 37MB Setup.exe. The following screenshots and dialog take you through the complete installation as it is for the current version of MySQL 5.0. I am using Windows XP Professional as my host operating system.

> ❄ **DROP SHIELDS**
>
> Before starting the installation, either turn off your personal firewall or edit the rules such that you allow port 3306 to your computer. If you don't understand this, just ignore it for now and you can adjust later in the process.

1. Double-click the Setup.exe file to begin the installation process. See Figures C.1 and C.2.

Figure C.1
The first dialog after running Setup.exe.

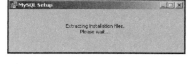

Figure C.2
Click Next.

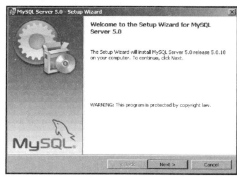

2. Click Next. The screen shown in Figure C.3 prompts you to choose a setup type.

Figure C.3
Setup Type screen.

3. Choose your setup type. I chose Complete on this screen to have the installer install all of the components. Figure C.4's screen prompts you to install when you are ready.

Figure C.4
Ready to Install screen.

4. Click Install on the Ready to Install screen. As the dialog screen says, this may take a few minutes. Once it is finished, the screen in Figure C.6 appears. Figure C.5 shows the installation process.

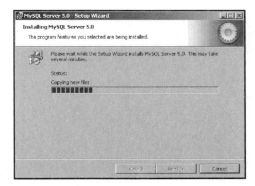

Figure C.5
Installing MySQL.

5. Decide whether you want to create a mysql account; see Figure C.6. In Figure C.7, you are prompted to continue to set up MySQL after installation is done.

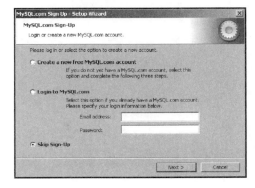

Figure C.6
MySQL.com account sign-up (optional).

Figure C.7
Install complete.

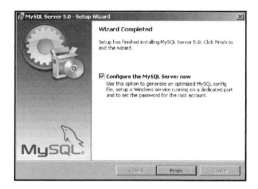

6. Click Finish to set up the server. I suggest setting up the server at this point, although it is possible to configure it after installation. The MySQL Configuration Wizard is shown in Figure C.8.

Figure C.8
MySQL Configuration Wizard.

7. Click Next to Continue; you go to the screen in Figure C.9 to select a configuration type.

Figure C.9
Select a configuration type.

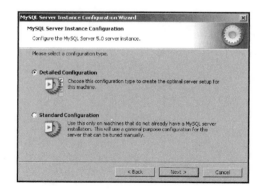

8. Choose Detailed Configuration and Click Next. The Detailed option gives you the most information and flexibility. Figure C.10 prompts you to choose a server type.

Figure C.10
Select a server type.

9. Choose a server type. I chose Developer Machine. Your choice should fit your needs. On the screen in Figure C.11, you choose the type of databases you want to use in your implementation.

Figure C.11
Database usage.

10. Select your database usage. For this course and general use, I choose Multifunctional. If I am using MySQL for web applications, I choose Transactional Database Only. As shown in Figure C.12, you select a location for your data.

11. Choose the location of your InnoDB tablespace by using the pull-down menu. I chose C:\Data. The number of concurrent connections defines how many users may use the database simultaneously. See Figure C.13.

Figure C.12

InnoDB tablespace set-tings.

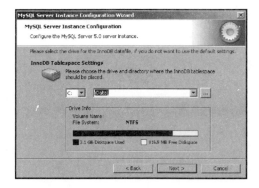

Figure C.13

Concurrent connections.

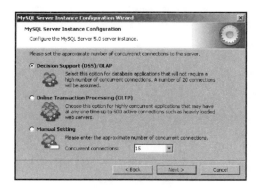

12. Choose the number of concurrent connections. For most purposes, I choose the first one. The third choice is good if you are building web applications to maximize throughput for users. Unless you have a specific need to choose otherwise, accept the defaults shown in Figure C.14.

13. Select the networking options. I accepted the default TCP/IP port (3306) and enabled strict mode.

14. Accept the defaults in Figure C.15.

15. Select the character set. I chose the standard Latin1 character set for this server. Your choice may vary according to your language needs. Figure C.16 shows the best options for a Windows install.

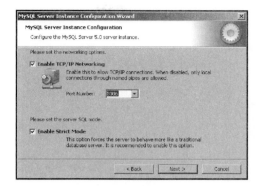

Figure C.14
Networking options.

Figure C.15
Default character set.

Figure C.16
Windows options.

16. Click all options on this screen for a more convenient installation. I like having MySQL installed as a service and having all of the path inclusions performed automatically.

17. Change the administrative password for MySQL as shown in Figure C.17.

Figure C.17
Security options.

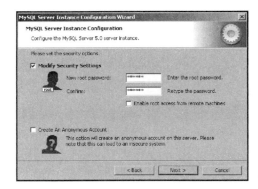

18. Change the root password. Do not create an Anonymous account. Remote access by the root user is not recommended but possible. The screen shown in Figure C.18 is prompting you to execute the installation with your options enabled.

Figure C.18
Ready to execute.

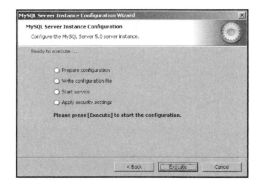

19. To finish the Installation, click Execute when you are ready to continue. If there is a connectivity problem, you will receive the error shown in Figure C.19.

Figure C.19
Connection error.

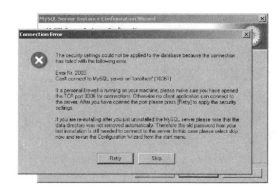

You may get a connection error if you didn't edit your firewall rules or turn it off completely. To complete the installation, I had to turn off my firewall (Windows firewall), click Retry, let the installation fail, uninstall MySQL, and reinstall. The second time around this warning did not appear. You can also try Skip on this error screen.

20. Click Finish. Figure C.20 shows the final MySQL installation screen. The MySQL Server will start and be available to you immediately—no reboot required. Figure C.21 shows how to log in to your new MySQL Server instance.

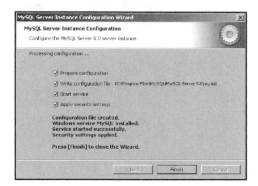

Figure C.20
Processing configuration.

Figure C.21
Log in to MySQL.

21. Open a command window by clicking Start, Run.

22. Type cmd and click OK. Log in as shown in Figure C.22.

The mysql prompt shown in Figure C.22 verifies that everything is installed and you are logged in to the server, ready to issue SQL commands.

Figure C.22

Logged In.

Unix/Linux

For Unix or Linux, MySQL AB provides a very long list of binary distributions including almost every conceivable platform. I suggest that, unless you have some special need, you download and use one of them. If you have a special need that is not supported by default, then you will need to download a source distribution and compile it. This section describes how to install a MySQL 5.0 binary distribution on a Linux computer. I am using Fedora Core 3 for my Linux distribution. Installation on any Unix or Linux computer will be very similar.

Currently, downloads can be found at: http://dev.mysql.com/downloads/mysql/5.0.html. The distribution that I usually select for Linux is listed just under the Windows version on this page as Linux (non RPM package). For each of the listed platforms, you will see a Standard, Max, and Debug package. I always use the Standard package. My distribution of choice is Linux (x86) Standard Package, the second choice in this list:

* Linux (non RPM package)
* Linux (x86, glibc-2.2, "standard" is static, gcc)
* Linux (x86)
* Linux (AMD64/Intel EM64T)
* Linux (IA64)
* Linux (POWER/PowerPC)
* Linux (S/390X)

My downloaded file is mysql-standard-5.0.18-linux-i686-glibc23.tar.gz. Choose the directory where you will use MySQL. Two possibilities are /usr/local or /opt. I prefer to install mine in /opt. You need to be logged in as root or have sudo access to complete the installation; the # prompt will reflect that I am logged in as root. There are no screenshots for this installation, as it takes place at the command line. I am assuming, for the sake of simplicity, that your mysql file is in your home directory. If it is not, realize that the path to the mysql file will have to be changed to fit your situation.

```
#  cd /opt
#  tar zxvf ~/mysql-standard-5.0.18-linux-i686-glibc23.tar.gz
(extracts the MySQL files into the /opt directory).
#  ln -s mysql-standard-5.0.18-linux-i686-glibc23 mysql
(creates a symbolic link to mysql).
#  groupadd mysql
(Adds a new group, mysql).
#  useradd -g mysql mysql
(Adds a new user, mysql).
#  cd mysql
#  scripts/mysql_install_db --user=mysql
(Installs the default databases, users, tables, etc.).
#  chown -R root  .
(changes user ownership of all files to the root user).
#  chown -R mysql data
(changes user ownership of all data files to the mysql user).
#  chgrp -R mysql .
(changes group ownership of all files to the mysql user).
#  bin/mysqld_safe --user=mysql &
(Starts the MySQL Server)
```

If your prompt seems to hang after this last command is entered, just press the Enter key to release it. You have successfully installed and started the MySQL Server. Now you may log in and begin interacting with the MySQL Server.

```
#  /opt/mysql/bin/mysql -uroot  <ENTER>
```

Initially, the MySQL Server has no default password for root. If you feel that this is a problem (and it is if security is an issue), enter the following command while logged in to your MySQL Server to change it:

```
mysql> UPDATE mysql.user SET Password = PASSWORD('newpwd') WHERE User =
'root';
```

This sets the root password for both root accounts (localhost and remote) for the MySQL Server. This command reloads the privileges from the grant tables in the mysql database. When you exit and log in again, you will have to log in with the new password.

```
mysql> FLUSH PRIVILEGES;
```

Appendix D

Orca Installation

This appendix shows you how to install Orca, a performance monitoring and prediction tool on Linux and Windows. To me, Orca is the best tool for measuring performance parameters at any price, but since it is free, it is even better.

Linux

Orca presents system performance reports in a graphical format in HTML pages. By default it presents graphical plots for the following parameters: Average # Processes in Run Queue (Load Average) & number of CPUs, CPU Usage, New Process Spawn Rate, Number of System & running Processes on CPU per CPU, Memory Page ins & outs rate, Swap ins & outs rate, Context switches & Interrupts rate per CPU, Interface Input Bits Per Second, Interface Output Bits Per Second, Interface Input Packets Per Second, Interface Output Packets Per Second, Interface Input Errors Per Second, Interface Output Errors Per Second, Interface Input Dropped Per Second, Interface Output Dropped Per Second, Interface Output Collisions, Interface Output Carrier Losses, IP Traffic statistics, IP Error statistics, TCP Connection statistics, TCP Traffic statistics, TCP Error statistics, ICMP statistics, UDP statistics, Disk System Wide Reads/Writes Per Second, Disk System-Wide Transfer Rate, Disk Reads/Writes Per Second, Disk Transfer Rate, Disk Space Percent Usage, Physical Memory usage percent, and Swap usage percent.

Orca is quick and easy to install and set up. It takes about 30 minutes, which includes reading the INSTALL file. Generously provided by Dr. Blair Zajac, the Orca web site can be found at www.orcaware.com. Blair describes Orca as "a tool useful for plotting arbitrary data from text files onto a directory on a Web server." It has the following features:

* Configuration-file based.
* Reads white space-separated data files.
* Watches data files for updates and sleeps between reads.
* Finds new files at specified times.
* Remembers the last modification times for files so they do not have to be reread continuously.
* Can plot the same type of data from different files into different or the same PNGs.
* Can create different plots based on the filename.
* Parses the date from the text files.
* Creates arbitrary plots of data from different columns.
* Ignores columns or use the same column in many plots.
* Adds or removes columns from plots without having to deleting *Round Robin Database (RRD)* files.
* Plots the results of arbitrary Perl expressions, including mathematical ones, using one or more columns.
* Groups multiple columns into a single plot using regular expressions on the column titles.
* Creates an HTML tree of HTML files and PNG plots.
* Creates an index of URL links listing all available targets.
* Creates an index of URL links listing all different plot types.
* No separate CGI setup required.
* Can be run under cron or can sleep itself waiting for file updates based on when the file was last updated.

A default installation gives you hourly, daily, weekly, monthly, quarterly, and yearly summary data represented graphically and in tabular form. Its graphics provide you with summary information that is complete, yet visually simple enough to do a quick scan of many servers in a short amount of time. For each parameter that is measured, you get a graphic image that contains the X and Y coordinates properly labeled with your data in tabular format showing Current, Average, Minimum, and Maximum values for the specified time selected. See Figure D.1.

Orca utilizes RRDTool, written by Tobias Oetiker, for logging and graphing. Orca is bundled with RRDTool and other required Perl modules in case you don't have them installed already. The requirements that need to be met prior to installation are very few: You need a working web server and Perl installed. During installation, the missing Perl modules are installed for you into an Orca-specific library directory so as not to conflict with any existing package-management systems. The source trees for all the components are under the packages directory in case you would like to install them manually. The Procallator "package" is also installed with Orca. Procallator is the Linux-specific script that runs periodically to gather data from the /proc filesystem on Linux.

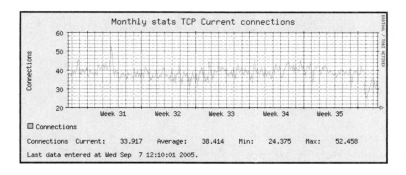

Figure D.1
Sample Orca parameter graph.

The following list outlines the requirements for installing Orca on Linux. Version numbers are subject to change.

- ❈ Perl 5.005_03 or higher
- ❈ RRDtool's RRDs Perl module, preferably 1.0.50 with local patches, or 1.2.x
- ❈ Data::Dumper 2.101
- ❈ Date::Parse 2.24
- ❈ Devel::DProf 19990108
- ❈ Digest::MD5 2.33
- ❈ Math::IntervalSearch 1.05
- ❈ Storable 2.15

Installation

These steps assume you have Perl and a web server already installed and working on your system.

1. Download the latest snapshot release located at www.orcaware.com/orca/pub/snapshots/.

2. Download, un-bzip2, and untar the file.

3. cd into the source directory that was created.
   I suggest that you read the INSTALL file before continuing with your actual installation, in case you need some special parameter for the configure script. At a minimum, you need to

know where you want your HTML files to go prior to using Orca. I chose my default web directory /var/www.

4. Go ahead and create /var/www/procallator, or Orca will complain that the directory does not exist when you run it for the first time. The HTML files and graphics are created in this directory.

5. Once you are prepared for the installation, issue the following commands:

```
# ./configure -with-html-dir=/var/www
# make
# make check (optional, but recommended)
# make install
```

There's already a makefile target named procallator_run_at_boot_using_chkconfig to start Procallator at boot time on Red Hat, Centos, and chkconfig-based systems. Dr. Zajac is adding different makefile targets to start Procallator at boot time for Debian and Ubuntu systems. He is also working on startup scripts for Orca. That is all there is to the basic installation, which places the executables in /usr/local/bin by default. At this point, you can issue the procallator command to begin data collection while you go into the configuration phase.

6. To begin collecting data, issue the following:

```
# /etc/init.d/procallator start
```

Procallator starts in background mode and begins data collection using default locations and parameters.

Orca Configuration

The procallator.cfg file is in /usr/local/etc, assuming you used the default configure -prefix setting. It contains the file locations and variables that you can change to meet your specific needs. You can–and should–change the following items to customize your site.

Change the email address to one that will be regularly monitored in case something goes wrong.

```
warn_email              root@localhost
```

If you want hourly plots, change the 0 to 1, and vice versa, for any of the other time plots. I generally use the hourly plot for watching a system that may be in "trouble."

```
# These parameters specify which plots to generate.
generate_hourly_plot        0
generate_daily_plot         1
generate_weekly_plot        1
```

```
generate_monthly_plot      1
generate_quarterly_plot    1
generate_yearly_plot       1
```

This shows up at the top of every page of data. It can be a graphic logo or just a title.

```
html_page_header        <h3>Put your site's logo here.</h3>
```

This title only shows up on the index.html:

```
html_top_title              Orca Host Status
```

This footer is included on every page including the index.html:

```
html_page_footer
<font face="verdana,geneva,arial,helvetica">
These plots brought to you by your local system administrator.
</font>
```

The find_files parameter points to the base data directory for raw data. By default this directory is /usr/local/var/orca/procallator. Under this directory, you will find your raw data directory. Its name is the same as the hostname. The raw data files are named as proccol-YYYY-MM-DD-00X. Each night, the last opened raw data file is compressed as either proccol-YYYY-MM-DD-00X.gz or proccol-YYYY-MM-DD-00X.bz2 to conserve disk space. If you want to modify the directory's location, manually edit the /usr/local/bin/procallator script, change the $DEST_DIR setting, and edit the find_files value in procallator.cfg.

Data Collection

Once you have edited the procallator.cfg file to your satisfaction, you are now ready to use Orca. If you started the data collector (procallator) at the end of installation, you should now have enough data to plot (procallator by default measures the system on five minute intervals, so you may have to wait for the first measurement to be taken). To give Orca a try, enter the following command:

```
# orca -o /usr/local/etc/procallator.cfg
```

This command tells orca to run once (-o) and refers it to the configuration file that you just edited. This first pass creates necessary directories and files in your /var/www/procallator directory. When Orca has finished processing the data, you get the message "Orca has completed." You can now check out your performance data at http://your-server/procallator/.

There will probably not be much to look at in terms of actual data, but all of the default plots and pages are now created and ready for you to inspect. Your index.html page should look something like Figure D.2.

Notice that the title of the box is, or should be, your hostname. In the example case, the hostname is debian. If you click one of the links, you are taken to the performance data pages for that timeline. Figure D.3 shows one of the hourly graphics for my host, home.

Figure D.2

The Orca index page.

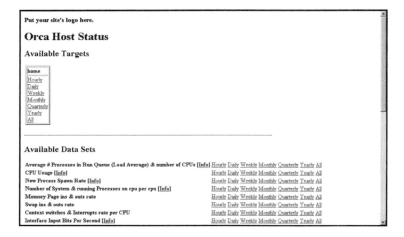

Figure D.3

Sample.

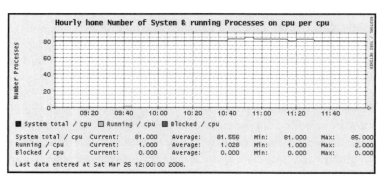

The graphics are self labeling and include the name of the host to which they refer. This comes in handy when you are looking at multiple hosts in a short amount of time. To see a real-life example of Orca on multiple hosts, point your browser to www.orcaware.com/orca/example_sites.html.

You should set up Orca to run hourly if you want the hourly plots to be updated that often. My cron entry is as follows:

```
@hourly /usr/local/bin/orca -o /usr/local/etc/procallator.cfg
```

If you only want Orca to run daily (at midnight) use this:

```
@daily /usr/local/bin/orca -o /usr/local/etc/procallator.cfg
```

Of course, you may use any time you wish. These are just given as examples.

Troubleshooting

Installing, configuring, and using Orca and Procallator are very simple. There isn't much to troubleshoot for Orca for a default install. If, however, you need to customize something, there can be issues with the number of columns in the RRD files compared to those that Orca is using.

Column data is a very common issue and is covered in the Orca FAQ at www.orcaware.com/orca/docs/FAQ.html. There are a couple of issues not covered in the FAQ with which you may need assistance. The first is gaps that may show up in your data. The second is that sometimes you may need to completely regenerate your data for any number of reasons. Both of these issues have the same resolution: Remove the RRD files and reprocess your data. Look in your procallator.cfg file to find the location of rrd_dir. The default location is /usr/local/var/orca/rrd/procallator/.

Under this directory is the subdirectory procallator_hostname, where the RRD files are kept. To regenerate the data, remove all of the RRD files. Then issue this command, which regenerates the RRD files without recreating the HTML and graphics:

```
# /usr/local/bin/orca -o -no-html -no-images  /usr/local/etc/procallator.cfg
```

Then process the RRD files normally creating the HTML and graphics:

```
# /usr/local/bin/orca -o /usr/local/etc/procallator.cfg
```

The reason to do this two-step process is to spare system resources. If you process a great deal of data, creating the RRD files, HTML, and images may run your machine critically low on swap space. If your data has gaps caused from the data collector being down, you will not be able to fill in the gaps. By putting the data collector in your startup scripts, you ensure that even after a reboot, your data will not suffer wide gaps. Some startup scripts are provided for you in the source tree under the data_gatherers directory. It is also wise to put in a process checker script to make sure the data collector does not go down and cause gaps. If the process dies, have the script restart the procallator and email you an alert. If you choose to have Orca running continuously—that is, without the -o command-line option—Orca sends out emails when it sees that a data file has not been updated within a few minutes.

Performance Monitoring

You, as a database administrator, should regularly check system performance. As stated earlier, Orca makes this easy. You can check a number of hosts at a glance, then move on to the most problematic areas for production systems.

You first need to learn what a healthy system's graphics look like so you can easily and readily recognize performance issues. When I check performance using Orca, I use the weekly performance charts, noting any spikes or suspicious trends in performance. If I detect anything unusual, then I go to the daily charts. Figure D.4 shows a system with CPU performance spikes. Since I am familiar with this system, I know these spikes are associated with my daily scheduled run of up2date.

Figure D.4

Average number of processes in run queue and number of CPUs.

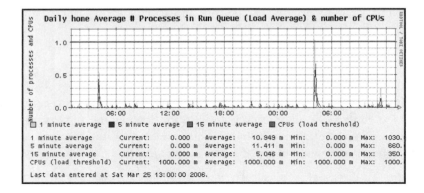

I like to check the daily graphs because they give me a very fine-grained look at the last 24 hours' worth of performance data. Hourly graphs give you the finest-grained look at your data, although I don't regularly check them unless the daily graph gives me a reason to check more closely. Beyond those specific performance graphs, I check sar, mpstat, and iostat values to more clearly diagnose any problems detected from the daily or hourly graphs. Quarterly and yearly charts are very useful for detecting performance trends. These are most valuable for observing performance degradation over time, as well as providing hard evidence that hardware additions, upgrades, or replacements need to be made; they are extremely handy when printed out and taken into managerial meetings. One word of caution should be noted here: Make every effort to perform careful analyses and do some performance tuning before recommending upgrades or replacements.

Diligent performance monitoring means being vigilant and learning the quirks and personalities of all the systems under your control. Orca is one way to maintain vigilance and delivers a lot of capability for no cost. My experience with Orca and Procallator comes from direct work with these tools in a very large enterprise environment where availability and performance directly affect the bottom line. For anyone who needs to check performance of even a few systems on up to hundreds, I strongly recommend that you give Orca a try.

Windows

The installation instructions for gathering performance data can be evaluated and posted via Orca on the Windows operating system. This should work on all versions of Windows from Windows NT 4.0. I have rewritten and enhanced the original instructions to give you an entire working system that is easy to set up and to get working.

You need a working Unix/Linux system with Orca installed and working as shown earlier to process the files produced from your Windows systems. I have gone through these instructions, grabbing screenshots along the way, to better illustrate what you need to do. It is easy to start gathering data on a Windows system. Unless you have some specific needs, I suggest using the simple setup described here.

This tool used to be referred to as orcaNT. It is now named winallator for two reasons: First, since it is a data-measurement tool and not a data-plotting tool, it deserves a name for a data gatherer. Second, the orcaNT portion of the original orcaNT package was just a patch to orca.pl that removed the call to ps aux and reduced the package requirements. To follow in the tracks of the other *allator tools, this package was renamed winallator.

Performance Monitor Setup

1. From a command prompt, Cygwin Shell, or Start > Run, type the following:

   ```
   perfmon
   ```

2. Click OK to start the Performance Monitor tool. See Figure D.5.

3. On the left pane of the Performance Monitor tool, click Performance Logs and Alerts, as shown in Figure D.6.

4. In the right pane, right-click Counter Logs and choose New Log Settings From.

5. Browse to where you unzipped the latest Orca snapshot to find winallator.htm. Select it and click Open.
   Once winallator.htm is loaded, you see the dialog shown in Figure D.7.

6. Give the new log settings a name (your computer name is a good choice) that does not appear in the Performance Monitor window, and then click OK.
   The dialog in Figure D.8 appears. The loaded settings record a number of measurements into log files in the C:\WinallatorLogs directory. The directory is created later. Leave the settings on this page as they are, but click the Log Files tab to see the screen shown in Figure D.9.

7. From the drop-down menu, choose Text File (Comma Delimited).

8. In the End File Names With: drop-down menu, select yyyymmddhh, and then click the Schedule tab to see the screen in Figure D.10.

Figure D.5

Performance monitor.

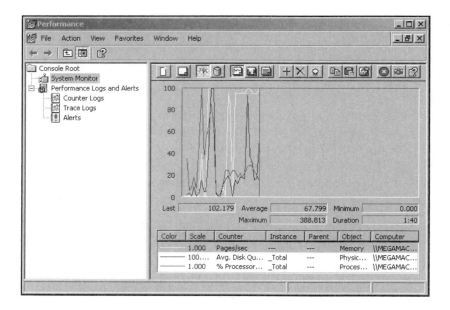

Figure D.6

Counter logs.

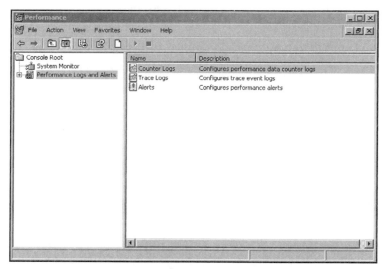

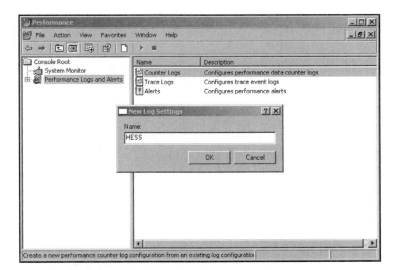

Figure D.7
Loading winallator.htm.

Figure D.8
Log preferences.

9. At the top of this dialog, you see the 6/22/2004 date. Use the drop-down menu to choose today's date.

Figure D.9

Log file settings.

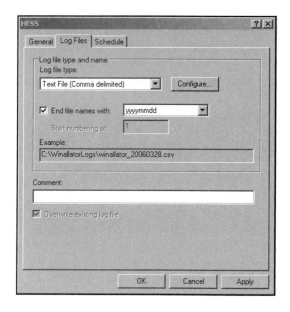

Figure D.10

Schedule settings.

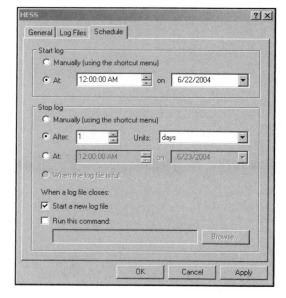

10. From the resulting calendar, choose today's date. Leave the other settings as they are.

11. To end the simple setup, click OK.

Data is recorded immediately into the C:\WinallatorLogs directory. If they are not, then right-click the new Winallator name and select Start.

If you need more or different parameters measured than the defaults in winallator.htm, consult the README file included in the Orca snapshot file that you downloaded. In my file tree, it is in data_gatherers\winallator.

Unix/Linux Server Setup for Windows Performance Log Processing

To process your log files from Windows machines, you need a functioning Unix or Linux server running Orca, as described in the first section in this appendix. I have written this section according to what works for me. Feel free to change the scripts and procedures to fit your individual needs.

1. On the Linux server, perform these operations as the root user:

   ```
   #  mkdir -p /orca/windows/data
   #  mkdir -p /orca/windows/staging
   #  mkdir -p /orca/windows/rrds
   #  mkdir /var/www/winallator
   ```

2. Edit winallator.cfg in the /usr/local/etc directory.
   It should be there after installing Orca, but if not look under the source tree for Orca under the data_gatherers/winallator directory; there is one there for you.

3. Copy the file to /usr/local/etc and rename it winallator.cfg.

4. Make the necessary changes in it the same way you did for the procallator.cfg, with the following exceptions:

   ```
   base_dir                    /orca/windows/
   find_files                  /orca/windows/data/(.*)/winallator_\d{10}\.csv
   ```

   You must use these locations if you use my scheme from earlier in this appendix.

5. Place percol_convert.pl and windows_orca_update.sh somewhere on the system and make them executable.
   I suggest putting them in /usr/local/bin, but you may choose another location. percol_convert.pl is the Perl script that converts the Windows log files into an Orca-compatible format. windows_orca_update.sh does all the work for you. You need invoke only the windows_orca_update.sh script to completely process the Windows log files into Orca format and create the RRDs, HTML pages, and graphs.
   If you follow these instructions, then you can find your HTML files at http://yourserver/winallator/. I am going to include the percol_convert.pl and the windows_orca_update.sh

scripts here, but they are also available online from my web site at www.kenhess.com and the Course Publishing web site (search for SQL Power!).

6. Contents of the percol_convert.pl script follow. You won't need to edit this:

```perl
#!/usr/bin/perl

use Time::Local;

$PERFMON="$ARGV[0]";
( -r $PERFMON ) or die "Log file ($PERFMON) is not readable.\n  Stopped";
open PERFMON or die "Could not open $PERFMON.\n  Stopped";

$linecount=1;                           # create counter to handle header line

while (<PERFMON>) {
  chomp;                                           # strip end-of-line
  chop();                                          # strip additional MS
end-of-line
  s/"//g;                                            # remove the quotes
  @Fld = split(',', $_);                            # split on commas

  if ($linecount==1) {                               # this is the
header line
    $linecount++;                                   # dont run this
section again
    printf("timestamp locltime");         # start with replacement
time headers
    for ($i=1; $i<=$#Fld; $i++) {           # loop through all but
first field
      $n = $Fld[$i];
      $n =~ s/^\\\\[A-Za-z]+[0-9]+\\//;                # strip server
name
      $n =~ s/\\pagefile.sys//;                   # strip \pagefile.sys
      $n =~ s/\\\?\?\\//g;                            # strip \??\
      $n =~ s/://g;                                 # strip :
      $n =~ s/\(Compaq.*NIC/~NIC/;               # shorten Compaq
interface title
```

```
    $n =~ s/ /_/g;                              # replace space
with _
    $n =~ s/\\/_/g;                           # replace \ with _
    $n =~ s/__/_/g;                           # shorten double _
    $n =~ s/\(_Total/~Total/g;                # replace (_Total
with ~Total
    $n =~ s/\(/~/g;                           # replace ( with ~
    $n =~ s/\)/~/g;                           # replace ) with ~
    printf(" %s",$n);                          # print the modified
header
    }
  } else {                                       # data lines start
now
    ($date,$time)=split(' ',$Fld[0]);           # extract time
data from first field
    ($mon,$day,$year) = split('\/',$date);       # date is mm/dd/
yyyy format
    ($hour,$min,$sec) = split(':',$time);        # time is
hh:mm:ss.nnn format
    $sec =~ s/\..*$//;                          # drop fractional
seconds
    $epochsec = timelocal $sec,$min,$hour,$day,$mon-1,$year-1900;
# calculate epoch
    printf("%s %s:%s:%s",$epochsec, $hour, $min, $sec); # print the new
time data
    for ($i=1; $i<=$#Fld; $i++) {               # loop through every
remaining field
      if ( ! $Fld[$i] || $Fld[$i] eq " " ) {
        $Fld[$i] = 0;                            # replace empty or space with
zero
      }
      printf(" %s",$Fld[$i]);                    # print all remaining fields
    }
  }
  printf("\n");                                  # end every line with an end-of-line
}
```

```
close (PERFMON);
```

Contents of the windows_orca_update.sh script. You may need to edit this script. I have provided prompts for you in the file.

```
#!/bin/sh


#################################
## Windows Server orca update. ##
#################################


## Change these parameters to fit your environment ##

## Location of the Perl conversion script ##
CONVERT="/usr/local/bin/percol_convert.pl"

## The directory where you put your Windows files to be processed ##
IN_DIR="/orca/windows/staging"

## The directory where your files will go to be processed by Orca ##
OUT_DIR="/orca/windows/data"

## Location of bzip2 ##
COMPRESSOR="/usr/bin/bzip2"

## Location of orca ##
ORCA="/usr/local/bin/orca"

## Location where you want your logs ##
LOG="/var/log/orca.log"


#################################
## Don't change anything below ##
#################################


##  Find New windows .csv data files in /staging, convert to orca readable
##  format, and move to /data, then compress .csv files in /staging.
for SERVER in `ls $IN_DIR/`
```

```
do
        if [ ! -d $OUT_DIR/$SERVER ]
        then
                mkdir -p $OUT_DIR/$SERVER
        fi
        for FILE in `ls $IN_DIR/$SERVER/*.csv`
        do
                FILE=`basename $FILE`
                $CONVERT $IN_DIR/$SERVER/$FILE > $OUT_DIR/$SERVER/$FILE
                $COMPRESSOR $IN_DIR/$SERVER/$FILE
        done
done

        for FILE in `ls $IN_DIR/$SERVER/*.csv`
        do
                FILE=`basename $FILE/$SERVER`
                $CONVERT $IN_DIR/$SERVER/$FILE > $OUT_DIR/$SERVER/$FILE
                $COMPRESSOR $IN_DIR/$SERVER/$FILE
        done

##  Run orca and compress files in /data
$ORCA -o -v /usr/local/etc/winallator.cfg >/$LOG
for SERVER in `ls $OUT_DIR`
do
        for FILE in `ls $OUT_DIR/$SERVER/*.csv`
        do
        FILE=`basename $FILE`
        $COMPRESSOR $OUT_DIR/$SERVER/$FILE
        done
done
```

7. **Transfer your data files from the Windows machines to the Linux server into the /orca/ windows/staging directory.**
   You do this once you have all of the directories made, the scripts in place, and the winallator.cfg edited. Since the files will be created once per day and rotate at midnight, I suggest copying or FTPing the data files from the Windows machines to the Linux server just after midnight. Once all your logs for a particular day are in the /orca/windows/staging

directory, they need to be processed with the windows_orca_update.sh script. I suggest setting up an automated process (script and schedule) to copy the files into the staging directory on the Linux server.

8. Set up a cron entry on the Linux server to run after all log files are in the staging directory. The following is a potential crontab entry that you can use provided all your Windows files are in the staging directory before 12:15 A.M. each day:

```
15 0 * * * /usr/local/bin/windows_orca_update.sh
```

9. Check your graphs each day for each server so you are aware of any issues that may be arising.

Even for 80 servers, I used to check mine in about two hours per day. This included investigating any issues that I noted from my spot checks.

Appendix E

PHP Installation

This PHP installation how-to assumes that you have installed

* MySQL
* Apache (version 2.x)

If the web server is not Apache (or is Apache 1.x), please refer to the installation instructions for other web servers in the PHP source tree. I cover installation on Windows using Internet Information Services (IIS) in the next section. The setup for Apache on Windows is the same as it is for Linux, so there is no need to repeat those instructions.

Unix/Linux

The following instructions are a step-by-step guide to installing PHP on a Unix or Linux system. In general, Linux systems compile PHP without any issue. Some Unix systems give errors if you are missing prerequisite programs such as gcc. The configure errors are very good in PHP and any errors are explicit enough to guide you to the packages that you need to install on your system in order to continue.

1. Point your browser to www.php.net/downloads.php and download the latest version of PHP under Complete Source Code.
   Download your choice of the tar.gz or the tar.bz2 format. I usually just save these to my home directory.

2. Enter one of the following depending on the distribution of PHP that you downloaded:

```
tar zxvf php-5.x.x.tar.gz


tar jxvf php-5.x.x.tar.gz
```

Your source tree unpacks in your current directory under php-5.x.x.

3. cd to php-5.x.x.

 NOTE

These instructions are for a fairly generic setup, so if you need something different please consult the
INSTALL file in the current directory.

4. Type the following:

```
./configure --prefix=/usr/local --enable-ftp --with-mysql=/usr/local/
mysql --with-apxs2=/usr/local/bin/apxs
```

This part can take a few minutes to run, as it is really checking out your system for certain
types of support. If it stops prematurely, you have to troubleshoot it by installing the
package(s) it deems as required for the installation of PHP. Usually, the problem is a typo
in the preceding configure command-line statement. Type it exactly as shown.

5. When this part of the installation completes successfully, type the following:

```
make ; make install
```

Here, you are actually stacking two commands on a single command line. The make com-
mand compiles PHP for your system based on the configure script's information gathering.
The make install command installs PHP documentation, libraries, other support files, and the
PHP-related compiled binaries into /usr/local/bin.

6. Once the installation has completed successfully, copy the php.ini-dist to the /usr/local/lib
directory:

```
cp php.ini-dist /usr/local/lib/php.ini
```

7. For the examples in this book, make the following change to the php.ini file in /usr/
local/lib:
Originally:

```
register_globals = Off
```

Change to:

```
register_globals = On
```

I am aware of the issues with this setting, but this is for testing and it should be okay for your use. The PHP installation and configuration are complete.

To have Apache work with PHP, you must make some slight changes to the Apache configuration file: httpd.conf.

8. Add the following lines to your httpd.conf file:

```
LoadModule php5_module          modules/libphp5.so
AddType application/x-httpd-php .php .phtml
```

9. Find the DirectoryIndex entry and add index.php to it:

```
DirectoryIndex index.php index.html index.html.var
```

10. Restart Apache with this command:

```
apachectl restart
```

PHP and Apache should now be set up to run .php files on Unix/Linux.

Windows

Follow these instructions to install PHP on Windows.

1. Point your browser to www.php.net/downloads.php and scroll down to the Windows Binaries section.

2. Click the PHP Zip Package link and choose one of the mirrors presented on the next page.

3. Click one of the links and save the file to your hard drive in a directory that you will remember.

4. Find that file and double-click to unzip it (or right-click, then click Extract All, if you have not installed a third-party compression program). See Figure E.1.

5. Click Next on The Compressed (zipped) Folders Extraction Wizard.

6. On the Select a Destination screen, type in C:\php to set the installation location shown in Figure E.2.
   You may choose a different drive or location if you wish, but remember the location.

7. Click Next to extract to the location you specified.

8. Click Finish to open the c:\php folder.

9. Copy the php.ini-dist file to the C:\WINNT or C:\WINDOWS directory, depending on your installation.

10. Rename the file to php.ini.

11. Open the php.ini file and find the following lines:

```
; Directory in which the loadable extensions (modules) reside.
extension_dir = "./"
```

Figure E.1

Extracting the PHP Zip file.

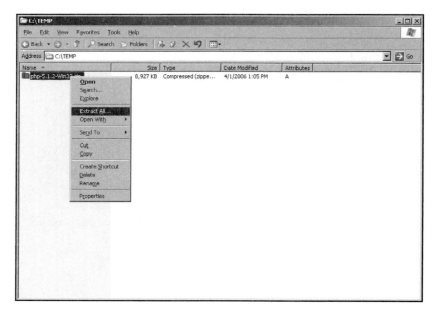

Figure E.2

Select a destination.

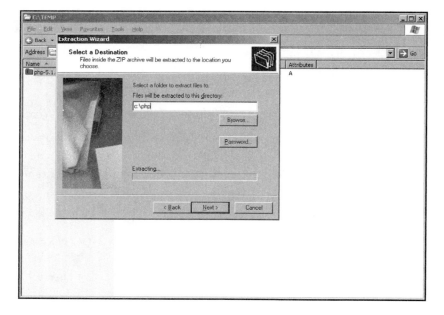

12. Change the extension_dir to "c:\php\ext". Enclose the extension directory in quotes, as shown.

13. Then make the following change:
    Originally:
    ```
    register_globals = Off
    ```

    Change to:
    ```
    register_globals = On
    ```

14. Save and close the file.

15. Close all those windows and right-click My Computer > Properties.

16. Click the Advanced Tab to see Figure E.3.

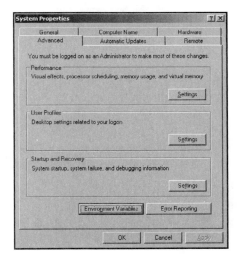

Figure E.3
System Properties.

17. Click the Environment Variables button near the bottom of the screen.
    In the Environment Variables window, you see two sets of environment variables.
    The lower window is for system variables. Scroll down in the System Variables window until you find Path.

18. Click Path and click the Edit button, as shown in Figures E.4 and E.5.

19. Add c:\php (or the path where you installed PHP). See Figure E.6.

Figure E.4

Environment variables.

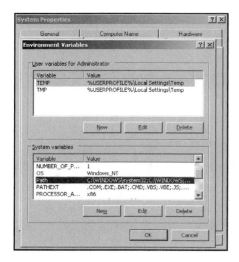

Figure E.5

Edit system variable.

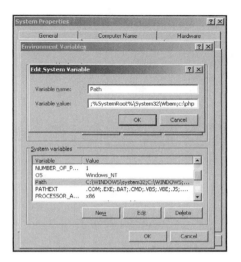

Figure E.6
Add PHP path to system path.

20. Click OK.

21. Click OK two more times to leave the Environment Variables and System Properties screens.

22. Open a command prompt by clicking Start > Run, typing cmd, and clicking OK.

23. When the command prompt opens, type:

```
php -v <ENTER>
```

You should see a response similar to the one in Figure E.7. The last step in setting up PHP for your Windows system is to configure IIS to recognize and use PHP files.

Figure E.7
PHP version information.

24. Go to Start > Programs > Administrative Tools > Internet Information Services (IIS) Manager.

25. Once the IIS Manager is open, click the (+) next to the Computer Name, click the (+) next to Web Sites, and then click Default Web Site, as shown in Figure E.8.

Figure E.8

IIS Manager.

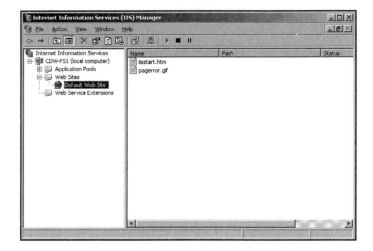

26. Right-click Default Web Site > Properties to see Figure E.9.

Figure E.9

Default web site properties.

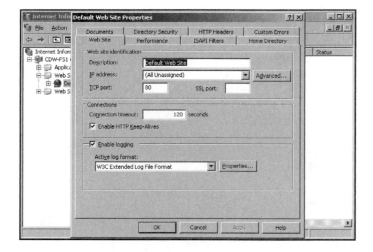

27. Click the ISAPI Filters tab, then click Add. See Figure E.10.

28. Type PHP into the Filter Name box.

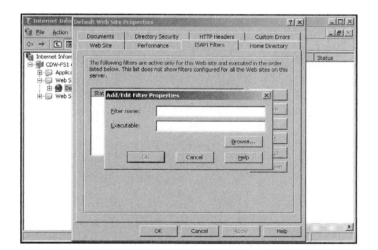

Figure E.10
Add or edit filter properties.

29. Click the Browse button to find the C:\php directory (or the directory where you installed PHP) and find the php5isapi.dll file.

30. Highlight php5isapi.dll and click Open. Figure E.11 shows the correct settings.

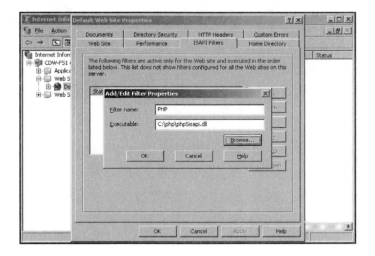

Figure E.11
ISAPI filter settings for PHP.

31. Click OK to keep these settings.

32. Click the Home Directory tab, then click the Configuration button to see Figure E.12.

Figure E.12

Application configuration mappings.

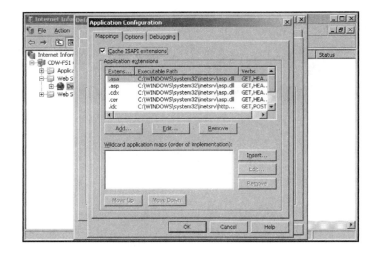

33. Click Add to see Figure E.13.

Figure E.13

Add or edit application extension mapping.

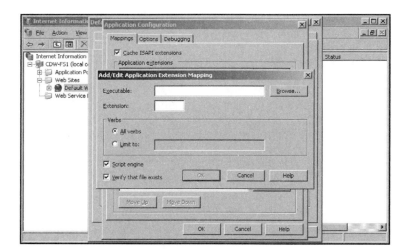

34. Click Browse to find C:\php. Locate and highlight php5isapi.dll and click Open.

35. In the extension box, type .php. The correct settings are shown in Figure E.14.

36. Click OK two times to accept all changes, and then restart IIS.
    For IIS 6.0 and above, you also need to make the following change.

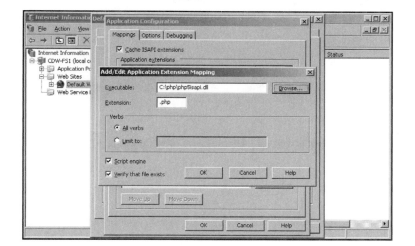

Figure E.14
Add or edit application extension mapping settings.

37. In the Internet Information Services (IIS) Manager tool, click Web Service Extensions. In the right pane, you see a number of extensions, buttons, and links. Refer to Figure E.15 for comparison.

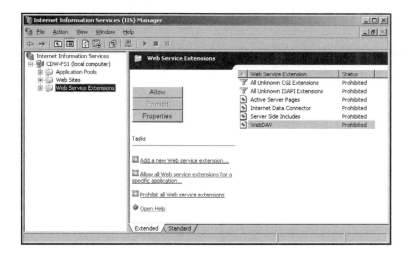

Figure E.15
Web service extensions.

38. In the right pane, click the Add a New Web Service Extension link.

39. Type PHP in the Extension Name field.

40. Click the Add button, then the Browse button.

41. Go to C:\php to locate php5isapi.dll and click Open. The screen should look like Figure E.16.

Figure E.16

Web service extension settings.

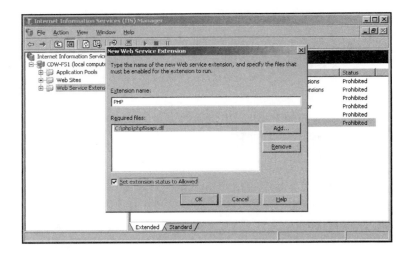

42. Click OK and to see your new Web Service Extension in the right pane.
    You have successfully set up and configured PHP to work with your system and IIS.

Follow these steps if you would like to test your installation:

1. Find the wwwroot (probably C:\Inetpub\wwwroot) and create a new text document named test.php.

2. Open test.php with Notepad.

3. Type in the following code:
```
<? phpinfo(); ?>
```

4. Save and close test.php.

5. Point your browser to http://yourserver/test.php. You should see a screen very similar to the one in Figure E.17.
   Congratulations! Your server is ready to serve .php files.

PHP Version 5.1.2

System	Windows NT CDW-FS1 5.2 build 3790
Build Date	Jan 11 2006 16:35:21
Configure Command	cscript /nologo configure.js "--enable-snapshot-build" "--with-gd=shared"
Server API	ISAPI
Virtual Directory Support	enabled
Configuration File (php.ini) Path	C:\WINDOWS\php.ini
PHP API	20041225
PHP Extension	20050922
Zend Extension	220051025
Debug Build	no
Thread Safety	enabled
Zend Memory Manager	enabled
IPv6 Support	enabled
Registered PHP Streams	php, file, http, ftp, compress.zlib
Registered Stream Socket Transports	tcp, udp
Registered Stream Filters	convert.iconv.*, string.rot13, string.toupper, string.tolower, string.strip_tags, convert.*, zlib.*

This program makes use of the Zend Scripting Language Engine:
Zend Engine v2.1.0, Copyright (c) 1998-2006 Zend Technologies

Powered By

Figure E.17
The PHP info page.

Functions

Functions are common components of any DBMS that provide enriched and expanded capability for the database administrator and user. There are functions for numeric and string manipulation, comparisons, flow control, aggregation of data, date and time, and many others. You can also program your own functions via SQL, known as a *user-defined function (UDF),* or through the C or C++ programming language to be compiled into the MySQL source code. In this appendix, you explore the various built-in functions, reading examples of each along the way. I finish out the appendix by showing you how to create your own UDFs and explain how you can use SQL to create them.

For the examples in this chapter, you need to create a new table named DEMO. You add to it as you go through the chapter, so it begins simply:

```
CREATE TABLE DEMO (ID int(4) PRIMARY KEY AUTO_INCREMENT, Total int(4));
```

And you need to add some data to it:

```
INSERT INTO DEMO VALUES ('', 40), ('', 120), ('', 35), ('', 18), ('', 5);

SELECT * FROM DEMO;

+----+-------+
| ID | Total |
+----+-------+
|  1 |    40 |
```

```
|  2 |    120 |
|  3 |     35 |
|  4 |     18 |
|  5 |      5 |
+----+-------+
```

Numeric Functions

The *numeric functions* included in MySQL consist of the arithmetic operators and mathematical functions. By using the built-in numeric functions in a DBMS, you are taking advantage of calculable data whose results are returned very rapidly. These built-in functions are compiled as part of the source code for the DBMS and therefore execute with very high efficiency. This method of doing calculations is far superior to other methods, such as using a web-oriented languages like Perl, Java, or PHP.

Arithmetic

The *arithmetic,* or *algebraic,* operators are functions that allow you to manipulate data in familiar ways such as addition, subtraction, multiplication, and division. The interesting thing about these operators is that to use them in an SQL context, you must use a SELECT keyword to issue operations involving them without a table column.

Addition

To perform operations involving addition, use the plus (+) operator:

```
SELECT 5 + 2;

+------+
| 5 + 2 |
+------+
|     7 |
+------+
```

This statement performs the addition operation and displays the result for you. You may also use parentheses if you are accustomed to doing so:

```
SELECT (5 + 2);

+---------+
| (5 + 2) |
+---------+
|       7 |
+---------+
```

Using addition with column data is very easy:

```
SELECT 5 + Total FROM DEMO;
```

```
+-----------+
| 5 + Total |
+-----------+
|        45 |
|       125 |
|        40 |
|        23 |
|        10 |
+-----------+
```

As you can see, this adds 5 to each value in the Total column. This is one way to add a value to a single column:

```
SELECT 5 + Total FROM DEMO WHERE ID = 1;
```

```
+-----------+
| 5 + Total |
+-----------+
|        45 |
+-----------+
```

There are many ways to add values to column data. Here are a few more examples:

```
SELECT 5 + Total FROM DEMO WHERE Total = 120;
```

```
+-----------+
| 5 + Total |
+-----------+
|       125 |
+-----------+
```

```
SELECT 5 + Total FROM DEMO WHERE Total > 20;
```

```
+-----------+
| 5 + Total |
+-----------+
|        45 |
|       125 |
```

```
|          40 |
+-----------+
```

Show the before and after of an operation:

```
SELECT Total, 5 + Total FROM DEMO WHERE Total < 100;
```

```
+-------+-----------+
| Total | 5 + Total |
+-------+-----------+
|    40 |        45 |
|    35 |        40 |
|    18 |        23 |
|     5 |        10 |
+-------+-----------+
```

```
SELECT Total, 5 + Total AS New_Total FROM DEMO WHERE Total < 100;
```

```
+-------+-----------+
| Total | New_Total |
+-------+-----------+
|    40 |        45 |
|    35 |        40 |
|    18 |        23 |
|     5 |        10 |
+-------+-----------+
```

Subtraction, Multiplication, and Division

I have combined the other arithmetic operators into a single section due to the similarity of their behavior to the addition operator.

```
SELECT Total, 5 + Total AS New_Total, Total -5 AS New_Diff, Total * 5 AS
New_Product, Total/5 AS New_Quotient FROM DEMO;
```

```
+-------+-----------+----------+-------------+---------------+
| Total | New_Total | New_Diff | New_Product | New_Quotient  |
+-------+-----------+----------+-------------+---------------+
|    40 |        45 |       35 |         200 |        8.0000 |
|   120 |       125 |      115 |         600 |       24.0000 |
|    35 |        40 |       30 |         175 |        7.0000 |
```

```
|    18 |        23 |        13 |          90 |       3.6000 |
|     5 |        10 |         0 |          25 |       1.0000 |
+-------+----------+----------+-------------+--------------+
```

SELECT Total, Total - 5 AS DIFF, Total/(Total -5) AS QUOT FROM DEMO;

```
+-------+------+--------+
| Total | DIFF | QUOT   |
+-------+------+--------+
|    40 |   35 | 1.1429 |
|   120 |  115 | 1.0435 |
|    35 |   30 | 1.1667 |
|    18 |   13 | 1.3846 |
|     5 |    0 |   NULL |
+-------+------+--------+
```

Note the NULL value is due to division by 0. Mathematically, division by 0 is undefined, but MySQL perceives this as a NULL value and returns it as such.

Insert the following into the DEMO table:

INSERT INTO DEMO VALUES ('', NULL);

Take a look at what happens when performing operations on NULL data. Re-enter the command that you used earlier:

SELECT Total, 5 + Total AS New_Total, Total -5 AS New_Diff, Total * 5 AS New_Product, Total/5 AS New_Quotient FROM DEMO;

```
+-------+-----------+----------+-------------+--------------+
| Total | New_Total | New_Diff | New_Product | New_Quotient |
+-------+-----------+----------+-------------+--------------+
|    40 |        45 |       35 |         200 |       8.0000 |
|   120 |       125 |      115 |         600 |      24.0000 |
|    35 |        40 |       30 |         175 |       7.0000 |
|    18 |        23 |       13 |          90 |       3.6000 |
|     5 |        10 |        0 |          25 |       1.0000 |
|  NULL |      NULL |     NULL |        NULL |         NULL |
+-------+-----------+----------+-------------+--------------+
```

Are these results accurate? The answer is no. When you add a number to a NULL value, for instance, the answer should be the number. NULL is a non-value and should be evaluated as 0 in such instances. The workaround for this problem is in this appendix's "Control Flow" section and is used as an example there.

Mathematical

Mathematical functions are the higher-level functions that are popular in geometric and trigonometric calculations. These functions include sine, cosine, tangent, absolute value, rounding, logarithm, natural logarithm, ceiling, floor, exponents, and so on. I give examples of each type, but you are encouraged to experiment on your own. You should be very pleased with some of the mathematical functions included as standard if you work with the type of data that can be manipulated with these functions. I look at each function in alphabetical order.

Absolute Value

The *absolute value* function takes the number input and returns the positive value for that number. If the number is positive, the returned value is the input number. x is any positive or negative number:

```
ABS(x)

SELECT ABS(5);
```

```
+--------+
| ABS(5) |
+--------+
|      5 |
+--------+
```

For any negative number:

```
SELECT ABS(-5);
```

```
+---------+
| ABS(-5) |
+---------+
|       5 |
+---------+
```

Insert the following into DEMO:

```
INSERT INTO DEMO VALUES ('', -33);

SELECT ABS(Total) FROM DEMO;
```

```
+-----------+
| ABS(Total) |
+-----------+
|         40 |
|        120 |
|         35 |
|         18 |
|          5 |
|       NULL |
|         33 |
+-----------+
```

Arc Cosine
x between -1 and 1 or NULL is returned:

```
ACOS(x)
```

```
SELECT ACOS(0);
```

```
+-----------------+
| ACOS(0)         |
+-----------------+
| 1.5707963267949 |
+-----------------+
```

```
SELECT ACOS(1.1);
```

```
+-----------+
| ACOS(1.1) |
+-----------+
|      NULL |
+-----------+
```

Arc Sine
x between -1 and 1 or NULL is returned:

```
ASIN(x)
```

```
SELECT ASIN(0);
```

```
+---------+
| ASIN(0) |
+---------+
|       0 |
+---------+
```

SELECT ASIN(1.5);

```
+-----------+
| ASIN(1.5) |
+-----------+
|      NULL |
+-----------+
```

Arc Tangent

x is any positive or negative number:

ATAN(x)

SELECT ATAN(1);

```
+------------------+
| ATAN(1)          |
+------------------+
| 0.78539816339745 |
+------------------+
```

SELECT ATAN(10);

```
+-----------------+
| ATAN(10)        |
+-----------------+
| 1.4711276743037 |
+-----------------+
```

For the tangent of two variables, use ATAN (y,x):

SELECT ATAN(10,5);

```
+-----------------+
| ATAN(10,5)      |
+-----------------+
```

```
| 1.1071487177941 |
+-----------------+
```

CEILING
Returns the lowest integer that is not less than x:

```
CEILING(x)
```

```
CEIL(x)
```

```
SELECT CEILING(1.25);
```

```
+--------------+
| CEILING(1.25) |
+--------------+
|            2 |
+--------------+
```

```
SELECT CEILING(-5.68);
```

```
+---------------+
| CEILING(-5.68) |
+---------------+
|            -5 |
+---------------+
```

Cosine
x is any positive or negative number and x is in radians:

```
COS(x)
```

```
SELECT COS(1);
```

```
+------------------+
| COS(1)           |
+------------------+
| 0.54030230586814 |
+------------------+
```

Cotangent
x is any positive or negative number:

```
COT(x)
```

```
SELECT COT(10);

+-----------------+
| COT(10)         |
+-----------------+
| 1.5423510453569 |
+-----------------+

SELECT COT(0);

+--------+
| COT(0) |
+--------+
|   NULL |
+--------+
```

CRC32

CRC32 calculates a cyclic redundancy check value and returns a 32-bit unsigned value. The result is NULL if the argument is NULL. The argument is expected to be a string and, if possible, is treated as a string if it is not.

CRC32(*expr*)

```
SELECT CRC32('SQL Power!');

+---------------------+
| CRC32('SQL Power!') |
+---------------------+
|          2608307353 |
+---------------------+
```

CRC values are generally used to compare before and after data transmission to make sure that data has not suffered corruption or loss during the transmission.

DEGREES

This function converts radians to degrees. x is any positive or negative number in radians, and the returned value is degrees:

DEGREES(*x*)

```
SELECT DEGREES(3.1416);
```

```
+----------------+
| DEGREES(3.1416) |
+----------------+
|   180.0004209183 |
+----------------+
```

EXP

Returns the value of e (the base of natural logarithms) raised to the power of x:

EXP(*x*)

SELECT EXP(1);

```
+----------------+
| EXP(1)          |
+----------------+
| 2.718281828459 |
+----------------+
```

SELECT EXP(0);

```
+--------+
| EXP(0) |
+--------+
|      1 |
+--------+
```

FLOOR

Returns the largest integer that is not greater than x:

FLOOR(*x*)

SELECT FLOOR(1.25);

```
+-------------+
| FLOOR(1.25) |
+-------------+
|           1 |
+-------------+
```

SELECT FLOOR(-5.68);

```
+--------------+
| FLOOR(-5.68) |
+--------------+
|           -6 |
+--------------+
```

LN, LOG
Returns the natural logarithm of x:

```
LN(x), LOG(x)
```

Returns the logarithm of x for an arbitrary base b:

```
LOG(b,x)
```

```
SELECT LN(0);
```

```
+-------+
| LN(0) |
+-------+
|  NULL |
+-------+
```

```
SELECT LN(1);
```

```
+-------+
| LN(1) |
+-------+
|     0 |
+-------+
```

```
SELECT LOG(10,10);
```

```
+------------+
| LOG(10,10) |
+------------+
|          1 |
+------------+
```

LOG2
Returns the base 2 logarithm of x:

```
LOG2(x)
```

```
SELECT LOG2(1);

+---------+
| LOG2(1) |
+---------+
|       0 |
+---------+

SELECT LOG2(0);

+---------+
| LOG2(0) |
+---------+
|    NULL |
+---------+
```

LOG10
Returns the base 10 logarithm of x:

```
LOG10(x)

SELECT LOG10(1);

+----------+
| LOG10(1) |
+----------+
|        0 |
+----------+

SELECT LOG10(0);

+----------+
| LOG10(0) |
+----------+
|     NULL |
+----------+
```

Modulo
Returns the remainder of the division of x by y:

```
MOD(x, y)
```

```
SELECT MOD(16,5);
```

```
+-----------+
| MOD(16,5) |
+-----------+
|         1 |
+-----------+
```

Modulo also works with fractional remainders:

```
SELECT MOD(16,5.31);
```

```
+--------------+
| MOD(16,5.31) |
+--------------+
|         0.07 |
+--------------+
```

PI

The default return value gives six-place accuracy although, internally, MySQL keeps track of the double-precision value. The returned default pi value is 3.141593. This statement returns the six-place accuracy value of pi:

```
PI(x)
```

```
SELECT PI();
```

```
+----------+
| PI()     |
+----------+
| 3.141593 |
+----------+
```

To obtain a higher returned accuracy, use a higher-precision number in a calculation involving pi:

```
SELECT PI() * 3.0000000000;
```

```
+---------------------+
| PI() * 3.0000000000 |
+---------------------+
|        9.4247779608 |
+---------------------+
```

POW

Returns the value of x raised to the power of y:

```
POW(x,y)

SELECT POW(2,3);

+----------+
| POW(2,3) |
+----------+
|        8 |
+----------+

SELECT POW(2,8);

+----------+
| POW(2,8) |
+----------+
|      256 |
+----------+
```

RADIANS

x is any positive or negative number in degrees and the returned value is radians:

```
RADIANS(x)

SELECT RADIANS(180);

+-----------------+
| RADIANS(180)    |
+-----------------+
| 3.1415926535898 |
+-----------------+
```

RAND

Returns a random floating-point value v between 0 and 1 inclusive (that is, in the range $0 \leq v \leq 1.0$). If an integer argument x is specified, it is used as the *seed value,* which produces a repeatable sequence. This could be helpful in generating marketing lists for callbacks or mailings if you include the address.

```
RAND(x)
```

If you need truly random numbers, don't use a seed value (value for x), as those values repeat each time you use the same seed value:

```
SELECT RAND();
```

```
+-------------------+
| RAND()            |
+-------------------+
| 0.69357606646938  |
+-------------------+
```

To select a random sample from a table, you can use something like this:

```
SELECT First_Name, Last_Name, Phone FROM Authors ORDER BY RAND() LIMIT 3;
```

```
+------------+-----------+--------------+
| First_Name | Last_Name | Phone        |
+------------+-----------+--------------+
| Robert     | Balzer    | 512-555-5131 |
| Anne       | Cohen     | 512-555-1555 |
| Lenard     | Dawson    | 512-555-7055 |
+------------+-----------+--------------+
```

```
SELECT First_Name, Last_Name, Phone FROM Authors ORDER BY RAND() LIMIT 3;
```

```
+------------+-----------+--------------+
| First_Name | Last_Name | Phone        |
+------------+-----------+--------------+
| Lynn       | Steele    | 512-555-2951 |
| Robert     | Balzer    | 512-555-5131 |
| Glen       | Harris    | 512-555-7755 |
+------------+-----------+--------------+
```

ROUND

Returns the argument x, rounded to the nearest integer:

```
ROUND(x)
```

Returns x rounded to y decimals. If y is negative, rounding takes place y digits left of the decimal point of the value x.

```
ROUND(x,y)
```

```
SELECT ROUND(1.033);

+--------------+
| ROUND(1.033) |
+--------------+
|            1 |
+--------------+

SELECT ROUND(1.533);

+--------------+
| ROUND(1.533) |
+--------------+
|            2 |
+--------------+

SELECT ROUND(1.033,2);

+----------------+
| ROUND(1.033,2) |
+----------------+
|           1.03 |
+----------------+

SELECT ROUND(1.033,-2);

+-----------------+
| ROUND(1.033,-2) |
+-----------------+
|               0 |
+-----------------+

SELECT ROUND(133.033,-2);

+-------------------+
| ROUND(133.033,-2) |
+-------------------+
|               100 |
+-------------------+
```

SIGN

Returns the sign of the argument as -1, 0, or 1, depending on whether *x* is negative, 0, or positive:

```
SIGN(x)

SELECT SIGN(88);

+----------+
| SIGN(88) |
+----------+
|        1 |
+----------+

SELECT SIGN(-88);

+-----------+
| SIGN(-88) |
+-----------+
|        -1 |
+-----------+

SELECT SIGN(0);

+---------+
| SIGN(0) |
+---------+
|       0 |
+---------+
```

SIN

Returns the sine of *x*, where *x* is given in radians:

```
SIN(x)

SELECT SIN(0);

+--------+
| SIN(0) |
+--------+
|      0 |
+--------+
```

```
SELECT SIN(1);
```

```
+----------------+
| SIN(1)         |
+----------------+
| 0.8414709848079 |
+----------------+
```

SQRT
Returns the square root of any non-negative value of x:

```
SQRT(x)
```

```
SELECT SQRT(9);
```

```
+---------+
| SQRT(9) |
+---------+
|       3 |
+---------+
```

```
SELECT SQRT(-9);
```

```
+----------+
| SQRT(-9) |
+----------+
|     NULL |
+----------+
```

TAN
Returns the tangent of x, where x is given in radians:

```
TAN(x)
```

```
SELECT TAN(0);
```

```
+--------+
| TAN(0) |
+--------+
|      0 |
+--------+
```

```
SELECT TAN(1);
```

```
+------------------+
| TAN(1)           |
+------------------+
| 1.5574077246549 |
+------------------+
```

TRUNCATE

Returns the number x, truncated to y decimals. If y is 0, the result has no decimal point or fractional part. y can be negative in order to truncate (make 0) y digits left of the decimal point of the value y.

TRUNCATE(*x*,*y*)

```
SELECT TRUNCATE(55.88,1);
```

```
+-------------------+
| TRUNCATE(55.88,1) |
+-------------------+
|              55.8 |
+-------------------+
```

```
SELECT TRUNCATE(55.88,-1);
```

```
+--------------------+
| TRUNCATE(55.88,-1) |
+--------------------+
|                 50 |
+--------------------+
```

```
SELECT TRUNCATE(55.88,-2);
```

```
+--------------------+
| TRUNCATE(55.88,-2) |
+--------------------+
|                  0 |
+--------------------+
```

```
SELECT TRUNCATE(55.88,2);
```

```
+------------------+
| TRUNCATE(55.88,2) |
+------------------+
|            55.88 |
+------------------+
```

Cast

Cast functions and operators, the implicit or explicit temporary modification of a column's data type, are nothing new to programmers. Casting is useful when making comparisons or doing operations to use data of another type to match the other data types in the comparison. For instance, if you have a text data type but want the text compared in a case-sensitive manner, cast the text as binary to make the data case sensitive. To cast a data type in SQL, you need a function to perform the cast. In this section, I show you the operators and functions to cast columns as different data types.

BINARY

The BINARY operator casts the string following it to a binary string. This is one way to force a column comparison to be done byte by byte rather than character by character. This causes the comparison to be case sensitive even if the column isn't defined as a BINARY or BLOB data type. BINARY also causes trailing spaces to be significant in the comparison.

```
BINARY string
```

You can use these functions in queries to get at their full usefulness in comparisons. Consider the following query:

```
SELECT ISBN, Title, Price, Sales FROM Works WHERE Title LIKE 'Y%';
```

```
+------------+---------------------------+-------+--------+
| ISBN       | Title                     | Price | Sales  |
+------------+---------------------------+-------+--------+
| 1231231234 | You Had Me At Shalom       | 16.99 | 600000 |
| 1266778899 | You Are Never Your Own Boss | 12.95 | 210000 |
+------------+---------------------------+-------+--------+
```

This query worked as expected. Now lowercase the 'Y%' and rerun the query:

```
SELECT ISBN, Title, Price, Sales FROM Works WHERE Title LIKE 'y%';
```

```
+-------------+----------------------------+-------+--------+
| ISBN        | Title                      | Price | Sales  |
+-------------+----------------------------+-------+--------+
| 1231231234  | You Had Me At Shalom       | 16.99 | 600000 |
| 1266778899  | You Are Never Your Own Boss| 12.95 | 210000 |
+-------------+----------------------------+-------+--------+
```

This query returned the results though you used a lowercase y. Are these the results you expected? They should be because the Title column is a CHAR data type, which is not case sensitive. To make the Title column case sensitive without using a permanent change via the ALTER keyword, you can use the BINARY operator to make this temporary change just for this query.

```
SELECT ISBN, Title, Price, Sales FROM Works WHERE BINARY Title LIKE 'y%';
```

```
Empty set (0.00 sec)
```

By changing the Title column to a BINARY data type for this query, you have made it case sensitive, therefore causing it to produce no results.

Issue the query again but change the lower case 'y%' to an uppercase 'Y%':

```
SELECT ISBN, Title, Price, Sales FROM Works WHERE BINARY Title LIKE 'Y%';
```

```
+-------------+----------------------------+-------+--------+
| ISBN        | Title                      | Price | Sales  |
+-------------+----------------------------+-------+--------+
| 1231231234  | You Had Me At Shalom       | 16.99 | 600000 |
| 1266778899  | You Are Never Your Own Boss| 12.95 | 210000 |
+-------------+----------------------------+-------+--------+
```

BINARY is the only type that may be cast on it own. In the next section, you are introduced to the other data types and how to cast them.

CAST

The CAST function takes one data type and changes it to another type explicitly:

```
CAST(expr AS type)
```

The CAST function allows you to cast the following data types:

- ❊ BINARY[(N)]
- ❊ CHAR[(N)]
- ❊ DATE
- ❊ DATETIME
- ❊ DECIMAL
- ❊ SIGNED [INTEGER]
- ❊ TIME
- ❊ UNSIGNED [INTEGER]

For a BINARY cast, the query from the last section looks like the following:

```
SELECT ISBN, Title, Price, Sales FROM Works WHERE CAST(Title AS BINARY) LIKE 'y%';

Empty set (0.00 sec)

SELECT ISBN, Title, Price, Sales FROM Works WHERE CAST(Title AS BINARY) LIKE 'Y%';
```

```
+------------+----------------------------+-------+--------+
| ISBN       | Title                      | Price | Sales  |
+------------+----------------------------+-------+--------+
| 1231231234 | You Had Me At Shalom       | 16.99 | 600000 |
| 1266778899 | You Are Never Your Own Boss | 12.95 | 210000 |
+------------+----------------------------+-------+--------+
```

If you attempt to convert one data type into another, incompatible data type, you receive a message similar to this:

```
SELECT ISBN, Title, Price, Sales FROM Works WHERE CAST(Title AS DATE) LIKE 'Y%';

Empty set, 7 warnings (0.00 sec)
```

You get an error as if you just have no data in your query rather than an actual error. There are non-fatal warnings, however.

You may view the warnings of the latest query by issuing this command:

```
SHOW WARNINGS;
```

```
+---------+------+------------------------------------------------------------+
| Level   | Code | Message                                                    |
+---------+------+------------------------------------------------------------+
| Warning | 1292 | Truncated incorrect datetime value: 'Bruises On My Heart'  |
| Warning | 1292 | Truncated incorrect datetime value: 'How To Write Great Queries' |
| Warning | 1292 | Truncated incorrect datetime value: 'Topiaries Are Tops'   |
| Warning | 1292 | Truncated incorrect datetime value: 'Good Night, Good Chocolate' |
| Warning | 1292 | Truncated incorrect datetime value: 'You Had Me At Shalom' |
| Warning | 1292 | Truncated incorrect datetime value: 'You Are Never Your Own Boss' |
| Warning | 1292 | Truncated incorrect datetime value: 'Doodling As Art'      |
+---------+------+------------------------------------------------------------+
```

CONVERT

CONVERT is sort of an enhanced CAST keyword. It can be used to cast a column as a different data type and for comparing strings of different data types:

```
CONVERT(expr, type)
```

```
CONVERT(expr USING transcoding_name)
```

You may use CONVERT in a similar way to CAST in your query from previous sections.

```
SELECT ISBN, Title, Price, Sales FROM Works WHERE CONVERT(Title,BINARY) LIKE 'Y%';
```

```
+------------+---------------------------+-------+--------+
| ISBN       | Title                     | Price | Sales  |
+------------+---------------------------+-------+--------+
| 1231231234 | You Had Me At Shalom      | 16.99 | 600000 |
| 1266778899 | You Are Never Your Own Boss | 12.95 | 210000 |
+------------+---------------------------+-------+--------+
```

Control Flow

Control flow is a way of performing logical tests within the database. This type of *testing*, or *branching*, is possible with embedded programming, but is more efficient when performed in the database. This type of SQL is efficient but not nearly as flexible as embedded programming—but using the two together creates very powerful solutions. In this section, I show you how to use the CASE, IF, IFNULL, and NULLIF functions.

CASE

Programmers are no doubt comfortable with CASE, but for nonprogrammers: CASE performs a comparison of values in an almost IF...THEN kind of way and yields results based on the test returning a true or false:

```
CASE value WHEN [compare-value] THEN result [WHEN [compare-value] THEN
result ...] [ELSE result] END

CASE WHEN [condition] THEN result [WHEN [condition] THEN result ...] [ELSE
result] END
```

In the Books table example, you can use CASE to perform an operation very common on many web sites and in catalogs: The actual prices are not shown but a message to 'Call' is posted instead.

Objective

Show a list of titles with prices. If the price is above $10.00, put the words "CALL FOR PRICING" in the list instead of the actual price.

First, figure out the details of the request. The first test is to check for books priced above $10.00 and if that test is true, then return the message "CALL FOR PRICING" instead of the price. You now have Price > 10 for the test. The second test is Price < $10.00. If true, then return the actual price. Since this example has only two tests, you can actually test one of the cases and assume that everything else fails. The completed SQL syntax is shown here:

```
SELECT CASE WHEN Price>10 THEN 'CALL FOR PRICING' ELSE Price END AS 'Book
Sale' FROM Works;

+------------------+
| Book Sale        |
+------------------+
| CALL FOR PRICING |
| CALL FOR PRICING |
| 9.99             |
| CALL FOR PRICING |
| CALL FOR PRICING |
| CALL FOR PRICING |
| 7.99             |
+------------------+
```

CASE works quite well when you have multiple choices or tests to perform on data. Some find its syntax less intuitive than IF...THEN type testing. There are times when one is preferable over the other; try both with your data to see which works best for you.

IF

The IF function is a single test function that tests a condition and, if true, yields the positive result. If false, it yields the default, or false, result.

```
IF(expr1,expr2,expr3)
```

Expression 1 (*expr1*) is evaluated as an integer, so this IF function is strictly for integers. You can use anything for *expr2* and *expr3*.

```
SELECT Title, IF (Sales > 50000,'Success','Failure') AS SALES FROM Works;
+---------------------------+---------+
| Title                     | SALES   |
+---------------------------+---------+
| Bruises On My Heart        | Success |
| How To Write Great Queries | Failure |
| Topiaries Are Tops         | Failure |
| Good Night, Good Chocolate | Failure |
| You Had Me At Shalom       | Success |
| You Are Never Your Own Boss | Success |
| Doodling As Art            | Failure |
+---------------------------+---------+
```

If *expr1* has to be something other than an integer, then you have to use a comparison function.

IFNULL

Since many people do not like to have NULL values show up when data is presented, the IFNULL function can change a NULL value to anything you want:

```
IFNULL(expr1,expr2)
```

If *expr1* is not NULL, then *expr1* is returned; otherwise, *expr2* is returned. The expressions can be numeric or string.

```
SELECT IFNULL(Total,'No Value') AS Totals FROM DEMO;

+----------+
| Totals   |
+----------+
| 40       |
```

```
|  120      |
|  35       |
|  18       |
|  5        |
|  No Value |
|  -33      |
+-----------+
```

The following example is one that I promised you from the "Arithmetic" function section and it illustrates how to exchange a 0 for the NULL value:

```
SELECT IFNULL(Total,0) AS Total, 5 + IFNULL(Total,0) AS New_Total,
IFNULL(Total,0) -5 AS New_Diff, IFNULL(Total,0) * 5 AS New_Product, IFNULL
(Total,0)/5 AS New_Quotient FROM DEMO;
```

```
+-------+-----------+----------+-------------+--------------+
| Total | New_Total | New_Diff | New_Product | New_Quotient |
+-------+-----------+----------+-------------+--------------+
|    40 |        45 |       35 |         200 |       8.0000 |
|   120 |       125 |      115 |         600 |      24.0000 |
|    35 |        40 |       30 |         175 |       7.0000 |
|    18 |        23 |       13 |          90 |       3.6000 |
|     5 |        10 |        0 |          25 |       1.0000 |
|     0 |         5 |       -5 |           0 |       0.0000 |
+-------+-----------+----------+-------------+--------------+
```

NULLIF

NULLIF returns NULL if *expr1* = *expr2*; otherwise, it returns *expr1*:

```
NULLIF(expr1,expr2)
```

String

String functions are designed to operate on character-type data. String-valued functions return NULL if the length of the result would be greater than the value of the max_allowed_packet system variable. For functions that operate on string positions, the first position is numbered 1.

I have to admit that I am hard pressed to find practical applications for all of the supported functions in MySQL, and the string functions are no exception. Some are essential and some have been implemented for very specific applications in mind. Some are so specific that one might even consider them to be obscure. I am compelled to present them all to you, no matter how esoteric, and give examples of each.

ASCII

The ASCII function returns the ASCII numeric value of the leftmost character in a string:

```
ASCII(str)

SELECT ASCII('abc');
```

```
+--------------+
| ASCII('abc') |
+--------------+
|           97 |
+--------------+
```

BIN

BIN returns the string representation of the binary value of x:

```
BIN(x)

SELECT BIN(10);
```

```
+---------+
| BIN(10) |
+---------+
| 1010    |
+---------+
```

BIT_LENGTH

BIT_LENGTH returns the length of a string in bits:

```
BIT_LENGTH(str)

SELECT BIT_LENGTH('Test');
```

```
+--------------------+
| BIT_LENGTH('Test') |
+--------------------+
|                 32 |
+--------------------+
```

CHAR

CHAR returns the string equivalent of a number or set of numbers. The character set may be supplied as an argument.

```
CHAR(x … [USING charset])

SELECT CHAR(68,66,65);


+----------------+
| CHAR(68,66,65) |
+----------------+
| DBA            |
+----------------+
```

CHAR_LENGTH

CHAR_LENGTH returns the string length in characters. Spaces are included in the count.

```
CHAR_LENGTH(str)

SELECT CHAR_LENGTH(Title) FROM Works;


+--------------------+
| CHAR_LENGTH(Title) |
+--------------------+
|                 19 |
|                 26 |
|                 18 |
|                 26 |
|                 20 |
|                 27 |
|                 15 |
+--------------------+
```

COMPRESS

COMPRESS is used to compress string data. Do not use char or varchar for compressed string types; use BLOB instead.

```
COMPRESS(string_to_compress)
```

The best examples come directly from the MySQL manual since I have not found an application for it myself:

```
SELECT LENGTH(COMPRESS(''));
```

```
+----------------------+
| LENGTH(COMPRESS('')) |
+----------------------+
|                    0 |
+----------------------+
```

```
SELECT LENGTH(COMPRESS('a'));
```

```
+-----------------------+
| LENGTH(COMPRESS('a')) |
+-----------------------+
|                    13 |
+-----------------------+
```

CONCAT

CONCAT is one of the most useful functions that I have ever used. I use it extensively to put data together for reports. *Concatenate* means to string things together. The CONCAT function adds strings together as if they were in the same column. This is very useful for a variety of applications. One is shown in this example:

```
CONCAT(str1, str2, …)
```

The best example produces readable first and last names for a report:

```
SELECT CONCAT(First_Name, ' ',Last_Name) AS Author FROM Authors;
```

```
+---------------+
| Author        |
+---------------+
| Anne Cohen    |
| Glen Harris   |
| Lynn Steele   |
| Robert Balzer |
| Lenard Dawson |
+---------------+
```

```
SELECT CONCAT(First_Name, ' ',Last_Name) AS Author FROM Authors ORDER BY
Last_Name;
```

```
+---------------+
| Author        |
+---------------+
| Robert Balzer |
| Anne Cohen    |
| Lenard Dawson |
| Glen Harris   |
| Lynn Steele   |
+---------------+
```

CONCAT_WS

CONCAT_WS is a special case of CONCAT that includes separator support. The WS stands for *with separator*. You notice that in the examples I gave for CONCAT, I had to use ' ' for the separator. This function allows you to specify it first and only once.

```
CONCAT_WS(separator, str1, str2,…)
```

```
SELECT CONCAT_WS(' ',First_Name,Last_Name) AS Author FROM Authors ORDER BY
Last_Name;
```

```
+---------------+
| Author        |
+---------------+
| Robert Balzer |
| Anne Cohen    |
| Lenard Dawson |
| Glen Harris   |
| Lynn Steele   |
+---------------+
```

You can imagine, if you had several strings to concatenate, how long and confusing the statement would be with ' ' between each string.

CONV

This function converts a number from one base to another and returns the string equivalent of the number:

```
CONV(x, from base, to base)
```

```
SELECT CONV(10,10,2);
```

```
+---------------+
| CONV(10,10,2) |
+---------------+
| 1010          |
+---------------+
```

ELT

ELT returns string 1 if *x* = 2, string 2 if *x* = 2, and so on:

```
ELT(x,str1,str2,str3,...)

SELECT ELT(2,'SQL','Power','Book');
```

```
+----------------------------+
| ELT(2,'SQL','Power','Book') |
+----------------------------+
| Power                      |
+----------------------------+
```

EXPORT_SET

According to the MySQL manual, EXPORT_SET returns a string in which for every bit set in the value *bits,* you get an *on* string; you get an *off* string for every reset bit. Bits in *bits* are examined from right to left (from low-order to high-order bits). Strings are added to the result from left to right, separated by the *separator* string (the default being the comma character: ,). The number of bits examined is given by number_of_bits (defaults to 64).

```
EXPORT_SET(bits,on,off[,separator[,number_of_bits]])

SELECT EXPORT_SET(5,'Y','N',',',4);
```

```
+----------------------------+
| EXPORT_SET(5,'Y','N',',',4) |
+----------------------------+
| Y,N,Y,N                    |
+----------------------------+
```

```
SELECT EXPORT_SET(6,'1','0',',',10);
```

```
+----------------------------+
| EXPORT_SET(6,'1','0',',',10) |
+----------------------------+
| 0,1,1,0,0,0,0,0,0,0        |
+----------------------------+
```

FIELD

FIELD returns the index of *str* in the list of strings. It returns 0 if *str* is not found.

```
FIELD(str,str1,str2,str3,...)

SELECT FIELD('ej', 'Hej', 'ej', 'Heja', 'hej', 'foo');


+------------------------------------------------+
| FIELD('ej', 'Hej', 'ej', 'Heja', 'hej', 'foo') |
+------------------------------------------------+
|                                              2 |
+------------------------------------------------+
```

FIND_IN_SET

The function returns the numeric position of the *str* if found in the *strlist*. It returns 0 if the string is not found.

```
FIND_IN_SET(str,strlist)

SELECT FIND_IN_SET('b','a,b,c,d');


+---------------------------+
| FIND_IN_SET('b','a,b,c,d') |
+---------------------------+
|                         2 |
+---------------------------+
```

HEX

HEX returns the string representation of the hexadecimal value for a number or a string:

```
HEX(number or string)

SELECT HEX('FF');


+-----------+
| HEX('FF') |
+-----------+
| 4646      |
+-----------+

SELECT HEX(10);
```

```
+---------+
| HEX(10) |
+---------+
| A       |
+---------+
```

INSERT

It is unfortunate that the INSERT function is also a regular SQL keyword, but it can be valuable nonetheless. INSERT returns the string *str*, with the substring beginning at position *pos*, and *len* characters long replaced by the string *newstr*. It returns the original string if *pos* is not within the string length. INSERT also replaces the rest of the string from position pos if len is not within the length of the rest of the string, and returns NULL if any argument is NULL.

INSERT(*str*,*pos*,*len*,*newstr*)

SELECT INSERT('interesting', 3, 4, 'BELL');

BELL was inserted into interesting, starting at the third character, and replaced four characters.

SELECT INSERT('interesting', 5, 2, 'BELL');
```
+-----------------------------------+
| INSERT('interesting', 5, 2, 'BELL') |
+-----------------------------------+
| inteBELLsting                     |
+-----------------------------------+
```

This time BELL was inserted at the fifth position, replacing only two characters. An interesting application of this function is to produce user passwords that are easy to remember but difficult to guess.

INSTR

This function returns the first occurrence of the substring in the string by position:

INSTR(*str*, *substr*)

SELECT INSTR('fantastic','fan');
```
+-------------------------+
| INSTR('fantastic','fan') |
+-------------------------+
|                       1 |
+-------------------------+
```

```
SELECT INSTR('instrument','ment');
```

```
+---------------------------+
| INSTR('instrument','ment') |
+---------------------------+
|                         7 |
+---------------------------+
```

In the first example, the substring fan was found at the first position in the word fantastic. The substring ment is found at the seventh position or letter in instrument.

LCASE, LOWER

This function takes a string that is in uppercase and changes it to lowercase. This is handy for maintaining consistency when presenting data.

```
LCASE(str)
```

```
LOWER(str)
```

```
SELECT LCASE('POWER');
```

```
+----------------+
| LCASE('POWER') |
+----------------+
| power          |
+----------------+
```

```
SELECT LCASE('POWer');
```

```
+----------------+
| LCASE('POWer') |
+----------------+
| power          |
+----------------+
```

LEFT

LEFT returns the leftmost number of characters in a string specified by *len*:

```
LEFT(str,len)
```

```
SELECT LEFT('facetious',4);
```

```
+---------------------+
| LEFT('facetious',4) |
+---------------------+
| face                |
+---------------------+
```

LENGTH

LENGTH returns the length of a string in bytes. Multi-byte characters are counted as multi-byte. In other words, if you have a character that is two bytes in length, it is counted as two bytes. CHAR_LENGTH counted multi-byte characters as single byte characters.

```
LENGTH(str)

SELECT LENGTH('Power');
```

```
+-----------------+
| LENGTH('Power') |
+-----------------+
|               5 |
+-----------------+
```

LOAD_FILE

LOAD_FILE reads the contents of a file as a string. The file must be readable, located on the local machine, its full path must be given, and the FILE privilege must be attributed to the user performing the operation:

```
LOAD_FILE(filename)
```

On Windows, you must use two *whacks*, or backslashes, when specifying the path:

```
SELECT LOAD_FILE('C:\\TEMP\\TEST.TXT')
```

```
+--------------------------------+
| LOAD_FILE('C:\\TEMP\\TEST.TXT') |
+--------------------------------+
| This is a text file.           |
+--------------------------------+
```

On Unix/Linux, just specify the path normally:

```
SELECT LOAD_FILE('/tmp/test.txt');
```

```
+----------------------------+
| LOAD_FILE('/tmp/test.txt') |
+----------------------------+
| This is a text file.       |
+----------------------------+
```

LOCATE

LOCATE finds the first occurrence of a substring and returns its position to you. If you specify the position, pos, then that is the starting position from which to search the string:

```
LOCATE(substr, str)
```

```
LOCATE(substr, str, pos)
```

```
SELECT LOCATE('fan','fantasticfan');
```

```
+-----------------------------+
| LOCATE('fan','fantasticfan') |
+-----------------------------+
|                           1 |
+-----------------------------+
```

```
SELECT LOCATE('fan','fantasticfan',5);
```

```
+-------------------------------+
| LOCATE('fan','fantasticfan',5) |
+-------------------------------+
|                            10 |
+-------------------------------+
```

LPAD

LPAD will *left pad* a string with characters to a specified length. If the specified length is less than the size of the string, then only the number of characters given in the length is returned:

```
LPAD(str, len, padstr)
```

This inserts the whole padstring because I am using a length of 11 characters which is the string plus the padstring:

```
SELECT LPAD('testing',11, 'TEST');
```

```
+-----------------------------+
| LPAD('testing',11, 'TEST')  |
+-----------------------------+
| TESTtesting                 |
+-----------------------------+
```

This query only inserts three letters of the padstring because of the length of 10 characters:

```
SELECT LPAD('testing',10, 'TEST');
```

```
+-----------------------------+
| LPAD('testing',10, 'TEST')  |
+-----------------------------+
| TEStesting                  |
+-----------------------------+
```

Since the length of three is less than the string, no padding took place and the original string was truncated to the length of three characters:

```
SELECT LPAD('testing',3, 'TEST');
```

```
+---------------------------+
| LPAD('testing',3, 'TEST') |
+---------------------------+
| tes                       |
+---------------------------+
```

LTRIM

LTRIM trims the leading (leftmost) spaces from a string:

```
LTRIM(str)
```

```
SELECT LTRIM('      testing');
```

```
+----------------------+
| LTRIM('      testing') |
+----------------------+
| testing              |
+----------------------+
```

MAKE_SET

The MySQL manual offers the following for MAKE_SET: "Returns a set value (a string containing substrings separated by ',' characters) consisting of the strings that have the corresponding bit in *bits* set. *str1* corresponds to bit 0, *str2* to bit 1, and so on. NULL values in *str1*, *str2*, ... are not appended to the result."

```
MAKE_SET(bits,str1,str2,...)

SELECT MAKE_SET(1,'a','b','c');

+-------------------------+
| MAKE_SET(1,'a','b','c') |
+-------------------------+
| a                       |
+-------------------------+

SELECT MAKE_SET(1 | 4,'hello','nice','world');

+---------------------------------------+
| MAKE_SET(1 | 4,'hello','nice','world') |
+---------------------------------------+
| hello,world                           |
+---------------------------------------+
```

MID, SUBSTRING

MID is given here:

```
MID(str, pos, len)
```

SUBSTRING is given here:

```
SUBSTRING(str, pos, len)

SELECT MID('temperamental', 8, 6);

+---------------------------+
| MID('temperamental', 8, 6) |
+---------------------------+
| mental                    |
+---------------------------+
```

This example shows a *negative position*. This means six characters from the end of the string:

```
SELECT MID('temperamental', -6, 6);
```

```
+-----------------------------+
| MID('temperamental', -6, 6) |
+-----------------------------+
| mental                      |
+-----------------------------+
```

OCT

OCT returns the string representation of a number's octal value:

```
OCT(x)
```

```
SELECT OCT('50');
```

```
+-----------+
| OCT('50') |
+-----------+
| 62        |
+-----------+
```

```
SELECT OCT('10');
```

```
+-----------+
| OCT('10') |
+-----------+
| 12        |
+-----------+
```

ORD

ORD returns the value of the leftmost character. If the character is not multi-byte, then ORD returns the same value as ASCII.

```
ORD(str)
```

```
SELECT ORD('Test');
```

```
+-------------+
| ORD('Test') |
+-------------+
|          84 |
+-------------+
```

QUOTE

This function quotes a string to produce a result that can be used as a properly escaped data value in an SQL statement:

```
QUOTE(str)
```

Any string with characters that need to be escaped, like single or double quotes, need a leading backslash to escape them:

```
SELECT QUOTE('It\'s');
```

```
+---------------+
| QUOTE('It\'s') |
+---------------+
| 'It\'s'        |
+---------------+
```

REPEAT

REPEAT returns a string consisting of the string *str* repeated *count* times:

```
REPEAT(str, count)

SELECT REPEAT('SQL', 4);
```

```
+-----------------+
| REPEAT('SQL', 4) |
+-----------------+
| SQLSQLSQLSQL     |
+-----------------+
```

REPLACE

REPLACE replaces the parts of the string, *str*, using a *from_str* and a *to_str*. The search is case sensitive.

```
REPLACE(str, from_str, to_str)

SELECT REPLACE('SuperHero', 'Super', 'Regular');
```

```
+------------------------------------------+
| REPLACE('SuperHero', 'Super', 'Regular') |
+------------------------------------------+
| RegularHero                              |
+------------------------------------------+
```

```
SELECT REPLACE('SuperHero', 'super', 'Regular');
```

```
+------------------------------------------+
| REPLACE('SuperHero', 'super', 'Regular') |
+------------------------------------------+
| SuperHero                                |
+------------------------------------------+
```

REVERSE

REVERSE returns a string with the characters reversed:

```
REVERSE(str)
```

```
SELECT REVERSE('sample');
```

```
+-------------------+
| REVERSE('sample') |
+-------------------+
| elpmas            |
+-------------------+
```

RIGHT

RIGHT returns the rightmost number of characters in a string specified by *len:*

```
RIGHT(str,len)
```

```
SELECT RIGHT('facetious',4);
```

```
+---------------------+
| RIGHT('facetious',4) |
+---------------------+
| ious                |
+---------------------+
```

RPAD

LPAD will *right pad* a string with characters to a specified length. If the specified length is less than the size of the string, then only the number of characters given in the length are returned:

```
RPAD(str, len, padstr)
```

This inserts the whole padstring because I am using a length of 11 characters, which is the string plus the padstring.

```
SELECT RPAD('testing',11, 'TEST');
```

```
+--------------------------+
| RPAD('testing',11, 'TEST') |
+--------------------------+
| testingTEST              |
+--------------------------+
```

This query only inserts three letters of the padstring because of the length of 10 characters:

```
SELECT RPAD('testing',10, 'TEST');
```

```
+--------------------------+
| RPAD('testing',10, 'TEST') |
+--------------------------+
| testingTES               |
+--------------------------+
```

Since the length of three is less than the string, no padding took place and the original string was truncated to the length of three characters:

```
SELECT RPAD('testing',3, 'TEST');
```

```
+--------------------------+
| RPAD('testing',3, 'TEST') |
+--------------------------+
| tes                      |
+--------------------------+
```

RTRIM

RTRIM trims the *trailing* (rightmost) spaces from a string:

```
RTRIM(str)
```

```
SELECT RTRIM('testing        ');
```

```
+----------------------+
| RTRIM('testing     ') |
+----------------------+
| testing              |
+----------------------+
```

SPACE

SPACE returns *x* number of spaces:

```
SPACE(x)

SELECT SPACE(5);
```

```
+----------+
| SPACE(5) |
+----------+
|          |
+----------+
```

SUBSTRING

SUBSTRING extracts a substring from a string starting with the position you specify. The two forms that use FROM are standard SQL forms and are used in the examples. You can choose from one of the following four:

```
SUBSTRING(str,pos)

SUBSTRING(str FROM pos)

SUBSTRING(str,pos,len)

SUBSTRING(str FROM pos FOR len)

SELECT SUBSTRING('Information' FROM 5);
```

```
+--------------------------------+
| SUBSTRING('Information' FROM 5) |
+--------------------------------+
| rmation                        |
+--------------------------------+
```

```
SELECT SUBSTRING('Information' FROM 5 FOR 3);
```

```
+---------------------------------------+
| SUBSTRING('Information' FROM 5 FOR 3) |
+---------------------------------------+
| rma                                   |
+---------------------------------------+
```

SUBSTRING_INDEX

SUBSTRING_INDEX returns the substring from string, *str,* before count occurrences of the delimiter, *delim.* If count is positive, everything to the *left* of the final delimiter (counting from the left) is returned. If count is negative, everything to the *right* of the final delimiter (counting from the right) is returned. SUBSTRING_INDEX() performs a case-sensitive match when searching for *delim:*

```
SUBSTRING_INDEX(str, delim, count)

SELECT SUBSTRING_INDEX('Testing the functionality', ' ', 2);
```

```
+-----------------------------------------------------+
| SUBSTRING_INDEX('Testing the functionality', ' ', 2) |
+-----------------------------------------------------+
| Testing the                                         |
+-----------------------------------------------------+
```

```
SELECT SUBSTRING_INDEX('Testing the functionality', ' ', 1);
```

```
+-----------------------------------------------------+
| SUBSTRING_INDEX('Testing the functionality', ' ', 1) |
+-----------------------------------------------------+
| Testing                                             |
+-----------------------------------------------------+
```

TRIM

TRIM returns the string *str* with all *remstr* prefixes and/or suffixes removed. BOTH is the default specifier if BOTH, LEADING, or TRAILING is not given. The *remstr* is optional and, if not specified, spaces are removed. Choose one of the following two:

```
TRIM({BOTH | LEADING | TRAILING} [remstr] FROM] str)

TRIM(remstr FROM str)
```

TRIM performs the same functions as LTRIM and RTRIM with the added feature of BOTH and the ability to specify other characters to remove as well as spaces.

```
SELECT TRIM('xx' FROM 'xxxxxtestxxxx');
```

```
+-------------------------------+
| TRIM('xx' FROM 'xxxxxtestxxxx') |
+-------------------------------+
```

```
|  xtest                          |
+--------------------------------+

SELECT TRIM(LEADING 'xx' FROM 'xxxxxtestxxxx');

+------------------------------------------+
|  TRIM(LEADING 'xx' FROM 'xxxxxtestxxxx')  |
+------------------------------------------+
|  xtestxxxx                               |
+------------------------------------------+
```

UCASE, UPPER

The UCASE function converts a string to uppercase characters. Choose one of the following two:

UCASE(*str*)

UPPER(*str*)

```
SELECT UCASE('Test');

+---------------+
|  UCASE('Test') |
+---------------+
|  TEST         |
+---------------+
```

UNCOMPRESS

The UNCOMPRESS function uncompresses a string compressed by the COMPRESS function:

UNCOMPRESS(*string_to_uncompress*)

```
SELECT UNCOMPRESS(COMPRESS('Testing'));

+---------------------------------+
|  UNCOMPRESS(COMPRESS('Testing'))  |
+---------------------------------+
|  Testing                        |
+---------------------------------+
```

UNCOMPRESSED_LENGTH
Returns the length of a compressed string before compression:

```
UNCOMPRESSED_LENGTH(compressed_string)

SELECT UNCOMPRESSED_LENGTH(COMPRESS(REPEAT('abc',30)));
```

```
+------------------------------------------------+
| UNCOMPRESSED_LENGTH(COMPRESS(REPEAT('abc',30))) |
+------------------------------------------------+
|                                             90 |
+------------------------------------------------+
```

UNHEX
UNHEX performs the opposite operation as HEX, taking a hexadecimal value and returning a binary string:

```
UNHEX(str)

SELECT UNHEX('53514C');
```

```
+----------------+
| UNHEX('53514C') |
+----------------+
| SQL            |
+----------------+
```

STRCMP: String Comparison
STRCMP compares two strings. If they are equal in size, a 0 is returned; if *expr1* is larger, a 1 is returned; if *expr2* is larger, a -1 is returned.

```
STRCMP(expr1, expr2)

SELECT STRCMP('test', 'test');
```

```
+----------------------+
| STRCMP('test', 'test') |
+----------------------+
|                    0 |
+----------------------+
```

```
SELECT STRCMP('Test', 'test');

+-----------------------+
| STRCMP('Test', 'test') |
+-----------------------+
|                     0 |
+-----------------------+

SELECT STRCMP('test1', 'test');

+------------------------+
| STRCMP('test1', 'test') |
+------------------------+
|                      1 |
+------------------------+

SELECT STRCMP('test1', 'test2');

+-------------------------+
| STRCMP('test1', 'test2') |
+-------------------------+
|                      -1 |
+-------------------------+
```

Date and Time

The Date and Time functions are among the most important and useful that you will deal with when using a database. Date manipulation has always been a difficult issue for programmers. Adding, subtracting, figuring day of the week for a future date, and predicting the date that is some number of days in the future are greatly simplified by MySQL. Standard dates in MySQL are presented as YYYY-MM-DD.

ADDDATE

ADDDATE returns the date a number of days in the future or past. When used with INTERVAL, a number of days (DAY), weeks (WEEK), months (MONTH), or years (YEAR) and so on can be specified. Choose from one of the following two:

```
ADDDATE(date, INTERVAL expr type)

ADDDATE(expr, days)
```

```
SELECT ADDDATE('2006-04-20', 60);

+---------------------------+
| ADDDATE('2006-04-20', 60) |
+---------------------------+
| 2006-06-19                |
+---------------------------+

SELECT ADDDATE('2006-04-20', INTERVAL 12 WEEK);

+------------------------------------------+
| ADDDATE('2006-04-20', INTERVAL 12 WEEK)  |
+------------------------------------------+
| 2006-07-13                               |
+------------------------------------------+
```

ADDTIME

ADDTIME() adds *expr2* to *expr1* and returns the result. The *expr1 variable* is a time or datetime expression, and *expr2* is a time expression:

```
ADDTIME(expr1, expr2)

SELECT ADDTIME('2006-04-15 23:59:59.999999', '1 1:1:1.000002');

+----------------------------------------------------------+
| ADDTIME('2006-04-15 23:59:59.999999', '1 1:1:1.000002')  |
+----------------------------------------------------------+
| 2006-04-17 01:01:01.000001                               |
+----------------------------------------------------------+
```

CURDATE

CURDATE returns the current date in the standard MySQL format:

```
CURDATE()

SELECT CURDATE();

+------------+
| CURDATE()  |
+------------+
| 2006-04-20 |
+------------+
```

CURTIME

CURTIME returns the current time:

```
CURTIME()

SELECT CURTIME();

+-----------+
| CURTIME() |
+-----------+
| 20:39:46  |
+-----------+
```

DATE

If you are given a data point that includes the date within a datetime type field, DATE extracts it for you:

```
DATE(expr)

SELECT DATE('2006-04-20 20:39:00');

+---------------------------+
| DATE('2006-04-20 20:39:00') |
+---------------------------+
| 2006-04-20                |
+---------------------------+
```

DATEDIFF

DATEDIFF returns the number of days between *expr1* and *expr2*. You may use datetime, but only the date part is used in the calculation:

```
DATEDIFF(expr1, expr2)

SELECT DATEDIFF('2006-04-20', '2006-06-27');

+------------------------------------+
| DATEDIFF('2006-04-20', '2006-06-27') |
+------------------------------------+
|                                -68 |
+------------------------------------+
```

DATE_ADD, DATE_SUB

DATE_ADD adds an amount of time to a date:

```
DATE_ADD(date,INTERVAL expr type)

SELECT DATE_ADD('2006-04-20', INTERVAL 5 DAY);

+---------------------------------------+
| DATE_ADD('2006-04-20', INTERVAL 5 DAY) |
+---------------------------------------+
| 2006-04-25                            |
+---------------------------------------+
```

DATE_SUB subtracts an amount of time from a date:

```
DATE_SUB(date,INTERVAL expr type)

SELECT DATE_SUB('2006-04-20', INTERVAL 5 DAY);

+---------------------------------------+
| DATE_SUB('2006-04-20', INTERVAL 5 DAY) |
+---------------------------------------+
| 2006-04-15                            |
+---------------------------------------+
```

Table F.1 shows the *type* and *expr* arguments.

Table F.1   Type And Expression Arguments

type	expr
MICROSECOND	MICROSECONDS
SECOND	SECONDS
MINUTE	MINUTES
HOUR	HOURS
DAY	DAYS
WEEK	WEEKS
MONTH	MONTHS
QUARTER	QUARTERS
YEAR	YEARS
SECOND_MICROSECOND	'SECONDS.MICROSECONDS'

type	expr
MINUTE_MICROSECOND	'MINUTES.MICROSECONDS'
MINUTE_SECOND	'MINUTES:SECONDS'
HOUR_MICROSECOND	'HOURS.MICROSECONDS'
HOUR_SECOND	'HOURS:MINUTES:SECONDS'
HOUR_MINUTE	'HOURS:MINUTES'
DAY_MICROSECOND	'DAYS.MICROSECONDS'
DAY_SECOND	'DAYS HOURS:MINUTES:SECONDS'
DAY_MINUTE	'DAYS HOURS:MINUTES'
DAY_HOUR	'DAYS HOURS'
YEAR_MONTH	'YEARS-MONTHS'

DATE_FORMAT

DATE_FORMAT formats the date value according to the format string:

```
DATE_FORMAT(date, format)
```

Table F.2 shows the list of specifiers that may be used in the format string.

Table F.2   Format String Specifiers

Specifier	Description
%a	Abbreviated weekday name (Sun....Sat)
%b	Abbreviated month name (Jan...Dec)
%c	Month, numeric (0..12)
%D	Day of the month with English suffix (0th, 1st, 2nd, 3rd, ...)
%d	Day of the month, numeric (00...31)
%e	Day of the month, numeric (0...31)
%f	Microseconds (000000...999999)
%H	Hour (00...23)
%h	Hour (01...12)
%I	Hour (01...12)
%i	Minutes, numeric (00...59)
%j	Day of year (001...366)
%k	Hour (0...23)
%l	Hour (1...12)

Specifier	Description
%M	Month name (January...December)
%m	Month, numeric (00...12)
%p	AM or PM
%r	Time, 12-hour (hh:mm:ss followed by AM or PM)
%S	Seconds (00...59)
%s	Seconds (00...59)
%T	Time, 24-hour (hh:mm:ss)
%U	Week (00...53), where Sunday is the first day of the week
%u	Week (00...53), where Monday is the first day of the week
%V	Week (01...53), where Sunday is the first day of the week; used with %X
%v	Week (01...53), where Monday is the first day of the week; used with %x
%W	Weekday name (Sunday...Saturday)
%w	Day of the week (0=Sunday...6=Saturday)
%X	Year for the week, where Sunday is the first day of the week, numeric, four digits; used with %V
%x	Year for the week, where Monday is the first day of the week, numeric, four digits; used with %v
%Y	Year, numeric, four digits
%y	Year, numeric, two digits
%%	A literal '%' character

```
SELECT DATE_FORMAT('2006-04-20', '%W %M %D %Y');


+------------------------------------------+
| DATE_FORMAT('2006-04-20', '%W %M %D %Y') |
+------------------------------------------+
| Thursday April 20th 2006                 |
+------------------------------------------+
```

DAY, DAYOFMONTH
DAY returns the day of the month in the 1–31-type format:

```
DAY(date)
```

```
SELECT DAY('2006-04-20');
```

```
+-------------------+
| DAY('2006-04-20') |
+-------------------+
|                20 |
+-------------------+
```

DAYNAME

DAYNAME returns the name of the day (Sunday, Monday, and so on) from the date:

DAYNAME(*date*)

SELECT DAYNAME('2006-04-20');

```
+-----------------------+
| DAYNAME('2006-04-20') |
+-----------------------+
| Thursday              |
+-----------------------+
```

DAYOFWEEK

DAYOFWEEK returns the numeric value of the day of the week, from 1–7:

DAYOFWEEK(*date*)

SELECT DAYOFWEEK('2006-04-20');

```
+-------------------------+
| DAYOFWEEK('2006-04-20') |
+-------------------------+
|                       5 |
+-------------------------+
```

DAYOFYEAR

DAYOFYEAR returns the numeric day of the year, from 1–365:

DAYOFYEAR(*date*)

SELECT DAYOFYEAR('2006-04-20');

```
+-------------------------+
| DAYOFYEAR('2006-04-20') |
+-------------------------+
|                     110 |
+-------------------------+
```

EXTRACT

EXTRACT can select date and time information using the same specifiers as DATE_ADD:

```
EXTRACT(type FROM date)

SELECT EXTRACT(DAY FROM '2006-04-20');
```

```
+--------------------------------+
| EXTRACT(DAY FROM '2006-04-20') |
+--------------------------------+
|                             20 |
+--------------------------------+
```

```
SELECT EXTRACT(YEAR_MONTH FROM '2006-04-20');
```

```
+---------------------------------------+
| EXTRACT(YEAR_MONTH FROM '2006-04-20') |
+---------------------------------------+
|                                200604 |
+---------------------------------------+
```

FROM_DAYS

FROM_DAYS returns a date from a given number of days:

```
FROM_DAYS(x)

SELECT FROM_DAYS(732787);
```

```
+-------------------+
| FROM_DAYS(732787) |
+-------------------+
| 2006-04-21        |
+-------------------+
```

FROM_UNIXTIME

FROM_UNIXTIME returns a standard date and time format from a Unix timestamp. Choose one of the two following:

```
FROM_UNIXTIME(unix_timestamp)

FROM_UNIXTIME(unix_timestamp, format)
```

```
SELECT FROM_UNIXTIME(1145519000);


+---------------------------+
| FROM_UNIXTIME(1145519000) |
+---------------------------+
| 2006-04-20 02:43:20       |
+---------------------------+

SELECT FROM_UNIXTIME(1145519000,'%Y-%m-%d');


+------------------------------------+
| FROM_UNIXTIME(1145519000,'%Y-%m-%d') |
+------------------------------------+
| 2006-04-20                         |
+------------------------------------+
```

GET_FORMAT

GET_FORMAT returns the date formats. See Table F.3 for function calls and format results.

```
GET_FORMAT(DATE|TIME|DATETIME, 'EUR'|'USA'|'JIS'|'ISO'|'INTERNAL')

SELECT GET_FORMAT(DATE,'USA');


+-----------------------+
| GET_FORMAT(DATE,'USA') |
+-----------------------+
| %m.%d.%Y              |
+-----------------------+
```

Table F.3 Function Calls And Format Results

Function Call	Result
GET_FORMAT(DATE,'USA')	'%m.%d.%Y'
GET_FORMAT(DATE,'JIS')	'%Y-%m-%d'
GET_FORMAT(DATE,'ISO')	'%Y-%m-%d'
GET_FORMAT(DATE,'EUR')	'%d.%m.%Y'
GET_FORMAT(DATE,'INTERNAL')	'%Y%m%d'
GET_FORMAT(DATETIME,'USA')	'%Y-%m-%d-%H.%i.%s'
GET_FORMAT(DATETIME,'JIS')	'%Y-%m-%d %H:%i:%s'

Function Call	Result
GET_FORMAT(DATETIME,'ISO')	'%Y-%m-%d %H:%i:%s'
GET_FORMAT(DATETIME,'EUR')	'%Y-%m-%d-%H.%i.%s'
GET_FORMAT(DATETIME,'INTERNAL')	'%Y%m%d%H%i%s'
GET_FORMAT(TIME,'USA')	'%h:%i:%s %p'
GET_FORMAT(TIME,'JIS')	'%H:%i:%s'
GET_FORMAT(TIME,'ISO')	'%H:%i:%s'
GET_FORMAT(TIME,'EUR')	'%H.%i.%S'
GET_FORMAT(TIME,'INTERNAL')	'%H%i%s'

HOUR
HOUR returns the hour from a time:

```
HOUR(time)

SELECT HOUR('10:10:00');

+------------------+
| HOUR('10:10:00') |
+------------------+
|               10 |
+------------------+
```

LAST_DAY
LAST_DAY returns the last day of the month from a date or date and time:

```
LAST_DAY(date)

SELECT LAST_DAY('2006-04-20');

+------------------------+
| LAST_DAY('2006-04-20') |
+------------------------+
| 2006-04-30             |
+------------------------+
```

MAKEDATE

MAKEDATE returns a MySQL formatted date from a year and a day of year. The *dayofyear* means the actual number of the day within the year, from 1–365:

```
MAKEDATE(year, dayofyear)

SELECT MAKEDATE(2006, 110);

+--------------------+
| MAKEDATE(2006, 110) |
+--------------------+
| 2006-04-20         |
+--------------------+
```

MAKETIME

MAKETIME returns a formatted time from the hour, minute, and second:

```
MAKETIME(hour, minute, second)

SELECT MAKETIME(10,05,00);

+--------------------+
| MAKETIME(10,05,00) |
+--------------------+
| 10:05:00           |
+--------------------+
```

MICROSECOND

MICROSECOND returns the microseconds from the time or datetime expression *expr* as a number in the range from 0 to 999999:

```
MICROSECOND(expr)

SELECT MICROSECOND('12:00:00.123456');

+------------------------------+
| MICROSECOND('12:00:00.123456') |
+------------------------------+
|                       123456 |
+------------------------------+
```

MINUTE

MINUTE returns the minute value from a time:

```
MINUTE(time)
```

```
SELECT MINUTE('10:24:00');
```

```
+-------------------+
| MINUTE('10:24:00') |
+-------------------+
|                24 |
+-------------------+
```

MONTH

MONTH returns the numeric month from a date:

```
MONTH(date)
```

```
SELECT MONTH('2006-04-20');
```

```
+---------------------+
| MONTH('2006-04-20') |
+---------------------+
|                   4 |
+---------------------+
```

MONTHNAME

MONTHNAME returns the actual month name from a date:

```
MONTHNAME(date)
```

```
SELECT MONTHNAME('2006-04-20');
```

```
+-------------------------+
| MONTHNAME('2006-04-20') |
+-------------------------+
| April                   |
+-------------------------+
```

NOW

NOW returns the current date and time:

```
NOW()
```

```
SELECT NOW();
```

```
+---------------------+
| NOW()               |
+---------------------+
| 2006-04-21 12:18:36 |
+---------------------+
```

PERIOD_ADD

PERIOD_ADD adds N months to period P (in the format YYMM or YYYYMM). It returns a value in the format YYYYMM. Note that the period argument P is not a date value:

```
PERIOD_ADD(P, N)
```

```
SELECT PERIOD_ADD(200604, 5);
```

```
+----------------------+
| PERIOD_ADD(200604, 5) |
+----------------------+
|               200609 |
+----------------------+
```

PERIOD_DIFF

PERIOD_DIFF returns the number of months between periods P1 and P2. The arguments should be in the format YYMM or YYYYMM. Note that the period arguments P1 and P2 are not date values:

```
PERIOD_DIFF(P1, P2)
```

```
SELECT PERIOD_DIFF(200604,200607);
```

```
+---------------------------+
| PERIOD_DIFF(200604,200607) |
+---------------------------+
|                        -3 |
+---------------------------+
```

QUARTER

QUARTER returns the quarter a date is in, from 1–4:

```
QUARTER(date)

SELECT QUARTER('2006-04-20');

+----------------------+
| QUARTER('2006-04-20') |
+----------------------+
|                    2 |
+----------------------+
```

SECOND

SECOND returns the second from a time, from 1–59:

```
SECOND(time)

SELECT SECOND('10:05:26');

+-------------------+
| SECOND('10:05:26') |
+-------------------+
|                26 |
+-------------------+
```

SEC_TO_TIME

SEC_TO_TIME returns the time from a given number of seconds from midnight:

```
SEC_TO_TIME(seconds)

SELECT SEC_TO_TIME(11235);

+-------------------+
| SEC_TO_TIME(11235) |
+-------------------+
| 03:07:15          |
+-------------------+
```

STR_TO_DATE

This is the reverse of the DATE_FORMAT() function. It takes a string, *str,* and a format string, *format.* STR_TO_DATE() returns a DATETIME value if the format string contains both date and time parts, or a DATE or TIME value if the string contains only date or time parts:

```
STR_TO_DATE(str, format)

SELECT STR_TO_DATE('04/20/2006', '%m/%d/%Y');
```

```
+-------------------------------------+
| STR_TO_DATE('04/20/2006', '%m/%d/%Y') |
+-------------------------------------+
| 2006-04-20                          |
+-------------------------------------+
```

SUBTIME

SUBTIME subtracts an amount of time (*expr2*) from a datetime (*expr1*):

```
SUBTIME(expr1, expr2)

SELECT SUBTIME('2006-04-20 23:59:59','10:15:20');
```

```
+-----------------------------------------+
| SUBTIME('2006-04-20 23:59:59','10:15:20') |
+-----------------------------------------+
| 2006-04-20 13:44:39                     |
+-----------------------------------------+
```

SYSDATE

SYSDATE returns the current system time and date:

```
SYSDATE()

SELECT SYSDATE();
```

```
+---------------------+
| SYSDATE()           |
+---------------------+
| 2006-04-21 13:10:37 |
+---------------------+
```

TIME

TIME returns the time from a datetime expression:

```
TIME(expr)

SELECT TIME('2006-04-20 13:44:39');
+----------------------------+
| TIME('2006-04-20 13:44:39') |
+----------------------------+
| 13:44:39                   |
+----------------------------+
```

TIMEDIFF

TIMEDIFF returns the difference of two time expressions:

```
TIMEDIFF(expr1, expr2)

SELECT TIMEDIFF('2006-04-20 23:59:59','2006:06:27 00:00:00');

+-------------------------------------------------------+
| TIMEDIFF('2006-04-20 23:59:59','2006:06:27 00:00:00') |
+-------------------------------------------------------+
| -1608:00:01                                           |
+-------------------------------------------------------+
```

TIMESTAMP

TIMESTAMP returns a date value with a datetime. Choose one of the two following:

```
TIMESTAMP(expr)

TIMESTAMP(expr1, expr2)

SELECT TIMESTAMP('2006-04-20');

+-----------------------+
| TIMESTAMP('2006-04-20') |
+-----------------------+
| 2006-04-20 00:00:00   |
+-----------------------+

SELECT TIMESTAMP('2006-04-20', '13:44:39');
```

```
+-------------------------------------+
| TIMESTAMP('2006-04-20', '13:44:39') |
+-------------------------------------+
| 2006-04-20 13:44:39                 |
+-------------------------------------+
```

TIMESTAMPADD

TIMESTAMPADD adds the integer expression *int_expr* to the date or datetime expression *datetime_expr*. The unit for *int_expr* is given by the interval argument, which should be one of the following values: FRAC_SECOND, SECOND, MINUTE, HOUR, DAY, WEEK, MONTH, QUARTER, or YEAR.

```
TIMESTAMPADD(interval, int_expr, datetime_expr)

SELECT TIMESTAMPADD(HOUR,2,'2006-04-20');
```

```
+-----------------------------------+
| TIMESTAMPADD(HOUR,2,'2006-04-20') |
+-----------------------------------+
| 2006-04-20 02:00:00               |
+-----------------------------------+
```

TIMESTAMPDIFF

TIMESTAMPDIFF returns the integer difference between the date or datetime expressions *datetime_expr1* and *datetime_expr2*. The unit for the result is given by the interval argument. The legal values for interval are the same as those listed in the description of the TIMESTAMPADD function.

```
TIMESTAMPDIFF(interval, datetime_expr1, datetime_expr2)

SELECT TIMESTAMPDIFF(WEEK, '2006-04-20', '2006-06-27');
```

```
+------------------------------------------------+
| TIMESTAMPDIFF(WEEK, '2006-04-20', '2006-06-27') |
+------------------------------------------------+
|                                              9 |
+------------------------------------------------+
```

TIME_FORMAT

Used like DATE_FORMAT but only time-related specifiers are valid:

```
TIME_FORMAT(time, format)
```

```
SELECT TIME_FORMAT('10:00:00', '%H %k %h %I %l');
```

```
+-------------------------------------------+
| TIME_FORMAT('10:00:00', '%H %k %h %I %l') |
+-------------------------------------------+
| 10 10 10 10 10                            |
+-------------------------------------------+
```

TIME_TO_SEC

This function returns the time in seconds:

```
TIME_TO_SEC(time)
```

```
SELECT TIME_TO_SEC('14:39:23');
```

```
+-------------------------+
| TIME_TO_SEC('14:39:23') |
+-------------------------+
|                   52763 |
+-------------------------+
```

TO_DAYS

Given a date, *date* returns a *daynumber* (the number of days since year 0):

```
TO_DAYS(date)
```

```
SELECT TO_DAYS('2006-04-20');
```

```
+-----------------------+
| TO_DAYS('2006-04-20') |
+-----------------------+
|                732786 |
+-----------------------+
```

UNIX_TIMESTAMP

This function returns the Unix timestamp. Choose one of the two following formats:

```
UNIX_TIMESTAMP()
```

```
UNIX_TIMESTAMP(date)
```

```
SELECT UNIX_TIMESTAMP();
```

```
+-----------------+
| UNIX_TIMESTAMP() |
+-----------------+
|       1145648422 |
+-----------------+
```

```
SELECT UNIX_TIMESTAMP('2006-04-20');
```

```
+------------------------------+
| UNIX_TIMESTAMP('2006-04-20') |
+------------------------------+
|                   1145509200 |
+------------------------------+
```

UTC_DATE
UTC_DATE returns the current UTC date in YYYY-MM-DD format:

```
UTC_DATE()
```

```
SELECT UTC_DATE();
```

```
+------------+
| UTC_DATE() |
+------------+
| 2006-04-21 |
+------------+
```

UTC_TIME
UTC_TIME returns the current UTC time in HH:MM:SS format:

```
UTC_TIME()
```

```
SELECT UTC_TIME();
```

```
+------------+
| UTC_TIME() |
+------------+
| 19:44:09   |
+------------+
```

UTC_TIMESTAMP

UTC_TIMESTAMP returns the current UTC date in YYYY-MM-DD format and the time in HH:MM:SS format:

```
UTC_TIMESTAMP()

SELECT UTC_TIMESTAMP();

+---------------------+
| UTC_TIMESTAMP()     |
+---------------------+
| 2006-04-21 19:46:20 |
+---------------------+
```

WEEK

Returns the week number for the date given:

```
WEEK(date)

SELECT WEEK('2006-04-20');

+--------------------+
| WEEK('2006-04-20') |
+--------------------+
|                 16 |
+--------------------+
```

WEEKDAY

Returns the weekday index for date (0 = Monday, 1 = Tuesday, ... 6 = Sunday):

```
WEEKDAY(date)

SELECT WEEKDAY('2006-04-20');

+-----------------------+
| WEEKDAY('2006-04-20') |
+-----------------------+
|                     3 |
+-----------------------+
```

YEAR

Returns the year for a date:

```
YEAR(date)
```

```
SELECT YEAR('2006-04-21');
```

```
+--------------------+
| YEAR('2006-04-21') |
+--------------------+
|               2006 |
+--------------------+
```

YEARWEEK

Returns the year and the week in a date:

```
YEARWEEK(date)
```

```
SELECT YEARWEEK('2006-04-21');
```

```
+------------------------+
| YEARWEEK('2006-04-21') |
+------------------------+
|                 200616 |
+------------------------+
```

Encryption

The encryption functions are invaluable to those of you who want to store data in an encrypted format. Fortunately, the several options are shown in the following examples. Be sure to store your encrypted values in a BLOB column. These functions are generally in alphabetical order, but since many are paired functions, I have placed the paired functions in the same section.

AES_ENCRYPT, AES_DECRYPT

AES_ENCRYPT (Advanced Encryption Standard) is the most secure type of encryption currently available for MySQL. Choose one of the two following options:

```
AES_ENCRYPT(str,key_str)
```

```
AES_DECRYPT(crypt_str,key_str)
```

```
SELECT AES_ENCRYPT('test','password');
```

```
+------------------------------+
| AES_ENCRYPT('test','password') |
+------------------------------+
| &W÷S/`wDvx÷)æ¢                |
+------------------------------+
```

ENCODE, DECODE

ENCODE and DECODE are simple encryption and decryption algorithms. Use a BLOB column for data generated with ENCODE and DECODE:

```
ENCODE(str,pass_str)

SELECT ENCODE('test', 'password');

+---------------------------+
| ENCODE('test', 'password') |
+---------------------------+
| m5:±                       |
+---------------------------+

DECODE(crypt_str,pass_str)

SELECT DECODE('m5:±', 'password');

+---------------------------+
| DECODE('m5:±', 'password') |
+---------------------------+
| test                       |
+---------------------------+
```

DES_ENCRYPT, DES_DECRYPT

DES_ENCRYPTS encrypts the string with the given key using the Triple-DES algorithm. On error, this function returns NULL. Note that this function works only if MySQL has been configured with SSL support. (Mine was not, so I cannot give any examples.)

```
DES_ENCRYPT(str[,(key_num|key_str)])

DES_DECRYPT(crypt_str[,key_str])
```

ENCRYPT

ENCRYPT uses the Unix crypt system call to encrypt a string. The *salt* value should be at least two characters in length. If no *salt* argument is given, a random one is used:

```
ENCRYPT(str [, salt])

SELECT ENCRYPT('password');
```

```
+---------------------+
| ENCRYPT('password') |
+---------------------+
| dNQmxZbDJyHZI       |
+---------------------+
```

MD5

The MD5 function calculates the MD5 128-bit checksum for the string, *str:*

```
MD5(str)

SELECT MD5('password');
```

```
+----------------------------------+
| MD5('password')                  |
+----------------------------------+
| 5f4dcc3b5aa765d61d8327deb882cf99 |
+----------------------------------+
```

PASSWORD, OLD_PASSWORD

PASSWORD calculates and returns a password from the plain-text password string. OLD_PASSWORD maintains compatibility with older (pre-4.1) clients:

```
PASSWORD(str)

OLD_PASSWORD(str)

SELECT PASSWORD('password');
```

```
+-------------------------------------------+
| PASSWORD('password')                      |
+-------------------------------------------+
| *2470C0C06DEE42FD1618BB99005ADCA2EC9D1E19 |
+-------------------------------------------+
```

SHA

SHA (Secure Hash Algorithm) returns the SHA encrypted value for the string, *str*. Cryptographically SHA is the more secure equivalent of MD5 encryption:

```
SHA(str)

SELECT SHA('password');
```

```
+-----------------------------------------+
| SHA('password')                         |
+-----------------------------------------+
| 5baa61e4c9b93f3f0682250b6cf8331b7ee68fd8 |
+-----------------------------------------+
```

Miscellaneous

These functions don't really fit anywhere else but are useful to the DBA and developer alike. While some of them seem a bit esoteric, I am including them because you may find them valuable in the future and you should be aware of them.

DEFAULT

DEFAULT returns the default value for a column. If there is no default value, you receive an error:

```
DEFAULT(col_name)

SELECT DEFAULT(Title) FROM Works;
```

```
+---------------+
| DEFAULT(Title) |
+---------------+
| NULL          |
| NULL          |
| NULL          |
| NULL          |
| NULL          |
| NULL          |
| NULL          |
+---------------+
```

```
SELECT DEFAULT(ISBN) FROM Works;

ERROR 1364 (HY000): Field 'ISBN' doesn't have a default value
```

FORMAT

FORMAT formats the number *x* to a format like '#,###,###.##', rounded to *y* decimals, and returns the result as a string. If *y* is 0, the result has no decimal point or fractional part:

```
FORMAT(x, y)

SELECT FORMAT(1234567.55555, 3);
```

```
+--------------------------+
| FORMAT(1234567.55555, 3) |
+--------------------------+
| 1,234,567.556            |
+--------------------------+
```

GET_LOCK

GET_LOCK tries to obtain a lock with the name given in *str* and with a timeout value given in *timeout*. The function returns 1 if successful, and a 0 if not. A NULL is returned in the case of an error. The named lock is released if another GET_LOCK is issued in the same session, or if your connection terminates:

```
GET_LOCK(str, timeout)

SELECT GET_LOCK('test', 5);
```

```
+---------------------+
| GET_LOCK('test', 5) |
+---------------------+
|                   1 |
+---------------------+
```

INET_ATON

INET_ATON (Internet Address To Number) returns an integer that represents the IP address (*expr*). The IP address is entered as the full address with dot notation:

```
INET_ATON(expr)

SELECT INET_ATON('10.0.1.250');
```

```
+-------------------------+
| INET_ATON('10.0.1.250') |
+-------------------------+
|               167772666 |
+-------------------------+
```

INET_NTOA

INET_NTOA (Internet Number To Address) returns the IP address from a 4- or 8-byte integer:

```
INET_NTOA(expr)

SELECT INET_NTOA('167772666');
```

```
+------------------------+
| INET_NTOA('167772666') |
+------------------------+
| 10.0.1.250             |
+------------------------+
```

IS_FREE_LOCK

IS_FREE_LOCK checks a named lock (*str*). If there is a lock by that name, the function returns 0. If the lock is free, it returns 1; otherwise, it returns NULL:

```
IS_FREE_LOCK(str)

SELECT IS_FREE_LOCK('test');
```

```
+---------------------+
| IS_FREE_LOCK('test') |
+---------------------+
|                   0 |
+---------------------+
```

IS_USED_LOCK

IS_USED_LOCK checks a named lock (*str*). If there is a lock by that name, the function returns the connection identifier of the client that holds the lock; otherwise, it returns NULL:

```
IS_USED_LOCK(str)

SELECT IS_USED_LOCK('test');
```

```
+---------------------+
| IS_USED_LOCK('test') |
+---------------------+
|                  41 |
+---------------------+
```

MASTER_POS_WAIT

You can use MASTER_POS_WAIT to control master/slave synchronization. You specify a position in the master log and the function blocks until the slave applies updates to that point. The number of log events it had to wait for to get to that position is the return value. You get NULL in these cases: if the slave SQL thread is not started; the master information is not initialized; the arguments are incorrect; the slave SQL thread stops while MASTER_POS_WAIT waits; or there is an error. You get -1 upon exceeding the timeout. If the slave is past the specified position, the function returns immediately. If you have specified a timeout value, the function stops waiting when timeout seconds have elapsed. You must set a timeout greater than 0; it or a negative timeout means no timeout.

```
MASTER_POS_WAIT(log_name,log_pos[,timeout])
```

RELEASE_LOCK

RELEASE_LOCK releases the named lock (*str*). If the lock is released, the function returns a 1; 0 returns if the lock was not established by this thread; you get NULL if there was no such lock:

```
RELEASE_LOCK(str)

SELECT RELEASE_LOCK('test');
```

```
+----------------------+
| RELEASE_LOCK('test') |
+----------------------+
|                    1 |
+----------------------+
```

SLEEP

The SLEEP function pauses an action for a number of seconds (*duration*) and then returns 0. If a SLEEP operation is interrupted, a 1 is returned:

```
SLEEP(duration)

SELECT SLEEP(5);
```

(5-second pause)

```
+----------+
| SLEEP(5) |
+----------+
|        0 |
+----------+
```

UUID

UUID returns a 128-bit Universally Unique Identifier. The number generated is a string of five hexadecimal numbers. UUID always returns a unique number because the first number is a timestamp:

```
UUID()

SELECT UUID();

+--------------------------------------+
| UUID()                               |
+--------------------------------------+
| 0d2b236a-236b-1029-b19e-0050da0f6715 |
+--------------------------------------+

SELECT UUID();

+--------------------------------------+
| UUID()                               |
+--------------------------------------+
| 0ef493a2-236b-1029-b19e-0050da0f6715 |
+--------------------------------------+

SELECT UUID();

+--------------------------------------+
| UUID()                               |
+--------------------------------------+
| 1013c6fe-236b-1029-b19e-0050da0f6715 |
+--------------------------------------+
```

Appendix G

Answers to Chapter Review Questions

Chapter 1

Multiple Choice
1. b, 2. d, 3. c, 4. d, 5. b, 6. d, 7. c, 8. a, 9. b, 10. c

Concepts
1. Database vendors have had to make tradeoffs between features and performance. They have not adhered 100 percent with the ANSI standard, so that it is a subset. It is a superset of that subset because there are expanded and enhanced features not included in the standard.
2. Portability is always a positive thing and SQL is no different. Portability makes migration and data interchange much easier and less expensive.
3. SQL is a language because it has syntax and semantics.

Chapter 2

Multiple Choice
1. b, 2. a, 3. d, 4. b, 5. c, 6. d, 7. a, 8. c, 9. a, 10. d

Concepts

1. All relations are tables because the definition for a relation is a table that meets certain requirements. A table is not a relation if it does not meet the requirements for the relation definition; for example, each row of a relation is unique.

2. No. Two tables may have a related column via a primary key/foreign key relationship, but referential integrity is only maintained if the relationship is defined in the table definition.

3. The unique index is smaller because there are no repeated values. Size and uniqueness of the values make a unique index very efficient.

Chapter 3

Multiple Choice

1. d, 2. c, 3. a, 4. c, 5. a, 6. a, 7. d, 8. a, 9. b, 10. c

Concepts

1. An ACID-compliant database is recovered in good condition since atomicity is an all-or-nothing process. There won't be any half transactions or open transactions due to the atomic nature of the database. Durability guarantees recovery after a crash because it only looks at committed transactions for recovery to a pre-crash state.

2. I would like speed, reliability, low TCO, low maintenance, great support from the vendor, and a low hardware overhead.

3. There aren't may products that fit this entire list, but you will most likely have to compromise on price if you expect all of the others.

Chapter 4

Multiple Choice

1. a, 2. b, 3. d, 4. c, 5. b, 6. a, 7. a, 8. d, 9. c, 10. a

Chapter 5

Multiple Choice

1. c, 2. a, 3. a, 4. d, 5. d, 6. a, 7. c, 8. b, 9. b, 10. d

Concepts

1. I would choose MyISAM because of the speed. Web users have a short attention span and therefore one needs the fastest access possible.

2. For any site that deals with currency, always use InnoDB for its transaction-safe engine and ACID compliance.

Chapter 6

Multiple Choice

1. b, 2. a, 3. a, 4. d, 5. a, 6. c, 7. b, 8. d, 9. b, 10. a

Concepts

1. DML has to do with putting data into a database, looking at data, updating data, and removing data. DML is where the action is in a database. Most queries are of the SELECT type because that is what a database is used for: asking questions and getting answers.

2. To prevent such issues, I would always test my code before entering it into an application.

Chapter 7

Multiple Choice

1. d, 2. b, 3. a, 4. a, 5. d, 6. b, 7. b, 8. c, 9. d, 10. b

Concepts

1. SAVEPOINT provides a ROLLBACK point in a transaction instead of rolling back the whole transaction.

2. Read-only rights are granted with a SELECT statement so a user can read data but not make any changes to it.

Chapter 8

Multiple Choice

1. d, 2. a, 3. a, 4. c, 5. a, 6. d, 7. b, 8. c, 9. b, 10. b

Concepts

1. Save the spreadsheet as a comma-separated text file. If there is an option for enclosing the individual data points in double quotes ("), use it and save the file. Create a table with the appropriate fields and column types. If you use an auto-increment column in the table, precede the first data point with a comma or the data won't go into the database correctly. Use LOAD DATA INFILE to import the data into the database.

2.

```
SELECT    Authors.First_Name,    Authors.Last_Name,    SUM(Works.Sales) *
Works.Price AS Total_Sales_$ FROM    Works    INNER JOIN Authors ON
(Works.Author_ID = Authors.Author_ID) GROUP BY    Authors.First_Name,
Authors.Last_Name;
```

```
+------------+-----------+---------------+
| First_Name | Last_Name | Total_Sales_$ |
+------------+-----------+---------------+
| Anne       | Cohen     |   10194000.00 |
| Glen       | Harris    |     279860.00 |
| Lenard     | Dawson    |     141858.00 |
| Lynn       | Steele    |    6796000.00 |
| Robert     | Balzer    |    6567810.00 |
+------------+-----------+---------------+
```

Chapter 9

Multiple Choice

1. d, 2. c, 3. b, 4. a, 5. a, 6. a, 7. d, 8. b, 9. b, 10. b

Concepts

1. The best argument for using a view is that it hides the underlying structure of the database from the user, thereby making your database more secure. Views can also be altered or dropped without destroying the underlying tables from which they were derived.

2. Views in MySQL are updateable by default, so you only need to create one. To update a view, you must have the proper permissions to do so.

Chapter 10

Multiple Choice
1. d, 2. b, 3. b, 4. b, 5. b, 6. d, 7. c, 8. a, 9. d, 10. d

Concepts

1. Since the local users are attached via a switch, then the switch, cabling, and NIC on the server must be functioning correctly. I would check the router that is attached to the Internet to ensure proper connectivity, check with other users to see if they are experiencing any difficulty with Internet traffic, check with the telecommunications company responsible for the Internet connection and, finally, check to see if we need to upgrade our Internet connection outbound speed.

2. I would install a performance monitor, like Orca, to check performance. I would check to make sure there is sufficient RAM for the growing database. I would also do some table maintenance to optimize the tables. In the case of a Windows server, I would defragment the file system on which the data and MySQL server reside. I would probably also look into a CPU or disk upgrade depending on the data from Orca.

Chapter 11

Multiple Choice
1. b, 2. b, 3. d, 4. a, 5. b, 6. d, 7. c, 8. a, 9. c, 10. a

Concepts

1. Normalization is the process of creating or editing a database such that redundant data is eliminated and inconsistencies are kept to a minimum while maintaining adequate performance. To have a scalable database, it must conform to the definition of a normalized database.

2. Aside from performance checks and maintenance issues, I would go through the normalization process with the database.

3. I would normalize and split the table into multiple tables with just a few columns each.

Chapter 12

Multiple Choice
1. a, 2. c, 3. c, 4. b, 5. c, 6. a, 7. b, 8. b, 9. b, 10. c

Chapter 13

Multiple Choice

1. c, 2. a, 3. c, 4. a, 5. d, 6. b, 7. b, 8. c, 9. a, 10. b

Concepts

1. Stored procedures cut down the network traffic of having queries go across the network to be submitted to the database. The queries are already optimized by the query optimizer and don't have to wait for the optimizer during the query. There is one single place to edit and maintain SQL statements: the database.

2. As stated in question 1, the queries don't have to be transferred across the network to be submitted to the database.

Chapter 14

Multiple Choice

1. d, 2. b, 3. d, 4. a, 5. a, 6. d, 7. b, 8. b, 9. d, 10. c

Concepts

1. The most important thing to consider when designing a data warehouse is the data audience, or user. The user is the one who knows and understands the business intelligence and the needs of the organization for which she is gathering the information.

2. Much the same as what happened to the example's author: a redesign of the database and a revision of the application. The user is the most important aspect of any undertaking involving data at any level. Users are the consumer and your customer.

Index